D1732716

A Wellesley Affair

A Wellesley Affair

Richard Marquess Wellesley and the Conduct of Anglo-Spanish Diplomacy, 1809–1812

John Kenneth Severn

A Florida State University Book

University Presses of Florida
Tallahassee

LIBRARY
The University of Texas
At San Antonio

University Presses of Florida is the central agency for scholarly publishing of the State of Florida's university system. Its offices are located at 15 NW 15th Street, Gainesville, FL 32603. Works published by University Presses of Florida are evaluated and selected for publication by a faculty editorial committee of any one of Florida's nine public universities: Florida A&M (Tallahassee), Florida Atlantic University (Boca Raton), Florida International University (Miami), Florida State University (Tallahassee), University of Central Florida (Orlando), University of Florida (Gainesville), University of North Florida (Jacksonville), University of South Florida (Tampa), University of West Florida (Pensacola).

Library of Congress Cataloging in Publication Data

Severn, John Kenneth, 1948–
    A Wellesley affair.

    "A Florida State University book."
    Bibliography: p.
    Includes index.
    1. Wellesley, Richard Colley Wellesley, Marquis,
1760–1842. 2. Great Britain—Foreign relations—
1800–1837. 3. Great Britain—Foreign relations—Spain.
4. Spain—Foreign relations—Great Britain. 5. Statesmen—Great Britain—Biography. I. Title.
DA536.W3S48   327.41046 [B]   80–25416
ISBN 0–8130–0684–8

Copyright © 1981 by the Board of Regents
of the State of Florida

Typography by Williams Typography
Chattanooga, Tennessee

Printed in U.S.A.

Contents

List of Illustrations

Preface

Richard Marquess Wellesley, governor-general of India, ambassador extraordinary to Spain, foreign secretary in the Perceval cabinet, and Lord Lieutenant of Ireland, has long been a controversial figure in British history. Traditionally historical interest in him has centered on his term as governor-general. The continued development of British power in the subcontinent, and the ever mounting problems associated with British colonialism, aroused interest in Lord Wellesley as the man who laid the foundation of Britain's Indian empire. The result was the publication of a selection of Wellesley's private papers, in 1847 and 1904, and two biographies, in 1880 and 1889. These were followed in the twentieth century by another publication of the Indian papers, a historical monograph on the Wellesley governor-generalship, and, most recently, a personal biography also dealing primarily with the years in India. Because this eight-year period in Wellesley's life was so productive and so important to British history, it is no accident that it is dealt with in such detail. Yet, in the important years of 1809–12, he applied his talents to the conduct of British diplomacy, and this part of his career has been largely ignored.

In 1809 Britain was entering the sixteenth year of her desperate struggle with France, and for the first time she possessed a viable military front, opened the previous year in the Iberian Peninsula. Nevertheless, early enthusiasm over the potential for success in Iberia had turned to

despair. Many in Britain predicted ultimate disaster for British arms and
called for their withdrawal. Lord Wellesley was not among these. Although the Peninsular War was exerting undue strain on Britain's
economy with few tangible results, and the Spanish alliance was not
functioning smoothly, he believed that England must persevere in her
efforts in Iberia and, if possible, extend them. Wellesley considered the
Peninsular War the key to ultimate victory over France, a belief which
he employed in the years 1809– 12, first as ambassador to Spain and
then as foreign secretary.

Wellesley's term as ambassador began at a time when the Anglo-
Spanish alliance was suffering from ill feeling and mutual distrust. The
British army under the command of Sir Arthur Wellesley was starving
because of deficiencies in the Spanish supply system, and Spain was
irritated over Britain's reluctance to cooperate in military adventures.
Wellesley's tasks were to see that the British army received proper
support, to convince Spain of Britain's good faith toward the alliance,
and to urge the Spanish to undertake military and governmental reform. Time and circumstances would prevent Wellesley from completely attaining these goals, but his embassy was certainly not without
merit or accomplishment. After weeks of difficult negotiating, Wellesley
would depart Spain confident that the alliance was again on firm
ground. More important, he would leave with a unique appreciation of
Spain's value in the struggle against Napoleon and of the problems in
dealing with the proud Iberians.

As foreign secretary, Wellesley continued to keep a close watch over
Spanish affairs. Spain in fact became the foundation of his foreign policy.
Accordingly the Marquess appointed his youngest and most trusted
brother, Henry, to the British Embassy in Seville. Thus, with Lord
Wellesley as foreign secretary, Wellington as commander in chief of
Britain's peninsular forces, and Henry Wellesley heading up the Spanish
embassy, British diplomacy in Spain would bear the personal mark of the
Wellesley family. Together the brothers provided Great Britain with
decisive and consistent representation. Lord Wellesley's responsibilities
as foreign secretary, however, were not confined to devising and implementing a foreign policy; he was also continuously called upon to defend
that policy. This defense brought Wellesley into conflict not only with the
parliamentary opposition but also with many members of the cabinet
whose commitment to the Peninsular War was not as great as his own.
This political struggle, decisive to the war against France, forms an
important part of this study.

It is a perplexing question why historians have ignored the role of the man responsible for policy making in a crucial period of British diplomatic history. That the years 1809–12 were often counterproductive for the British army was certainly a factor. There were of course victories in the peninsula, but most appeared Pyrrhic, with Napoleon continuing to extend his sway over the continent. The fruits of Wellington's patient military strategy would not become apparent until after the Marquess departed. Wellesley also suffered from the fact that his term as foreign secretary came between those of George Canning and Viscount Castlereagh, both of whose subsequent fame exceeded his own. Moreover, Wellesley's personality did not endear him to historians: He was considered arrogant, indolent, and profligate, attributes which brought him more ridicule than praise. Interpreting contemporary judgments of his personality as assessments of his work, many historians have chosen either to ignore his contributions to British foreign policy or to attribute them to Canning or Castlereagh. Finally, Wellesley has always been obscured by his younger brother, Arthur, Duke of Wellington. Aside from the fact that Wellington was an extraordinary general, the tangible achievements of the warrior have always been more alluring to historians than the relatively intangible achievements of the diplomat.

The degree to which each of these factors affected history's negligence of Lord Wellesley can only be conjectured. It is, however, certain that his life in the years 1809–12 needs attention, not only because his contributions were significant but also because, by ignoring Wellesley, historians have only superficially touched on Anglo-Spanish diplomacy during the period. A close study reveals that these years were pivotal ones for Great Britain, when she had to decide, amidst gloomy political, economic, and military conditions, whether she would maintain her efforts against Napoleon in Spain. It is, therefore, the purpose of this study to examine this crucial period of Anglo-Spanish diplomacy and to reveal and evaluate Lord Wellesley's role in it.

In the process of researching and writing this study, I have incurred considerable debts. I would first like to express my appreciation to the directors and staffs of the Strozier Library at Florida State University, the Public Record Office of Great Britain, the British Museum, the All Souls College Library, Oxford, and the Archivo Histórico Nacional in Madrid, whose assistance and cooperation made the research for this study a pleasurable experience. I wish also to thank Mrs. Iris Butler Portal and Professor William W. Rogers for their timely advice and encouragement.

To Professor Donald D. Howard go my very special thanks. As

teacher and friend, he inspired, directed, and encouraged my work through its various stages. Without him, this study would never have found its way into print.

Finally, I shall always be thankful for the moral and financial support of my wife, Deborah, and my parents, Dr. and Mrs. Kenneth Severn. For sharing with me the emotional highs and lows which are a part of historical research and writing, and urging me on toward the project's completion, I dedicate this book to them.

1

The Formative Years

Richard Colley Wellesley's political career began with difficulties experienced by many other young, aspiring politicians in eighteenth-century Britain. With democracy still many years off, an oligarchy governed Britain. The king ruled with a Parliament comprised of a privileged minority responsible only to a privileged electorate. Under this system, a political career was open to any Protestant of rank or wealth. If, in addition, a man possessed brilliance and ambition, a position of leadership within the political structure could be obtained with relative ease—providing political allegiance was properly placed. Men with neither wealth nor rank found the pursuit of a political career frustrating; without advancement based on ability, many capable men watched less able individuals move ahead of them. Richard Wellesley's experiences with such frustration were to have a lasting effect on his political career.

The lack of progress in the initial stages of his political career was especially rancorous to Richard Wellesley; besides having supreme confidence in his own abilities, he had been raised with great expectations of success. His family was of Anglo-Irish extraction. Originally from Wells, in Somerset, the Wellesleys obtained land and position in Ireland during the reign of Henry II. There they began ambitiously to accumulate wealth through services rendered to the crown and judicious marriages with other Anglo-Irish families. As a result, by the eighteenth century, the Wellesleys were a family of wealth and prestige in Ireland.[1]

In 1728 the Wellesley estate was inherited by the first Richard Colley Wellesley. The man, unfortunately for subsequent generations, was a spendthrift. He squandered enormous amounts of money on improvements to the grounds of the family estate and on entertainment for his family and friends. Although the elder Richard Colley Wellesley's flamboyant tastes and unproductive life drained the family treasury, he left his son, Garrett Wellesley, a substantial income of £8,000 a year. Garrett also inherited many of his father's personal traits. He enjoyed art, company, and comfort and suffered from a poor grasp of finances. A kind man whose heart was invariably larger than his pocketbook, Garrett married in 1759 an ambitious and quick-tempered sixteen-year-old girl named Anne Hill. One year later Anne gave birth to her first son, Richard. The same year Garrett Wellesley was raised in the Irish peerage to Viscount Wellesley of Dungan and Earl of Mornington.[2]

Richard Wellesley rarely uttered a kind word about his parents. Yet, having produced five remarkable sons, they must have possessed some positive characteristics. Richard was soon followed by the second son, William. More famous under his later name, William Wellesley-Pole, he was a prominent member of the Irish and English Parliaments and was chief secretary to Ireland in 1809. The third son was Arthur, the illustrious Duke of Wellington, joint victor over Napoleon at Waterloo. The least auspicious was Gerald, the fourth son, an accomplished scholar and prominent Anglican cleric. Henry was the fifth and last son. In his youth, he was an indispensable assistant to Richard, and later he held ambassadorships in Madrid, Vienna, and Paris.[3]

It would appear then that Anne Wellesley was an attentive and ambitious mother. Although she distinctly lacked maternal affection, she wanted the best for her children, especially her first, Richard, who she hoped would secure and extend the family fortune. No expense was spared in raising Richard. He was born with the proverbial silver spoon in his mouth. A thorough and expensive education began at age five, when he was sent to a small boarding school in the village of Portarlington to study reading, writing, geography, and French. Although fragile and subject to chronic illness, Richard was intelligent, resolute, temperamental, and self-confident. Easily bored with the school's curriculum, young Wellesley found that the best way to stay interested was to tutor his classmates. This was a boon to his self-esteem, and it stirred him to greater efforts in mastering his studies.[4]

At the age of eleven, Richard went to Harrow, but his career there was brief. Involved in a conspiracy to bar out a new headmaster, he was

Richard Marquess Wellesley (1760–1842), by J. P. Davis. Reproduced with permission of the National Portrait Gallery.

expelled. Distressed at the time, Richard later regarded the expulsion as one of the fortunate occurrences of his life, for on leaving Harrow he entered his beloved Eton. Seven important years were spent at Eton, where he excelled as a student. Enthusiastic over his studies, Richard became an accomplished classicist. He worked hard, his talents were recognized, and his mind and character developed; moreover, he formed a lasting friendship with one of his fellow students, William Wyndham Grenville.[5]

Upon graduation, Wellesley enrolled at Christ Church, Oxford. There he continued to distinguish himself in the classics, winning the Chancellor's Prize for Latin Verse. He maintained his friendship with William Grenville and cultivated a new one with Henry Addington.[6] On May 22, 1781, his father, Garrett Wellesley, died. Richard's life changed abruptly. He had new responsibilities and soon left Oxford, without a degree, to care for his family. But far from being distraught, he remained an optimistic young man.

The death of his father did not have a deep emotional effect upon Richard Wellesley, now Lord Mornington. Knowing only the abundance of his youth, accustomed to success, confident of his ability, he expected shortly to assume an active role in British politics. Instead harsh, new realities faced Richard on his return. Garrett Wellesley had been a successful, accomplished musician. Indeed, his compositions "When for the world's repose my Chloe sleeps," "Come fairest Nymph," and "Here in cool grot" were familiar throughout the British Isles and had won him an appointment as doctor and professor of music at Trinity College. Unfortunately, Garrett's musical pursuits brought little financial reward, and he left the family heavily in debt.[7] Thus the year 1781 found Richard Wellesley without money, wholly bereft of political influence, and responsible for the management of a large and difficult family. At this point, his dreams of a great political future must have seemed chimerical.

Mornington did not succumb to the despair and disillusionment that would accompany his disappointments in later life. Instead, he actively involved himself in Irish politics, taking his father's place in the Irish House of Lords. He soon became an expert in Irish affairs, and in 1782 he went to London to act as an intermediary between the Irish and British Parliaments. Because Irish politics fascinated Wellesley, he was content with his role in the Irish House of Lords.[8] But, when William Pitt became prime minister in 1783, his cousin, William Grenville, familiar with Richard's talents, encouraged Pitt to bring young Mornington into

Parliament. As a result, he won election to the House of Commons in 1784 from the rotten borough of Bere Alston.[9]

Lord Mornington looked forward to an exciting governmental career, but there were barriers in his way. Cabinets in late-eighteenth-century Britain depended upon carefully arranged parliamentary majorities. Because party lines were not distinct, a ministry needed a broad base of appeal to maintain its majority. Anyone included in the government had to possess political influence, in the form of either great wealth or patronage controlled through rank. Mornington possessed neither. His Irish peerage, which assured him of an important role in Irish politics, meant nothing in Britain, and he was financially paralyzed by a debt-ridden estate and the maintenance of an expensive family. As a result, Wellesley, though endowed with great ability and enthusiasm, was of little use to Pitt except as another vote in the Commons. He became disillusioned by his dependence on a sociopolitical system that he could neither fit into nor control. Mornington was merely another back-bencher—one of Pitt's men. In 1785 he sought but failed to secure the vice-treasureship of Ireland. The following year there was a perceptible improvement in his fortunes; Pitt appointed him a junior lord of the treasury, but the position fell far short of his ambitions.[10]

Family matters added to Wellesley's frustrations. He reveled in political problems, but domestic worries distressed him. Although he never shirked family responsibilities, he resented them as a distraction and a reminder of his inability to rise in British politics. In 1786 his main worry was about Arthur. William, the first brother, had inherited the estates of a cousin, William Pole, and was financially secure, but Arthur was a problem. He had been sent to Eton but had shown little progress or promise. The expense of Eton was great, and Arthur was withdrawn when younger brothers Gerald and Henry, who were academically inclined, were ready to enter school. Family funds simply could not support three boys at Eton. Another future had to be determined for Arthur. After prolonged consideration, Mornington and his mother decided on a military career for him, and Arthur enrolled as a cadet at the Royal Academy of Equitation at Angers in Anjou.[11] It was the beginning of an illustrious career.

The year 1786 was significant also as the year Mornington met Hyacinthe Gabrielle Roland, the woman who would be his mistress and bear him five children before their marriage in 1794. The perceptive Lord Curzon once wrote, "One of the main sources of weakness in Wellesley's career, upon which his biographers appear uniformly to have

turned a blind eye, was his relations with women."[12] Indeed, women
were a constant source of personal distress or public embarrassment to
Wellesley for most of his life, and Hyacinthe was no exception. Her
background is somewhat obscure, but it is known that her father was
Irish and her mother French. Brought up in Paris, where her mother
was an actress, Hyacinthe eventually migrated to Britain. As a woman,
according to Iris Butler, "Hyacinthe Wellesley's own letters reveal her as
a clever, fascinating and virtuous woman, lacking in wisdom and stability
but with noble qualities."[13] She was also beautiful and charming. For
Wellesley, it was an enjoyable relationship, but in time it would become a
liability.

The next two years were difficult for Lord Mornington. A quarrel
resulted in the loss of his seat in the House of Commons.[14] Further, his
health began to deteriorate, the family debt in Ireland grew, and his
younger brothers caused several embarrassments. To compound his
problems, he had a growing family of his own. Hyacinthe had given birth
to a son, Richard, in 1787, and in February 1788, her first daughter,
Anne, was born. Wellesley's future looked bleak, but in 1788 his friends
Pitt and Grenville secured for him the royal borough of Windsor. He was
returned to the Commons, and none too soon.[15]

The 1789 session of Parliament would be an important one. George
III had lapsed into apparent insanity, necessitating the formation of a
regency. The Prince of Wales would be regent, but he was trusted
neither by the king nor by Pitt and his party. So the prime minister
introduced a bill, known as the Regency Bill, limiting the powers of the
regent, and it passed after prolonged debate.[16] When the king recovered,
he was grateful for this piece of parliamentary maneuvering. Mornington, who had supported the bill vigorously, expected some form of
reward; but none came, and his career remained static. Convinced of his
abilities and raised with expectations of a brilliant future, Wellesley faced
the prospect of perpetual obscurity. Perhaps his difficulties were caused
by his overwhelming family problems. In any case, he decided to escape.
Plans were made for a tour of the continent, and shortly after the birth of
their fourth child, Gerald, Richard and Hyacinthe departed England,
first for Spa. The trip was a great success. Richard stabilized his nerves,
recovered his health, and by chance witnessed the functioning of the new
revolutionary government in France.[17]

Before returning to Britain, Mornington secured an appointment for
Henry in the diplomatic service, and with that his brothers were all well
placed.[18] Shortly thereafter he sailed for England, optimistic over his

William Pitt the Younger (1759– 1806), by J. Hoppner. Reproduced with permission of the National Portrait Gallery.

future. His closest friends, Pitt, Addington, and Grenville, were in the
key governmental positions, and Wellesley undoubtedly felt he could
rely on them for his promotion. But the old liabilities remained. He
possessed no patronage, no English estates. He was heavily in debt, and
his liaison with Hyacinthe was looked upon with disfavor by the king's
intimate circle of friends. Moreover, Wellesley did not fit in well socially
with his chosen political associates. He did not drink, gamble, or hunt—
the favorite pastimes of eighteenth-century Britain. Undaunted, Mornington returned to Parliament to support such new liberal causes as the
abolition of the slave trade and Catholic emancipation. Having witnessed
the effects of the French Revolution firsthand, however, he opposed
parliamentary reform and spoke against Grey's reform bill. Wellesley,
though liberal in sentiment, was a realist and a great believer in public
order. He did not believe it was the time for governmental changes.[19]

With an eye on political advancement, Mornington supported the
government's stand on all parliamentary issues and involved himself in
parliamentary planning by making himself a frequent visitor to the Pitt
estate. But these efforts proved futile. His advancement remained negligible until 1793, when he was appointed to the Privy Council and to the
India Board of Control. He took particular interest in the latter, school-
ing himself thoroughly in Indian affairs. Rarely did he attend the meetings of the Board of Control (a penchant that would follow him through
life), but he was always well informed on its proceedings. His first
important governmental role came when he was chosen to speak for the
ministry on its opposition to revolutionary France. The speech, ponder-
ous and lengthy by modern standards, was considered a great success.[20]

The next three years were rather uneventful for Wellesley, with his
advancement, as usual, progressing more slowly than he wished. In 1794
he decided to marry Hyacinthe. This gesture was less a romantic one
than an attempt to eliminate one of his liabilities; but Wellesley remained
in debt and lacked the requisite patronage for real power.[21] His last
speech in the House of Commons came in 1795 when he supported the
Seditious Meetings Act.[22] Mornington then became deeply involved in
Irish affairs because of the prospect of a French-sponsored revolt in
Ireland. In 1796 he purchased a colonelcy for Arthur, who went off to
serve in India. But family problems were still far from settled, as Richard
now had three sons of his own ready to begin school. Sorely pressed
financially, he needed money; and money could come only through
advancement. Wellesley again looked to his friends Pitt, Grenville, and
Addington, but there was little they could do.

The House of Commons in 1793, by Karl-Anton Hickle. Reproduced with permission of the National Portrait Gallery. Pitt is addressing the House. Lord Wellesley is seated turned away in the front row, fifth to Pitt's right.

Then unexpectedly Wellesley's career changed for the better: Pitt appointed him governor of Madras with reversion to the governor-generalship of Bengal. Lord Cornwallis was to be governor-general, but a quarrel between him and the board of directors led to his resignation before setting out for India. Lord Mornington would sail as the new governor-general. The position was both prestigious and potentially lucrative—far more than Wellesley could have hoped for in Parliament. The year 1797 proved to be more eventful. On November 3 Mornington was awarded a long-sought English peerage, becoming Baron Wellesley.[23]

New opportunity lay in India. For the first time Wellesley could prove his ability. But while he eagerly awaited departure, Hyacinthe grew insecure. With five children to care for, for her to accompany her husband would be impractical. Moreover, she had a dreadful fear of the ocean and looked with horror on a four- to six-month sea voyage. Hyacinthe implored her husband to stay in England, failing to recognize the importance of the governor-generalship. Wellesley did not wish to leave her behind, but he could not forgo this opportunity. Both became distraught over the impending departure, and thus even in a moment of glory and satisfaction, domestic problems plagued Richard Wellesley. Only when she realized that the governor-generalship might bring relief to the family's beleaguered finances did Hyacinthe become reconciled to Richard's leaving. Still it was a distraught Wellesley who embarked on November 10, 1797, aboard His Majesty's frigate *La Virginie*.[24]

As governor-general, it would be Wellesley's responsibility to protect the East India Company's interests and to ensure unimpeded trade. To prepare for the task, he spent the long journey studying Indian history. Already well informed on Indian affairs through his position on the India Board of Control, Wellesley developed a valuable understanding of the strange, new people with whom he would have to deal. He understood the sources of conflict among the various Indian states as well as the primary and secondary interests of each. More important, being a pragmatic man, he appreciated the power and position of the several parties struggling for hegemony in India and the resources at their disposal. By the time of his arrival, Wellesley was confident that he could govern effectively. He was also fortunate to have the capable assistance of his two brothers Arthur and Henry, the former in a military capacity, the latter in a diplomatic and advisory role.[25]

Lord Mornington inherited an India restless with discontent. The trouble sprang from the unfortunate circumstances that had faced his predecessor, Sir John Shore. Shore became governor-general in 1793, at a time when the policy of nonintervention called for in Pitt's India Act of 1784 was at its height. The act, requiring the consent of Parliament before a British declaration of war or annexation in India, was based on two premises: that the Indian nations were not aggressive, and if left to their own resources would create a balance of power in the subcontinent; and that the Indian wars, so disruptive of commerce in the past, were the result of the aggressiveness of the India Company itself.[26] Initially the policy worked well, but by 1793 it was being undermined by political developments in both India and Europe—Mahadji Sindia, the outstanding leader of the Maratha nation had died, and a rejuvenated France had again become aggressive in the subcontinent. The renewal of French influence in India and internal dissensions in the Marathan Confederacy destroyed prospects of stability in central India. Shore was unable to perceive the change, and by the time of his recall India was in turmoil.[27]

Wellesley brought to India the belief "that in eastern countries divided command, divided authority, bring chaos."[28] He also carried with him a phobia of France, which he directed against both French aggression and ideology. When he arrived in India, it became apparent that none of the irresoluteness and timidity that characterized Shore's administration would continue. Wellesley felt that a power balance in India was unlikely. Only through British supremacy, he believed, could the peace necessary for the proper conduct of commerce be achieved and maintained. Thus his personal policies were simple: first, French influence in India must be eliminated, so that no foothold could be established for an invading army or for political intrigue; second, the concept of an Indian balance of power must be replaced by British supremacy.[29] Although Mornington's fear of France was real, it was no accident that he used the first policy to achieve the second. In India, Richard Wellesley became one of the first Britons to apply the concept that political and economic empires were inseparable—a concept pursued so indefatigably by the Victorians. Wellesley's imperialism differed from that of the Victorians in that it was not evangelic. He did not try to change the societies with which he came into contact—only to dominate them.[30]

The main instrument Wellesley employed to implement his policy of domination was the subsidiary treaty, which in one form or another was negotiated with various Indian states. The treaties were uncomplicated: an Indian nation threatened by one or more of its neighbors was furnished aid in the form of British troops garrisoned within the borders of the Indian state to guarantee its territorial integrity. In return, the

Indian state provided Britain with either a cash payment or a cession of agreed-upon land.[31] The effects of such treaties were obvious: the Indian signees were undoubtedly protected from invasion, but they were also irrevocably dependent on British power. Further, the treaties allowed the British a much larger standing army than the India Company could otherwise afford and secured for the governor-general more reliable political intelligence. The despotic overtones of the treaties never concerned Wellesley, as he was convinced that British supremacy served the best interests of all concerned.

Despite an exhausting voyage, Wellesley arrived in Calcutta full of enthusiasm. Being nearly six months removed from the India Company's authority, he also had the independence to pursue his own schemes.[32] Shortly after his arrival, he contended with the powerful south Indian state of Mysore under the capable leadership of Tippu Sultan. Tippu had long been antagonistic toward the British, but to Lord Mornington, Tippu's greatest sin was a strong attachment to France. In addition to his close diplomatic ties with the French government, Tippu retained several French military and political advisers in his capital, Seringapatam. Wellesley considered this intolerable and made plans to destroy French influence in Mysore by badgering Tippu into a political agreement. Tippu was too intelligent and stubborn for this tactic, and after weeks of fruitless negotiating Wellesley resorted to force. His military preparations included a diplomatic offensive to isolate Tippu. To the north of Mysore lay the extensive dominions of the Nizam of Hyderabad, a land plagued with a weak government and hostile neighbors—Mysore and the Marathas. Mornington took advantage of the Nizam's insecurity, and concluded the first of his subsidiary treaties. By a brilliant stroke of diplomacy, Wellesley secured the alliance of Mysore's immediate neighbor and discouraged the powerful Marathas from coming to Tippu's aid. The British army, commanded by Major General George Harris and Colonel Arthur Wellesley, then invaded Mysore and destroyed Tippu and his army at the Battle of Seringapatam. Wellesley subsequently placed a British puppet on the throne of Mysore, and French influence in south India came to an end.[33]

The Mysore campaign showed Wellesley at his best. He pursued his plans with clear-sighted vigor, prepared well, and made few mistakes. The result was a stabilization of Indian politics and a vast extension of British hegemony in India. As he eagerly awaited praise and approbation from Britain, Wellesley began to settle other outstanding issues. In southeast India a succession crisis beset the state of the Carnatic.

India before Wellesley (1798)

Political instability there, as Mornington perceived it, hampered the India Company's trade. He intervened, and the divided people of the Carnatic were helpless before British power. By placing a man of his own choosing on the throne, Wellesley established British control over the Carnatic and the whole of south India. Employing the same issues and methods, he secured the west coast city of Surat. Next he directed his attention toward the state of Oude, where he coerced the ruling house into signing a subsidiary treaty requiring the cession of peripheral lands to the British.[34]

In a matter of months, Richard Wellesley had enhanced British power and prestige in India to an extent beyond that ever before imagined. Awaiting his just reward, he failed to perceive that events in India did not arouse much enthusiasm at home, where European affairs dominated interest.[35] Nor could he imagine the directors of the East India Company not being impressed with his work. But the directors had sent Wellesley to India to secure greater profits, and he had managed only to increase expenditure and drain the company's treasury. They failed to recognize that Mornington was attempting to secure years of uninterrupted prosperity by eliminating the sources of disruption. Hence, instead of eulogies of praise from a grateful nation, what Wellesley received was a hesitant note of approval and the suggestion that he cut expenditures.[36] He was astonished. At home he was not given the chance to demonstrate his abilities, and in India, where these were amply displayed, they went unrecognized. To compound his frustrations, Wellesley received a succession of bitter letters from his wife.

Separation had strained relations between Richard and Hyacinthe. They were lonely, and each blamed the other for the resultant grief. In her letters Hyacinthe accused Richard of infidelity, urged him to cut short his stay in India, demanded that he send money home, and admonished him for ignoring their children. It was all extremely distressing to Richard, and his health began to deteriorate. His body broke out in boils; unable to sleep, he developed a fever and in general suffered from nervous exhaustion.[37]

Wellesley eventually received recognition for his efforts, but only after the details of his accomplishments became fully known in Britain. Pitt secured for him an elevation in the Irish peerage to a marquessate, and the East India Company awarded him £100,000.[38] Surprisingly, the new Marquess flew into a rage. What he wanted, what he felt he deserved, and what he had instructed his family and friends to try to secure for him was an English marquessate, because this alone would give him the parliamentary prestige he previously lacked. To Lord Wellesley an Irish marquessate was politically and socially useless, and he considered its bestowal an insult. He hurried letters off to London, complaining of unjust treatment.[39] As for the £100,000, he considered this an insult as well. Wellesley claimed, with some justification, that it was granted at the army's expense, and under that pretext he declined the money.[40] The refusal of the £100,000 revealed a great deal about Richard Wellesley as a man. Money meant little to him, although he enjoyed finery and was constantly in debt. What was important were matters involving personal honor and prestige—things that appealed to his pride. Vanity was Richard Wellesley's outstanding trait, and produced his greatest weaknesses—occasional self-delusion and intellectual dishonesty. Wellesley was morally honest, and he considered accepting the £100,000 not right.[41]

London society viewed Wellesley's refusal of the money with amusement. People wondered what this vain little man was trying to prove.[42] Most who had traveled to India had returned with enormous, illegitimately acquired fortunes. Such was accepted practice. Wellesley had had the opportunity to return with an honest fortune and had rejected it over a matter of principle. Hyacinthe Wellesley was not amused. She could scarcely believe that Richard could be so thoughtless as to abandon an opportunity to eliminate his debts and establish financial security for life. Again she sent a flurry of hostile letters, and he became more disturbed.[43]

Wellesley entered a period of personal isolation after this affair, but he continued to deal with Indian affairs, initiating a program of farsighted administrative reforms. The Marquess felt that maladministration in India lay not so much in the system as in the people entrusted with the task of governing. The vast majority of the East India Company's employees knew nothing of Indian culture and history and were ignorant of native languages. Their basic nature was to profit from their positions, usually at the expense of fair and effective government. Wellesley concluded that if tranquillity was to be established and maintained in India, confidence and trust had to replace suspicion between Indian and Briton. The first step would be to educate the East India Company's employees. To this end, Wellesley established the College of Fort William, where prospective company employees could be instructed in Indian languages, history, culture, and politics. This project represented one of the first British attempts at civil service reform. By basing appointments on students' ability and performance at Fort William, Wellesley saw an opportunity to establish a respectful, efficient, and honest administration that would benefit both India and the East India Company. Again, however, the company looked unfavorably upon his plans. The directors felt that the cost of maintaining the school was too high, and they resented an inevitable loss of patronage.[44]

Meanwhile, there were new political problems to deal with—the Marathas of central India. Wellesley's aggressive politics had brought British influence to the Maratha's borders on the north, south, and east—a proximity which alarmed its inhabitants. The potential for trouble had not escaped Wellesley's notice, but he hoped to deal with it peaceably. Given the state of Marathan politics, a peaceable solution appeared possible. The death of Mahadji Sindia had diffused Marathan leadership, and the Marquess hoped to play upon the jealousies of the various leaders. But, like Tippu Sultan, the Maratha leaders were not fooled by the subsidiary treaties, nor would they succumb to threats of force. Negotiations reached an impasse, and war ensued.[45] The Marathas, even under threat of war, failed to unify, and the British armies proceeded against them in piecemeal fashion. Generals Harris and Wellesley carried out successful campaigns, eliminating most of the Marathan armies. Only Holkar, the most cunning and aggressive of the Marathan leaders, remained unscathed. The Marquess and Holkar negotiated without success, and war resumed. This time the wily Marathan defeated a British army beset with logistical problems.[46] It was the first and only defeat suffered by the British army during Wellesley's term as governor-general, and in spite of the several successful campaigns that followed, it was enough to give strength to his enemies on the India board.

Wellesley's adversaries were numerous. He could not count one friend on the board of directors. These men did not understand the implications of his policies—nor did they wish to understand. Their concern was not the state of the India trade in fifty years but, rather, immediate profit. As governor-general, Lord Wellesley had been expensive, fighting numerous wars, establishing his college, and building a new Government House. Although each project in its own way would ensure future profits, collectively they did little for the company at the moment. Further, most of the board's members rankled at Wellesley's independence and arrogance. Thus the board decided that these policies must end and with them Lord Wellesley's governor-generalship. Under normal conditions, the Marquess could have counted on the support of friends in government, but in 1804 Pitt led a weak ministry that did not include Grenville. He could not afford to offend the India interests in Parliament by supporting Wellesley.[47] Without allies, the Marquess found himself recalled. He departed India in August 1805.[48]

Lord Wellesley's term as governor-general is difficult to judge objectively. It is arguable that both his administration and his achievements were on the whole reactionary and pernicious. Those who believe in the virtues of constitutionalism, self-determination, and the rights of subject people will see little to admire in his material additions to the East India Company's territories. Regardless, Wellesley's term as governor-general was productive, and it revealed much about him as a person. The Marquess never doubted what he wished to accomplish, and he was convinced that in the pursuit of a goal the end justified the means. He demonstrated great administrative ability and tenacity in achieving his ends and displayed an imagination in his policies that revealed a comprehensive grasp of major issues. He was extremely effective in dealing with subordinates, freely delegating responsibility to those whom he trusted. At the same time Wellesley kept initiative in his own hands and did not shirk his own responsibilities. His tenure as governor-general also revealed, however, a dictatorial, vain, proud, yet insecure man, a man subject to depression in times of adversity. Eight years alone in India revealed and developed both his strengths and his weaknesses.

Wellesley returned to Britain believing his work as governor-general had secured a profitable future for Britain in India. Thinking that some of his countrymen would be of the same opinion, he expected a lavish welcome from family, friends, and appreciative members of government. Yet, when he stepped ashore at Portsmouth, he found only his wife and family. Grievously disappointed, the Marquess had no way of knowing that the bleak homecoming was but a portent of two miserable years to follow.

Wellesley returned to a political situation drastically different from the one he had left in 1797. The coterie of politician friends that stood at the pinnacle of power when he departed for India no longer existed. Pitt was prime minister, but he headed a government weakened by the defection of Grenville over the issue of Catholic Emancipation.[49] Wellesley did not relish the prospect of confronting the dilemma of divided loyalty, but this problem resolved itself with Pitt's death in January 1806. For the Marquess, however, the outstanding difference was in his own position as it had been in 1797 and as it was 1806. He returned with an English peerage, an elevation in the Irish peerage, and newly found wealth. Moreover, he had a following in Parliament made up of those who saw

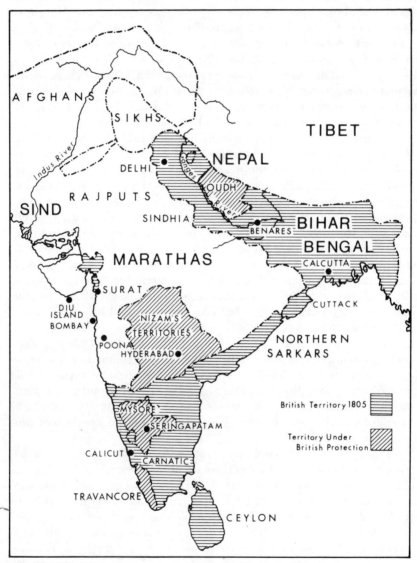

India after Wellesley (1805)

him as a statesman of genius, some past subordinates who maintained their allegiance, and two loyal brothers, William and Arthur. At a time when party lines were indistinguishable, a personal following such as this meant political strength, and as a result Wellesley had reason to be optimistic over his political future.

With Pitt's death, King George III turned to Grenville to form a ministry. On January 23, 1806, Wellesley offered his services to his old friend, who in turn made plans to appoint the Marquess foreign secretary.[50] Then, two days later, Wellesley wrote to Grenville: "A man of the name of Paul [1] (whose character you probably know) rose yesterday in the House of Commons, and gave notice of a motion for Monday, when he says he proposes to move for papers with a view of founding charges against Lord Wellesley. It is said that he is supported by Francis, even by Windham, and that the Prince of Wales has also ordered all his friends to attend for the purpose of countenancing the miserable attack of this obscure and low man. Certainly this is not the mode in which I expected to be treated."[51] Indeed not—first the snub on his return and then an attack on his policies! Despite efforts by Grenville to curtail the investigation into Wellesley's policies, Paull made good his threat. Though the inquiry failed to arouse much interest, it nonetheless had a profound effect on the Marquess. His vanity and honor injured, Wellesley declined a post in Grenville's Ministry of All the Talents and, further, refused to take his seat in the House of Lords until the issue was resolved.[52]

In 1806 Parliament was absorbed with European affairs and labor unrest at home. It had little time for the dubious charges made against Wellesley. Still Paull persisted, and when he was defeated in the 1806 elections such radical Whigs as Sir Francis Burdett, Lord Folkestone, Samuel Whitbread, and Sir Thomas Turton continued the action he had initiated.[53] In 1807 the Ministry of All the Talents foundered on the Catholic issue, and a new ministry under the nominal leadership of the Duke of Portland was ushered in. The duke offered Wellesley a cabinet post, which he again declined, owing to the "peculiar delicacy" of his situation.[54]

The investigation dragged inconclusively through 1807. Parliament began to weary of the proceedings, and by 1808 the Marquess regained enough confidence to take his seat in the House of Lords.[55] Finally, on March 15, 1808, Sir John Anstruther moved a resolution of approval and thanks to Lord Wellesley with regard to his policies in Oude. It carried 189 to 29.[56] The following June a vote of censure on Wellesley's policy in the Carnatic was defeated 124 to 15, and a vote of approval

carried 98 to 19.[57] With this vote, the investigation came to an end. The
Marquess was relieved but bitter. He again felt unjustly deprived of his
rightful place in British government.

To compound his troubled state of mind, a domestic quarrel of
immense proportions paralleled the parliamentary investigation.
Richard and Hyacinthe both expected to resume their life together
where it had left off in 1797, but eight years had transformed them both.
By 1806 they had become emotionally hardened and more impatient;
there was trouble between them from the moment Richard stepped off
the boat at Portsmouth. Hyacinthe did not understand Richard's disappointment over his rather private reception. While he had envisioned a
hero's welcome, she had expected a warm, tender reunion. As a result,
she reacted caustically, an understandable yet inappropriate response.
The verbal war that followed ceased only when the two combatants
separated in 1809. In a letter to his wife, Richard, in one of his more
tender moments, explained:"The only ray of light that can illuminate
the remainder of my life is to provide for the happiness of you and my
children. . . . The tragedy of my political situation, added to my bad
health in this horrible climate, stamps my entire conduct with the melancholy and coldness which you seem to think are directed only towards my
family. . . . my dearest wish is for peace in my home, and a retired life,
having failed to reach the goal towards which my education, my birth,
my work and my services were directed. My situation deserves in-
dulgence from all who love me. You would have found me very different
if my misfortunes had not poisoned my peace of mind."[58] Lack of
recognition, the parliamentary inquiry, and a bitter marriage combined
to have a devastating effect on Lord Wellesley. He became indolent and
melancholy, suffering a near nervous breakdown.[59]

Estranged from his wife and unoccupied in politics, the Marquess
began the licentious life style for which he became notorious. He openly
maintained concubines and led a generally raucous existence—indeed a
tragic period of Wellesley's life. Paralyzed by attack from home and
Parliament, he accomplished little for two years. His activities amused
some and bedeviled others. Arthur Wellesley wrote unsympathetically to
his brother William: "I am convinced that his fornication has kept him
out of office. In spite of his Idleness he would have been in office before
now if he had not taken to whoring."[60] A less critical public dismissed his
private life as irrelevant, and some citizens urged him to become active in
British politics again. A man, describing himself as an independent
Englishman, wrote:

It is reported that the Marquis of Wellesley has been offered a
leading situation in the government, and that his extreme delicacy
has induced him to refuse it, till the charge against his administration in India was settled in Parliament—I thought that Lord
Wellesley's mind was superior to menda infamia, and that the call
of his King and Country would command his services—What,
because a poor wretch thought proper to bring a charge against
him, and some narrow minded commercial men, from little motives of resentment as India Directors, supported it; can this affect
such a man as Lord Wellesley? And cannot the inquiry be brought
on in Parliament whether Lord Wellesley is in or out of the administration? Ought this to prevent the ablest man now in the
Kingdom, alas Pitt is gone, from serving his country, at the moment
when every energy and every nerve should be exerted to serve it,
without one moment's delay. . . . Now the nation looks up to Lord
Wellesley, he and Mr. Hastings were the ablest men who governed
India; Lord Wellesley there proved his talents as a statesman, let
him then take the station to which the King calls him, and let not
the nation be disappointed.[61]

Wellesley needed such encouragement. A man of proven ability, his
career had been characterized by unfulfilled ambition. He was dejected,
and inactivity only perpetuated his depressed state of mind. The frustrations of his career and marriage were difficult for him to overcome, and
it was not until late 1807 that he began to put these things behind him.
Emerging from his political isolation, he contributed to the debates in
the House of Lords and took a marked interest in foreign affairs. But
supremely confident of his ability and accustomed to the political independence he enjoyed in India, the Marquess desired a cabinet post
where, he believed, he could freely implement his many ideas. It would
be the tragedy of Lord Wellesley's life that he did not realize that in
England such a position would never exist for him.

In 1808 there was no ministerial post available for Wellesley. It was not
until the spring of 1809 that his friend George Canning held out the
hope that space might be made for him in the Portland cabinet. In the
meantime, the Marquess agreed to return to public service as
ambassador to Spain in the summer of 1809—a time when the
Peninsular War was entering its most crucial stage for Britain.

2

Appointment to the Ambassadorship

Britain's Iberian campaign began in the summer of 1808 amidst a spirit of public unanimity and optimism, but by January 1809 that spirit had given way to gloomy despair. Military setbacks, coupled with the enormous expense of war, led many Britons to reevaluate their views on the conflict. Many questioned if victory was possible and, if so, whether winning was worth the necessary sacrifice. These questions, growing out of the events of 1808, led to a great political debate in 1809—a debate which did not subside until Napoleon's retreat from Russia in 1812. The debate was pursued by those who predicted ultimate disaster for British arms, and their constant challenge to the government's policy of continuing the war came to dominate British politics in those years. It was this debate and the nuances surrounding it that brought Lord Wellesley out of his self-imposed political isolation and, in part, led to his appointment as ambassador to Spain in 1809. It, therefore, is essential to examine the political and diplomatic events of the years 1807–9.

The Peninsular War had its origins in the year 1807, when, at Tilsit, Napoleon and Czar Alexander I of Russia agreed on peace. Only Britain remained at war with France, and Napoleon prepared to starve her into submission by strictly implementing an economic blockade known as the Continental System. Britain, for her part, hoped to protect her shores and commerce while maintaining the ability to strike at Napoleon wherever he might show weakness.[1] Realizing that Britain's foreign policy was based on overwhelming sea power, Napoleon moved swiftly to challenge her naval superiority. His plans included a comprehensive ship-building program and the incorporation into his own navy of the considerable Danish fleet anchored at Copenhagen. George Canning, the British foreign secretary, correctly perceived Napoleon's intentions as a serious threat to Britain's vital security. As a preventive measure, he dispatched Admiral James Gambier with a British squadron in September 1807 to take control of the Danish fleet—peaceably, if possible. The stubborn Danes resisted the British intrusion, obliging Gambier to bombard Copenhagen before he could seize the fleet. While the operation was a success in the sense that it deprived Napoleon of naval reinforcements, it also provoked a public outcry in London.

Many Britons were at best halfhearted in their support of the war. The outspoken Whig leader Charles James Fox, for instance, espoused peace with France from the war's outbreak until his death in 1806. Similarly, William Grenville, who had joined the Whigs over the Catholic question, only reluctantly continued Pitt's foreign policy as head of the Ministry of All the Talents. The ominous agreement at Tilsit caused most Whigs to give up hope for a successful conclusion to the war. Party lines were drawn on the issue, and Grenville, speaking for the opposition in 1807, called for peace. When the Copenhagen expedition became known in London, the opposition indignantly condemned Gambier's bombardment as high-handed, illegal, and immoral.[2] But outrage was not confined to public utterances; the issue was brought before Parliament for debate.

Wellesley had long been a vigorous proponent of the war against France, and the year 1807 found him unchanged. His refusal to take his seat in the House of Lords and his strong personal attachment to Lord Grenville had kept him from speaking out on the subject, but the proposed debate on the Copenhagen expedition stirred him out of political retirement.[3] Taking his seat in the Lords, Richard rose in strong support of Canning. Allaying the doubts some Britons had over the legality and morality of capturing the Danish fleet, Wellesley explained concisely the necessity of the action. He described Napoleon's designs, the means he possessed to accomplish them, the concurrence of Denmark with those schemes, and the imminent danger that threatened Britain should the designs be implemented. The vote on the expedition resulted in an overwhelming victory for the government.[4] Whether Wellesley's speech contributed to the result can only be conjectured, but for him it was a momentous occasion. The oration gave him confidence, reestablished his position in British politics, and resulted in a final political split with his closest friend, William Grenville. Wellesley subsequently remained politically active, overseeing the defense of his India policies and closely observing the European scene.[5]

Portugal, Britain's long-time ally, became Napoleon's newest target. He planned to invade, close her ports, and seize the fleet. Canning realized that he could do nothing to prevent the French army's march into Portugal, but he could save the fleet and along with it the Portuguese royal family if he moved swiftly. The energetic foreign secretary proved equal to the task. At the end of November 1807, General Andoche Junot took Lisbon, only to find that a British fleet had preceded him. Gone was the coveted Portuguese navy, along with the royal family, which had fled to Brazil.[6]

The successful expeditions to Copenhagen and Lisbon did not, however, hide the fact that (except for Sweden) France was in complete control of the continent. Napoleon's obsession became Canning's frustration. No longer were there political rifts on the continent for Canning to exploit; other countries were reluctant to challenge France, even with British arms and money. Then, in the spring of 1808, Napoleon inadvertently created the situation that Canning had been awaiting.

Napoleon, determined to subdue Britain, had begun searching for weaknesses in his own efforts. He wondered where Britain, with her continental trade severed, would turn for substitute trade. The Spanish colonies seemed the obvious answer. Indeed, Britain had long fostered illicit trade with these colonies; when that trade failed, she encouraged the colonies to revolt under her protection.[7] Bonaparte consequently believed that a truly effective strangulation of British trade must include the closing of Spain's colonial ports. Theoretically, because Spain was his ally, this should not have been a difficult task. Yet the Spanish government had little control over her own colonies. Napoleon believed that better control might be established through the application of his own administrative ability, power, and prestige, but first, he had to gain control of Spain.

Because Napoleon considered Spain an unreliable ally, he had long planned to establish more direct control over Spanish affairs. What form such control would assume he had not determined. Nevertheless, preparing for any eventuality, he had filtered French troops into Spain on the heel of Junot's passage to Portugal. By March, there were nearly 100,000 French troops in Spain, with Marshal Joachim Murat at the head of an army of 40,000 advancing toward Madrid. Even so, it was the

Robert Stewart, Viscount Castlereagh and 2d Marquess of Londonderry
(1769–1822), by T. Lawrence. Reproduced with permission of the National
Portrait Gallery.

Spanish who precipitated Napoleon's take-over. On March 17, 1808, in a palace revolution, Crown Prince Ferdinand deposed his father, Charles IV, as King of Spain. Napoleon, who had a hearty disliking for Ferdinand, finally decided to remove the Bourbons from the Spanish throne. Taking advantage of the confusion that followed the royal coup, and of the presence of his troops on Spanish soil, Napoleon summoned both Ferdinand and Charles to the French city of Bayonne. There Charles IV surrendered his rights to the throne, and Ferdinand, coerced by Napoleon, followed suit. By the Treaty of Bayonne, all those in line of succession likewise renounced their claims. Joseph Bonaparte would be the new King of Spain.[8]

Spanish leaders tacitly accepted the coup, but their countrymen did not. On May 2, 1808, Madrid experienced a violent insurrection. Although ruthlessly suppressed by Marshal Murat, "Dos de Mayo" became a signal for widespread revolt throughout Spain. Bonaparte responded by sending additional soldiers to pacify the country, but, to everyone's surprise, the initial engagement between insurgent forces and the French resulted in a startling victory for the Spanish. The entire army of General Pierre Dupont surrendered following the Battle of Baylen. News of the surrender aroused Spanish enthusiasm. All over Spain people armed themselves, and in most every town and district a junta was formed to organize resistance.[9]

Meanwhile, Canning and all of Britain carefully watched the events in Spain. First indications that Napoleon was planning a significant move were reported on March 4, 1808.[10] It was known then that there were heavy concentrations of French troops in the large cities of northern Spain and that Bonaparte was to meet with the Spanish royal family in Bayonne. But it was not until May 23 that the Bayonne settlement became known along with the revolt of Dos de Mayo.[11] Britain was shocked. The *Times* called upon the Spanish to resist and urged the British government to provide them with support. On June 1 it editorialized: "The obligation to assist the people of Spain against this destroyer of mankind, rests stronger on the present administration of this country, on the account of the reproaches with which they stigmatized their predecessors in office, for deserting the cause of the Continent."[12] Canning, elated with the events in Spain, was quick to respond: "We shall proceed upon the principle, that any nation of Europe that starts up with a determination to oppose a power which . . . is the common enemy of all nations, whatever may be the existing political relations of that nation and Great Britain, becomes instantly our essential ally."[13] The opposition was as incensed over the French coup as the government, so Canning enjoyed the unanimous support of Parliament.[14]

On June 6 two representatives from the province of the Asturias arrived in London to solicit assistance, particularly arms and ammunition.[15] Canning and Viscount Castlereagh, secretary of war, prepared to send British war matériel and money to Spain. At the same time a British army under the command of Sir Arthur Wellesley, originally destined for revolutionary activity in South America, readied for an assault on the peninsula.[16] The target was Junot, whose communications had been severed by the Spanish insurrection. All of this, however, took time; Briton and Spaniard alike, especially the parliamentary opposition, became impatient with the Portland ministry. The *Times* commented:

> Never was there a period when the way to immortal honor and permanent security lay so open to the councils of this country, as it does at the present; and most anxiously do we wish that we may adequately avail ourselves of so favorable a juncture. But let us be fully aware, that it is not merely by praising the Spaniards, or stigmatizing their Oppressor, that we can support their cause—a cause the most glorious in the defense of which man ever bled: no, if they fight the enemy of every human right, we must fight him too, or we cannot hope either to partake of their glory or promote their success. If they meet him and his forces in their own country, we ought to meet them too, wherever they are to be found, and to draw away, or detain in other parts, as many of them as we are able to cope withal; for let it be observed, that though the Spaniards may have gallantly declared that they will fight for their own rights with their own arms, they have never yet been rash enough to say, that they wish the whole force of the enemy to be let loose upon them; and that they would not have us provide employment for a single Frenchman in any other quarter. yet, whoever casts his eyes round him upon the measures pursued by this country, would almost suppose, that those honourable men who have arrived here from Spain, had come for the express purpose of soliciting us to keep all our troops at home. No expeditions, no ship, no not even a rocket has yet been sent off from England. . . .[17]

British troops landed in Portugal in August 1808, scarcely a month after the Spanish victory at Baylen, and defeated Junot's army north of

Lisbon at the Battle of Vimeiro. But as Sir Arthur prepared to complete
the victory with a vigorous pursuit of Junot's dispersed army, Sir Harry
Burrard superseded him. Sir Harry, later to be superseded by Sir Hew
Dalrymple, lacked Arthur's skill and tenacity, and Junot was allowed to
retreat in good order.[18]

All Britain waited anxiously for news of Wellesley's army. On September 2 the *Times* announced the Battle of Vimeiro, and Britons began to
celebrate. The celebration was, however, interrupted by news of an
agreement signed by Dalrymple and Junot, known as the Convention of
Cintra,[19] which acknowledged the French defeat but obliged Britain to
transport Junot's defeated army to France. Such a concession was in-
comprehensible to many Britons, who were convinced that Junot and his
troops should instead be sent to Britain as prisoners of war. They had
received news of Wellesley's victory with satisfaction. Coupled with the
successes of the Spanish insurgents, these victories had restored the
optimism and enthusiasm of the British people for a conflict which was
beginning to tire them. Thus when news of the Convention of Cintra
reached London, British citizens were appalled and dismayed.[20]

The indignant public response was somewhat unreasonable. Six days
before news of the victory at Vimeiro became known in London, the
Times had explained: "The public anxiety to hear some account of the
progress of Sir Arthur Wellesley hourly increases. Those who are unac-
quainted with the real strength of the French force at Lisbon confidently
speculate upon the immediate surrender of Junot. We are not of this
opinion. Junot is an officer of great energy and decision, and will most
probably defend himself to the utmost. He has had sufficient time to
render his position very formidable, and to provide the means of a
vigorous and protracted defense."[21] When Burrard allowed Junot to
retreat after Vimeiro, the *Times*'s prediction essentially came true. So the
error in Portugal was a tactical one, and although the Convention of
Cintra belied the fact that the French army had been beaten in battle, it
did free Portugal of French occupation. Nevertheless, the furor in
Britain became so great that Dalrymple, Burrard, and Wellesley were
recalled to account for the convention before a court of inquiry.[22]

Lord Wellesley had carefully followed Peninsular events, especially
after Arthur's appointment to command the British expeditionary force.
Wellesley favored a concentration of energies against Napoleon, and
Iberia seemed to him as good a place as any for a vigorous effort.
Throughout the months of August and September he remained well
informed of Arthur's activities.[23] He basked in the glory of his brother's

success, and when the Convention of Cintra led to Arthur's recall, the Marquess prepared to battle for his brother's reputation. He realized that many who had attacked his India policies were eagerly turning their attention to Arthur. Samuel Whitbread, an inveterate Wellesley antagonist, wrote to Thomas Creevey, "I grieve for the opportunity that has been lost of acquiring national glory, but am not sorry to see the Wellesley pride a little lowered."[24] William Cobbett was more succinct: "Now we have the rascals on the hip. It is evident that *he* [Arthur Wellesley] was the prime cause—the *only* cause—of all the mischief, and that from the motive of thwarting everything *after he was superseded.* Thus do we pay for the arrogance of that damned infernal family. But it all comes at last *to the House of Commons.*"[25]

Dalrymple and Burrard returned to London before their young subordinate. They announced that Arthur was the inspiration behind the convention, when in fact Dalrymple was the author. Wellesley and his brother William rushed a letter to Arthur urging him to return to London as soon as possible. The Marquess wrote, "Sir Hew's line of conduct is so extraordinary, that it is impossible for any other person than yourself to meet it."[26] In the meantime, the Portland Ministry was deciding how to cope with the opposition's challenge to the convention. There seemed to be two choices: they could sacrifice the three generals by not supporting them, or they could try to salvage what they could of their generals at the risk of a parliamentary attack by the opposition.[27] An outraged Canning favored the former: "This Convention must be directly ours, or our commanders'. We must judge them—or the public will judge us."[28] Castlereagh believed otherwise, and his opinion prevailed in the cabinet.[29]

The Wellesley brothers, realizing the gravity of the situation, planned Arthur's defense. In their minds, the best course was to demand a comprehensive and open inquiry—one going at least as far back as Arthur's landing in Portugal. A thorough inquiry, they hoped, would lead to Arthur's vindication; about Portugal, he had the least to hide and the most for which to be proud.[30] William wrote to Arthur: "Unless the public mind is restored to health, you never can recover your place in the public estimation; and to restore the public mind I am sure it is necessary for you to take the pains of having your conduct placed fairly before the public."[31] The Wellesleys, who along with their friends now formed a powerful political coterie, were victorious. After a comprehensive and protracted investigation, ending in December 1808, Arthur was absolved of all wrongdoing.[32] Obviously the episode was pivotal for the career of Arthur Wellesley, but it was also important for the Marquess. His position on the Peninsular War was made clear, and he had revealed a surprising amount of political strength.

The recall of Dalrymple, Burrard, and Wellesley did not signal the end of British involvement in the peninsula. On their departure, the command of 40,000 British troops had been passed to Sir John Moore. On the surface at least, Moore inherited a favorable military situation. The Spanish victory at Baylen and the evacuation of French forces from Portugal had placed the French on the defensive. Thus Moore was ordered to enter Spain to cooperate in a Spanish offensive.[33]

Cooperation, however, proved a difficult task. The Spanish were hard pressed to coordinate their own activities. Local juntas refused to cooperate either with one another or with the Supreme Junta in Seville. Further, although many Spanish leaders were enthusiastic, they often lacked good judgment and were given to exaggeration. Even when Napoleon, alarmed at the course of events in the peninsula, marched an additional 100,000 soldiers into Spain, the Spanish remained supremely confident. The British representative to the Supreme Junta, John Hookham Frere, only added to the problem. Devoted to the Spanish cause, Frere zealously urged Moore into Spain, believing that a combined Anglo-Spanish force could halt Napoleon's advance.[34] Moore was less certain of success. Placed in a perilous position by Napoleon's advance and the Spanish army's failure to stop it, he wrote to Frere: "The movement I am making is of the most dangerous kind. I not only risk to be surrounded at any moment by superior forces, but to have my communications intercepted with the Galicias. I wish it to be apparent to the whole world . . . that we have done everything in our power in support of the Spanish cause, and that we do not abandon it until long after the Spaniards abandoned us."[35]

In spite of all this, Moore, upon learning that the French thought him in retreat toward Portugal, risked an advance through Salamanca to Valladolid. He believed that by advancing on the emperor's communications, he could draw the French army to the north, delaying its advance on southern Spain and Portugal.[36] Napoleon was unconcerned with communications, but he realized that Moore had greatly overextended himself against overwhelming odds. Ordering his army northward, he moved quickly to crush the British army. Moore, in turn, seeing the danger to which he had exposed his army, beat a hasty retreat to Corunna, where preparations had been made for the army's evacuation. Napoleon led the pursuit as far as Astorga, where Marshal Soult, the Duc de Dalmatia, took command. After a tortuous retreat, Moore arrived in Corunna and, while waiting for his fleet to arrive, gave battle to Soult. Soult was repulsed, but the British army sailed out of Corunna without its commander; Sir John Moore died in battle on January 16, 1809.[37]

The British public viewed the Moore expedition as yet another setback. Gone was the dream of a quick, decisive Anglo-Spanish victory over France, and with it the enthusiasm of the previous summer. Politically, the response was similar. Before the Battle of Corunna, the opposition had been prepared to support the war; after Corunna, it no longer believed the war could be won.[38] The returning soldiers of Sir John Moore's army only reinforced this belief with graphic descriptions of Spanish cowardice and Anglophobia.[39] With good cause, the Portland ministry girded itself for a parliamentary attack challenging the Convention of Cintra and the government's overall peninsular policy.

When Parliament convened in January 1809, Portland's ministers seized the offensive. On January 23 the Earl of Liverpool moved in the Lords the "Thanks of the House" to Arthur Wellesley for "the skill, valour, and ability employed by him on the 17th and 21st of August, and particularly on the later day, in the Battle of Vimeiro." The motion received the House of Lords's unanimous assent.[40] Hoping to circumvent altogether the question of the Convention of Cintra, Liverpool two days later introduced another motion of "thanks," this time to Sir John Moore, David Baird (Moore's second in command), and John Hope (in command when Moore was wounded). Liverpool praised Moore, extolling his virtue, courage, and brilliance as a commander.[41] Responding for the opposition, the Earl of Moira concurred with Liverpool's motion but took the opportunity to question the events which led to Corunna. "What! did our troops go to Spain only to make their escape? What was now to become of those great interests the protection of which was the greatest boon that Providence could have bestowed on a sinking country. British blood and treasure, and the invaluable lives of British officers and soldiers, had been sacrificed to no purpose, and without in the least assisting the great cause which the country had been pledged to support. Thus were we doomed to witness the extinction of every hope of continental alliance and cooperation. . . . To what but the ignorance and incapacity of ministers were all those calamities to be attributed?"[42]

In the House of Commons, Samuel Whitbread took the initiative for the opposition by calling on Castlereagh to publish the dispatches of Sir John Moore.[43] Except for those papers which he deemed too delicate, Castlereagh agreed, but he quickly changed the subject, moving for the construction of a monument to the memory of Sir John Moore. The motion carried and was followed by another successful motion of thanks to Arthur Wellesley.[44] If the motions had been introduced, as they were in the House of Lords, with the hope that the government's policies would not be called into question, the hope was illusory. The opposition attacked mercilessly, with Lord Erskine being particularly eloquent: "But for their immortal renown, it would have been better for them, certainly much better for their country, to have shot them up on the parade of St. James' park, than to have sent them, not to suffer the noble risque of soldiers—and in a practicable cause, but to endure insufferable, ignoble, and useless misery, in a march to the very center of Spain, when they who sent them knew that Bonaparte had above 100,000 men before them."[45] The opposition did not, however, confine its attack to oratory but concentrated on the publication of Sir John Moore's correspondence, which, it was hoped, would discredit the government. Further, it asked for reports on men, supplies, and aid invested in Spain. The government responded slowly.[46]

The pace of the opposition's assault gained momentum in February. Opposition M.P. George Ponsonby moved for a parliamentary investigation into Sir John Moore's campaign. Ponsonby had several complaints. He questioned why in the initial stages of the Spanish revolt, when nearly everyone in England wanted to support Spain, the government had made no definite commitment. Then, once the decision to support Spain had been made, why had the government not made a close study of what the Spanish were capable of doing on their own? Ponsonby suggested "that if the Spaniards were insensible of the cause of their degradation, and indifferent as to its removal, it was in vain for England to calculate upon materially exciting the spirit, or effectually aiding the exertion of such a people."[47] Ponsonby then expressed what was in the minds of most members of the opposition: "What, I would ask, would be the situation of England itself at this hour, if the domineering establishment of the priesthood had not been removed, if the baneful effects of the feudal system had not ceased to exist, and if a liberal system of equal laws had not been established, which secures every man the property of his own labor; which excites industry by guarding its produce; which encourages genius by rewarding its exertion; which constitutes the happiness, the glory, the fame, and the consequence of this great nation? With such a picture in our contemplation, how was it possible to suppose that the Spaniards could make a glorious struggle, could submit to severe privations, could act greatly, under the influence of the Inquisition, and

George Canning (1770– 1827), by T. Lawrence. Reproduced with permission of the National Portrait Gallery.

of no hope of bettering their condition?"[48] He wondered if Britain was justified in maintaining an old, corrupt, debilitated government.

Beyond the basic questions posited by Ponsonby, the opposition wanted to know why, once a British force was sent to Spain, communications were not improved so that the actions of the Spanish and British forces could be better coordinated. And why was Frere sent as representative to Spain when he had no understanding of military affairs? The questions went on. Why was Moore not given enough money to obtain the necessary provisions for his army? Once in Spain, how was Moore's army received? Why was Moore not given the independence to run his own campaign? If complete success was impossible from the outset, why was a campaign undertaken at all? Why was Moore asked to advance against overwhelming odds for questionable gains? Why stay in Spain when the Spanish did not appear to want British aid?[49] In sum, the opposition's attack came from two directions. Strategically it opposed the manner in which the campaign in Spain was conducted; philosophically it opposed supporting the ultraconservative sociopolitical system that was Spain's.

The Portland ministry based its defense on the premise that Britain's operations in the peninsula, particularly in Spain, were more limited than the opposition had surmised. The ministry argued that it had but three options when reacting to the events in Spain: aid would be granted only in the form of arms, money, clothing, and ammunition, based on the supposition that the Spanish were capable of defending themselves; every British soldier would be sent to the peninsula, and no pecuniary aid would be withheld; aid would be supplied in the form of both men and supplies, but a strong military reserve would be kept in Britain. The ministry informed the opposition that it considered the first contrary to British honor and the second unsound because it would leave Britain defenseless. The British army, then, was sent to act as an auxilliary force only, "and surely the British government was not to be blamed because the Spanish forces had not, unhappily, been able to hold out till the arrival of the military succours which were sent out to their assistance."[50] This was of course not to say that the Spanish lacked spirit. Rather, the government maintained that the Spanish will to resist was as great as ever.

The ministry ascribed the poor performance of the British army to the rapidly changing military situation in Spain. The army reacted slowly to these changes because of poor roads and because it was accompanied by its own supply train. The French, on the other hand, traveled in an area with good roads and merely seized what they needed in the form of supplies. As for the results of the campaign, it was necessary to draw the French northward to allow the Spanish the necessary time to organize their defenses in the south and to give the Portuguese respite from attack. Moore's manuever had accomplished this. Castlereagh concluded the ministry's defense by accusing the opposition of trying to obstruct the government's policies and asked that the motion for inquiry be defeated.[51] Wellesley, present at these debates, concurred.

Lord Milton responded for the opposition. Convinced that the country wanted an inquiry into the failures in Spain, he explained that "for his own part he should not hesitate to declare, that whether his friends were in power or out of power, he should at all times be a strenuous advocate for the necessity of vigilant inquiry into the conduct of public affairs."[52] Lord Milton's technique was one often employed by opposition parties in British politics: challenging the actions of the party in power under the guise of protecting political rights. George Canning was unimpressed. In a bitter retort in the House of Commons, Canning accused the opposition of spreading lies, overgeneralization, misinformation, and rumor. He argued that, rather than seeking the truth, the opposition merely wished to discredit the government. Further, he was appalled that the opposition would question British involvement in Spain on philosophical grounds: "To assist the patriotic efforts of the Spanish nation was the sole object, and they did not wish to inflict upon that country any change as the price of that assistance. God forbid! that we should ever be so intolerant, as to make a conformity to our own opinions the price of our assistance to others, in their efforts for national independence."[53] A division on Ponsonby's motion for inquiry came at 3:30 Saturday morning, February 25. The motion was defeated by ninety-three votes.[54]

Rebuffed, the opposition tried another tactic—an assault on John Hookham Frere, the British representative in Spain and close personal friend of George Canning. Frere's attraction to the opposition lay in the fact that he had had an extremely unpleasant relationship with Sir John Moore. The envoy believed that Moore had been dilatory in his operations in Spain and was generally ill disposed toward the Spanish cause. In a series of letters that ended only with Sir John's death, Frere had lectured Moore on what he felt should be the general's proper conduct.[55] Thus, because of his own questionable conduct and his close identity with the Portland ministry, Frere was an ideal subject on whom the opposition could focus its attention.

To discredit Frere and, in turn, the government, the opposition first needed to accumulate evidence of wrongdoing. On March 16, Earl Grey announced that he would move that the Moore-Frere correspondence be produced. Attempting to disguise the reason for his request, Grey claimed he was seeking information on the army's delay in embarkation from Corunna.[56] No one was deceived. Liverpool informed Grey before the House of Lords that all letters passing between Moore and Frere were contained in the general's private correspondence and therefore could not be produced. He explained that all information on the British army's movement at Corunna could be found in the dispatches of the officers employed there.[57]

Grey was incensed. He could not be convinced that letters passing between Frere and the commander in chief were private. Suddenly the opposition had new ammunition—the government's resistance to revealing the details of its involvement in Spain. Their position grew even stronger when on March 24 Britain learned that French forces had seized the Spanish port city of Ferrol and with it a part of the Spanish fleet.[58] To the opposition, this was further evidence of governmental negligence and Spain's reluctance to cooperate. Consequently Lord Grenville demanded that all Spanish material—not just the letters between Moore and Frere—be placed before the House of Lords.[59] The Earl of Darnley was more specific. He moved for the production of the Moore-Frere correspondence along with that of Sir David Baird, Charles Stuart, George Canning, and General Brodrick. These papers, he hoped, would show that the failures in Spain were the ministry's responsibility.[60]

Under such heavy pressure, Liverpool informed the House of Lords that he would produce the Moore-Frere correspondence and whatever else was desired. He excepted the Stuart letters because the government did not have them and the Canning papers because of national security.[61] The government's evasion on the Stuart and Canning correspondence gave the appearance that it was withholding vital information. In fact the papers were not released because it was feared that they would reveal that the Spanish were uncooperative and at times belligerent. Under persistent opposition pressure, a tired Liverpool stated inanely, "As the papers themselves increased, the desire for more increased in the same proportion."[62]

Gradually and reluctantly the government produced most of the papers. Subsequent discussions centered on Frere's questionable involvement in military affairs. Frere was an inviting target for the opposition, because through him the government's policies could be closely examined; while a direct vote of censure on the government's Spanish policies appeared unlikely, forcing Frere's recall might accomplish nearly the same thing. For its part, the government defended Frere. That he had been somewhat less than discreet could not be denied, but Corunna had been Moore's own doing.[63]

Grey opened for the opposition on April 18, 1809, by stating his surprise that anyone could see the Moore-Frere correspondence and maintain that Moore had not been driven against his own inclination to march further than Salamanca.[64] Liverpool intervened to comment that Frere had only related Spanish sentiments to Moore, that he had no authority over the general, and that Moore knew it.[65] Grey, unconvinced, continued his attack. He questioned the government's conduct of the campaign from the beginning, and he stated that Frere was ". . . a gentleman, who, whatever may be his talents in other respects, and however painful and unpleasant it may be to me to make the observation, appears to be wholly unqualified, from his folly, ignorance and presumption, for that high and important station which he at present occupies."[66] Lord Grey based his charges on Frere's policies, which he judged erroneous, and on his attitude, which he judged insolent. Grey, forgetting his party's impatience in the summer of 1808, then suggested that the ministry had not sufficiently investigated the situation in Spain before investing so heavily in men and matériel. Liverpool's response was effective: "What! when the feeling of resistance against oppression was so strong and so general in Spain, would it have been honourable to the British character, had his majesty's ministers told the gallant Spaniards; 'We will not give you aid while you are in most want of it; while your efforts at emancipation are in infancy; but we will defer our assistance until you are in full strength and need it not?' "[67]

Liverpool ably defended the ministry. He argued that Moore's decision to advance was his own and was the correct one. He stated that Frere could not be blamed and that it was foolish to expect victory in one campaign.[68] Lord Erskine was unimpressed. He explained that while he respected the men in the administration, as ministers they were guilty of improvidently wasting the country's resources; he considered them responsible for the death of every British soldier who had fallen in Spain.[69] So grave a charge was followed by bitter invective from both sides of the House of Lords. The vote on Grey's motion for a censure of government policy in Spain failed on April 21, 1809, but the discussion about Frere continued.[70]

Earl Darnley asked if Frere was to be recalled. If not, he gave notice that he would move for such an action.[71] The ministry now had to evaluate its position. The Moore-Frere correspondence proved that Moore had acted on military considerations; it showed also that Frere's conduct had been questionable. Frere undoubtedly possessed talent, but he was vain, arrogant, and careless. He had been overly optimistic in his dealings with the Spanish, and had constantly misjudged their capabilities.[72] Thus there was reason for recalling him. Although Canning initially resisted, he too began to consider different options, since the inquiry into Frere's conduct at this point was the only issue against the government.

The opposition, noticing the effectiveness of the attack on Frere in the House of Lords, proceeded with the same arguments in the Commons. On April 20, 1809, Canning was questioned on Frere's conduct. Samuel Whitbread announced that he, like Earl Darnley, was contemplating the introduction of a motion for Frere's recall.[73] On April 27 Mr. Eden moved that all the Moore-Frere correspondence be introduced so that Frere's conduct might be better examined.[74] The opposition's tactics exasperated Canning, who soon came to believe that Frere was causing more trouble than he was worth and that it was time for his recall.

To recall Frere was to admit his misconduct and to acknowledge the government's error. Unwilling to grant the opposition the satisfaction of so great a victory, the ministry searched for a means to withdraw Frere gracefully. Canning suggested recalling him under the pretense that the situation in Spain required someone of sufficient rank to assume a full ambassadorship. Canning's colleagues agreed because, in addition to its obvious convenience, the suggestion contained an element of truth. The Spanish, acutely conscious of protocol, resented the presence of a mere minister plenipotentiary in Seville when they maintained a full ambassador in London.[75] Moreover, new problems in Anglo-Spanish relations necessitated the services of a diplomat more experienced and more prudent than John Hookham Frere.

Canning and Castlereagh had become increasingly disillusioned with the Spanish. Their generals were proving themselves incompetent and recalcitrant; their political leaders appeared inexperienced, divisive, inefficient, and, in many cases, corrupt. Thus the two British ministers began an overall reassessment of the British commitment in the Iberian Peninsula. The Moore campaign and its political results had convinced them that Spain required a more cautious approach.

In March a memorandum from Arthur Wellesley to Castlereagh

declared that if Portugal was designated the focal point of Britain's peninsular policy, it could be defended with 20,000 British troops and a reconstituted Portuguese army.[76] Castlereagh concurred, and at his urgings the ministry appointed Arthur Wellesley commander in chief of Britain's peninsular forces.[77] Arthur's instructions reflected a new ministerial attitude: "The defense of Portugal you will consider as the first and immediate object of your attention. But, ʑ the security of Portugal can only be effectually provided for in connexion with the defense of the Peninsula in the larger sense, His Majesty on this account, as well as from the unabated interest he takes in the cause of Spain, leaves it to your judgement to decide, when your army shall be advanced on the frontier of Portugal, how your efforts can best be combined with the Spanish, as well as the Portuguese troops in support of the common cause. In any movements you may undertake, you will, however, keep in mind that until you receive further orders, your operations must necessarily be conducted with especial reference to the protection of that country."[78]

The Portland ministry had no intention of abandoning Spain. Military supplies would still be forwarded, but any cutback in British aid would not be lost on the Spanish. It was therefore essential to convince them that Britain still supported Spain's cause. At the same time Spain had to be dealt with firmly and be made to realize the need for greater efficiency in her army and government. Such would be the task of the next British ambassador to Spain.

Lord Wellesley was ideally suited for the ambassadorship. He was well informed on Iberian affairs, and he, unlike Frere, was a political realist—decisive yet prudent. Wellesley's personality, point of view, prestige, and experience all made him suitable for the post. Moreover, a problem relating to Britain's newly defined involvement in the peninsula further revealed Wellesley's desirability. The Portland ministry, seeking to avoid a repeat of the Moore-Frere relationship, had carefully defined the status of commander in chief in the peninsula, giving Arthur Wellesley full responsibility for all military decisions.[79] But military decisions were to be completely separated from diplomatic decisions. The implicit danger was that contradictory decisions on the part of soldier and diplomat could create military and diplomatic chaos. To avoid such an occurrence, cooperation was essential, and what better way of guaranteeing it than by appointing the commander in chief's brother as ambassador?

It was fairly obvious then that the appointment should go to Lord

William Wyndham Grenville, 1st Baron Grenville (1759– 1834), by J. Hoppner. Reproduced with permission of the National Portrait Gallery.

Wellesley, but there was a question of whether Wellesley would be amenable to an ambassadorship. While the Marquess was less than enthusiastic, there were positive aspects to the appointment which would act as inducement: he could again work in conjunction with his brother; he could be in the center of exciting, important events; and he could escape his wife.[80] Yet why would a man who had lately been offered posts in two successive cabinets accept a mere ambassadorship? Why would Wellesley labor in India only to return to a post lower than the one he had left? For a man of Lord Wellesley's pride and vanity, there had to be further incentive. There was, and it was related to what would become one of the most extraordinary episodes in British political history.

In March 1809 George Canning revealed to the Marquess a proposal to bring him into the Portland cabinet. Canning had been nurturing this plan for several months. Since the outbreak of the Peninsular War, he and Castlereagh had repeatedly clashed over the conflicting responsibilities of the Foreign Office and War Office. At that time the functions of the two offices were ill defined and overlapping. When encroachment occurred, friction invariably resulted, as had happened with Canning and Castlereagh. Canning was undeniably temperamental and impetuous, but he genuinely considered Castlereagh a mediocre minister of war. Consequently Canning resolved to reorganize the Portland ministry by moving Castlereagh to another post and replacing him with Lord Wellesley.[81]

It is not surprising that Canning looked to Wellesley to take over the War Office, since the two were good friends. Other than Pitt and Grenville, Canning was the one political colleague the Marquess respected and to whom he often deferred. Canning likewise appreciated Wellesley's abilities, and although the two men frequently disagreed, mutual respect preserved their friendship.[82] Thus, with Wellesley's permission, Canning revealed his plans to the Duke of Portland early in April and threatened to resign if they were not soon accomplished. Bewildered, Portland confided in Lord Bathurst. Together they decided that the cabinet could not stand without Canning. But, reorganizing a cabinet in the middle of a parliamentary session could prove equally fatal, and they urged Canning to defer implementing his plan until the prorogation of the current session. Canning reluctantly agreed to their request.[83]

Canning informed the Marquess of the proceedings. Faced with the problems of keeping Wellesley busy and out of the way while the political manueverings continued and of rescuing the government from the unhappy prospect of the opposition forcing Frere's recall, Canning offered Wellesley the ambassadorship. Wellesley accepted, assured that the mission to Spain would be temporary and that recall would be prompt when a way was found for his entrance into the ministry.[84] A relieved Canning made the official appointment on April 30, 1809. The British public responded enthusiastically. The *Times* commented: "We consider the appointment as an unequivocal pledge given to the nation by Ministers that they are resolved to adopt no half measures, to pursue no system of cold or timid precaution, to leave no outlets for irresolution or vacillation. Lord Wellesley cannot be an instrument for such purposes; he possesses one of the cardinal virtues, fortitude, which we would at the present moment place above the others, because it is that which the necessities of the hour render indispensable."[85]

Although Lord Wellesley was appointed ambassador extraordinary on April 30, he did not embark for Spain until July 24. Wellesley's detractors suggested that his delay stemmed from an abortive attempt to secure passage to Spain for a mistress named Miss Leslie.[86] The Marquess did make such an attempt, but it hardly preoccupied him for nearly three months. Instead, Wellesley and his apologists preferred to ascribe the delay to ill health. Again, there was truth in this rationale, because the Marquess had suffered his first attack of gout.[87] It is, however, clear that Wellesley's late departure was due primarily to Canning's continuing political intrigue, which required Wellesley's presence in London.

Shortly after Wellesley's appointment, Canning again tried to force cabinet reorganization upon Portland. Helpless, Portland turned to George III, who sympathetically promised to consider a solution to the problem. But the king dallied, and on May 31 the impatient Canning tendered his resignation. George III refused to accept it, suggesting later to Canning that a restructuring of cabinet offices might prove more beneficial to Britain's interests than a reshuffling of cabinet personnel. Specifically, the king recommended that the political responsibilities of the War Office be given to the Foreign Office. To compensate, the War Office would be combined with the Board of Control.[88] The idea was impractical and hardly what Canning desired, but, unwilling to contradict the king, Canning temporarily deferred to the plan. In addition, Portland urged Canning to temporize, pointing to Castlereagh's deep involvement in the planning of a major military expedition to the Scheldt estuary—the ill-fated Wlcheren campaign. Forced to agree, Canning saw no further reason for the Marquess to remain in London.[89]

Unfortunately, the prolonged delay between Wellesley's appointment and his departure had coincided with a deterioration in Anglo-Spanish relations. The sobering reality of Napoleon's power and the prospect of a protracted campaign had ended the euphoria that previously existed in both Spain and Britain. Familiar suspicions and hostilities were renewed. There was persistent discord over encounters between British and Spanish ships on the high seas and alleged British support of revolutionary movements in the Spanish colonies.[90] Spain's inability to defend the harbor of Ferrol and her refusal to allow Britain to garrison Cádiz also caused ill feeling.[91] Most of the points of conflict seemed to stem from each ally's misconception of the other's obligations.

Since the outset of the war, Spain had expected from Great Britain an unlimited supply of monetary and material aid, and Britain had hoped that Spain would make such subsidies feasible by opening her colonial trade to British commerce. But when a treaty was concluded in January 1809, it contained provisions for neither.[92] Spain, jealous of her colonial trading monopoly, refused to commit herself to open trade unless Britain agreed to a specified yearly subsidy. Canning refused to go this far, preferring to use British aid as a lever in his negotiations.[93] As a result, Anglo-Spanish relations were based on merely a vague pledge of mutual friendship and cooperation. Diplomacy became a day-to-day affair, resulting in numerous misunderstandings.

Allied tensions mounted through the spring of 1809. Canning, already disturbed over Spain's refusal to open her colonial trade, became angry when she delayed granting a license for the purchase of specie needed to carry on the war effort.[94] The Spanish, on their part, were relentless in their demands for British aid. Canning received innumerable requests for arms, money, and supplies, requests which were notable for their frequency and excessiveness. The outbreak of war between France and Austria in 1809, and the resultant Austrian appeal for British aid, put an additional burden on Britain's already beleaguered finances. Thus Canning had repeatedly to deny Spain's requests or at least to equivocate on them.[95] Spain became increasingly disillusioned, but Frere, knowing of his recall, was indifferent to the trend. Sympathizing with the Spaniards, he failed to explain Britain's position.[96] Vigorous representation was clearly needed in Seville to clarify the situation.

Wellesley sailed on July 24, 1809, hoping to satisfy Spain that Britain's interest in her was undiminished. This, however, would be a difficult task, as the instructions which the Marquess carried reflected the current state of Anglo-Spanish relations. Specifically, Wellesley had the unenvi-

able duty of informing the Spanish that little British aid could be expected in the upcoming months. He could guarantee that the supply of
arms, stores, ammunition, and clothing would continue unabated, but
monetary and military assistance would be negligible.[97] The cutback had
become a matter of policy necessitated by practical and political considerations, but the Marquess hoped to convince the Spaniards that the
Austrian war was the primary cause of the reduction in subsidy. In fact,
helping Austria had become an expensive matter. Aside from a monetary subsidy and shipments of equipment, the Portland ministry had also
decided to open a second front to assist Austria with the expedition to the
Scheldt. Although the operation involved a considerable investment in
men and money which could have been better employed in the peninsula, Wellesley would tell the Spaniards that the Walcheren expedition
amounted to direct aid to Spain because of the diversion it created for
France.[98] It was an excuse that Spain was unlikely to accept.

To compound his problems of presenting this realistic yet gloomy
picture of Britain's capacity to support Spain, Wellesley would have to
urge the Spanish to greater exertions against France. Military activities
were to be encouraged as were practical reforms in the military and
governmental structures. Canning instructed the Marquess to "avoid
any appearance of a desire to interfere, unnecessarily, with the internal
concerns and interests of Spain," but experience had revealed a great
need for reform.[99] Consequently, at the first opportunity, Wellesley was
to suggest improvements which might help a more effectual prosecution
of the war. He was also to recommend a liberalization of Spain's government and commerce. Such an occurrence would put to rest reservations
harbored by several members of the opposition over the nature of the
Spanish regime. It would also have more practical results: Canning
believed that "the removal of such grievances or restrictions on political
and personal liberty as the Junta may already have made up their minds
to recommend, if granted soon, would tend to give weight and energy to
the authority of the Government."[100] It is clear that Canning wanted to
effect changes in the Spanish government and military establishment,
but, as he stated in the Commons several months earlier, he was unwilling to force Spain into these changes. Then again, Canning had little
with which to coerce the members of the Supreme Junta.

Undoubtedly Lord Wellesley realized that he was stepping into a
difficult situation. He would be dealing with a disorganized, vastly inefficient government, on which he would be forced to make demands for
which he could provide no return. There was little prospect for great

diplomatic success. He could only hope for continuation of harmony within the alliance. But Wellesley had learned much from the parliamentary debates of the previous winter and spring. He realized that even if the Spanish failed to perform adequately in the field or did not make efforts to promote the interests of the alliance, support at home could be maintained—that is, if British military and diplomatic affairs were conducted openly, consistently, honestly, and, to some extent, successfully. Above all, he would have to protect British interests scrupulously. Spain would receive no unwarranted quarter from Lord Wellesley.

3

Military Negotiations with
the Supreme Junta

Lord Wellesley sailed into Cádiz harbor on July 31, 1809, aboard His Majesty's ship *Donegal.* He immediately notified John Hookham Frere and the Supreme Junta of his arrival and at ten o'clock the following morning went ashore. Cádiz gave the Marquess a glittering reception: bells tolled, people lined the city's streets, and, so that his first steps on Spanish soil might symbolically be over Spain's oppressor, a French flag was strategically placed at Wellesley's point of disembarkation.[1] Duly impressed, the new ambassador wrote to Canning: "I was received at Cádiz with every demonstration of public honour, and with the most cordial and enthusiastic expressions of veneration for his Majesty's person and respect for his government, of zealous attachment to the British alliance, and of affectionate gratitude for the benefits already derived by the Spanish nation from the generosity of his Majesty's councils, and from the persevering activity, valour and skill of his officers and troops."[2]

Spain had an obligation to provide any British representative with a proper reception. Yet Wellesley's, which most contemporary accounts called extraordinary, was a direct result of how the Spanish perceived the former governor-general. He was reputed to be a tough, disciplined diplomat, and, from the extensive personality analyses sent by Spain's London legation, it was clear that Wellesley would conduct Britain's Spanish affairs much differently than had Frere.[3] That the junta was

46

apprehensive over this fact was made manifest in its official acknowledgment of the appointment. Satisfaction with Frere's conduct was amply expressed, while Wellesley's appointment was given cordial but hesitant approbation.[4] Still, Spanish leaders were not so foolish as to expect Frere's reappointment. It was therefore in their interest to ingratiate Lord Wellesley to Spain's cause, and what better way than through an appeal to his known vanity?

The flattery had its desired effect. Wellesley, in his first letters from Spain, betrayed an optimism that the goals of his mission could be accomplished.[5] He was, however, not to be long deceived. Even as he traveled to Spain, his brother Arthur was participating in a joint Anglo-Spanish campaign, the results of which would greatly complicate future relations between the allies.

Arriving on the peninsula on April 22, 1809, to assume command of the British army, Sir Arthur had promptly begun operations to free Portugal. On May 12 he moved on the army of Marshal Nicolas Soult, then occupying the north Portuguese city of Oporto. A combination of surprise and good luck brought success, and Soult was forced into a headlong retreat through the Portuguese mountains, across the Spanish frontier.[6] This accomplished, Sir Arthur turned his attention to a French corps under Marshal Claude Perrin Victor, poised menacingly near the Portuguese frontier for a march on Lisbon. An attack on Victor would involve fighting on Spanish soil but, in Arthur's judgment, not to the extent that it would jeopardize the security of Portugal. Rather, he argued that its defense necessitated such a campaign. Receiving permission in June to link up with a Spanish army under General Gregorio de Cuesta, Sir Arthur entered Spain on July 4, 1809.[7] One week later he met with Cuesta to plan the operation.

At the July 11 meeting, the two generals agreed to join forces on July 21 and to advance together on Victor near the Spanish village of Talavera de la Reina.[8] Yet the ostensible spirit of allied unanimity soon faded, and Arthur came to doubt the campaign's future.

Throughout his military career Arthur had given special attention to his commissariat, believing that "a starving army is actually worse than none."[9] While operating in Spain, he considered it especially important that the commissaries be well supplied, because allowing the army to live off the land would earn only the enmity of his allies. Consequently, before entering Spain, Arthur requested the Supreme Junta's guarantee that provisions and transport facilities would be amply provided within easy reach of the British army. Eager for Sir Arthur's assistance, the junta

Spain and Portugal

complied. Nonetheless, by mid-July supplies, provisions, and transport facilities had all become scarce.

Sir Arthur immediately complained.[10] The junta promised to improve logistics but with little effect. Wellesley, his situation deteriorating, pondered withdrawing to Portugal. But he was committed to the campaign and aware of the adverse consequences which would attend a retreat. "It is certain," he explained, "that the people of England will never hear of another army entering Spain, after they will have received the accounts of the treatment we have met with; and it is equally certain that without the assistance, the example and the continuance of a British Army, the Spanish armies, however brave will never effect their object."[11] Although greatly annoyed, Sir Arthur continued his advance on Talavera.

On July 22, Sir Arthur learned that Victor's corps consisted of only 20,000 men. With the allied armies numbering over 50,000 troops, Arthur perceived the possibility of a rout. He proposed an attack for the following morning, but Cuesta would not cooperate. While the allies quarreled, Victor retreated to join General Horace Francois Sebastiani's 4th Corps, as well as additional reserves from Joseph Bonaparte's garrisons in Madrid, swelling the French army to 46,000 men.[12] Already enraged over Spain's failure to supply the British army, Arthur now complained, "I find General Cuesta more and more intracticable every day; it is impossible to do business with him, and very uncertain that any operation will succeed in which he has any concern."[13] On July 24 Cuesta urged an advance on Madrid, but now Sir Arthur, knowing that Victor had been reinforced, refused to cooperate. Optimistic, the stubborn Cuesta marched on alone, but when confronted by Victor's enlarged army he retreated precipitously to Talavera, closely pursued by the French. At daybreak on July 27, Victor attacked the allied positions. The battle raged for two days until the French were forced to retire. In the fighting, Britain lost over 5,000 men, while French casualties totaled 7,000.[14]

The following day Cuesta urged a pursuit of the retreating French. Wellesley, however, seeing his army exhausted from two days of vicious fighting and two weeks of insufficient rations, preferred to remain in the easily defensible positions around Talavera.[15] On July 30 he received news that a reconstituted French force under Marshal Soult was advancing on his rear, threatening to cut communications with Portugal. Sir Arthur decided to make a short retreat. Bereft of adequate transportation, he left 1,500 sick and wounded British soldiers to Cuesta's care.[16]

By this time Wellesley's disillusionment with his ally had reached the breaking point. He openly chastised Cuesta for allowing Victor to retreat toward reinforcements and was openly verbal over Spain's failure to provide supplies.[17] Writing to Frere, he complained: "Although my troops have been on forced marches, engaged in operations with the enemy, the success of which I must say depended upon them, they have had nothing to eat, while the Spanish army have had plenty."[18] Likewise, the Spanish were not enthralled with Sir Arthur. The junta's secretary of state, Don Martín de Garay, severely criticized him for his lack of cooperation throughout the campaign, especially in not following up the Battle of Talavera with the vigorous pursuit suggested by Cuesta. The criticism left Wellesley livid and convinced of a previous conjecture: that a joint Anglo-Spanish military venture could never succeed. Occupying a defensive position southwest of Talavera, he stated flatly that he would never again cooperate with the Spanish armies.[19] Thus, when Lord Wellesley entered Cádiz on August 1, 1809, Anglo-Spanish relations were at their lowest point since the outbreak of the Peninsular War.

The Marquess was unaware of the extent to which the alliance had been undermined. He had of course been informed of the victory at Talavera, and Frere had relayed some of Sir Arthur's numerous complaints.[20] But details were scarce; so while efforts were being made to procure a suitable ambassadorial residence in Seville, Wellesley remained in Cádiz, attempting to acquaint himself more fully with the events of the previous three weeks.[21] It soon became evident that the situation demanded his prompt and undivided attention. In addition to past problems, Sir Arthur's complaints were increasing daily. Besides the alleged lack of provisions, Cuesta had added to Wellesley's ire by retreating from Talavera, leaving behind the sick and wounded British soldiers he had pledged to protect.[22] Outraged, Sir Arthur bitterly denounced the Spanish, who in turn reacted indignantly.[23] Martín de Garay advised the Marquess that Sir Arthur was overreacting; Cuesta's movements, he argued, were fully justified, and the British army was being amply supplied. Lord Wellesley, however, had information that the British army had not received bread for five days and then only 4,000 pounds.[24]

The Marquess summoned his brother to a conference, hoping to gain a clearer idea of the army's condition.[25] But Sir Arthur declined, explaining: "I wish I could see you, or could send somebody to you; but we are in such a situation, that I cannot go to you myself, and I cannot spare the only one or two people to converse with whom would be of any use to you. I think, therefore, that the best thing you can do is to send somebody to me as soon as you can; that is to say, if I remain in Spain, which I declare I believe to be almost impossible, notwithstanding that I see all the consequences of withdrawing."[26] Nevertheless, Sir Arthur graphically described his situation. He reiterated the desperate needs of the army and told of a breakdown in its discipline. Soldiers were plundering the countryside and in many cases were joined by their officers. So wretched was the army's state that Sir Arthur claimed, "With the army which a fortnight ago beat double their numbers, I should now hesitate to meet a French corps of half their strength."[27]

As soon as Wellesley procured a residence, he set out for Seville. Frere informed him on arrival that relations between Sir Arthur and Cuesta had further deteriorated. Cuesta, Frere explained, was insulted by the commander in chief's repeated charges of Spanish incompetence and neglect.[28] Moreover, the Spanish general was less than impressed with the conduct of the British army. On August 10 he wrote to Sir Arthur, accusing British soldiers of looting Spanish supplies. "Today the English have taken one hundred Quintals of Biscuit which was coming to us from Seville. They have detained another quantity of horses, which were coming to us laden from Puente de Moesther, and the day before yesterday they received four hundred and fifty Quintals more. The towns and Shepherds also must contribute that article while they rob us with their troops & I rec. that it is impossible to provide a supply of bread for our own."[29] Sir Arthur could not deny that the Spanish needed provisions as badly as the British did or that his troops were guilty of looting. But he categorically refuted Cuesta's charge that British troops were plundering Spanish supplies, insisting, instead, that the Spanish troops were guilty of intercepting supplies destined for the British army.[30] Frustrated and increasingly disillusioned, Sir Arthur once again threatened to withdraw into Portugal: "It is useless to complain, but we are certainly not treated as friends, much less as the only prop on which the cause in Spain can depend. But besides this want of good will, which can easily be traced to the temper and disposition of the General commanding the Spanish army, and which ought to be borne with patience if there was any hope of doing good, there is such a want of resource in the country, and so little question of bringing forward what is to be found, that if the army were to remain here much longer it would become totally useless."[31] Thus, while the Marquess presented his credentials to the Supreme Junta, Sir Arthur claimed that he could neither trust Spanish generals in the field nor count on the junta for the feeding of his troops. The Spanish maintained that his charges were exaggerated and his conduct self-serving. Such disagreement was obviously not in the best

interests of the alliance; it became Wellesley's task to reestablish a basis
for mutual trust. If that could not be done, he must convince the Spanish
that Britain was not abandoning Spain's cause. Only when this was
accomplished could he turn his attentions to the original goals of the
mission.

In pursuing these objectives, it would be necessary for the ambassador
to adopt aggressive diplomacy. Wellesley sensed that only by maintaining
the offensive in his discussions with Spanish officials could he hope for
an improvement in Spain's treatment of the British army. Therefore, on
August 12, Wellesley, referring to the situation as a crisis, demanded that
Martín de Garay take immediate steps to alleviate the British army's
plight. To begin, it was necessary to call into action the corps of the
Marquis de la Romana and of the Duque del Parque and any other force
which might be moved to the north of Spain. The idea was to oblige the
French to reduce their forces in Estremadura. Such action, Wellesley
maintained, would remove the immediate threat to the allied armies and
allow them to regroup and reorganize. At the same time, he emphasized
the absolute necessity of providing the British army with a regular
supply of provisions and means of transport. He insisted that only when
these demands were met would the British army be formidable enough
to resume offensive operations in Spain.[32] Wellesley was fully aware that
his brother had no intention of renewing offensive operations in the
near future, but he felt that the prospect of such an event would stimulate Spain to greater activity.[33]

The Spanish response was immediate. Garay informed Wellesley that
orders had been issued for the prompt implementation of all his demands. He insisted that Spain had been faithful to her pledge to keep the
British army supplied, but in so doing he showed a note of skepticism:
"The said commissaries go with ample powers and funds to provide and
prepare all the succours that are necessary, and which the scarcity of the
country may permit, which, desolated by the enemy, sacked by the
soldiers, having suffered the weight of war for eight months, and not
being moreover of the most fruitful, is not in a state to supply all that
might be desirable."[34]

Garay's response apparently satisfied Wellesley, even though his son
had warned, "You will find in Garay above all a pretended friend but in
heart a rancourous enemy."[35] The following day Lord Wellesley dispatched Brigadier General William Doyle and Major Armstrong to Sir
Arthur's camp with Garay's response and the following message: "I am
inclined to believe that this Government is disposed to make every effort

compatible with its powers, with the state of the country, and with the inveterate defects of the military department in Spain."[36] It was a subtle way of telling Sir Arthur that while some deficiencies might persist, Spain was not lacking in good intentions. Wellesley therefore urged his brother to remain in his present position. Doyle and Armstrong stayed with Arthur to act as liaisons between his headquarters and Seville.[37]

The junta's promises for supplies and transport soon proved fallacious. Arthur reported his army on half rations and his cavalry completely without forage. He warned that "Either the British Army must be fed and supplied with the necessaries which they require, or I shall march them back into Portugal."[38] Wellesley relayed the message to the junta, imploring it to take action.[39] General Cuesta became alarmed, realizing that a British retreat would expose his army to French attack. To mollify Sir Arthur, he proposed a plan to supply both the British and Spanish armies by establishing a common magazine at the village of Truxillo. There supplies would be distributed to both armies according to their numbers. To ensure impartiality of distribution, the magazine would be run by representatives from each army.[40]

Sir Arthur rejected the proposal. Suspicious by nature, he immediately detected the plan's many weaknesses. He calculated that only about one-fourth of his army's needs could be supplied from the Truxillo magazine. The remaining three-fourths would have to be procured from the countryside, where the Spanish army would obviously have preference. In addition, he could see that the Spanish would have no difficulty diverting shipments destined for Truxillo directly to their own camp. Consequently, Sir Arthur informed Cuesta that he would have to come up with a more foolproof proposal.[41]

While Lord Wellesley implored the Spanish to ease his brother's logistical problems, he busied himself with another important matter. Since his first days in Spain he had been urged to secure the removal of General Cuesta.[42] Sir Arthur considered Cuesta utterly incompetent, and history has to a certain extent confirmed his appraisal. But many knowledgeable people of the day were impressed by the old soldier's abilities. George Erving, the United States representative in Seville, commenting upon Cuesta's appointment, noted that the utmost confidence had been placed in the general and that he was esteemed as a good tactician, a great disciplinarian, and an enterprising yet cautious leader.[43] After Talavera, Erving reconsidered. He admitted Cuesta's failings as a tactician, but still believed him to be a good leader and disciplinarian. He found Cuesta's greatest weaknesses to be pride and obstinacy but noted, "Wellesley [Arthur] is not deficient in pride." Erving also believed that Cuesta, even more than Sir Arthur, was making an effort to keep the alliance running smoothly.[44]

Regardless of Cuesta's merits, the Marquess, realizing his brother's low opinion of the Spanish general, cautiously agreed to do what he could to have him replaced.[45] Earlier Frere had suggested Cuesta's removal, so Wellesley did not hesitate to revive the subject.[46] He was pleased to find that Martín de Garay did not object to Cuesta's dismissal, but both men realized the goal had to be pursued with discretion. Any action against a prominent general could potentially cause serious embarrassment to both the junta and Great Britain. The junta, in particular, did not feel strong enough to summarily dismiss Cuesta merely on Britain's request. Garay and Wellesley concluded that Cuesta's poor performance had to be proved publicly. Otherwise the precise time would have to be chosen for Cuesta to be retired in a manner which would be both decorous and, for the junta, safe.[47] Fortunately Cuesta himself solved their problem: on August 11, after suffering a paralytic stroke which immobilized one of his legs, he expressed a desire to resign his command.[48]

After Secretary of War Don Antonio Cornel confirmed Cuesta's retirement, the problem became one of finding a suitable successor. Because Arthur Wellesley's friend the Marquis de la Romana was employed elsewhere, Lord Wellesley hoped the Duke of Albuquerque would be elevated to the command. Unfortunately, Albuquerque was not an admirer of the Supreme Junta, and, because of past animosity, Cuesta's immediate subordinate, General Francisco Eguia, was appointed to his place.[49]

With Eguia's appointment, there was a basic change in Wellesley's negotiating position. The Supreme Junta, in its efforts to secure Cuesta's removal and in its proposal for the British army's supply, had shown a willingness and eagerness to attend to Britain's complaints. These positive acts on Spain's part demanded reciprocity. Wellesley had to demonstrate that Britain too was prepared to sacrifice for the alliance. Thus when Eguia, on taking command, submitted what amounted to a revision of Cuesta's Truxillo plan of supply, the Marquess advised his brother to cooperate. Sir Arthur complied, but in writing to Eguia he stated: "I am apprehensive, that from the nature of the proposed arrangement, it is impracticable of execution; but at your Excellency's desire, I have sent Lieut.-Colonel Waters, of the staff, and Mr. Venyss, of the Commissary General's department, to Truxillo, where they will meet any officers who will be appointed by you, and in concert with Mr.

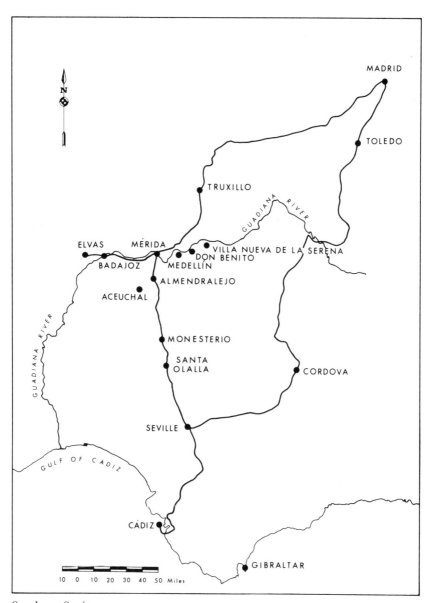

Southern Spain

Layno de Jones, the Intendant employed by Government with the British army, will settle such an arrangement as may be practicable."[50] It was hoped this would signal a fresh start for Anglo-Spanish military affairs, but Sir Arthur was wary. He expected the junta to take direct and immediate action toward the supply of his army—vague promises would not appease him.[51]

Lord Wellesley retained a guarded optimism. Relating the events of his first several days to George Canning, he explained: "I have reason to believe that great exertion has since been made by this government for the purpose of giving speedy effect . . . to the commencement of an improved system of supply and movement for the troops in the field. But the impoverished state of the country, the weakness of the government and the inveterate defects of the military department in Spain render any speedy improvement impracticable, and induce me to apprehend great difficulty even in the ultimate success of any plan, which can now be suggested."[52] The future course of Anglo-Spanish relations had obviously become clearer to Wellesley. As a realist, he foresaw the necessity of bringing about military and governmental reform; yet as ambassador, his immediate responsibility was the support of his brother's army and the maintenance of harmony within the alliance.[53] It was therefore necessary for him to devise a plan to accomplish both in the event that Spain's plans for supplying Sir Arthur's army failed.

While the Marquess agonized over the army's welfare, the junta began to panic over Spain's military situation. Spanish politicians and soldiers alike looked with horror upon the British commander in chief's repeated threats to retreat into Portugal. It was widely believed that such an eventuality would create an untenable military situation, since it would render southern Spain highly vulnerable to French attack. This prospect aggravated the junta's already declining popularity.[54] To compensate, it decided to embark on an ambitious military offensive, hoping to regain lost credibility through a series of military victories. The strategy would have the added feature of holding the British army in Spain, for such an undertaking would require its active support. The junta's problem naturally would be to secure a British promise to adhere to the plan. In an effort to regain his ally's confidence, Garay reported to Wellesley that a troop of biscuit makers had been dispatched to the British army in Estremadura. Denying any past discrepancies, Garay claimed that these were additional efforts to improve the army's supply and transportation. Besides the immediate relief promised by the biscuit makers, Garay claimed he had already sent 300 quintals of salt meat, 100 pounds of beef tongue, convoys of rice, salt, fish, cheese, flour, barley, and biscuit, and 1,500 mattresses. Future needs would be furnished from a Spanish depot stocked with cattle, wheat, flour, barley, and biscuit and administered by the director of royal provision, Don Alexander García Gómez. Similar arrangements would be made for the Portuguese army of General Beresford while operating in Spain. In addition, Garay advised Lord Wellesley that during future campaigning, all towns through which the British army might pass would be required to provide for the army while it was in the area.[55]

Relaying the information to his brother, Wellesley saw the new proposal as a partial solution to the army's logistical problems. The plan was by far the most comprehensive and practical yet presented. Sir Arthur, on the other hand, remained pessimistic, largely because of past experiences with the junta's promises.[56] His pessimism was justified, for within hours after presenting the plan of supply, Garay, in an ill-judged display of opportunistic diplomacy, requested British cooperation in the Supreme Junta's proposed autumn campaign.[57]

Garay's request came on August 18, 1809. The junta's plan was based on the premise that the armies of Soult, Victor, and Mortier were beginning to retreat, offering an excellent opportunity for an allied attack.[58] The plan was, however, ludicrous from its inception, for it was based on a wholly imaginary premise. In fact, it is hard to believe that the junta was unaware of this fact, because at the time it proposed the offensive an alarmed General Francisco Venegas reported the beginning of a French offensive against his army.[59] In fact, the French were gathered in force and not disposed to making any sort of withdrawal.

Britain could not of course consider committing herself to such a campaign until she determined the reliability of Spain's promises and certainly not before the British army was again on combat footing. Sir Arthur's ideas were more definite. He unequivocally refused to take part in any campaign, holding to an earlier commitment never again to participate in a cooperative operation with the Spanish.[60] Unwilling to accept this refusal, the junta offered him 300 fresh horses along with the lavish promise for supplies.[61] The commander in chief scorned the bribe. Consequently, the Spanish promises evaporated, and instead of being relieved, the plight of the British army grew worse. A heretofore hopeful Wellesley received the gloomy intelligence that during the past month his brother's army had not received even ten days' supply of bread, the cavalry only three deliveries of fodder. Sir Arthur further informed the Marquess that several units sent out on foraging missions were stopped by Spanish patrols and relieved of what they had already collected. Outraged by these incidents, Sir Arthur advised his brother: "Under these circumstances I can remain in Spain no longer; and I request you to give notice to the Government that I am about to withdraw into Portugal."[62]

While Wellesley contemplated other alternatives, in the end he honored Sir Arthur's request and sent word of the decision to both the Supreme Junta and General Eguia.[63] The Spanish reacted indignantly. To draw attention away from their own deficiencies, they fabricated the story that the British were withdrawing because Spain would not cede to Britain the cities of Cádiz and Havana as a condition for military assistance. At the same time the junta made every effort to conceal complaints over its failure to provide provisions and transport for Sir Arthur Wellesley's army.[64] In Eguia's camp, the alarm over the impending retreat was just as great. Sir Arthur had informed Eguia of his intentions on August 18 and suggested that the general take measures to secure his army's position.[65] Eguia responded with a visit to British headquarters in an undisguised effort to change Sir Arthur's mind. In the ensuing two days, Eguia exhausted his limited imagination trying to persuade Sir Arthur to remain in his present position, making impossible promises about provisions.[66] All failed, and an extremely angry Eguia wrote to General Wellesley: "If, however, not withstanding this answer, your Excellency should persist in marching your troops into Portugal, I shall be convinced that other causes, and not the want of subsistence, have induced your Excellency to decide in taking such a step."[67]

Eguia was not alone in his assessment of the British position. George Erving wrote, "their pretext is the want of provisions, but the fact is that they are as abundantly supplied as the country is able to supply."[68] In fact, Erving thought the Spanish were worse off than the British, owing to the fact that British troops had repeatedly intercepted convoys destined for the Spanish army. Erving could not substantiate this claim but pointed out that it "may well be believed of an army the general of which tells the people whom he comes to assist, that he can answer for the *valor* of his troops, but not for their *morality!*"[69]

In reality both armies were short of provisions. Bread was scarce, and rarely did a soldier see wine, brandy, meat, or salt, especially after the Battle of Talavera. A British officer, while encamped at Jaraicejo, wrote of the supply problem: "The time which we passed at this spot, although sufficiently monotonous, was such as one is not likely to forget. To the best of my belief, not one issue of bread was made to the troops during the fortnight; but an exceedingly coarse kind of flour, mixed with bran and chopped straw, and in very small quantities was distributed by the commissariat. This was moistened with water, and made into a sort of pan-cake, was baked on a camp-kettle lid, and speedily devoured. The only regret was the quantity was so small. If any person who belonged to the troops stationed at Almarez at that period can say that his appetite was satisfied on any one day of the fourteen spent there, I can only remark that he was infinitely more fortunate than his neighbors."[70]

Arthur Wellesley scoffed at the suggestion that the sufferings of the Spanish army were commensurate with those of his own, but Colonel Philip Keating Roche, the British military representative traveling with Eguia's army, admitted that the Spanish were not faring well.[71] In fact, British, Spanish, and French alike were suffering from want of provisions, "the country being exhausted in all directions." There were noticeably fewer complaints from the Spanish camp only because those hardy men were used to deprivation. Indeed, even the Spanish soldier's ordinary diet would have been considered starvation by a Briton. The average Englishman relished a diet including beef, but the common Spaniard existed on a staple of vinegar, garlic, lamp oil, and cayenne pepper, mixed with boiling water and poured over a dishful of bread.[72] In any event, Eguia's accusations exhausted what little patience Sir Arthur still possessed. Writing to Lord Wellesley, he vented his outrage: "These reports and insinuations against me may do very well for the people of Seville: but the British Army will not soon forget the treatment it has received; and I know there is not a general officer in it, and I believe not an officer or soldier, who does not think that I should have neglected its interests, and even should have risked its existence, if I had delayed its departure for another day."[73]

Wellesley had now determined that the state of the British army was as bad as his brother described. The army would have to withdraw to a point within range of reliable depots or face dissolution. But the closest such magazines were in Portugal, and the Marquess had come to realize that a retreat of such magnitude would increase Spanish leaders' suspicions of British intentions at a time when he believed the alliance more than ever had to be preserved in good harmony. Rumors of a Franco-Austrian armistice were rampant in Seville. Wellesley knew the rumors had substance and realized that Napoleon would shortly be able to concentrate his energies on Spain. Thus, with the prospect of the Anglo-French conflict being fought exclusively on the Iberian Peninsula, it was no time to jeopardize the Spanish alliance. Wellesley therefore set about to complete a plan which he had been nurturing for several days. He hoped simultaneously to alleviate the consternation of the Spanish government without exposing the British army to unnecessary danger and to allow both parties the time and means to reorganize, reform, and whatever else was needed in order to prepare for another campaign.[74]

On August 21, 1809, Lord Wellesley sent his two-pant plan to Martín de Garay: first, a "Plan to enable the British Army to procure the Means of Movement," and, second, a "Plan for the British Army taking up a Position upon the Left Bank of the Guadiana."[75] Essentially Wellesley had concluded that Spain's failure to provide the British army with transport and provisions derived primarily from a total absence of efficient administration within the government. Orders had repeatedly been issued to supply English needs, but the necessary means had never been taken to ensure the execution of those orders. Neither was it ascertained if the orders had been carried out or, if not, why not. "Accordingly," the Marquess commented, "The result of the well-intentioned but inefficient zeal of the officers of government has been totally inadequate to the exigencies of the occasion."[76] Wellesley's plan reflected this analysis.

He presented to the Supreme Junta minimum requirements for the transportation and subsistence of the British army. For every 25,000 men operating in Spain, there were to be 1,000 mules and 100 carts to provide transport of hospital stores, military chests, and five days' rations. These were not to be considered as part of the train necessary to conduct supplies and provisions from magazines to the army. Magazines were to be established in six different locations on two separate lines. Depots nearest the army were to be established at Villa Nueva de la Serena, Don Benito, Almendralejo, and Aceuchal. These would contain supplies of flour, biscuit, rice, bacon, barley, oats, wine, and brandy, all drawn from the country at hand. The second line of depots was to be established at Monesterio and Santa Olalla, their provisions, primarily biscuit, wine, and brandy, to be drawn entirely from Seville and its vicinity.[77]

The formula for administering these depots was simple. To procure provisions for the magazines, steps were to be taken to purchase grain under a governmental requisition which would ensure delivery at fair prices. Accounts were to be collected on all articles of provision existing in Estremadura, so that these might be collected when necessary. The collection of provisions and transport in Estremadura would be carried out by appointees of the Supreme Junta and Arthur Wellesley; those resources collected in and around Seville and Cádiz would be under the auspices of the appointees of the Junta and Lord Wellesley. At the head of each line of depots would be a military officer, assisted by six or eight commissaries—all named by the British commander in chief.[78]

Communications between the depots and the army would be established by convoys consisting of a brigade of carts, escorted by an officer and by a sufficient number of men to protect it. Once the lines of communication were established, regular daily reports were to be made, both to Arthur Wellesley and to the Supreme Junta in Seville, on the state of each magazine and each convoy. These returns were to contain a list of the nature and quantity of each article conveyed, the time of departure and arrival of each convoy, and the name of the officer commanding the escort, who would be responsible for the convoy's punctual delivery. Finally, Wellesley, cognizant of both the Spanish and British character, suggested the establishment of a system of rewards for meritorious service.[79]

With regard to military operations, Wellesley suggested the allied armies retire to a position on the left bank of the Guadiana River from Villa Nueva de la Serena to Badajoz. Specifically, the English army would occupy Mérida as an advanced post, with the army extending from Almendralejo on the right to Badajoz on the left. This position would provide sufficient protection for Portugal and have the added benefit of protecting Seville and the left flank of the Spanish army. The Spanish would occupy positions from Medellín to Villa Nueva de la Serena. To occupy these positions would allow both armies temporary means of subsistence while the plan of supply was being implemented, and dissensions over forage or supplies of any kind would be eliminated by keeping the armies separated.[80]

Wellesley designed his plan primarily to allow the British army time to refresh and reorganize and ultimately to resume offensive operations. But while Sir Arthur restored his army to its former condition, he could not be bothered with the innumerable Spanish requests for his cooperation in their own plans. The success of Wellesley's plan depended upon the patience and cooperation of the contracting forces, especially the Spanish. But experience had taught Wellesley that he could not depend on Spanish patience, so he made a final demand on the Supreme Junta: "But in order to give full effect to every part of this plan, the general commanding the Spanish army should be positively ordered to conform in every respect, to such instructions as he might receive from Sir Arthur Wellesley, and should be directed to occupy such positions, and to

Arthur Wellesley, 1st Duke of Wellington (1769– 1852), by T. Lawrence. Reproduced with permission of the Victoria and Albert Museum.

pursue such a plan, either of offense or defense, as Sir Arthur Wellesley may propose."[81]

Wellesley realized that there were aspects to his plan upon which the Spanish would find agreement difficult—in particular the final provision which subordinated the Spanish commander in Estremadura to Wellesley's brother. Nevertheless, when the Marquess presented his proposal to Martín de Garay on August 21, he had reason to believe that it might be successfully implemented.[82] For several days he had witnessed a decisive shift of diplomatic initiative to British hands. The junta, desperately attempting to gain British adherence to its military plans through extravagant promises of supplies and provisions, had all but admitted its own failures in the same endeavor. Moreover, the continuous pleas for vigorous military activity illustrated the junta's concern for popular opinion and convinced Wellesley that its plight was desperate. The junta was on the defensive; it knew that Sir Arthur would hold steadfastly to his threats to withdraw and that in Lord Wellesley lay the only hope of preventing such a retreat. The price for keeping the British army in Spain would therefore be the guarantee to collect provisions and transport facilities and to abrogate responsibility for their final distribution in favor of British authorities. In addition, Arthur Wellesley would be given final authority for military decisions taken in Estremadura. Wellesley assumed the junta would pay the price. He was not so sure of Sir Arthur's acquiescence.

Wellesley was confident that his plan would provide for the British army's safety while an attempt was made to alleviate the supply problem. Yet he knew that if his brother was to make a purely military decision, he would be inclined to discard the scheme entirely. Thus, when on August 22, 1809, Wellesley sent the plan to Sir Arthur for consideration, he employed his considerable powers of persuasion to influence his brother's decision. The thrust of Wellesley's approach was to convey the extent of the public alarm in Seville occasioned by the threatened retreat. The Marquess admitted that much of this panic had been contrived by the Supreme Junta but pointed out that the adverse effects of public hostility toward Great Britain, justified or not, could not be discounted. Wellesley left little doubt that he believed that Sir Arthur could justify a retreat, but explained: "Viewing, however, so nearly the painful consequences of your immediate retreat into Portugal, I have deemed it to be my duty to submit to your consideration the possibility of adopting an intermediate plan, which might combine some of the advantages of your return into Portugal without occasioning alarm in Spain, and without endangering the foundations of the alliance between this country and Great Britain."[83] The final decision lay with Arthur Wellesley. Yet while Arthur's decision was to be based on the practical needs of the army, the Marquess implied that he expected his brother to compromise.

Wellesley anticipated immediate replies from both his brother and Martín de Garay. To his dismay, however, two days after delivering the plan to the Supreme Junta, he possessed not even so much as an acknowledgment of its receipt.[84] This annoyed the anxious Wellesley, since he deemed immediate implementation essential to the plan's success. Consequently he sent a curt note to Garay demanding prompt action.[85] Garay's reply, explaining that the junta wished to investigate the situation before coming to a final decision, could hardly have been calculated to relieve the ambassador's anxiety.[86] Sir Arthur was not so dilatory. Unfortunately, his response was a complete misinterpretation of his brother's intentions.

Sir Arthur could see the advantages of remaining in Spain, short of the Portuguese frontier, while new attempts were made for the supply and transport of his army. He did not, however, think that these advantages justified the sacrifice that he considered inherent in the plan's military proposals.[87] When Sir Arthur joined Cuesta's army in mid-July, he had in essence committed himself to cooperative military action in Spain so long as operations were conducted by mutual consent. What constituted mutual consent was ambiguous, but it certainly implied that Britain would need good reason to terminate her cooperation. Arthur believed that Spanish behavior during the Talavera campaign threatened the very existence of his army and justified such a termination. For this reason he separated his army from Cuesta's and announced his refusal to cooperate further. And, as mentioned, Sir Arthur also maintained that Spain's failure to supply him necessitated a retreat to reliable magazines in Portugal. In addition, it appears that the threatened retreat was inspired by a desire to effect a more distinct and permanent separation of the British and Spanish armies. Clearly the British commander in chief felt that he had exhausted his usefulness in Spain and now wanted complete independence to pursue his own plans. "By going within the Portuguese frontier," Sir Arthur explained, "I clear myself entirely from the Spanish army, and should have an opportunity hereafter of deciding whether I will cooperate with them at all, in what manner, and to what extent, and under what conditions, according to the circumstances of the moment."[88]

Sir Arthur believed that Wellesley, through his plan, intended to coordinate an Anglo-Spanish defense of the Guadiana. Not only was Arthur convinced of the indefensibility of this position, but, more important, he saw that a coordinated defense would necessitate joint operations with the Spanish army. This, above all else, he did not want. Sir Arthur considered his independence too great a sacrifice for a plan of supply which might prove as useless as its predecessors. Nonetheless, sending the analysis to his brother, Arthur agreed to remain in Spain until "I shall have received your Excellency's sentiments upon what I have submitted to your judgement."[89]

Wellesley immediately detected Arthur's misinterpretation. He had never intended to suggest the Guadiana as a permanent defensive position. Rather, he had hoped only that "under all the circumstances of the actual situation of the enemy's force, the position suggested might be safe, for a sufficient time, to enable you to try the result of the plan of supply for your army, which I had offered to this Government, and that the supplies which were provided in Portugal would at the same time be within your reach."[90] In addition, the positions that Lord Wellesley suggested the armies establish would ensure their separation. There was hope then that a clarification of Wellesley's intentions might persuade his brother to accept the plan. Unfortunately, changing conditions forced Wellesley to abandon his project as unfeasible.[91]

In an August 21 meeting with Martín de Garay, Lord Wellesley demanded and received assurances that while his proposals were being enacted, the Spanish would make every effort to keep the British army supplied. But as reports reached the Marquess daily of the army's deteriorating condition, he concluded that the Spanish promises were spurious.[92] To compound the problem, the junta, on August 25, after four days of procrastination, presented its own plan of supply.[93] Wellesley had submitted his plan with the understanding that it would be acted upon immediately and was unprepared to debate the merits of an alternative plan. Moreover, the Spanish plan was unrealistic, dealing solely with the administration of the magazines instead of their creation.[94] The Marquess believed the first step in meeting the needs of the British army was the collection of supplies, and the Spanish plan made no provision for this. The cumulative effects of these events disillusioned Wellesley. "A strict observation of the proceedings of the Junta and of its officers," he explained to Canning, "has convinced me, that I had formed too sanguine an expectation of their exertions, and too favorable an opinion of their sincerity."[95] Wellesley returned the plan with the riposte that the junta act on his own proposals.[96]

The ensuing three days produced no significant improvement in the situation. The British army continued to go without adequate supplies, and the junta failed to produce a decision on the British plan. With his patience exhausted, Wellesley wrote to the junta on August 30, informing it of his decision to advise Sir Arthur to retreat.[97]

Indeed, Wellesley sent such advice to his brother, now Viscount Wellington, but with some qualifications. The Marquess realized that Wellington's primary concerns were supplying his army and maintaining his independence from the Spanish. Therefore, in supporting the retreat to the Portuguese frontier, Wellesley hoped that his brother would provide a suitable concession which, while not being detrimental to his own position, would help combat unfavorable public reaction to the retreat. In particular, Wellesley entreated that "the longer you can delay your actual passing the Portuguese frontier, the less will be the ill-temper and alarm in this quarter; that, if you can take up your position within the Spanish frontier, it will be more satisfactory here." In return, Wellesley promised: "I shall add the impossibility of your resuming offensive operations. I shall also advise the Spaniards to adopt a defensive system, and shall say nothing of the possibility of your acting again in Spain on any defensive plan. Perhaps this might answer without any positive declaration that you never mean to cooperate again with them."[98] Originally Wellesley had hoped Wellington could issue a vague promise of future military cooperation in Spain if the supply and transportation problems were remedied and the military command reorganized. He had, however, been in Spain long enough to realize that vague promises were often subject to much misinterpretation and decided to dismiss the subject.[99]

While Wellington mulled over his brother's latest suggestions, the Supreme Junta made a final attempt to prevent the retreat. On August 30 Martín de Garay informed Wellesley that his plan of supply had been approved in its entirety. The junta would take immediate steps to establish the suggested magazines, and the Spanish army would assume the proposed position on the Guadiana.[100] At the same time Wellesley also had reports that his brother was finally receiving adequate supplies and provisions from Spanish sources.[101] As a result, the junta expected Wellington to halt his retreat and take up the position designated for his army. Normally these events might have prompted the Marquess to reconsider his decision, but the junta had compromised itself by demanding immediate preparations for an Anglo-Spanish offensive.[102] Wellesley considered this "an inadmissible and impractical condition" and informed Garay that the retreat would continue. Hoping to temper the Spanish reaction, he assured Garay that the bulk of Wellington's army would remain in Spain, near Badajoz.[103]

The news of Talavera and its results had by this time reached the Portland Ministry in London. From the numerous dispatches emanating from the Foreign and War Offices on August 12, it is apparent that the gloomy news caused much despair.[104] Already besieged by unfavorable publicity from the failure of the Walcheren campaign, the ministers were in no mood for unfavorable reports from the peninsula. The result was a hardened attitude toward Spain. Canning, in particular, was noticeably discouraged by the failure of British arms. He was convinced that it would ultimately be necessary to abandon Spain. In a letter to Wellesley labeled "Private and Confidential," Canning explained that the best to be hoped for was keeping the British army intact, behind the Portuguese frontier. This army along with that of the Portuguese would defend Portugal, leaving the defense of Spain to the Spanish. Canning saw in the Spanish nothing but ineptitude: "I am alarmed when I hear of their determination to take the field.—Under any leader, whom they now have, a system of extended operations, *by themselves,* seems hopeless and mischievous."[105] Canning went on in what could at best be described as duplicity toward the alliance:

> If the result should be that there is no mode in which the British Army can act in Spain, creditably and advantageously; the next object is to get creditably out of the difficulty. And I hope the instructions which I send you today will at least put that within your power. The refusal of either and still more of both of the conditions, if it is thought right to press them (*at the risque of their being accepted*) would afford a plain and strong ground, and one highly acceptable to this country, for withdrawing from the contest in Spain, and leaving the Spaniards to their own exertions. Whatever be the results of the discussions, I am persuaded that it is very necessary to let the Spaniards see, that, if they are not at once more active, and more tractable, we shall soon leave them to themselves. . . . my patience is put to a proof which I cannot stand.[106]

The instructions to which Canning referred were simple and straightforward. First, if Spain expected the further cooperation of British troops, then she would have to provide, to Wellesley's satisfaction, the necessary means of transport and a constant and regular supply of provisions. Second, if Wellington required it, the garrisoning of Cádiz and the centralization of the Spanish military command would have to be accomplished before further British military involvement.[107]

Canning's dispatches, which arrived on September 4, 1809, were somewhat out of date. Retreat from Spain had already been decided upon and, for the most part, carried out. Regardless, Wellesley was not so disillusioned as Canning and pointedly avoided following his suggestions. To avert compromising the few Anglophiles left in Spain, he refused to demand British occupation of Cádiz. Such a demand would have impaired the confidence of the Spanish nation in British sincerity and good faith by reinforcing the belief that the army had retreated for the purpose of enabling Britain to obtain that object. Further, the Marquess refused to press the issue because the demand at that point would have been denied, and such a denial would have presented a great obstacle to the success of the proposition in the future. Wellesley also avoided the problem of centralizing the Spanish army's command, since it was apparent that Wellington was in no position to accept such a command. If he could not accept it, the appointment would go to a Spanish officer, an event which might preclude introducing a British officer to that position in the future.[108]

Wellesley, obviously foreseeing an important role for Britain in Spain, instead set about to reestablish British credibility with the Spanish. Spain had naturally greeted with indignation the news of the final decision to retreat, though not to the extent of Wellington's first threat. The lack of panic was probably due to the manner in which the retreat was carried out and to the general inactivity of the French.[109] Nevertheless Lord Wellesley received intelligence on September 4, 1809, that unless Britain made some sort of official statement on the causes of Wellington's retreat, accusations spread by the Supreme Junta, French agents, and various other Anglophobes would eventually be accepted by most Spaniards.[110]

Until this time, both Wellesley and Wellington had scrupulously avoided publicizing their complaints against the Supreme Junta and the Spanish army. They realized that for its own well-being, the junta had to keep the national spirit high.[111] Consequently, when Wellington withdrew, many Spaniards accepted the junta's allegations ascribing his action to some sinister motivation. After all, there was historical precedence. Britain, in the past, had seized Gibraltar, attacked Buenos Aires and other New World possessions, and confiscated the Spanish fleet. Now, some presumed, Britain wanted Cádiz and Havana. To counter such sentiment, Wellesley published this statement: "I declare on the part of the British Govt. that the army under the command of Sir A. Wellesley has neither been supplied by the Civil Authorities nor aided by the Military Powers of Spain in any degree sufficient to enable him to contend with the French forces opposed to him in the field; and that those causes alone have compelled Sir A.W. to retire within reach of more adequate assistance, and to resume the Defense of Portugal as the sole object of his immediate operations."[112]

At the same time, Wellesley took the opportunity officially to justify Wellington's retreat. In a formal note to the Supreme Junta, he explained that since Moore's disastrous campaign, Britain's primary objective had been the defense of Portugal. Naturally this did not strictly confine British operations to Portugal, but it prevented the undertaking of a campaign which might expose Portugal to the enemy. Given this proposition, Wellesley declared that Wellington had begun the Talavera campaign assured that his action would not endanger Portugal. Instead, he was met with a dearth of transport and subsistence, which, after a month and a half, had the accumulated effect of weakening the army to the extent that Portugal's defense was threatened. For this reason alone, the Marquess maintained, and not for any disaffection for the alliance, Wellington retreated to the Portuguese frontier. Wellesley sent this dispatch on September 8, and with it he considered the affair finished; so also ended the first phase of his mission.[113]

Lord Wellesley had gone to Spain in an atmosphere of foreboding pessimism. On arrival in Cádiz, he found the Anglo-Spanish alliance strained to the breaking point by the quarrel between Sir Arthur Wellesley and Spanish officials. Although the new ambassador believed that his brother's complaints were justified, he also realized that Spain would consider unjustified and insulting the precipitate retreat to Portugal which Sir Arthur planned. He therefore set out to reestablish harmony in Anglo-Spanish relations by bringing about a reconciliation between the Spanish and Sir Arthur. Although he failed to produce that reconciliation, he displayed much skill and an amazing amount of patience in keeping an explosive situation under control.

In his extensive negotiations with the Supreme Junta during August 1809, Wellesley, unlike his predecessor, undeceived by countless promises, had remained firm in his demand for action. Yet he never despaired of Spain. Even after several desperately needed plans for the British army's supply had failed, he encouraged the Spanish and presented a remedial scheme of his own. Ultimately Sir Arthur withdrew to the

Portuguese frontier, but the retreat came about slowly and was completed only after Wellesley convinced himself and the Spanish that it was absolutely necessary. The Spanish were indignant and disappointed over the retreat, but, significantly, no irreparable damage had been done to the alliance. After September 8 Lord Wellesley was prepared to pursue his diplomacy afresh.

4

Political Negotiations with the Supreme Junta

Wellington's retreat to Badajoz signaled the end of the Talavera campaign and marked Britain's second unsuccessful military adventure in Spain in less than a year. To many observers it seemed to illustrate the futility of further British involvement. Yet Lord Wellesley was convinced that if Britain was to persist in the struggle with Napoleon, her primary efforts would have to be directed to the Iberian Peninsula. He candidly admitted that, given the immediate state of the Spanish government, the Anglo-Spanish alliance could not succeed; the Supreme Junta was simply incapable of simultaneously administering a country and conducting a war. Still, he was confident the Spanish will to resist Napoleonic aggression was as great as ever and the potential for success ever present. While it remained only to develop this potential, doing so would require drastic alterations in Spain's government and military system. Writing to Canning, the Marquess explained: "A relaxed state of domestic government, and an indolent reliance on the activity of foreign assistance, have endangered all the high and virtuous objects for which Spain has armed and bled. It must be now evident, that no alliance can protect her from the inevitable result of internal disorder and national infirmity; she must amend and strengthen her Government; she must improve the administration of her resources, and the structure and discipline of her armies, before she can become capable of deriving benefit from foreign aid: the matchless enterprize and skill of her most powerful, generous, and active ally, have been rendered fruitless in victory by the inefficiency of her own Government and army; and Spain has proved untrue to our alliance because she is not true to herself."[1]

Hence, from a practical standpoint, Wellesley took a lively interest in securing better government for Spain, determined not only to encourage change but to influence the direction it would take.[2] At the same time, he had to cope with the normal diplomatic responsibilities of the embassy. Often these affairs would either directly or indirectly affect his efforts at encouraging reform. The Supreme Junta's receptiveness to the ambassador's suggestions generally varied in relation to Britain's response to Spanish demands and with the general state of the military situation in Spain. Success usually depended upon Wellesley's ability to keep diplomatic initiative in his own hands, but numerous problems existing between the allies meant that he was constantly frustrated in his efforts to maintain that initiative. Still he persisted, believing that for the future of Spain and the alliance an alternative had to be found for the Supreme Junta.

This now infamous assemblage came into existence in the summer of 1808, shortly after the Battle of Baylen, a result of British pressure and Spanish initiative. Britain believed that she could not effectively aid a country which lacked a central government, and Spanish leaders realized that their country required a central authority to coordinate her material and moral resources against France.[3] In the absence of Ferdinand VII, being held by Napoleon in France, Spain needed an alternative form of leadership. Originally most Spaniards favored a regency, but no suitable regent could be found. Another solution was to convene the Cortes, or Parliament of Spain. Unfortunately, this body, like the old French Estates-General, was antiquated and had not met for so long that its revival would have been far too time-consuming to contend with the exigencies of the moment. Consequently, for lack of a better alternative, it was agreed that each of the provincial juntas would nominate two delegates to form a central junta. This body, numbering during its existence from twenty-four to thirty-five members, was given the title of Supreme and Central Government Junta of Spain and the Indies.[4]

The formation of the Supreme Junta was the first step in the consolidation of Spain's government following Napoleon's usurpation of the monarchy in 1808. Unfortunately, it fell woefully short of providing the necessary leadership for a country involved in a life-and-death struggle. Since its inception the junta, unable to provide a well-understood system of union between the provinces and itself, had failed to subordinate the fiercely independent provincial juntas to its authority. Accordingly, the provincial juntas rebelled against and spread propaganda against the Supreme Junta's decisions.[5] The consequences of this jealousy were first made apparent in Sir John Moore's campaign, when he, like Wellington, suffered greatly from Spain's failure to provide subsistence and to coordinate her military activities. As a result, in January 1809 the Supreme Junta made an attempt to limit the powers of the provincial juntas, but, as might be expected, it proved to be an exercise in futility.[6]

There were other problems. The Supreme Junta was originally intended to be only a stopgap government, one which would see to the orderly assemblage of the Cortes.[7] Once formed, however, the junta clung tenaciously to its power. It postponed calling the Cortes, giving rise to public criticism already stimulated by the junta's sometimes inept leadership.[8] William Jacob, a British traveler touring Spain in the spring of 1809, noted: "The best informed people here think that a revolution in the government is absolutely necessary to save the country. A change which, by concentrating the feelings of the people and directing them properly, without the cumbrous load of forms now existing, would do more to baffle the enemy than any effort which the present body are likely to desire."[9]

The lack of public support for the Supreme Junta led to many problems. Necessary taxes were uncollected; total mobilization was impossible; ministers, assuming their own genius, were overly independent; and centralized authority proved unattainable.[10] So acute were the problems that they prompted George Erving, a strong supporter of the Spanish cause, to state, "A more formidable enemy to the Spanish cause than the French is this perpetual jealousy of & want of confidence in the government."[11] Finally, on May 22, 1809, in an effort to mollify public opinion, the junta promised "that the legal known representation of the monarchy shall be reestablished in its former Cortes, which will be convoked in the course of the next year or sooner, if circumstances permit."[12] Because no date was set, the promise was nebulous.

Problems continued to pile up. The junta, lacking a strong power base, found it difficult to unite its own members in common agreement.[13] With power divided among thirty-five members, decisive action, so indispensable during wartime, was virtually unattainable. Colonel Cochrane Johnstone warned Wellesley in the spring of 1809: "Your Lordship will find upon your arrival at Seville that the Supreme Junta are split into different parties—their number is too great for the proper dispatch of business—a great deal of intrigue is going on."[14] Moreover, the junta wasted much time on trivialities and failed to direct its attention to the major issues. Even the staunchly pro-Spanish Lord Holland was forced to admit that the junta's members "were too much occupied with the ceremonies, forms and patronage of their new government."[15] To compound the problem, many members of the junta were inferior in character and ability, and even the capable few were so much absorbed in tradition that they failed to function efficiently.[16]

Lord Wellesley, familiar with the many deficiencies in the Spanish government long before his departure from England, knew that as ambassador he would have to confront them.[17] Canning too was convinced that subtle efforts would have to be made to improve the system of government, but he left it to the Marquess to determine what types of changes were to be urged.[18] The various events of the Talavera campaign turned Wellesley's attention to the subject sooner than he had expected. Not having firsthand experience with the Supreme Junta, he was in no position to suggest far-reaching governmental changes. Instead, he hoped to encourage the junta toward self-reform. For this reason, Wellesley complied with its various schemes to improve the system of supplying the British army, the failure of which was symptomatic of the junta's inability to govern effectively. By delaying Wellington's retreat, Wellesley gave the junta numerous opportunities to prove it was capable of greater efficiency. When the Spanish proposals failed, the ambassador provided his own, again hoping that the junta could adjust to its own inadequacies.[19] As has been seen, all came to naught, and Wellesley realized he could no longer conduct his experiments at the expense of the British army. He concluded that radical change was necessary if Spain was to apply her own and Britain's resources effectively in the struggle against France.[20]

Surprisingly, Wellesley did not initiate discussion on the subject. In mid-August, Martín de Garay, in private conference, requested his opinion on the state of the Spanish government, with special reference to the appointment of a regency and the assemblage of the Cortes.[21] In a series of private meetings that followed, Wellesley outlined his ideas. First, the Supreme Junta should immediately nominate a Council of Regency composed of not more than five members to assume executive power. Second, the junta should call a prompt election and assembling of the Cortes, the election to be superintended by those members of the junta not serving in the regency. Third, the junta should decree "a redress of grievances, correction of abuses and the relief of exactions in

Spain and the Indies, and also the heads of such concessions to the Colonies, as shall fully secure to them a due share in the representative body of the Spanish Empire." Finally, the regency's first act should be to improve Spain's military system. Apparently Garay expressed agreement with most of Wellesley's suggestions.[22]

It is not difficult to guess the junta's motives for initiating these discussions. They occurred at a time when the junta was gravely concerned over Wellington's threatened retreat to Portugal. As noted, the junta feared both a new French offensive and adverse public opinion. Consequently it made every possible effort to convince the British ambassador that the retreat would be a mistake. Garay's openness to reform appears to have been an extension of this effort. Yet, on closer analysis, the junta was conceding little, for the discussions never developed beyond the stage of private conversation between Wellesley and Garay. Nothing was committed to writing, and discussion on the subject abated when public alarm subsided over the military situation.[23]

Naturally the junta was more anxious to perpetuate its power than to abrogate it in favor of other authorities. But other reasons were posited for resisting significant change in government, especially change instigated by Great Britain. Many Spaniards doubted the notion that a regency and the Cortes could accomplish more than the junta; some believed that they would destroy what progress had already been made toward governmental reform. Others felt that Wellesley was merely attempting to assert a preponderant British influence in Spanish affairs through an alteration in government. As a skeptical George Erving explained, "In fine if this plan can be executed, the Marquis of Wellesley will in effect be Lord-Lieutenant of the Kingdom . . . and then the revolutionary energies upon which the cause of the patriots depends for success, will be completely extinguished."[24]

It was by this time common knowledge that the Marquess was trying to secure change, but few suspected or even considered that he was also trying to establish greater British control over the affairs of Spain.[25] This was precisely Wellesley's goal. In a memorandum written in late August or early September of 1809, he concluded that if ultimate success was to be achieved in the peninsula, then it would be necessary to

> enable and induce the Governments of Spain and Portugal to call forth the military resources and power of the Peninsula under one general system of action . . . to combine the strength of a large British force with the operations of such a system.

Experience has proved that these necessary means cannot be provided until we shall have obtained a decided influence over the civil governments of Spain and Portugal together with the efficient direction of the military force of both countries.[26]

It is not to be assumed that Lord Wellesley saw this as a permanent feature of Anglo-Spanish relations; to him it was merely a means to consolidate and coordinate the allied effort. A realist, he could see that British influence could be extended only in an intangible manner, through diplomatic pressures.[27] Napoleon had already discovered the consequences of taking too direct a role in Spanish affairs.

Spain's persistent failure to attend to the needs of the British army, Wellington's final retreat to the frontier, Canning's alarm over the situation, and the lethargy of the Supreme Junta all persuaded Wellesley to apply greater pressure in urging the Spanish to make substantial changes in their government and military system.[28] In his note of September 8 to Martín de Garay, the ambassador committed himself to the promotion of such changes. He informed the junta that the British army would not return to Spain until the military department was revised to cope with the various problems of logistics and strategy. This, he explained, could not be effected unless there was a correction in the executive power of Spain. And to employ the human and natural resources of Spain effectively, Wellesley believed it necessary to provide the people with a voice in government. In essence he was addressing his earlier suggestions for the formation of a regency and the calling of the Cortes.[29] Besides his determination to withhold active British military support until this was accomplished, there is also evidence that the Marquess contemplated withholding material aid as well. Apparently, however, he concluded that this would serve no useful purpose.[30]

Wellesley waited in a state of extreme agitation for the junta's response to his September 8 dispatch. The junta and its armies frustrated him; he disliked Seville, and, according to his own admission, his only enjoyment came from "scolding the Secretary of State regularly twice a day."[31] The junta, however, assured of its relationship with Great Britain, felt no compulsion to react positively to Wellesley's demands. This attitude stemmed from the news that the Franco-Austrian War had reached a decisive conclusion at Wagram.[32] While Spain would now have to face Napoleon's full fury, Wagram also meant that Britain's last hope lay in the peninsula. Like it or not, she would have to support Spain. Moreover, the junta realized that Wellesley was not in a position to demand reform. On the contrary, as a result of Wellington's military predicament and Britain's financial position, the ambassador himself was in desperate need of the junta's cooperation.

Wellington's problem was hypothetical. Since retreating to Badajoz, he had become concerned over French military intentions. In particular, he worried that Soult might undertake a siege of the fortress city of Ciudad Rodrigo. Such an operation, if successful, would completely separate the Spanish government from its northern provinces, place the French in complete control of Castile, and threaten the security of the Portuguese fort of Almeida. To avoid this calamity, Wellington wanted the junta to strengthen the army of Estremadura, and it became his brother's task to persuade it to do so.[33]

Martín de Garay answered Wellesley's request with vague assurances, now all too familiar, from which the ambassador knew he could expect nothing. Wellesley did not have to look far for an explanation of the junta's hesitant attitude. By request of the Junta of Estremadura, the Duke of Albuquerque commanded the army of that province. Albuquerque's hostility toward the junta was well known, and consequently that august body feared giving him too much power.[34] Wellington, acquainted with the circumstance, was not surprised: "I am much afraid, from what I have seen of the proceedings of the Central Junta, that in the distribution of their forces they do not consider military defense and military operations, so much as they do political intrigue and the attainment of trifling political objects. They wish to strengthen the army of Venegas, not because it is necessary or desirable on military grounds; but because they think the army, as an instrument of mischief, is safer in his hands than in those of another."[35]

Throughout September the junta failed to reinforce Albuquerque's small army of 12,000, obliging Lord Wellesley to make numerous solicitations. Not only were these efforts futile, but the junta began neglecting Albuquerque's provisions, bringing extreme misery to the Spanish troops. Actually, given the number and condition of Albuquerque's soldiers, his army was worthless.[36] Fortunately, the French remained inactive, awaiting reinforcements, and Wellington, who was prepared to protect either Ciudad Rodrigo or Seville, could attend to the immediate task of defending Portugal.[37]

At the same time, Wellesley's embarrassment was compounded by his uncomfortable position concerning finances. Britain, as usual, was suffering a severe shortage of specie. Consequently Canning instructed his ambassador to apply for a license to purchase $10 million in gold and silver from the Spanish American colonies. More specifically, the license would grant Britain the right to export the sum free of duty, arrange for its delivery, and make payment for it in London within thirty days of delivery at a rate of four shillings to the dollar. Wellesley hesitantly made the request on September 3, knowing that the only other similar transaction had resulted in utter disaster.[38]

In March 1809 the British government had dispatched His Majesty's ship *Undaunted* to Cádiz to receive a license for the purchase of specie on the free market in Veracruz at a rate of no more than four shillings, two pence to the dollar. Sir Cochrane Johnstone was sent to act as agent, but all negotiations for the license were to be handled by John Hookham Frere. Once obtained, the license was to be delivered to Johnstone, who would then proceed to Veracruz to effect the purchase. Most important, once the purchase was made, the specie was not to be paid for (by bills of exchange on the British treasury) until Johnstone was given a receipt certifying the specie was on board ship.[39]

Contrary to orders, Johnstone, on arriving in Spain, went immediately to Seville, where he negotiated directly with the Supreme Junta for the purchase of $3 million from the Royal Treasury in Veracruz, at a rate of four shillings to the dollar. The rate of exchange was favorable, but Johnstone made a fatal mistake in issuing the bills of exchange in Seville in return for the order.[40] Given the desperate state of British finances, this portended disaster because the bills would be placed into circulation long before London had received the specie.[41] To compound his error, Johnstone contracted to supply Spain with 150,000 muskets and 10,000 quintals of powder (which Britain could not spare) in part payment for the dollars received in Veracruz. The contract for arms was £193,750, and it can be safely assumed that Johnstone hoped to make a handsome profit on the deal. His corrupt dealings became more apparent when he took advantage of his situation to obtain a personal monopoly for supplying Spain with cattle.[42]

The British government found itself in an embarrassing position. While Johnstone's negotiations were a complete breach of his instructions, Britain was in a sense committed to them because the entire transaction had been sanctioned by Frere.[43] Still, Johnstone's arrangements were untenable as far as Britain was concerned. England could not honor the early issue of bills and certainly could not make available the extraordinary amount of arms and ammunition promised by Johnstone. Consequently Frere was instructed to advise the junta of the irregular nature of Johnstone's conduct and to ask that it not circulate the bills until word was received of the specie having been received on board the *Undaunted*. The junta reluctantly agreed, having already budgeted the bills of exchange.[44]

To placate the Spanish, Canning instructed Wellesley on his departure to obtain another license to purchase $2–$3 million in specie. Payment would be made by allowing the junta to circulate the appropriate number of Johnstone's bills, and when information arrived confirming the delivery of Johnstone's dollars, the Marquess would then regrant new bills in the same amount.[45] Unfortunately, when Wellesley assumed the ambassadorship in August, he became so totally preoccupied with his brother's problems that this was never done, and the junta was forced to hold the bills longer. At the same time, Canning, under great pressure from Spencer Perceval, sent the order to make application for the purchase of $10 million.[46]

Wellesley, impractical by nature, was annoyed at having to make this request, for it interfered with what he considered to be the more pressing matter of persuading the junta to introduce governmental changes. Already he was in a weakened diplomatic situation. Spain did not fear Britain's withholding material assistance, and he had been forced to request Spanish cooperation in sending reinforcements to Estremadura. Could he now ask for permission to purchase specie in South America when such a concession had previously caused the junta much inconvenience? The prospects for Wellesley accomplishing anything were bleak. The junta was quick to perceive its advantage and reacted accordingly. Garay refused to acknowledge the September 8 letter, and, responding to the request for $10 million, explained that Spain could not afford to grant such a vast sum. The Marquess, accustomed to having his way in India, was annoyed.[47]

Relations between Garay and Wellesley grew worse when the former began to renew Spain's request for British military assistance. On September 13 he insisted that the French were beginning a massive offensive and urged the ambassador to call Wellington into action. Aware that Wellington's army was the only diplomatic leverage he still possessed, Wellesley responded by refusing to acknowledge any of Garay's inquiries until the junta answered the September 8 letter.[48] Undeterred, the Spanish persisted in these requests; when the Marquess failed to acknowledge their pleas, they became antagonistic. The junta refused to provide Wellington with accurate intelligence on the size and movements of the Spanish armies and discontinued supplying any information on French movements.[49] Albuquerque's army was allowed to disintegrate slowly, no plans were made for the defense of Cádiz, and only a weak defense was established in the Sierra Morena, the last line of defense before Seville.[50] The junta's conduct so angered Wellesley that he requested his own recall if the present junta was not soon replaced.[51]

Despite his extreme displeasure with the junta, Lord Wellesley at no time suggested or urged its overthrow. Ironically, on September 17 he saved it from just such a fate. Several prominent politicians, disgusted with the Supreme Junta's conduct of the war, had devised a plan for its overthrow. The plot was well organized and backed by several army regiments stationed in Seville. Their plan called for seizing the junta, transporting its key members to Manila, and establishing a Council of Regency similar to that suggested earlier by Wellesley. On the eve of the proposed revolt, the conspirators elected to advise the Marquess of the plot. It was a fatal error. Besides abhorring revolution of any kind, even against a government he despised, Wellesley could not allow himself to be a party to such an activity. As ambassador, Wellesley would have been totally discredited if he became involved in a coup d'état. He thus resolved to inform the junta, but in doing so he was careful not to reveal the authors of the plot. Rather, he provided the junta with enough information to thwart the plot but not enough to apprehend the conspirators.[52]

The junta, relieved and grateful, offered to Wellesley, as an expression of its gratitude, the Order of the Golden Fleece. The Marquess declined, explaining he could not accept such an honor from an authority whose conduct toward the interests of Spain he could not approve.[53] Nonetheless, Wellesley, having secured the junta's indebtedness, attempted to use it as a means of encouraging reform. The junta, however, remained recalcitrant. "They were all gratitude *for an hour,*" the Marquess told Wellington, "but *now* that they think themselves secure, they have begun to cheat me again. . . . I told Garay this evening that I would not trust the protection of a favorite dog to the whole Spanish army. It is some satisfaction to abuse such miscreants, if you cannot reform them."[54] Anglo-Spanish relations subsequently remained unchanged throughout September.

On October 3, Wellesley, to his astonishment, received a reply to his letter of September 8. Written by Martín de Garay, the letter contained an unequivocal denial of Wellington's charges of Spanish negligence in supplying provisions and transport facilities and of Spain's reluctance to cooperate militarily. Garay charged, instead, that Wellington was responsible for most of his own problems and for the failure of the

Talavera campaign. In the end, however, Garay vaguely conceded that the junta had an obligation to consider some sort of reform in Spain's government. "This plain narrative is complete proof, how important and necessary it is to seek for means of conciliating the plan of a reform with the different interests which must concur in effecting it, and to deliver the common from evils greater than those we are desiring to avoid. Such is the intention of Government, and such has been its occupation for many days."[55] Reform, Garay continued, required both patience and prudence, and could not be effected immediately.

The junta's sudden willingness to consider reform can be attributed to the fact that negotiations for a treaty of subsidy had been transferred from London to Seville. It may be recalled that the treaty between Britain and Spain signed in January 1809 and later amended in March deferred negotiations for a subsidy agreement to a later date.[56] To compensate, Spain had submitted to Canning a request for an extravagant loan. Spain sought £10–£20 million to be raised by London's commercial community and to be paid in monthly installments over a period of a year. Provisions of repayment and interest were to be considered at the time of the transaction, and as security Spain offered her customhouses in Cádiz and Veracruz.[57]

Canning, shocked at the magnitude of the request, informed the Spanish ambassador, Pedro Cevallos, that the request could not be granted. Britain, he explained, was busy equipping her army, as well as Austria's and Spain's, and was in no position to grant such a loan.[58] Throughout the spring of 1809, British subsidies to Spain were minimal, consisting of the barest essentials. Only when Wellington entered Spain in July did they increase. Records for the months of July, August, and September show considerable amounts of muskets, ammunitions, uniforms, and various military accoutrements being shipped to Spain.[59] At this point Canning and his colleagues believed that they were making an adequate and optimum contribution to Spain.

The junta, wary of Britain's reliability, decided, however, to initiate negotiations for a definite treaty of subsidy. Accordingly, on July 31 Admiral Don Ruiz de Apodaca requested an audience with Canning to discuss such a treaty.[60] Canning agreed to meet on August 7, and the Spanish representative arrived bearing concrete proposals: each country would coordinate its military activities with the other; Britain would place at Spain's disposal 25,000 infantry and 5,000 cavalry to be employed as Spain saw fit, in Europe or America; Spain would have full control of the assistance granted, and need not account for the motives that determined how it was engaged; Britain would undertake naval activities in favor of Spain; Britain would supply Spain with naval stores as needed at the same price Britain had paid for them; Britain would immediately supply 150,000 muskets and then 10,000 every month until 500,000 troops were armed; Britain would supply 20,000 tents in three months and then 5,000 every month thereafter; Britain would supply $2 million every month until the conclusion of the war.[61]

Canning, who had hoped to avoid altogether the question of a subsidy agreement, was unprepared for so extravagant a proposal. Given the uncertain state of Europe, he believed that Britain had to be prepared to render aid wherever an opportunity might present itself; she could not completely commit herself to one area, as Apodaca's treaty would have her do. Moreover, Canning feared that a treaty of this magnitude would give Spain license to pursue policies independent of British interests. As foreign secretary, he wished to preserve the flexibility that he believed the promise of subsidies gave him.[62] Consequently he was ill disposed to discuss the issue and held the proposal for several weeks in an obvious attempt to stall the negotiations. Finally on September 16, after straining Spanish patience for nearly six weeks, Canning decided to absolve himself of the issue by entrusting Lord Wellesley with the negotiations.[63]

To Spain subsidies were an important issue, and undoubtedly the junta hoped to use Apodaca's proposals as a bargaining point. At this juncture, Garay, apparently trying to create a proper atmosphere for negotiations, issued the junta's response to Wellesley's letter of September 8. The Marquess, however, shared Canning's position. On receiving the Spanish proposals, he reacted immediately by presenting demands that he knew the junta would consider untenable. Pointing out the total absence of reciprocity in the proposed treaty, Wellesley insisted that Britain could continue her assistance to Spain only if the ports of South America were opened to British trade.[64] The positions of both sides left no room for negotiation, and the issue temporarily abated.

One might expect that the stalemate would have made the junta more recalcitrant than ever over British suggestions for governmental and military reform. In mid-October, however, the junta found itself in a weakened position. Public pressure in Spain was again mounting against the junta while simultaneously the British were becoming more impatient with Spanish affairs.[65] In addition, on October 13, Wellesley had requested a ship to be readied at Cádiz to transport him to London.[66] It soon became common knowledge in Seville that the ambassador was being recalled to take charge of the Foreign Office in a newly formed cabinet.[67] The prospect of Wellesley assuming so important a post, with a bitter memory of his negotiations in Seville, must have caused concern within the councils of the Supreme Junta. As a result, on October 23 the junta submitted a program for reconstituting the government, which it hoped would appease both public opinion and Lord Wellesley.[68]

The junta proposed the formation of a committee of seven members empowered to direct the country's military resources. The committee would have a rotating membership elected from the Supreme Junta. Although the junta sought to convince Wellesley that this committee would provide greater efficiency, the plan had several weaknesses, to which Wellesley was quick to call attention. First, he believed that the executive commission was merely a camouflage for the continuance of the junta's power. Not only was the committee self-perpetuating through the junta, but the junta also reserved for itself executive powers not delegated to the committee. In other words, the change was simply a facade, with the government's power base remaining unchanged. Second, the Marquess argued, the system was impractical. By dividing the executive powers between two agencies, the junta would only rob the government of unity of action. Instead of concentrating power, as Wellesley suggested, via a five-member regency, the new committee would subdivide the executive and promote "delay, counteraction and weakness in the operations of the Government." Predictably, the Marquess concluded: "It is my duty to declare to your Excellency, that the appointment of this committee affords me no confidence in the promised correction of any of those evils of which I complained . . . nor furnishes any security to the British Army, in any operation within the Spanish territory." He explained that to provide efficiency and force in the government it would be necessary to combine and consolidate all executive branches of the junta.[69]

As part of its plan, the junta had also informed the ambassador it would call for elections to the Cortes on January 1, 1810, and predicted that it would assemble on March 1, 1810. On this point also Wellesley was dissatisfied. He could not understand why, since the assembling of the Cortes had been first announced in May 1809, it could not meet sooner. To him, it was absolutely essential that the Cortes meet and provide the executive (whatever form it might take) with public support. Wellesley could not hide his disappointment over the junta's proposals: "These objects are inseparable from the interests of the alliance; and it is therefore with the deepest regret, that I witness any course of proceedings, tending to procrastinate those improvements in the condition of Spain, which alone can enable her to receive the auxiliary armies of Great Britain."[70]

The Marquis de la Romana, an old and loyal friend, promoted Wellesley's proposals within the junta. Wary that these might diminish its power, the junta rejected them and charged fallaciously that a regency "would disgust the colonies, trample on the King's rights, would never assemble the Cortes and be corrupted by the French."[71] The majority accepted this view, and on November 1, 1809, the junta voted to retain its commission of seven.[72] As a compromise, Romana unsuccessfully suggested creating a permanent deputation of five delegates to serve as an advisory board for a Council of Regency.[73]

Following his October 24 response to Garay's plans for reforming the junta, Wellesley busied himself with preparations for his departure. Acceptance of the Foreign Office appointment made it necessary for him to appoint his own replacement and to set Britain's Spanish affairs in order, as he would desire them to be as foreign secretary. On October 26 he announced that Bartholomew Frere, brother of John Hookham Frere, would act as the new minister plenipotentiary and requested an audience of departure with the Supreme Junta at the earliest convenient date.[74] Garay complied, but quiet hostility continued to exist between Wellesley and the junta. The Spanish persisted in their requests for active military assistance, and the Marquess was equally relentless in his refusals.[75] Five days later the junta announced that it could not accept Wellesley's suggestions for change in the government. In apparent frustration, Martín de Garay resigned as secretary of state and was replaced by Francisco de Saavedra.[76]

Meanwhile, Wellington, advised of the important position his brother would shortly assume, traveled to Seville to discuss peninsular affairs. A delighted Wellesley received him on November 2, 1809.[77] Neither brother ever commented extensively on their private discussions, and no record exists of their substance. It is clear, however, that the discussions centered on Britain's future in Iberia, because they resulted in an important memorandum which the Marquess wrote to himself on November 4. The memorandum became the basis of Lord Wellesley's policies as foreign secretary, and undoubtedly reflected a Wellesley view of Spain and Portugal. It called for a vast reinforcement of the British army, renovations in the Spanish government, and the eventual consolidation of the Spanish military command under Wellington. A sensitivity toward Spanish public opinion in both the colonies and the peninsula was apparent, as was a realistic appraisal of British domestic politics. But the heart of the memorandum was Wellesley's commitment to Spain: "However the conduct of the Spanish Government may increase the difficulties of cooperation, alienate the spirit of the English from their cause, and even apparently justify a total separation of the interests of the two nations, yet it must never be forgotten that in fighting the cause of Spain, we are struggling for the last hope of continental Europe."[78] It was a commitment which Lord Wellesley never abandoned.

On November 6, after an audience of departure with the Supreme Junta, the Marquess, accompanied by Wellington, proceeded to Cádiz.[79] There he told Saavedra that Wellington would temporarily remain at Badajoz but would shortly move north toward the Tagus River. To provide adequate protection for Seville when this occurred, he again advised the junta to increase the Army of Estremadura to 20,000 men. At the same time, he reiterated the necessity of instituting meaningful reforms in the Spanish government—in particular, those reforms first suggested in August.[80] This accomplished, Wellesley instructed Bartholomew Frere to persist in demanding an augmentation of the Army of Estremadura and to continue urging reform. Most important, he cautioned Frere "to avoid any declaration or expression which might tend to engage the British Government to permit our Army to cooperate with the Spanish troops within the territory of Spain."[81]

Before departing, as a final gesture of good faith, Wellesley informed the junta that 10,000 muskets had arrived from Britain for the Spanish armies and that he was placing at Spain's disposal 9,000 muskets and all the military stores contained at Cádiz. He added that Britain could not supply Spain with all the muskets and ammunition she desired but would make every attempt to maintain deliveries of other forms of aid. In return, he hoped Spain would grant a license for the purchase of $10 million in Veracruz.[82] The new foreign secretary then made his final farewells, thanked his staff, and departed on November 11. "He went to England," said Wellington, "in high spirits, & determined to exert himself to make a strong Gov't. for the King."[83]

In a broad perspective, it seems that little was accomplished during Wellesley's three months as ambassador to Spain. During those months the military situation in Spain deteriorated, the Supreme Junta continued its inept rule, Spanish military leadership remained incompetent, Britain secured no commercial or fiscal concessions from Spain, and the allies' mutual mistrust generally persisted. Yet closer examination reveals the mission's important tangible and intangible results. From the standpoint of Britain's military position in the peninsula, Wellesley's diplomacy enabled Wellington to terminate his involvement in Spain and retreat to the Portuguese frontier without arousing an inordinate amount of hostility among the Spanish. Wellington was then able, in the space of three months, to provision his troops, recondition his horses, repair his wagons and carts, and reestablish discipline and morale within his army.[84] At the same time he was able to devise and oversee the construction of an elaborate system of fortifications north of Lisbon, which came to be known as the Lines of Torres Vedras.[85] Finally, influenced by the Marquess, Wellington moderated his quick temper and showed greater diplomacy in subsequent dealings with the Spanish.

At no time did Wellesley expose the British army to unnecessary risks or compromise British interests. He had learned from the debate over Moore's campaign that the parliamentary opposition had more success attacking the ministry's handling of the war in Iberia than in attacking the war itself. Consequently the Marquess realized that even if the war did not progress as hoped, the government could maintain support for it as long as it conducted its own affairs with discretion. Thus, throughout his stay in Spain, Wellesley scrupulously protected the government's position by accumulating evidence, through his numerous dispatches, that any failures in Spain were attributable to Spanish error.[86] It was a brilliant foresight on Wellesley's part and would prove invaluable in the upcoming parliamentary session of 1810.

Perhaps the most important result of Lord Wellesley's brief tenure as ambassador to Spain was the experience he gained in dealing with the Spanish and the problems of war. From three months of first-hand observation, Wellesley saw that ensuring greater efficiency in Spanish affairs and more cooperation with Britain required changes in the Spanish government. He had come to realize that the Spanish were profoundly suspicious of British intentions and to some degree would have to be coerced into making needed revisions in government. As foreign secretary, Wellesley was determined to employ coercive measures in dealing with Spain, whether they were subtle or not. The Marquess realized, moreover, that success would not come easy in Iberia, and on this point he would not attempt to deceive his colleagues in Parliament. Yet he was convinced that to facilitate success, Britain must adopt a broader commitment to Spain, a policy which he would persistently urge in both the cabinet and Parliament.

There were important results of Wellesley's mission to Spain, and they were due primarily to his energies and abilities as a diplomat. He was often characterized by his contemporaries as indolent, extravagant, and arrogant. In Spain he retained his innate arrogance, and many of his proceedings were characterized by condescension. Still this arrogance might more accurately be described as self-righteousness, a trait exemplary of many important Britons of the day. The British, in general, treated the Spanish like children, who they felt were obliged to revere, respect, and obey Britain. Though Wellesley was guilty of this attitude, so were Canning, Castlereagh, and many other prominent British politicians. Wellesley was not extravagant in his life-style—not in Spain at any rate—where he constantly stayed within his budget, and he was certainly not indolent.[87] The volume of his dispatches illustrates considerable energy, as do the numerous conferences and meetings with various members of the junta for which he was responsible. Moreover, his dispatches reveal an uncommon brilliance. They are clear, concise, and beautifully written. Earl Bathurst, acting foreign secretary before Wellesley's return to London, commented upon them: "I really believe that in point of composition as well as of political observation they are as able as any, if not more able than any, which were written in the best times of diplomacy."[88] The ultimate compliment came from William Wilberforce, a man known and respected for his talent and independent thinking, who remarked to one of his friends: "I suppose you have never seen: but when the Duke of Wellington commanded in Spain, and his brother the Marquess Wellesley was sent to conduct the negotiation, the papers containing the dispatches of the two brothers were printed by Parliament, and I remember thinking that I had never seen anything at all equal to them in talent."[89]

5

To the Foreign Office

Lord Wellesley went to Spain assured of being recalled to assume a cabinet post, so it came as no surprise when in mid-October he was offered the Foreign Office. Yet the offer came under conditions far different from what Wellesley had expected. Canning's plans for reorganizing the Portland ministry had not succeeded. Instead, the political intrigue which he had begun in March resulted in the complete dissolution of the Portland cabinet. When the government reassembled, Canning found himself without a post, and it was the new prime minister, Spencer Perceval, who lured the Marquess back to London as foreign secretary. Though far removed from these events, Wellesley was an important force in the political maneuverings leading to the formation of the Perceval cabinet; his decisions helped to determine the character of the new ministry. Similarly, these events helped shape Wellesley's perceptions of the new government and his role in it.

Canning, it may be recalled, had agreed in June to refrain from pressing for Castlereagh's removal from the War Office until plans for the Walcheren campaign were completed.[1] Consequently Castlereagh continued in office unaware of the proceedings against him, and the cabinet functioned without incident until after the departure of the Walcheren expedition on July 28, 1809. Canning then clamored for action.[2] This time Portland agreed to cooperate, promising that Lord Camden would advise his nephew of what had occurred. But Camden, who in April had agreed to assume this responsibility, was unable to summon the courage to carry it out. After several days' procrastination Portland planned to inform Castlereagh personally, but before he could do so he suffered an epileptic fit and was disabled for several days.[3] Castlereagh, much to Canning's dismay, remained in the War Office.

Canning urged the remainder of his ministerial colleagues to take immediate action toward Castlereagh's removal. He found them no more cooperative than Portland. Almost to a man, they felt that Portland, old and sick, could no longer continue in his role as prime minister, and they hoped to combine Castlereagh's removal with the naming of a new prime minister. In this way Castlereagh could be painlessly moved to another post as part of a general reorganization which would accompany the formation of a new ministry. The plan, however well conceived, was temporarily thwarted when Portland recovered to resume his place in the cabinet. Canning, in turn, renewed his efforts to remove Castlereagh, and as reports began arriving of the disasters of the Walcheren campaign he became more insistent.[4]

On September 5 the prime minister met with Canning. After listening to impatient demands, Portland explained that the burdens of office had become too heavy for him and that he intended to resign.[5] It was then that Canning's ambitions changed from merely securing Castlereagh's removal from the War Office to seeking the premiership. Hoping to hasten the formation of a new cabinet, he sent his resignation to the king, ostensibly because no action had been taken on Castlereagh.[6] Yet Canning's intentions seemed obvious to many close observers. As early as September 3 William Wellesley-Pole conjectured in a letter to Lord Wellesley that Canning was maneuvering for the premiership.[7] Two days later Benjamin Sydenham, a close Wellesley associate, learned of the Canning-Castlereagh quarrel and predicted the total dissolution of the ministry, with Canning and Perceval struggling for leadership.[8]

After submitting his resignation, Canning refused to attend a subsequent cabinet meeting on September 7.[9] The agenda included an important discussion of foreign affairs, and Castlereagh, still ignorant of all that was happening, became suspicious over Canning's absence. That evening he queried his uncle, Lord Camden, and, after six months of being deceived, he was finally told the truth. Understandably upset, Castlereagh chose to resign, and on September 8 the Portland cabinet was in complete disarray.[10]

Political infighting then began in earnest. Canning told Perceval that the new prime minister would have to come from the House of Commons, for there the crucial voting would occur in the upcoming sessions of Parliament. In that case, there could be only two contenders for the position—Canning and Perceval. Canning announced he would not serve under Perceval and assumed that Perceval felt similarly toward him.[11] But Perceval did not go along with Canning's premise, nor did he believe that a cabinet could stand without Canning's support. He proposed an alternative, offering to serve under a third person, whom both he and Canning could support. Among the many candidates Perceval suggested was Lord Wellesley.[12] Canning rejected the idea, hoping George III would entrust him with the task of forming a new ministry.[13]

On September 12 in a personal audience with George III, Canning offered to form a new ministry, but the king made no decision, preferring to maintain the status quo for as long as possible. While George procrastinated, Perceval and Canning sought to strengthen old political alliances and muster new support. Each man realized that his obtaining a majority in Parliament was more difficult than usual because any new cabinet in which he served would lack the services of the other. In analyzing the political situation, both men realized that the most prominent Tory politician at that time not active in government was Lord Wellesley and concluded that a new cabinet could not stand without him. As a result, each began to vie for Wellesley's allegiance.[14]

Canning had the advantage at the outset. Already possessing a close relationship with the Marquess, he had been cultivating a friendship with the youngest Wellesley, Henry. On hearing of John Villiers's desire to retire as British representative to Portugal, Canning had appointed Henry in his place.[15] Henry accepted but wisely resigned shortly after Canning left the Foreign Office, thinking it only fair to allow the future foreign secretary to make the appointment.[16] While Canning had made the desired impression, Henry nonetheless refused to commit himself until he heard of his brother's intentions.

Perceval had no reason to despair. To his surprise, he had the unqualified support of William Wellesley-Pole. "Pole of his own accord," explained Charles Arbuthnot, "came to offer himself to Perceval, and between ourselves, seems to dislike the part taken by Canning."[17] It was safe to assume that Pole's support was due primarily to his dislike of Canning, for he and Castlereagh had been fast friends since the cabinet debate over the Convention of Cintra.[18]

Pole's support was pivotal, not only from the standpoint of his close and trusting relationship with the Marquess but also because of his influence over Wellesley's closest friend, Benjamin Sydenham.[19] Anticipating that the political chaos would open an important new post for Wellesley, Sydenham consulted with Pole on a course of action. Together they decided that the Marquess's future lay with Perceval and set out to undermine Canning's influence. On September 16 Sydenham wrote to Wellesley concerning recent developments. He explained that the king and cabinet were determined to keep Canning from the premiership and that Perceval would probably be the king's choice. Sydenham therefore impressed upon the Marquess the necessity of clarifying his engagements with Canning, because he believed Perceval was prepared to offer him either the Foreign Office or the War Office.[20]

Meanwhile, Canning, feeling his position weakening, produced a letter written by Wellesley which simply stated that if Canning was unable to strengthen the cabinet (through the removal of Castlereagh from the War Office), then he wished to be recalled from Spain.[21] Obviously Canning wished this letter to be construed as a sign of Wellesley's commitment to him. Sydenham, upon learning of Canning's action, immediately wrote to the Marquess in a determined effort to draw him away from Canning. He pointed out that Canning opposed Perceval's proposal for the formation of a ministry under Wellesley's leadership and that Canning had an all-encompassing concern with self-promotion. Finally, Sydenham reiterated his belief that Canning would never be called to the premiership.[22]

As Sydenham was writing, events of the past six months were drawing to an incredible conclusion. After resigning, Castlereagh had retired from public sight. On September 19 he emerged to challenge Canning to a duel, charging him with deceit in concealing his complaints and activities for so long. Canning was obviously not responsible for the failure to enlighten Castlereagh, but the latter, even on being told of this, refused to withdraw the challenge. Confronted with Castlereagh's vehemence, Canning accepted.[23]

With an eye to the future, Canning hoped to make the best of a bad situation by asking Henry Wellesley to be his second. Henry, wary of Canning's motives, declined but offered his services at the duel in any other capacity Canning might desire. Years later Henry wrote: "I have always been at a loss to account for Canning's motive for applying to me upon this occasion, for although I had known him all my life we had never lived in great intimacy—I have sometimes thought that he might have a political motive, and that he might think it of importance to him at this juncture to appear to be intimately connected with the Wellesleys—which, had I acted as his friend in this quarrel, the world might have been induced to believe."[24]

The duel took place in the early morning of September 21 at Putney Heath and concluded with Canning receiving a clean wound in the thigh.[25] The British public was shocked by the duel, and George III was both intrigued and outraged.[26] But the most important result of the duel was that, for the time being at least, both Canning and Castlereagh were unable to take an active role in the formation of a new ministry. Perceval realized this and began to consider alternatives in assembling a new group of ministers. Unsure of his support in Parliament, he first turned to the opposition leaders, Grey and Grenville, to explore the possibility of a coalition government.[27] Both declined. Believing conditions to be untenable for a Tory ministry, they assumed that the king would ultimately have to turn entirely to them.[28] Many believed that Perceval made this offer merely to stall for time until Wellesley's intentions were known.[29] It is unlikely that this was his sole motive, but he was considering an overture to the Marquess. Thus Perceval, upon being appointed prime minister on October 2, offered the Foreign Office to Wellesley. Sydenham, entrusted with the task of gaining Wellesley's acceptance, embarked for Spain on October 5.[30]

By that time the Marquess had received Sydenham's letters as well as information on the Canning-Castlereagh duel. He knew that he would soon have to declare his loyalty either to Canning or to Perceval. Wellesley was aware of his obligation to Canning and pondered its extent. He did not lack advice. "Canning has claims upon your friendship," explained Wellington, "because he was willing to sacrifice his own situation in order to bring you into power; but it is a question deserving your consideration whether you alone of all his friends and colleagues are to support his pretensions to be *the First Minister,* and are bound to sacrifice yourself to attain that object."[31] Clearly Wellesley's family wanted him to take the course that would most benefit him, and that course was with Perceval. Wellington and Pole both wanted their brother to accept the Foreign Office and hoped that ultimately he would move to the premiership. The opportunistic nature of such planning is best illustrated by a letter from Wellington to Pole: "I am not sorry that Wellesley was in Spain during these discussions. He could have taken no advantage of, at the same time that he would have been involved in them; which would have been a disadvantage; and as things now are he has time to hear how matters are settled, & to consider what line he will take under the settlement."[32]

Wellesley needed no advice. Long before Sydenham's arrival, he had decided against following Canning, correctly reasoning that Canning's actions in September had an entirely different motivation from those of March and April. Wellesley perceived a significant distinction between agreeing to serve with a minister "and an engagement to act under him either in or out of office for the purpose of forcing him into any particular station, against the wishes of his colleagues, of his party, of his Sovereign, and even against the opinions of all in my own favor."[33] The Marquess had been fully prepared to support Canning if he had resigned because the ministry was not strengthened and certainly had no objection to serving under him if Canning were prime minister. Yet this did not mean Wellesley could be called upon to support Canning in opposition because Canning could not be made prime minister. For years it had seemed to the Marquess that only fate stood between him and a cabinet post; he would not now allow Canning's designs to stand in his way.

Wellesley felt obliged to offer Canning an explanation for his decision. This he did in a long letter in which Canning, among other things, was taken to task for his unwillingness to serve under Wellesley. In reply Canning heatedly denied that the Marquess had been seriously considered as first minister—certainly not to the point that it was recognized by the cabinet and sanctioned by the king. "If the Cabinet had advised the King, and the King had approved the advice, to make you first Minister," asked Canning, "in God's name why are you not so?"[34] Despite this bluster, Canning could not have missed the point of Wellesley's argument—that he seemed less concerned with strengthening the cabinet than with forwarding his own ambitions.

Arriving in Seville with all the sordid, if biased, details of the eventful past two months and armed with Perceval's offer, Sydenham got Wellesley's consent to go to London to accept the seals of office.[35] In the meantime, Britain eagerly awaited Wellesley's decision. Conjecture was rampant. "The Wellesley family seem to be at the call of everyone," commented the Morning Chronicle on the confusion, "for Mr. Perceval, as well as Mr. Canning, says he can have them."[36] In general, the opposition press, such as the Morning Chronicle and the Edinburgh Review, believed that Wellesley would align with any government as long as he could take office; progovernment publications, such as the Morning Post and, to a certain extent, the Times, gave him credit for more integrity. On October 14 the Chronicle offered a biting commentary: "It is well known that the Noble Marquis loitered three months in London, after his appointment to the Spanish Embassy, in hopes of getting into the Cabinet through the secret arrangement of his *friend* Mr. Canning; and he is now expected to *hurry* home, that he may take advantage of the success of his *friend* Mr. Perceval."[37] The *Post* denied that the Marquess had loitered in London, maintaining that any delay was due primarily to the ministers who wished him to stay. Further, the paper affirmed that the Marquess considered both Canning and Perceval as friends, which strengthened its contention that had Wellesley been interested solely in an office he could have long since had one. "We hope, at least," the *Post* went on, "that if any sacrifice be made, the Noble Marquis will be more fortunate in obtaining justice for his motives, than he has been on other occasions, when everything that office and honours could confer was obviously within his reach."[38]

Throughout October the attacks on Wellesley continued. "If it should be asked," said the *Chronicle*, " 'What possible influence Mr. Sydenham, (who was only Secretary in India to Lord Wellesley), can have over the mind of the Noble Marquis?' The answer is obvious—the influence that a superior mind naturally possesses over that of an inferior."[39] When Wellesley's decision to accept the Foreign Office became known, the criticisms were coupled with debasement encompassing the whole of the Perceval ministry. Characterizing Wellesley as a giant and a hero in India, the *Chronicle* believed he "left Lilliput for Brobdinog" when he returned to London, but commented days later: "That he should appear a great man to his Majesty's present Ministers is exceedingly natural. All magnitude is relative. When Lord Wellesley comes to Downing-street, he will find himself back again in Lilliput, without having had the trouble of doubling the Cape."[40] This view of the ministry was not an objective assessment of its abilities, nor was it typical of public opinion. Still, it was hoped by some that Wellesley would be able to persuade his colleagues to make an effort to strengthen the government by appealing to divergent elements not included in the cabinet.[41]

When Wellesley arrived in Portsmouth on November 29, 1809, many Britons considered his addition to the cabinet inconsequential. Some believed Wellesley, even if not a member of the cabinet, would support Perceval as long as he maintained the effort in the peninsula.[42] Indeed, the Marquess would see withholding his support as tantamount to giving power to the opposition. This prospect, it was known, he abhorred, as the ascendancy of the Whigs would certainly lead to the abandonment of the war effort. Most observers, however, were confident that Wellesley would add stability to the new ministry. The *Times* remarked: "Lord Wellesley's acceptance of office is regarded by the supporters of the

Ministry as an event equally favorable to the future interest of the country and the permanency of the new arrangements. By his accession the keystone of the arch is supplied, which the current of public opinion, however violent or adverse its direction, can it is supposed, neither injure or undermine."[43] Those of a more pessimistic outlook believed that nothing could help Perceval. The opposition was too strong, they maintained, and only by seeking new leadership, instead of reshuffling the old, could a government stand.[44] Regardless, Wellesley proceeded to London optimistic and full of energy.

Much to the delight of his critics, Wellesley arrived in London obsessed with assuming a vacancy (created by the death of the duke of Portland) in the Royal Order of the Knights of the Garter.[45] Wellesley had always been overly concerned with titles and protocol. But in this case, the Knight of the Garter was an honor which Wellesley probably considered suitable compensation for his not being granted an English marquessate earlier. Unfortunately, in his campaign for the Garter the Marquess greatly embarrassed both himself and others. From the day he arrived in London, he impatiently urged Perceval to represent his case before George III. Reluctantly Perceval agreed, but found the king unreceptive.[46] Aside from the fact that he had never liked Wellesley, George III had other plans for the available Garter.[47] Nevertheless, Perceval eventually was able to persuade the king. Wellesley learned of the decision on December 1, but his pleasure was blunted by the knowledge that investiture would not be immediate. Since prompt investiture would tend to give royal approbation to his Spanish mission, Wellesley suggested his appointment be published in the *Gazette*. The king vehemently refused the unprecedented request, placing Perceval—caught between Wellesley's solicitations and the king's refusals—in an uncomfortable situation. The appointment was not officially announced until Wellesley's investiture several weeks later.[48] The Marquess had to find satisfaction in the fact that the news of the honor had been circulated verbally, even though not always in the kindest of terms.

This seemingly extraneous episode had one further result—it revealed to both Wellesley and Perceval their vast personal differences. Thereafter their relationship was characterized by little more than polite hostility. Wellesley's vain and autocratic nature had not diminished.

Wellesley officially accepted the seals of office on December 5, 1809.[49] Settling into his post, he turned his attention to Spain. As an integral part of his Spanish policy, the new secretary counted on the presence of his brother Henry in the embassy in Seville. Wellesley knew from experience that the Spanish responded to the British point of view only after the application of great diplomatic pressure. That there were few available means to bring such pressure to bear was illustrated by Wellesley's own failure to institute his cherished reforms in Spain's government and military system. There was always the possibility of utilizing British military assistance and the subsidy as diplomatic tools. But the Marquess knew Wellington was in no position to undertake an offensive, and Britain was more or less obliged to keep subsidies flowing. The apparent limitations of these potential tools of diplomatic leverage meant that difficulties would persist in the negotiations with Spain, at least for the time being.

Yet Wellesley knew that negotiations could be greatly influenced by the strength and position of the British representative in Spain. With this in mind, he turned to Henry, whose presence would create an ideal situation. As the brother of both the foreign secretary and the commander in chief of Britain's peninsular forces, Henry would have extraordinary influence—far beyond that of another representative. Spanish leaders, having already witnessed Wellesley's and Wellington's ability to coordinate their activities, would logically perceive Henry's actions as being sanctioned by the Marquess. Wellesley had employed this method of diplomacy in India, when he entrusted Henry with the critical negotiations for a subsidiary treaty with the state of Oude. "As his brother," Henry explained, "I would have greater advantages . . . than could be possessed by any other individual in India excepting himself, and this was, I believe, his principal reason for entrusting this important mission to me."[50] Henry correctly supposed that his eldest brother trusted him implicitly.

Informed that Henry was being considered for the embassy in Portugal, Wellesley wrote to him several days before departing Spain: "I advise you not to decide your own situation (unless you should be particularly desirous of going to Lisbon) until my arrival. You may rely on my using every effort to place you in a situation worthy of you, and acceptable to you."[51] On arrival in London, Wellesley promptly made his proposition. Henry acquiesced, and on December 12 George III appointed him envoy extraordinary and minister plenipotentiary to Spain.[52] Six days later the king also agreed to make Henry a member of the Privy Council "to give him greater weight in dealing with the Spanish" and appointed Charles Richard Vaughan secretary of legation.[53] On December 23 His Majesty's ship *Antelope* prepared to carry Henry Wellesley to Cádiz.

Henry's varied and interesting life had shaped his mind much the same as Wellesley's, and amply qualified him for the post he was to assume. The youngest prodigy of Garrett and Anne Wellesley, he was educated at Eton, where he showed promise as a scholar. Unfortunately, the poor state of his family's finances prevented his going on to college. Instead of attending Oxford, Henry studied military science at the Court of Brunswick. Although he never protested, Henry considered his inability to attend college a great disadvantage, "because I believe that the two or three years passed there by young men previous to their entering public life are of the greatest value, not only with the view to the acquirement of knowledge, but also to the forming of friendships and connections which, once formed, usually continue through life."[54]

From Brunswick, Henry traveled to Brussels and then to Spa, where, in consultation with the Marquess, he decided to enter the diplomatic service rather than pursue a military career. Henry's first diplomatic assignment (secured by Wellesley) was as an attaché at The Hague. Next, he was sent to Sweden as secretary of legation. For a year and a half he functioned as British chargé d'affaires in Stockholm until the outbreak of the war with France, when he was recalled to Britain to join his regiment. Subsequently Henry took part in the Battle of Hondschoote. He returned to London to be discharged from the army, having had his fill of military life.[55]

In February 1794 Henry went to Lisbon to escort his recently widowed sister, Anne, to London. On the voyage, the ship was captured by a French warship, whereupon he and Anne were taken to Brest and brought before a *représentant du peuple*, Jean Bon André, "one of the most ardent adherents of Robespierre." André subjected his captives to a tirade on George III and William Pitt. Henry commented afterward, "This speech, addressed to a young woman by a man of good education and one of the highest functionaries of the Republic, affords a good specimen of Republican taste and feeling."[56] Henry, Anne, and the other passengers were then imprisoned for a period of nearly nine months.

Following the death of Robespierre, the French government decided to allow the female prisoners to return to London on an American ship. Upon learning of this decision, Henry received permission to accompany his sister to the ship and there persuaded the captain to take him and several others aboard later that night. That evening, after bribing a jailer, Henry escaped in the company of thirteen others. On board ship, the captain informed him that the French were making thorough searches of every vessel leaving Brest. If Henry and his cohorts were

Henry Wellesley, 1st Lord Cowley (1773– 1847), by J. Hoppner. Reproduced
with permission of His Grace the Duke of Wellington and the Courtauld Institute of Art.

discovered, all, including women, would be returned to prison. Henry decided on another means of escape. He purchased a twenty-three-foot fishing boat, and the fourteen fugitives set out across the English Channel. The vessel ran into foul weather, and four men died—either from exposure or drowning—before the group landed near Falmouth.[57]

Henry spent the following year recovering from his harrowing escape and nurturing a bitter hatred of the French Revolution. In 1796 Lord Grenville appointed him a précis writer in the Foreign Office. He held this post for a year and a half, during which time he had the good fortune to accompany the Malmesbury mission to Lille in its effort to negotiate a peace with the French Directory. In the fall of 1797, Henry chose to accompany his brother to India. After providing Wellesley with five years of invaluable service, Henry returned to London to become a lord of the treasury. A few months later he was chosen as the new envoy extraordinary and minister plenipotentiary to Spain. Unfortunately, the outbreak of war between Britain and Spain prevented Henry from going to Madrid, and he subsequently became secretary to the treasury along with William Huskisson. Henry pointed to the long hours required by his treasury post as being responsible for a most distressing episode in his already eventful life. On March 6, 1809, his wife, Charlotte, ran off with William Paget, the future Marquess of Anglessy and hero at Waterloo. Actually, the elopement did not catch Henry unaware; he had known of the clandestine affair for at least a year.[58] Nonetheless, the final separation caused him a great deal of pain. He became despondent and resigned from the treasury post, explaining that his wife's desertion had left him incapable of continuing.[59]

Henry remained a political recluse until Canning chose him to replace Villiers in Lisbon. When Canning resigned, Henry promptly declined nomination. Following his intimate involvement in the Canning-Castlereagh duel, he seriously considered applying for a mission to Buenos Aires, but at his brother's urging he deferred making a decision until the political situation in Britain cleared. When Wellesley returned to London with the offer of the Spanish Embassy, Henry eagerly accepted.[60] It was a post well suited to his talents and inclinations.

Wellesley's instructions to his youngest brother betrayed an urgency which reflected the deteriorating political and military situation in Spain, the continuing difficulties within the alliance, and the domestic situation in Britain. Since Wellesley's departure, the French had been actively preparing for an offensive designed to subdue southern Spain. Instead of responding with a vigorous defense, the Spanish decided to pursue the unrealistic autumn offensive planned since August. At best, the campaign would have been hazardous, calling for a three-frontal attack from distant points, in the hope of engaging the enemy simultaneously on all fronts. The inferior ability of both Spanish troops and officers made coordinating the operation virtually impossible. Moreover, the Spanish would have to attack an enemy established in a concentrated, defensive position, under the command of competent officers and manned by experienced, confident troops.[61]

Surprisingly, the campaign began on an optimistic note: on October 18, 1809, at the Battle of Tamames, the Duque del Parque achieved the first Spanish victory against the French since Baylen. The victory was, however, hardly noteworthy—the French were able to retreat in good order.[62] Nevertheless, the junta, making the best of the victory, badgered Britain for more active support—for Spain in general and the campaign in particular.[63]

The Spanish were, however, still failing to fulfill even Britain's minimal requests. Saavedra, for instance, in response to Frere's concern for the Army of Estremadura, claimed that it had been brought to a strength of 12,000 effective infantry and 2,500 cavalry. Intelligence from Albuquerque revealed an ill-equipped, ill-fed infantry of 13,292 and 1,040 cavalry in miserable condition. Saavedra still apparently felt justified in requesting Wellington's active assistance in the Spanish campaign, pointing to the dangerous situation caused by the peace agreement recently signed between France and Austria. Frere forcefully refused and charged that the junta was attempting to use Wellington's refusal to cooperate as an excuse for any future Spanish failures.[64]

Undeterred, Saavedra continued to besiege Frere with requests for additional supplies of money, clothing, arms, ammunition, and the cooperation of British troops.[65] Frere, with strong support from Wellington, gave an unequivocal "no" to the last request, and he took the opportunity to press Spain for trading concessions before responding to the others. "By removing the impediments which obstruct the Commerce of Great Britain," suggested Frere, "the Spanish Gov't. can essentially improve Her resources, facilitating to her the means of furnishing the supplies of which Spain is so much in need, making perhaps the only return which under the present circumstances it is in her power to make, for the many and great sacrifices which have been offered up in her defense."[66] Spain, still suspicious of British motives, held steadfast in her refusal to make trading concessions, and the subject was soon dropped.

Meanwhile, the Spanish offensive proceeded with disastrous results.

General Carlos Areizegas, in command of 56,000 Spanish troops, was crushed by Generals Horace Sebastiani, Edouard Mortier, and Jean Joseph Paul Dessolles commanding 30,000 French, at the Battle of Ocaña.[67] Colonel Philip Roche, accompanying Areizegas, reported on the battle: "It is most melancholy to reflect upon the mad, unthinking, vain and self conceited folly, which has directed every operation the Spaniards undertake. . . . In my former letters your Lordship will see I predicted all these misfortunes, and I really cannot see anything short of a miracle which now can save the country."[68] The Battle of Ocaña had a sobering effect on Briton and Spaniard alike. Another attempt was made to overthrow the junta, whose popularity continued to wane with each defeat.[69] Britain began to despair of southern Spain's safety and pondered the feasibility of withdrawing the British and Spanish armies to Ceuta, Majorca, and Minorca if Spain fell to France. Particular attention was now paid to the Spanish fleets harbored in Cádiz, El Ferrol, and Cartagena, whose safety had heretofore been neglected.[70]

Frere continued to urge the junta to take immediate steps to provide for the defense of Andalusia, in particular the augmentation of Albuquerque's army, as the Battle of Ocaña had made it essential for Wellington to move northward to protect Portugal.[71] But the Spanish remained indifferent to the warnings. Then on November 29 came the stunning news of the destruction of the Duque del Parque's army by General François Kellermann at Alba de Tormes.[72] This, the end of the autumn campaign, meant the nearly total destruction of the Spanish army. With the exception of Andalusia, France controlled all of Spain and posed an ominous threat to Portugal. Wellington, astonished at Spanish ignorance of military affairs, declared: ". . . if they had preserved their two armies, or even one of them, the cause was safe. The French could have sent no reinforcements which could have been of any use; time would have been gained; the state of affairs would have improved daily. . . . But no! Nothing will answer excepting to fight great battles in plains, in which their defeat is as certain as is the commencement of the battle. They will not credit the accounts I have repeatedly given them of the superior numbers even of the French; they will seek them out, and they find them invariably in all parts in numbers superior to themselves."[73] As he retreated northward, Wellington advised the Spanish that their only hope was to mass what remained of the armies in strong, defensible positions and to have guerrillas continue to harass French communications.[74]

Britain continued to ship arms and supplies to Spain; in return, the

Spanish only persisted in more demands. The Supreme Junta's newest scheme after the disastrous defeats at Ocaña and Alba de Tormes was for Britain to land a force of 25,000 troops on the northern coast of Spain to divert French attention into Catalonia.[75] Lord Wellesley responded with indifference. At the same time, and contrary to its assertions, the junta still failed to reinforce Albuquerque's army in Estremadura. Instead of a strong army of 20,000, Albuquerque had at his disposal a nominal force of 18,000, of which only about 6,000 were deemed fit for service. The rest were in hospitals, absent, or unarmed. "The whole are in a wretched state in point of cloathing and equipments," reported Frere, "and have been without pay for the last three months."[76]

The Supreme Junta seemed incapable of constructive activity. The condition of Albuquerque's troops was typical of the remainder of Spain's army. No steps had been taken toward reforming or rebuilding the defeated armies, and the commanders remained in their positions against their own inclinations.[77] The junta was paralyzed with internal discord. The executive committee could not function under Romana's leadership because the junta overruled all its decisions; at the same time, capable, popular leaders were jealously kept from positions of influence. The Supreme Junta's ineptness increased until the junta of Seville felt compelled to remind it of its duties and obligations.[78] Such advice was ignored, and the situation continued to deteriorate. Finally, the extent of public discontent caused Bartholomew Frere to become concerned that the junta, fearing a coup d'état, might eventually turn to France for the support necessary to maintain itself.[79]

With the knowledge of these events and of the general condition of Spain, Wellesley drew up Henry's instructions for the political, military, and economic problems which Henry would encounter. Politically, the problem seemed obvious. Wellesley considered it absolutely essential to find a substitute for the Supreme Junta. The first step in this process would be for Henry to insist unequivocally that the Cortes assemble with the least possible delay. When this was accomplished, Wellesley suggested that Henry work to acquire influence over key members of the Cortes and to urge the prompt formation of a regency and the dissolution of the Supreme Junta.[80] A subtle change in method had developed since Wellesley's tenure in Spain. His earlier plans were based on the premise that governmental reform would emanate from the junta itself; now he apparently concluded that the junta would not voluntarily relinquish its authority but would have to be forced from power. Wellesley's anticipation that Henry would involve himself and assert his influence in assert his influence in Spain's political affairs set a pattern for foreign secretaries' expectations which would last for several years.

In military matters, Henry would confront the threatening position of the French armies. Of primary importance was the removal of the Spanish fleets from their vulnerable positions in El Ferrol, Cartagena, and Cádiz before they fell into French hands. There was a provision in the treaty of January 1809 dealing with such a circumstance, and Henry was instructed to bring it to the junta's attention.[81] Regarding military reforms, the new envoy was to urge the Cortes and regency, if and when they met, to commence a rapid reorganization of the army into a well-appointed, well-disciplined force. To secure the unqualified support and loyalty of the populace for the army, Wellesley suggested the abrogation of ancient but extant political and economic abuses. The foreign secretary guaranteed that military supplies would continue to flow into Spain but instructed Henry to consult with Wellington regarding their most effectual employment.[82]

Wellesley had always avoided economic problems, viewing them as a nuisance that could always be overcome. Nevertheless, in his few short weeks in London, the Marquess had become acutely aware of financial problems. On taking office, Perceval had directed his attention to a report by Huskisson outlining the state of the British economy in August 1809.[83] The situation was one of budgetary distress created by the war. Economists (including Perceval) believed that the war could be maintained only by the creation of new money through loans and the issuance of bills of exchange, or by an increase in the level of foreign trade, which would add to the revenues of British customhouses and bolster the consumer economy. Wellesley's instructions consequently dealt with both alternatives. Henry, on arrival in Spain, was to reapply promptly for a license to export $10 million from Mexico, and to initiate discussions on the elimination of the "impediments which have hitherto obstructed the return of gold and silver into this country." "We are amply entitled to claim the relaxation of the colonial laws of Spain in this particular instance," Wellesley explained, "as a return for the unexampled exertions of this country in the cause of Spanish independence."[84]

Wellesley's instructions directed Henry to begin serious discussions for instigating British trade with Spanish America. The fact that Britain had carried on a more profitable trade in this area when she was at war with Spain than when they were allies particularly annoyed the Marquess. Along the same line, Wellesley saw the immediate necessity of Spain's removing any obstructions to British trade with Amelia

Island, just off the coast of Spain's colony of Florida, where naval stores were in abundance. He considered these obstructions "deeply injurious to the prosperity of the British navy and inconsistent with the spirit of the alliance."[85]

Before Henry Wellesley embarked for Spain, another matter arose which was of the greatest importance to Lord Wellesley. On February 2 he received word that the Portuguese minister in Seville had inquired if the Cortes of 1789 had abrogated the Salic Law.[86] If it had, then the Princess of Brazil would have been in line to succeed to the Spanish throne and would be qualified to act as regent. Saavedra had responded that the question would be discussed when the Cortes convened, but Wellesley remained apprehensive since the appointment of a single regent from the royal family would pose several problems. First, should the regent prove unpopular with the Spanish people, he or she might inhibit Spain's efforts against France. Second, in the case of the Princess of Brazil, the governments of Portugal and Spain would be essentially united under one authority, which would weaken Britain's diplomatic position. Great Britain preferred to deal with her Iberian allies individually since age-old animosities still existed between the two countries, and invariably the military situation differed from one country to the other. Third, Britain feared the junta would use the appointment of a regent as a pretext for not assembling the Cortes.[87]

For these reasons, Wellesley instructed his brother to discourage any attempts to appoint the princess regent in the absence of Ferdinand VII. Similarly, he informed Henry of his concern over the Duke of Orleans's aspirations for the same post.[88] The duke had long intrigued to become commander in chief of the Spanish armies and regent of the kingdom—Canning had warned Wellesley of this in July 1809. Moreover, Orleans was well organized. He had a large following in the junta as well as agents furthering his interests throughout Spain.[89]

Orleans's claims presented unique problems. Disregarding the possibility that he might prove an incapable leader, his French ancestry would immediately make him unpopular with a large sector of the Spanish population. More important, Orleans might not relinquish his position amicably when peace was finally achieved and Ferdinand VII returned to Spain.[90] Before leaving Cádiz in November, Wellesley demonstrated his concern by warning the commander of the British fleet in that port, Admiral Purvis, "that it is by no means desirable to favor any project for facilitating the arrival of the Duke of Orleans in Spain. On the contrary it is advisable to prevent any such project, and I am to request that you will attend to this suggestion and that you will leave a copy of this letter with any person who may succeed you at Cádiz, and also transmit a copy to Lord Collingwood, or to the officer commanding in the Mediterranean."[91] Henry was provided with the same instructions.

Wellesley did not burden Henry with a vast list of official instructions, as Canning was likely to do. Through their discussions and past experiences working together, Henry knew what his brother expected, and the Marquess, in turn, was willing to rely on Henry's judgment, prudence, and ability. Henry departed Britain on February 12, knowing that the political and military situations in Spain were rapidly deteriorating.[92] The French were on the march southward, threatening the Sierra Morena and consequently Seville. In response the junta desperately sought Wellington's aid, but Frere pointedly suggested that they cease fretting over the absence of British military assistance and attend to the task of defending the passes of the Sierra Morena.[93] Instead, the junta occupied itself with devising ways to shift the blame for Spain's predicament from itself to Great Britain. As a result, the government fell into disarray. With the junta concerned only with self-justification, Spain reverted to the condition which had existed shortly after the revolution in 1808—each province acting independently of any central authority. "These provinces abandoned to their own exertions," explained Frere, "have increased their activity in proportion to the danger which threatens the country, and though they pay outward marks of deference to the authority of the Supreme Junta, the Government are very cautious of interfering in their operations."[94]

Spain seemed to be slowly slipping into anarchy—an ominous trend which would challenge Henry Wellesley. In the meantime, Lord Wellesley would vigorously attempt to rally a pessimistic cabinet and Parliament to Spain's cause. The stage was set for the opening of a new phase in Anglo-Spanish relations.

6

New Beginnings: Negotiations with Spain, January–June 1810

Lord Wellesley took office as foreign secretary assuming, with justification, that he would play a leading policy-making role in the Perceval cabinet. Perceval's desperate solicitations for his services could have persuaded even a man of lesser arrogance that his presence in the cabinet would be essential. Moreover, with the absence of Canning, Castlereagh, and Sidmouth, the new cabinet lacked brilliance. Aside from Perceval, Wellesley was certainly the most distinguished member. Wellesley was confident that Perceval and his colleagues supported his views on Spain and Portugal. Not only was he former ambassador to Spain and Wellington's brother; he also harbored popular strong anti-French sentiments, and he had been extremely vocal in urging an extension of Britain's war effort in the peninsula. He doubtless believed that Perceval would not have offered him the Foreign Office had the cabinet adhered to different views so he was surprised to find that his colleagues opposed an extended war effort. Instead, it seemed that the goal of the new government was to scale down Britain's efforts, passing more responsibility to Portugal and Spain. Liverpool explained to Wellington: "The expenditure of this country has become enormous, and if the war is to continue, we must look to economy. I do not believe so great a continued effort has ever been made by this country, combining the military and pecuniary aid together, as his Majesty is making for Portugal and Spain. The respective governments of these countries should be made sensible of the truth of this position, and should feel the necessity of making extraordinary exertions for their own support."[1]

The ministry's timidity can be explained by the facts that its rather questionable strength had yet to be tested in Parliament and that British finances were already under strain. Perceval warned Wellesley as he assumed office that there would be problems accumulating money for future operations in either Spain or Portugal.[2] For the moment the Marquess acquiesced, although it is apparent that he felt that this limitation could be overcome if the government gathered adequate strength in Parliament.[3] Until that strength developed, he remained willing to accept the prevailing sentiment of the cabinet.

The cabinet's problems in dealing with Parliament would be multiple. Added to its obvious weakness caused by the Canning-Castlereagh duel, the ministry would be forced to defend an event for which it was not directly responsible—the Walcheren expedition. Wellesley, for instance, had always opposed the expedition as diverting attention away from Iberia, which he considered the major theater of war.[4] Nevertheless, because many of the members of the new cabinet had much to do with the organization and planning of the expedition, and because the expedition was part of the overall policy of opposing French expansion, it had to be defended. Then, too, many Britons were beginning to despair over the war in general. Some government supporters even suggested that negotiations be opened with Napoleon in an effort to salvage Portuguese independence before Wellington was forced to retire.[5]

Perceiving the government's weakness and this general trend in public opinion, the opposition attacked mercilessly. Its goal was to win a vote of censure on both the Walcheren campaign and the government's policy in the peninsula and ultimately to force an abandonment of the war. The addition to the Perceval cabinet of the arrogant Wellesley, who had been generally disliked for years, seemed to ignite in the opposition stronger attempts to discredit the ministry. In addition to perceiving the war as futile, the opposition could not justify fighting in Spain to maintain an antiquated and corrupt sociopolitical system. The Whigs saw the Tories as either unwilling or unable to confront this apparent dichotomy in British policy and, as illustrated by the *Examiner,* viewed Lord Wellesley as a personification of this shortcoming:

> While Spain was languishing under a tyranical Junta and a
> fettered press, they [the Ministers] sent over an English Nabob,
> long celebrated in the fettering department, to regenerate the

nation—a pompous man of pleasure, who walked over the French flag, drank the Pope's health, ate a few dinners, ogled a few ladies, made a few hums and hows, and after *thus* regenerating Spain, came back to regenerate England, much in the same way. The brother of this "great man" still lingers in the Peninsula, waiting til he is compelled to make his last retreat, while the natives are everywhere discomfited, and his own soldiers, to whom a loaf is the first of luxuries, are starving upon fruit. But then he has fine titles. . . . We have seen Parliament at the nod of the most worthless set of Ministers since the time of Walpole.[6]

Wellesley, accustomed to such abuse, prepared his arguments for the upcoming session of Parliament. In the interim he busied himself acquainting Henry with the responsibilities of his new post and tending to the affairs of the Foreign Office—particularly those dealing with Spain. Spain's representative in London, Admiral Don Luis de Apodaca, persistently burdened the Marquess with requests for aid, complaints over the British detention of Spanish ships on the high seas, and protests of Britain's numerous violations of Spain's colonial trading laws[7]—but to no avail. British ships continued to stop and search any vessel suspected of trading with France, the justification being that many vessels were sailing fraudulently under the Spanish flag to avoid such encounters. As for illegal trading with the Spanish American colonies, the Continental System had forced the government to turn a blind eye to this activity.

In January 1810, Wellesley turned his attentions to the opening of Parliament. All parties eagerly awaited the opening, each apprehensive of what the session would hold in store. The opposition felt that its position was stronger than ever and, as a result, made efforts to organize its forces. "I think a great deal ought to be done to embrace as many persons as possible," wrote Lord Milton, "for, after all, nothing but a majority in Parlt. can lead to the practical benefit of getting rid of the present administration."[8] And of course turning out the ministry meant the elimination of Lord Wellesley from the government. "I trust the Marquis [Wellesley]," Milton continued, "will meet with the fate you predict for him. He is a great calamity inflicted upon England."[9]

Parliament convened on January 23; George III called for continued support of the war and commended his ministers for their past performance: "The most important Considerations of Policy and of good Faith require that as long as this great cause can be maintained with a Prospect of Success, it should be supported, according to the Nature and Circumstances of the Contest, by the strenuous and continued Assistance of the Power and Resources of His Majesty's Dominions; and His Majesty relies on the Aid of His Parliament in His anxious Endeavours to frustrate the attempts of France against the Independence of Spain and Portugal, and against the Happiness and Freedom of those loyal and resolute Nations."[10] The opposition, hoping to score an initial and decisive victory by rejecting the speech, saw it solidly accepted by ninety-six votes.[11] Although rejection of the king's opening speech was a rare occurrence, and despite the fact that the government would soon be called upon to justify its actions in Iberia and Walcheren, few members of the opposition concealed their disappointment. "Lord Grey came in drunk from the Duke of York's," wrote the flamboyant Thomas Creevey, "where he had been dining. He came and sat beside me on the same sofa, talked as well as he could over the division of the night before, and damned with all his might and main Marquis Wellesley, of whose profligate establishment I told him some anecdotes, which he swallowed as greedily as he had done the Duke's wine."[12]

Two days later, with the introduction in both Houses of a motion of Thanks to Wellington for the Battle of Talavera, the opposition launched an attack on the government. In the House of Lords, Lord Grey immediately interjected a motion for the publication of Wellington's instructions along with his dispatches. Grey claimed publication of these was necessary to determine whether Wellington had acted on his own or on orders from the ministry and whether the results of the battle merited a vote of Thanks. Lord Erskine seconded Grey, conjecturing that if "the result of fighting a battle should be, although a victory was claimed, the failure of the main purposes of the campaign, would it not be essential that they should have information with respect to the reasons for adopting that measure, before they voted thanks for a victory which had produced only disastrous consequences?"[13]

The government, seeking to avoid a thorough inquiry into the Talavera campaign, opposed the motion, with Liverpool claiming that the original motion was only a "tribute to the bravery of the army, and the skill of the commander."[14] There followed a vigorous discussion; Grey's motion failed.[15] Liverpool then reiterated his motion of Thanks, stating, "I wish to direct your attention solely to the conduct of the officer, and the army under his command, on the 27th and 28th of July."[16]

Still, the opposition persisted in its attack. The Earl of Suffolk charged that Wellington had acted imprudently by placing himself in the position he did, that he should have had better knowledge of the strength and movement of the various French forces, and that he should have called into action more of his own troops. Suffolk maintained that if Thanks were to be voted to anyone, they should go to the army and not to the general.[17] Earl Grosvenor concurred. In his opinion, votes of Thanks were to be granted not for valor and skill alone but should correspond to overall success as well: "Whenever consequences no way beneficial, still more injurious, resulted to the country, from any operation of an army, whatever admiration might attach itself to the conduct of that army during such operations, he did not perceive the propriety of their being publicly thanked by the Parliament."[18]

The debate proceeded wearily on until Wellesley rose to speak in favor of the motion. The Marquess disagreed with the approach used by Liverpool, believing the best course to be an open and comprehensive discussion of the campaign itself. Thus, after presenting glowing praises of his brother, Wellesley embarked on a detailed analysis of the goals of Wellington's operation culminating in the Battle of Talavera. The basis of the plan, he explained, was the defense of Portugal, threatened as it was by Soult's presence in the north and Victor's in the southeast. Once Soult was beaten, it was only natural for Wellington to turn against Victor. It was at this stage that he was invited to act in concert with Cuesta. This, Wellesley continued, could not have been refused in good grace, for Cuesta's army appeared formidable. Thus the Marquess claimed that the campaign was tactically sound until the Spanish disappointed Wellington. Even so, he added, Wellington made the best of a bad situation, for without Talavera, "it would have been impossible to prevent the enemy from over-running the South of Spain, or from making a fresh irruption into Portugal." This, coupled with the fact that Wellington was able to withdraw to an advantageous position on the Portuguese frontier, led Wellesley to conclude that a vote of Thanks was fully justified.[19]

After a futile attempt by Grey to refute Wellesley's argument, a vote was taken and the motion carried without a division.[20] The new foreign secretary's performance was well received by the ministry's proponents. Even some members of the opposition were reluctant admirers, as Lady Holland's reflections illustrate: "Lord Wellesley made his debut in the character of Minister upon the thanks of the House being moved to Lord Wellington. Some commend, and others disparage his speech; perhaps the middle line of praise would be nearest the truth. He was rather oriental in his style of praising his brother, but much may be owing to his feelings upon such a subject as that of his brother's merits undergoing a slighting review."[21]

In the House of Commons, Perceval, in spite of the effects of Wellesley's tactics, pursued a course similar to Liverpool's. "Because national
uniformity was necessary," he explained, "he would not introduce the
over-all plan of the campaign or other peripheral topics, and concentrate solely on the battle itself."[22] This was tantamount to admitting that
the campaign as a whole did not merit a vote of Thanks, and the
opposition was quick to agree. Many of the opposition's speakers
suggested that Wellington fought at Talavera for the sole purpose of
obtaining a title. The battle, they maintained, was exemplary of the
commander's indiscretion, not his valor.[23] Like the debate in the Lords,
the government's position in the Commons did not become secure until
the strategy of the entire campaign was revealed and the results
analyzed. These were provided by Castlereagh, who was responsible for
Wellington's orders. Castlereagh concluded that Wellington had carried
on a reasonably successful campaign, under trying circumstances, without putting "himself in a situation from which he might not at any time
have been able to regain his former position in Portugal."[24] The motion
for Thanks subsequently carried without a division, prompting a disappointed Thomas Creevey to comment: "All our indignation against
Wellington ended in smoak. Opposition to his thanks was so unpopular,
that some of the stoutest of our crew slunk away; or rather, they were
dispersed by the indefatigable intrigues of the Wellesleys and the tricks
of Tierney."[25]

Wellesley's position, that full disclosure was the best course to follow,
was triumphant, a fact which certainly inflated his already overblown
ego. The event also served to reinforce his conviction that the government had done nothing that could create embarrassment. With a full-
scale debate on the war in Spain a certainty, Wellesley urged the publication of the Spanish papers which he had scrupulously collected as
ambassador and brought home. A less confident Perceval resisted.[26]
Because the opposition had been able to carry a motion of inquiry into
the Walcheren campaign, he remained wary of his strength in Parliament and felt that the papers' publication would make the government
more vulnerable.[27] Wellesley, for the first time since assuming office,
openly lost patience with his timid prime minister. In a strongly worded
letter, he advised: "The moment is now arrived . . . we must satisfy both
Spain and England that our conduct has been right, and that the causes
of past misfortunes are not irremediable, because those causes are to be
traced to errors and faults, which may be corrected, and which we are
resolved to correct by the utmost efforts of our influence. If the Spanish
and Portuguese papers are to be supressed, I confess that it appears to

me, that we shall deprive ourselves of our main advantage in the conflict with the opposition. They will not be able to withstand the intrinsic and honest strength of our cause as founded on that information. But we shall be subject to every kind of prejudice, misrepresentation, and calumny if we refuse to produce evidence, of what we must assert."[28] Perceval succumbed to the logic and allowed the papers' publication.

To make good his argument and ensure the successful termination to a debate on Spain, the Marquess needed to take steps to correct the causes of past misfortunes in Spain. He had been pleased to learn of the junta's decision to convene the Cortes on March 1, 1810.[29] This would help put to rest the opposition's indignation over the corrupt nature of Spain's social and governmental institutions. But he remained concerned over the junta's determination to retain its powers. Unaware of the rapidly deteriorating political and military situation in Spain, Wellesley resorted to a clandestine operation designed to free Ferdinand VII from captivity. If successful, the need for either the junta or a regency would be eliminated.

Much mystery surrounds this bizarre and somewhat romantic attempt to free Ferdinand VII.[30] The operation was conceived by Charles Leopold, Baron de Kolli, a disaffected French nobleman. Baron de Kolli was first introduced to Lord Wellesley by Charles Arbuthnot, a family associate. The Baron's plan was to sail to Quiberon Bay on the coast of Brittany, where he and his accomplices would be put ashore. He would then proceed to Paris to establish contacts and complete his plans. His men, disguised as priests, would then make their way to Valençay, where Ferdinand was held captive, free him, and return to ship.[31] Because Kolli's plan lacked adequate financing, he turned to Wellesley, who in turn agreed to cooperate. On January 29, 1810, Wellesley wrote to Lord Mulgrave of the Admiralty requesting that Captain George Cockburn and his ship, H.M.S. *Implacable,* be placed at the disposal of the Foreign Office. Mulgrave's response was promptly affirmative.[32]

On February 2 Wellesley acquainted Cockburn with the mission and provided him with detailed instructions. The captain was to receive Kolli and his agents on board the *Implacable,* transport them to Quiberon Bay, and there await their return. If the mission was successful, Cockburn was to urge the king to return to Portsmouth for a briefing on the situation in Spain and the status of the Anglo-Spanish alliance. The monarch would then be transported to Cádiz. If Ferdinand declined, then Cockburn was to proceed directly to Cádiz, where the British minister would take charge of all consultations with the king. Should the mission fail, Cockburn was to return immediately to Britain.[33]

Subsequent days were spent arranging the financing of Kolli's mission. Money was needed to pay the agents for their services, for their support while in France, and for various other necessities, most particularly bribes. The operating funds had to be in French currency or in some other form not traceable to Britain. Consequently it was decided to supply Kolli with jewels, which could be easily bartered or exchanged. On February 27 Wellesley sent to Cockburn £800 in cash and £6,334 in jewelry. Two days later he sent another £6,093 in jewels. The Marquess ordered Cockburn to deliver these funds personally to the baron and to obtain an official receipt. As a precautionary measure against Kolli's playing the role of a double agent, his reimbursement was to be withheld until the mission was concluded.[34]

Kolli and his agents borded the *Implacable* on March 2, and, as arranged, Cockburn transferred the money to the baron's care. Four days later they set sail for Quiberon Bay. The mission arrived at its destination on the evening of March 7, and at 11:00 o'clock on the evening of March 9 Kolli went ashore "without the least disturbance or molestation." There he made contact with a general of the Vendean insurgents, Baron de Feriet. An efficient smuggler of British goods, the baron had reliable contacts on the coast. On a promise of recompense and favor for the Vendean cause, Feriet agreed to convey all communications between Kolli and Cockburn. These arrangements made, Kolli set out for Paris, accompanied by Feriet as far as Nantes.[35]

While Kolli established himself in Paris, Cockburn cruised the waters of Quiberon Bay. Kolli's goal in Paris was to gain as much support as possible from French malcontents and to arrange his entrance into Valençay. Unfortunately, because he was indiscreet in handling his money, French officials became suspicious. He was subsequently arrested and his private papers seized.[36] The plan foiled, Napoleon, for his own amusement and as a marvelous piece of propaganda, decided to follow it to its logical conclusion.

Napoleon dispatched to Valençay a French agent disguised as the baron. The agent presented Ferdinand with a letter from George III verifying Kolli's legitimacy, and assured him that everything was prepared for his escape. As Napoleon anticipated, Ferdinand's courage was not equal to the undertaking; "He obstinately refused to have anything to do with the supposed agent of Great Britain." The emperor sub-

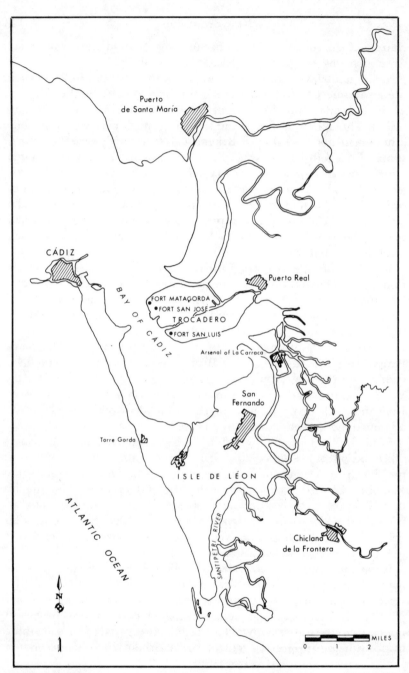

Cádiz in 1810

sequently published in the *Moniteur* the news of Kolli's arrest and Ferdinand's disgraceful behavior, although he failed to reveal the exact sequence of events.[37] Cockburn knew only that the mission had failed because of Ferdinand's intransigence, and he so informed Wellesley on May 25.[38]

There was little public or private reaction to the reports in the *Moniteur*. Most Britons seemed to discredit anything of such nature appearing in that Paris publication. The Marquess was not called to account in Parliament, and the aborted effort received only minimal attention in Spain.[39] In retrospect, the Kolli mission seems an ill-judged, rash decision on Wellesley's part. From the beginning there was only minimal hope for success, while the potential for embarrassment was great. It was, however, indicative of Wellesley's desperation to effect a change in Spain's government.

Meanwhile, Henry Wellesley arrived in Cádiz to find Spain's military and political situation drastically altered. The despised junta was gone, Seville had fallen, and French forces were besieging Cádiz. With the Spanish armies on the defensive following their defeats at Ocaña and Alba de Tormes, Joseph Bonaparte had decided to press his advantage by undertaking the conquest of Andalusia. His armies met little resistance. The passes of the Sierra Morena were taken on January 20, opening the roads to Seville and Cádiz.[40] The onslaught sent panic through the Supreme Junta as well as the British embassy. Efforts were made to secure Cádiz as a place of retreat in the event of Seville's fall. Frere demanded and obtained the destruction of the fortress of Santa Catalina near Cádiz, so that if it fell into French hands it could not prevent the passage of British and Spanish ships into and out of the Bay of Cádiz.[41] Apprehensive concerning their own survival, the citizens of Cádiz now requested British aid in the defense of the city—aid that they had been rejecting since the outbreak of the war. Frere gladly complied with this latest appeal, summoning a garrison of troops from Gibraltar.[42]

On January 24 the Supreme Junta left Seville to take up residence in Cádiz. Already discredited, it ignited a public uprising when it deserted. The citizens of Seville demanded that the Supreme Junta be abolished, that Saavedra be elected president, and that Romana organize a defense of the city.[43] Realizing that Seville was indefensible, and anxious to retreat himself, Frere convinced the insurrection's leaders that Saavedra's and Romana's skills were needed elsewhere and that the most practical course to follow was to appoint a regency and retire to Cádiz.[44] A similar insurrection followed in Cádiz, obliging Don Pedro Rivero to make this announcement:

There shall be a council of Regency composed of five persons, one of them for the Americas, but none of those who compose the Junta can be elected.

That these five persons are to be the Reverand Bishop of Orense Don Pedro de Quevedo and Quintana; the Chancellor of State and Secretary of State for Foreign Affairs Don Francisco de Saavedra; the Captain General of the Royal Armies Don Francisco Xavier de Castaños; the Chancellor of State and Secretary of State for the Navy Department Don Antonio Escaño; and the Chancellor of the Council of Spain and the Indies Don Estevan Fernandos de León in consideration of the Americas.[45]

On January 31, 1810, one day before Seville fell to the French, the Supreme Junta ceased to exist.

The French, however, had made a poor decision in occupying Seville before advancing on Cádiz. The latter, situated at the end of a long and narrow isthmus, was easily defended from land attack, provided it was properly garrisoned. In January the small contingent of regular Spanish troops at Cádiz could not have withstood a vigorous French assault. Perceiving this weakness, the Duque de Albuquerque had decided to forgo any attempt to relieve Seville and led his small army directly to Cádiz.[46] Had Soult decided on the same strategy, French troops could easily have arrived at Cádiz ahead of Albuquerque. As it was, Albuquerque arrived in Cádiz on February 3, a day ahead of the advancing French, and his weak army proved force enough to turn back the initial assaults.[47]

Still, Cádiz was much less than secure, and it eagerly received the first British reinforcements from Gibraltar on February 7. After conferring with Albuquerque on the employment of his army and receiving assurances of its safe embarkation prior to "any capitulation being entered into between the city of Cádiz & the enemy," General William Bowes landed his troops. Because the citizens of Cádiz still hesitated to allow British troops within the city, Bowes took up a position on the opposite end of the isthmus, on the Isla de León.[48]

Four days later Major General William Stewart arrived in Cádiz with 2,146 more troops sent by Wellington. In addition to the conditions set out by General Bowes, Wellington had requirements for his troops. He asked that they remain under the immediate and exclusive command of their own officers, that they act as much as possible as a unit, that they be relieved as often as deemed proper, that they not be removed from

Cádiz or the Isla de León, that they be fed from Spanish stores according to British rations, and that they have free access of communication with the transports, which would remain. The Spanish agreed, and the troops disembarked. Fortunately that same day 8,400 muskets, 6,715 sets of accoutrements, and 100,000 flints arrived from London.[49]

Gradually Cádiz became secure from French attack, with Albuquerque's army garrisoned within the city and over 3,000 British troops placed in defensive positions on the Isla de León. To this was added a regiment of 1,300 Portuguese troops, which landed on February 16, to be placed under General Stewart's command. At the same time, the garrison of Cádiz was fortunate to receive a shipment of 9,600 muskets and $6 million in specie for its own maintenance.[50] One week later the first transport of Spanish troops, remnants from the dispersed armies, arrived to aid the defense of Cádiz. Subsequently Albuquerque was named commander in chief of the Spanish forces and governor of Cádiz.[51]

Such was the situation when Henry Wellesley arrived in Cádiz on February 28, 1810, to be warmly received by the Duque de Albuquerque, General Venegas, and Admiral Villa Vincentia.[52] He was shocked to find that Seville had fallen, that Cádiz was essentially all that remained of free Spain, and that the junta had been abolished. Just as shocking was the political and military chaos prevalent in Cádiz. Authority was ill defined, and discipline absent in the Spanish army. Consequently Henry's immediate task was to bring order to Cádiz and to ensure her greater security. Initially he found the Spanish cooperative. For the first time they admitted British troops into the city and granted permission to send a garrison to defend Ceuta, at least until Spain could defend it herself.[53] These accommodations misled Henry; he was soon to become baffled and dismayed by the stubborn and uncooperative nature of the Spanish.

Britain was stunned by the news of Seville's fall. Many Britons came to believe that the cause in Spain was hopeless and that imminent doom hung over Portugal. A feeling of despair was apparent within the councils of the Perceval cabinet, where Liverpool constantly urged Wellington to secure a safe place of embarkation should that become necessary.[54] Fortunately no one in the ministry suggested negotiating a treaty with Napoleon to salvage Portuguese independence at the expense of Spain, although this was by no means an uncommon suggestion. Nonetheless, the disillusioning reports from the peninsula could not have come at a more inopportune time, since the government was preparing to introduce motions for subsidizing the Portuguese army.

Despite the uncertain state of British public opinion on the war, the ministry formalized its plans. On February 22 Wellesley moved in the Lords to take 30,000 Portuguese troops into Britain's pay at a cost of £980,000. Ill at the time of his speech, Wellesley did not deliver an effective appeal, but the subsequent debate resulted in an affirmative vote by a substantial margin.[55] In the House of Commons the debate was more heated. Perceval carried on a brilliant fight, but in so doing he betrayed a pessimism over the conflict in Iberia, a mood seemingly inherent in everyone but the Wellesleys. Perceval carefully explained that it was not merely a question of supporting Portuguese troops but rather one of defending the whole peninsula. The ultimate logic in his argument was that if Napoleon was not stopped in the peninsula, then he would have to be stopped on British shores at far greater expense. In other words, Perceval considered the Peninsular War to be only the better of two alternatives if the war was to be fought at all.[56]

The opposition struck back with its standard argument. Maintaining that the cause was hopeless, it pointed to the military disasters, the massive French reinforcements pouring into Spain, the wretched state of the British treasury, and what seemed to be a lack of potential for success in the Spanish and Portuguese armies. Samuel Whitbread's speech was exemplary of the opposition's position: "Spain has not done its duty—no matter from what cause—the people, had, however, some excuse—they had been under the selfish sway of an aristocracy, that only wanted to use them as an instrument to effect their own narrow purposes; their implicit confidence had been abused by the blind bigotry of an intolerant priesthood—a priesthood, that whatever it preached, practiced not the gospel it ought not alone to preach but practice; they often had had the sword in their hands as often as the crosier—and that they had had, he feared, in their hearts any thing but the meekness, humility, charity, and peace that their blessed master had inculcated by his pure precepts, enforced by the example of his apostle's [*sic*] life, and sealed by the last sufferings of his all atoning death."[57] The opposition simply could not reconcile supporting the Spanish inquisition and the social injustice that it spawned.

The government ignored the ideological tirades. Instead, it pointed to the resilience of the Spanish and Portuguese patriots and Britain's moral responsibility to support them as long as a spark of resistance remained. Its case was strong enough to carry the motion.[58] Lord Wellesley greeted the victory with guarded optimism. The debate revealed that the government still had strong support for the war, but it also illustrated a growing apprehension on the part of many parliamentarians (of both the government and the opposition) over Britain's ability to finance the war. Similarly the opposition was becoming more convincing in its position that Spain could never be successful or worthy of success in the war against France as long as the old social and governmental institutions remained. As a result, Wellesley became determined to secure commercial advantages in Spanish America for British merchants and to bring about reforms in Spain's government. He considered the abolition of the junta and the establishment of the regency only a beginning.

Unfortunately, Henry Wellesley was in no position to carry out his brother's desires. On arriving in Cádiz, Henry realized that there were other important matters requiring attention. He was particularly struck by the vulnerability of both the Spanish fleet and the French prisoners of war kept on barges in the bay. Britain could not afford to allow France to obtain the services of the considerable Spanish fleet anchored in Cádiz, and, because the fleet was performing no useful service in its present position, Henry wanted it moved to a place of greater security. Neither could Britain allow the escape of the over 4,000 prisoners, many of whom were officers who would prove a timely addition to the French armies, particularly that encamped before Cádiz.[59]

Earlier Lord Wellesley had alerted Henry to this situation, and now Admiral Purvis and General Stewart also expressed concern. Their concern became alarm when a storm hit Cádiz on March 4 which resulted in the destruction of several ships and the near loss of several prisoner barges.[60] "The necessity for as early a removal as possible from Cádiz," advised Stewart, "of every discription of incumbrance, whether it be under the head of a superfluous population of prisoners or of ships, appears to be a consideration at this moment paramount to all others."[61] Henry was of a similar opinion and, as a result, relayed the advice to General Castaños.

Castaños understood the necessity for such action, but found himself at a loss as to how it could be effected. He could send the prisoners neither to the Balearic Islands nor to Ceuta because both places were already overcrowded. The defenseless state of the Canary Islands ruled out that possibility. He concluded that the only practical solution to the problem would be to send all prisoners to Britain.[62] As for the Spanish fleet, he was reluctant to commit himself on its removal. Most Spaniards saw it as the only deterrent to a British takeover of Cádiz, although in fact it would have been ineffectual in resisting an attack. Unable to sanction such a one-sided suggestion, Henry offered a compromise. He promised that if Castaños would distribute half of the prisoners among Ceuta, the Balearic Islands, and the Canary Islands, then Britain would take responsibility for the other half. Henry also suggested sending 2,000 or 3,000 of General Blake's troops to Minorca on the fleet anchored at Cartagena. The result would be twofold—the island reinforced and the safety of the fleet secured.[63]

Henry lacked the authority to make such an offer but, lacking alternatives, decided on this course of action. He was certain that his actions would result in a reprimand, but he was also confident that the Marquess would protect him from severe censure. The episode was indicative of the independence and flexibility which Lord Wellesley's position gave to Henry.[64]

Although Castaños accepted the offer, Henry soon found that securing Spanish cooperation in implementing the plan would be more difficult. The problem was one characteristic of the defunct Supreme Junta—a breakdown in executive authority. In this case the conflict was between the junta of Cádiz and the regency over which of the two held final authority within the city. Complicating matters was the fact that the regency, supposedly the nation's supreme authority, operated from the Isla de León.[65] Henry, aware of this problem since his first days in Cádiz, commented: "The government too are following the example of their worthy predecessors. Owing to some misunderstanding with the Junta of this place, they cannot be prevailed upon to take up their residence here, but remain at the Isla de León conducting themselves more like the Junta of a miserable village, than the Regents of a Kingdom in a condition to require all the energy and exertion of the most vigorous minds."[66] By taking up residence on the Isla de León, the regency's prestige was diminished. The opposite happened to the junta, and the result was a paralyzed government.

Relations between the junta and the regency had never actually been good, but Henry had come to believe that if the regency was transferred to Cádiz the situation would be greatly simplified. Henry held good opinions of the gentlemen of the regency and believed that in better circumstances they could govern effectively.[67] Yet Castaños was reluctant to approve the move. He believed that as long as Albuquerque kept his headquarters in Cádiz, the regents should stay on the Isla de León to watch over military affairs there. Consequently Henry met with Albuquerque to arrange the transfer of his headquarters to the Isla de León so that the regency might move to Cádiz. Albuquerque could not understand the necessity of such a move but deferred to Wellesley's

wishes, removing the sole motive for the regency's staying on the Isla de
León.[68] Nevertheless both parties responded with characteristic slow-
ness, and it took the eruption of a serious feud between Albuquerque
and the junta of Cádiz finally to effect the transfer.

The feud originated with a letter to the regency from Albuquerque,
who accused the junta of Cádiz of obstructing his efforts to improve the
army and blamed the junta for not supplying, feeding, or paying his
soldiers.[69] Many of Alberquerque's accusations were well founded, but,
not satisfied with merely submitting the statement to the regency, he
imprudently published it. The revelations caused an uproar in Cádiz,
where the junta enjoyed considerable popularity and where it was generally felt that a maximum and adequate effort had been made to supply
the wants of the army and to provide for the defense of the Isla de León.
The junta therefore composed a comprehensive reply to Albuquerque.
Henry made every effort to suppress its publication but to no avail.[70]

In its retort, the junta accused Albuquerque of misrepresentation and
lying, concluding: "The Junta promises itself that your Excellency, is
thoroughly penetrated with the mistake under which you have labored,
excited by a desire that certainly is good essentially, but very dangerous
in its manner, for, the delicate circumstances in which we are placed,
require a very minute circumspection in all those measures, that the
public may become acquainted with, and to which, they may give
perhaps a false interpretation, or perchance an ambiguous one."[71]
Outraged, Albuquerque threatened to resign as commander in chief.
Henry argued against such an action, and the duque agreed to send
only a note to the regency justifying his charges. Unfortunately, indiscretion was pervasive; the regency, in turn, unwisely published the
letter with the stipulation that nothing further would be said on the
issue.[72] Predictably Albuquerque's unpopularity grew in Cádiz, resulting in numerous intrigues to remove him from his posts as governor of
Cádiz and commander in chief. Realizing the urgency of the situation,
Henry persuaded Albuquerque to move his headquarters immediately
from Cádiz to the Isla de León.[73]

This accomplished, Henry went before the regency to hasten the
transfer of its operation to Cádiz. He advised the regents that the longer
they delayed in making the move, the more their authority would be
undermined, especially with Albuquerque gone from the city. The regency finally agreed on March 22, 1810. Henry Wellesley looked forward to more vigorous and efficient leadership for Spain.[74]

Soon after this decision, Albuquerque precipitated another crisis.

Suffering from a wounded pride, he resigned his posts, but it was the regency's responsibility to accept or reject his resignation. It was obvious that his service to Cádiz and Spain made him deserving of honorable treatment. It was equally clear that his pride, vanity, and stubbornness would keep him in perpetual conflict with the junta of Cádiz. Consequently, rather than become involved in the quarrel, the regency wisely accepted his resignation. Albuquerque was thanked for a job well done and dispatched to London as ambassador extraordinary.[75] Castaños took over as commander in chief, appointing General Blake as his second in command on the Isla de León. Once these issues had been settled, Henry again turned his undivided attention toward moving the French prisoners of war and the Spanish fleet from the Bay of Cádiz, reiterating his demands to the new secretary of state, Don Eusebio de Bardaxi y Azara.[76]

Henry Wellesley's activity during his first month in Cádiz was extraordinary. Besides attending to the problems already discussed, he sought to strengthen Cádiz's defense. Like the Marquess, he saw that ultimately Spain's military success depended upon the reformation of her army. To this end, he hoped to secure an appointment for General Stewart as commander of the Spanish forces in Cádiz. Stewart, Henry believed, could provide the army with proper training and discipline.[77] The Spanish were not yet prepared to take such a step, and so, rather than press the issue so early, Henry directed his attention to Cádiz's more practical needs. What he found was pressing need for reinforcements. In consultation with Stewart, he determined that at least 10,000 reinforcements were necessary, and he wrote to the Marquess requesting that half of these be British. On the advice of Wellington, he set out to raise the other 5,000 in Cádiz.[78] At the same time, Henry sought to improve the naval defenses at Cádiz. His problem was that the commander, Admiral Purvis, was too old and too tired to cope with the situation, and most French successes in securing positions opposite Cádiz were due to the admiral's negligence. The situation became so acute by the end of March that all shipping had to be moved up-harbor to avoid attack. For this reason Henry asked the admiralty to make a change in the command.[79]

Henry also succeeded in securing a license to export desperately needed specie from Veracruz. Initially the Spanish denied the request on the grounds that there was insufficient specie in the Mexican treasury to comply with British desires. Henry countered by asking for all that Mexico could afford, the differences to be made up by purchases of specie on the open market.[80] The regency ignored the proposal; Henry,

impatient for a decision and prompted by a directive from Lord Wellesley, reiterated the request. "You will make use of every motive in your
power," wrote the Marquess, "to recommend to them the urgent importance of coming to a speedy decision upon a matter on which so essentially depends the facility with which Great Britain can continue to assist
the Spanish armies."[81] Persistence paid off: on March 28 the regency
granted a license to purchase $10 million of specie on the open market.
There was attached a duty of 17 percent to be paid when the accounts of
the two governments were settled at the war's end. Henry objected to this
extraordinary duty and, after proving it had no precedent, had it lowered to 11 percent.[82]

Wellesley, though pleased with his brother's progress in Cádiz, became
increasingly frustrated with his own position in London. The opposition
was gaining strength in Parliament as the investigation over the Walcheren campaign continued. Similarly Wellesley's colleagues were becoming
more timid in their support for the Peninsular War. There were two
reasons for their hesitation: a fear that the situation in the peninsula
might deteriorate and a reluctance to attempt to expand the British
effort because of their pessimism over securing parliamentary support
for the requisite increase in expenditure. Liverpool, for instance, continued to remind Wellington that he must at all costs preserve his army,
even if it meant abandoning Portugal earlier than he otherwise might.[83]
Such defeatism did not accord with Wellesley's concept of how the war
should be run; still, it was Perceval's preoccupation with finances which
annoyed Wellesley the most. On March 4 the prime minister suggested
that it was time to demand trading concessions in the Spanish American
colonies. Wellesley agreed that such a request was justified, but it must
have appalled him to hear Perceval conclude his suggestion by explaining that "if such liberty is not speedily obtained, I do not see how we shall
be able to pay our army out of the Kingdom."[84]

It must be recognized that Lord Wellesley was not a practical man. He
ignored such details as money in both his private and his public lives. If
something had to be done, he did it and thought about its cost later. He
conducted his governor generalship in India in this manner, which
became the cause of his recall. So too would it be the cause of his troubled
relationship with Spencer Perceval. Nonetheless, for the time being,
Wellesley complied with Perceval's suggestions and ordered Henry to
initiate discussions on a trade agreement.[85] But his inability to supply the
peninsula with sufficient reinforcements, supplies, and money angered
him. He therefore suggested reorganizing the cabinet to strengthen the

government at least to the extent that it would feel comfortable in asking Parliament for an increased expenditure for the peninsula. The Marquess suggested that overtures be made to Canning, Castlereagh, and Sidmouth; and to facilitate their return to the cabinet, he offered to serve in another capacity or to withdraw completely, whichever was deemed necessary.[86] Perceval could see no benefit in undertaking such discussions while the debate on the Walcheren campaign continued, and he deferred action on Wellesley's proposal. Wellesley, in turn, agreed to the postponement but determined to pursue the subject at another time.[87]

In the meantime the government was being challenged in the House of Lords regarding its decision to publish the Spanish dispatches. Those members of the opposition who reviewed the correspondence before final publication, seeing that it might bolster the government's position on the war, moved that it be suppressed. The challenge was led by Wellesley's old friend Lord Grenville. Grenville argued that the ministry had violated several basic tenets of diplomacy by publishing the correspondence. He believed that Britain would betray the alliance by perpetrating aspersions on the Spanish government and would compromise the safety of those whom the government held in confidence. He also maintained that Parliament had no right to investigate the ability and integrity of foreign army commanders, especially those of an ally—in this case, General Cuesta. Such action, Grenville added, would inhibit all future operations involving the combined allied forces. Most important, Grenville was certain that should the papers be made public, future British ministers would be shunned and all confidence in them withheld by foreign governments.[88]

After listening to Grenville's arguments, Wellesley rose in rebuttal. He conceded that the government had an obligation of good faith with its allies regarding the public disclosure of diplomatic proceedings. Yet the uniqueness of the situation, he pointed out, demanded the revelation of the way in which Great Britain's efforts to aid her peninsular allies had been frustrated. This, the Marquess claimed, could not be done without examining the events in the peninsula to determine and explain the reasons for both successes and failures, which could not be accomplished without the publication of the diplomatic correspondence. Wellesley further maintained his confidence that the papers would demonstrate how the ineptness and corruptness of the Spanish government were responsible for the unfortunate plight of the nation.[89]

Wellesley then struck at Grenville's specific objections, claiming them invalid owing to the extinction of the Supreme Junta. Moreover, accord-

Spencer Perceval (1762–1812), by J. Nollekens. Reproduced with permission of the Victoria and Albert Museum.

ing to the Marquess, the comments on the various public officials which appeared in the documents were now public knowledge in Spain and in general reflected the opinions of most Spaniards. Nor would an agent's life be in any more danger after than before publication, as most informants were well known and were in fact proud of that notoriety.[90]

Using Grenville as a means of attacking the opposition, Wellesley then charged him with ignorance and neglect. He castigated Grenville for his hypocrisy in referring to the Foreign Office's mismanagement of its affairs while he himself was grossly uninformed. "What then is the cause," asked the Marquess, "which has thus disturbed the noble lord's temper, and perverted his judgement? The noble lord cannot have read the papers, or he does not understand them."[91] Wellesley's presentation was effective, and Grenville's motion was flatly rejected.[92]

In Cádiz, Henry Wellesley continued to act vigorously. With his confidence in the regency's ability to govern, the prospects for success in Spain seemed brighter. Writing to the Marquess, he reported that the regency was beginning to show greater vigilance and activity. Attention was finally being directed toward supplying the armies with money and arms. Spanish troops were being paid regularly, their discipline was improving, and they were being clothed in a national uniform. In such a favorable atmosphere Henry decided, as previously instructed, to initiate discussions on a trade agreement with the new regency.[93] In so doing, Henry took pains to prevent any suspicion that Britain was trying to coerce Spain into such an agreement. Trust was imperative if the negotiations were to succeed. "The city of Cádiz is more connected with South America than all the rest of Spain put together," explained Henry, "and the establishment of our influence here will greatly facilitate any arrangements we may wish to make hereafter with South America."[94]

The question of trade first arose in early April when the regency discovered that it would shortly be out of funds. Bardaxi went to Henry with the news that Spain would soon require monetary assistance from Great Britain.[95] Unprepared for this revelation, Henry replied that he could offer no encouragement for the granting of such assistance, in the form of either a loan or a gift. Pointing to the difficulty of meeting such a request, Henry explained that the government would have to submit the measure to Parliament, "which would occasion discussions, which in the actual condition of Spain, it would be very desirable to avoid."[96]

Disappointed, Bardaxi pursued another course. He suggested concluding a convention defining the nature and extent of the assistance which Great Britain would provide. In return Bardaxi promised that

Spain would make reciprocal sacrifices. Henry advised that only a commercial agreement would be to Britain's advantage, and Bardaxi concurred.[97] Following these discussions, Henry wrote enthusiastically to his brother: "This is the moment for concluding a commercial arrangement with the Spanish government, which should be so formed as to make it easy to prove that, while it is advantageous to the interests of Great Britain, it is not injurious to those of Spain. . . . I am certain that the Spanish government and Bardaxi are anxious to meet me half way in any arrangement which may have for its object the mutual benefit of the two kingdoms. I shall therefore wait with anxiety for your instructions upon this subject."[98]

Lord Wellesley was not elated by the news. Not only was it contrary to his concept of how such a negotiation should proceed but it came at a time of increasing disagreement between him and Spencer Perceval. Unknown to Henry, while he was discussing finances and trade agreements with Bardaxi, Admiral Apodaca in London was presenting an official request for a loan of £2 million.[99] Wellesley considered the request reasonable, especially when compared with that presented the previous year for £10 million to £20 million. Yet Perceval promptly informed his foreign minister that it could not be granted in its entirety and certainly not without attaching some conditions. The prime minister explained that he had planned to ask the Parliament for a £3 million vote of credit to cover unforeseen services. He would use this credit to cover the loan. Two million pounds, however, would leave him short, and since he dared not ask for more he would propose a loan of £1.5 million. In addition, Perceval explained that he did not believe that such a loan and such a vote of credit could be carried in Parliament unless Spain came to some sort of liberal understanding concerning trade with the colonies, "at least during the period of the war and for such time longer as the debt due from Spain to this country shall remain unpaid."[100]

This approach conflicted with Wellesley's ideas. He knew that Spain would never agree to open her colonial trade in return for the fulfillment of her modest request. More important, he was determined to keep separate the promise of British assistance, whether in the form of a loan or definitive treaty, from the conclusion of a trade agreement. Wellesley was convinced that if Britain was to carry on a successful diplomacy in Spain, she would have to retain flexibility in the granting of aid. Spain would have to be persuaded to grant free trade by other means.[101] For this reason the Marquess refused to negotiate the loan with Perceval's conditions attached. He informed Apodaca that Britain could not grant the loan owing to her inability to meet even her own expenses. The $10 million to be purchased in Veracruz would provide only part of her needs, and Britain would have to continue negotiating bills of exchange. Wellesley explained that the situation might be materially altered if trade with the Spanish colonies was thrown open to Britain for the duration of the war, but he promised nothing.[102]

Thus when Henry's proposals arrived in London, Wellesley had already decided to separate matters of trade and subsidy. Yet Perceval remained anxious to conclude an agreement. He suggested that Henry pursue negotiations for a trade agreement, using a similar arrangement with the Prince of Brazil as an example. What Perceval sought was direct trade with the colonies, Spain itself, and her European islands at a duty of not more than 25 percent. The prime minister concurred with Wellesley that it would be unwise for Britain to commit herself to specific subsidies because the fiscal situation in Britain was too unstable to determine from one year to the next the amount of aid she could afford. Perceval did, however, believe it advisable to use the granting of a £1.5 million loan as leverage in negotiations for a trade agreement. He suggested the amount might be raised to £2 million only if some material aid could be included in the sum; as another alternative, loans might be negotiated for £1 million a year, for the duration of the war.[103] Again Wellesley could not agree with the prime minister and refused to relay such instructions to Cádiz.

Even had an agreement been reached between the two men, it would have been too late to be of help: the situation in Spain had changed once again. The regency had unexpectedly received new funds, and tensions had increased between it and the British embassy. Henry Wellesley was beginning to realize that he had misjudged the abilities and determination of the regents. In mid-April the regency, acting contrary to Wellesley's advice, appointed General Cuesta governor of the Balearic Islands and transferred management of all available resources to the junta of Cádiz.[104] To Henry, these were signs of the regency's weakness. An incompetent and outspoken opponent of the regency, Cuesta deserved no appointment, although perhaps it might quiet his supporters. And giving all fiscal responsibility to the junta merely confirmed the fact that the regency could not control the commercial interests of Cádiz. Henry realized this body would never agree to an opening of the colonial trade to Great Britain. Greatly disappointed, the young Wellesley apprised Bardaxi of his sentiments.[105]

Relations continued to worsen. On April 16 Castaños placed General

Joaquin Blake, a man known for his anti-British sentiments, in command of Spanish forces in Cádiz and on the Isla de León.[106] Shortly thereafter Lieutenant General Thomas Graham arrived in Cádiz to assume overall command of the British forces. Graham promptly suggested new measures for strengthening the defenses of Cádiz and the Isla de León. Regrettably, he found Blake uncooperative, forcing Henry to protest. Anglophobic sentiments appeared, and the Spanish again became suspicious of Britain's aims in Cádiz. "A party at Cádiz hostile to the British nation," explained Henry, "was endeavoring to instill into the minds of the lower classes of the inhabitants, that all the measures we proposed . . . were so many steps towards retaining permanent possession of Cádiz."[107]

Bureaucratic entanglements followed, illustrating the folly of splitting governmental responsibilities between the regency and the junta. In late April, Henry's own investigations showed that Cádiz's supply of grain was dwindling rapidly and that there was no immediate prospect of replenishment. The junta had completely ignored its responsibility to secure additional supplies.[108] Henry decided to act independently, concerned not only for Spain's welfare but for that of the British troops as well. He turned for help to Colin Campbell, the military governor in Gibraltar. Campbell lacked the grain to provide the city with relief, although he did arrange for the prompt shipment of supplies from Algiers. At the same time, Henry empowered the commissary general in Sicily to purchase as much wheat as possible in Sardinia and elsewhere in the western Mediterranean.[109]

Henry hoped that his quick actions, which held off a major crisis, would give him added leverage in his negotiations. On May 2, however, two Spanish ships, the *Algeciras* and the *Asia,* arrived in Cádiz from Veracruz with $7 million in specie. This sum greatly relieved the regency's financial anxieties and bolstered its sense of independence.[110] As a result, Henry, who was particularly intent upon securing the removal of the Spanish fleet from Cartagena and the final evacuation of French prisoners from Cádiz, received countless empty promises from the regency.

With the French advance into Andalusia, the threat to Cartagena was indeed real. If it fell, France would find herself in possession of a fleet of seven ships of the line. For this reason Henry urged Bardaxi to order the fleet's removal to Minorca.[111] Bardaxi agreed that it should be done but said that Spain did not have enough seamen for the task. Henry turned to Purvis, who also claimed to be short of manpower; he suggested that

Spain use men from its Cádiz fleet. Spain refused that alternative but agreed to allow Spanish sailors who had fled the French into Gibraltar to help in Cartagena. This problem settled, Bardaxi issued, on April 26, 1810, the necessary orders to move the fleet.[112] Regrettably, when he issued such orders, he had no realistic assessment of when they would be effected. Several days passed and no attempt was made to move the fleet. Pressed for time, a frustrated Henry Wellesley urged action but to no avail. It was not until June 2, six weeks after Henry first approached the Spanish on the matter, that the fleet finally moved.[113]

The regency proved equally dilatory in removing French prisoners of war from Cádiz. Henry had struck the bargain for their removal at the end of March and had promptly carried out his obligation, but by the end of May, despite Henry's urgent solicitations, the regency had not removed the first prisoner from Cádiz. It seemed nothing could motivate the regency to action—not even the escape of several hundred prisoners on May 26.[114] Out of desperation, Henry informed the regency that either the remaining 2,000 prisoners should be sent to Ceuta, along with British reinforcements, or they would be sent to England aboard Spanish ships of the line.[115] As the Spanish were already suspicious of British intentions at Ceuta, they chose the latter alternative. On May 31 the final evacuation began.[116]

Henry Wellesley's first three months in Spain had produced in him both optimism and despair. Beginning his mission with the energy and confidence which often characterizes a newly appointed representative, he quickly learned that to obtain results he would have to act decisively and forcefully in his dealings with the Spanish. Secure in the knowledge that he had Lord Wellesley's full support, Henry did not hesitate to adopt this approach, with some success. Through his urgings the Cartagena fleet was moved to a place of greater security, Cádiz's defenses were improved, French prisoners of war were moved, and the regency was established in Cádiz. These problems satisfactorily solved, Henry could look forward to negotiations on trade, reorganization of the army, and governmental reform.

Wellesley was still experiencing frustration in London. The British public was despondent over events in the peninsula, and the opposition press had begun to play on these sentiments, arguing that it was time for Britain to come to terms with reality. French expansion did not consist of Napoleon alone, it maintained, and would go on even in his absence. Accordingly, the opposition urged the government to conclude a treaty of peace with Napoleon before Britain destroyed herself in a futile cause.[117] Although the ministry did not succumb to this argument, there was a marked tendency toward pessimism within its ranks. Because Wellesley's colleagues already doubted their ability to maintain a majority in Parliament, they were reluctant to expand the war effort in such an atmosphere. Wellesley was therefore unable to provide Spain with all the supplies needed, and Wellington found himself short of provisions, money, and manpower, despite assurances that his position was secure.[118] Wellington knew the source of the problem: "If we had a strong government in England, and the command of money, and arms I think we might still oblige the French to evacuate the Peninsula,"[119] the first condition being a prerequisite for the other two.

For his part the Marquess, convinced that the government had to be strengthened, renewed the efforts he had begun in March to bring Canning, Castlereagh, and Sidmouth into the cabinet. On May 3 he again offered to resign to facilitate this maneuver.[120] It is apparent, however, that his real goal was to bring Canning alone into the government to provide another strong voice in the cabinet to urge a more vigorous prosecution of the war. Of Castlereagh and Sidmouth, Wellesley valued only the latter, but he realized an overture could not be made to Canning without making a similar one to Castlereagh.

Perceval disagreed with Wellesley's analysis of the political situation. Satisfied with the ministry's position in Parliament, he did not believe that the addition of Canning without Castlereagh or Sidmouth (or any other combination of the three) would be of much consequence.[121] Perceval was probably right, for it did not appear that Canning and Castlereagh were yet ready to serve together. As it was, all three men were supporting the government on most key issues. Thus if one was included in the cabinet without the others, their unanimous support might be lost, and Perceval, much to Wellesley's dismay, refused to act on his request. It must be kept in mind, however, that Perceval was not preparing to embark on as controversial a policy as Wellesley was advocating.

It is obvious that, from the beginning of his term as foreign secretary, Lord Wellesley was not at ease with the government's situation vis-à-vis the Parliament, nor was he satisfied with his own status within the cabinet. He did not get along well with his colleagues, especially Perceval, with whom he constantly quarreled over money, strategy, and politics. Yet Wellesley was active in these first months in office. He played prominent roles in the parliamentary debates, and his dispatches to the peninsula were far more numerous than those of his predecessor, George

Robert Banks Jenkinson, 2d Earl of Liverpool (1770–1828), by T. Lawrence.
Reproduced with permission of the National Portrait Gallery.

Canning. Wellesley's major weakness was that he had become preoccupied with peninsular affairs, trusting other important areas of British interest to his subordinates.

To the delight of his critics, the Marquess did not ignore his social life. He openly kept mistresses and hosted frequent parties, quickly establishing himself once again as the focal point of London gossip. His personal conduct infuriated Wellington, who believed, like many others, that it interfered with his work. Writing to Pole, he offered this somewhat hypocritical judgment: "I wish that Wellesley was *castrated;* or that he would like other people attend to his business & perform too. It is lamentable to see Talents & character & advantages such as he possesses thrown away upon whoring."[122] This criticism was too harsh. Despite his personal life-style, Wellesley's first months in office were characterized by skill, determination, and vigor.

Moreover, Wellesley's personal habits were not now so scandalous, for on February 10, 1810, he and his wife, Hyacinthe, had signed a deed of legal separation. Nine days later the Marchioness departed Apsley House, leaving the Marquess free of marital obligation. So ended a relationship which had once held much promise. The marriage had never recovered from the shock of seven years of separation and Wellesley's acute disillusionment when he returned from India. Barely tolerating one another in the years that followed, Richard returned from Spain in 1809 determined to obtain the separation. Hyacinthe, for her part, hoped to maintain the status quo because of the effects separation might have on her children, but eventually she succumbed to her husband's resolve. The deed of separation provided her with a handsome annuity which cut deeply into Richard's limited financial resources until her death from pneumonia on November 5, 1816.[123]

7

Wellesley Diplomacy: Negotiations with the Castaños Regency, June–September, 1810

For the Wellesleys the summer of 1810 would prove to be one of bristling political and diplomatic activity. In London the Perceval ministry, having warded off numerous challenges to its foreign policy, would face the long-awaited parliamentary investigation into the government's handling of the war in Spain. Lord Wellesley welcomed the debate, confident that the government would emerge strengthened, perhaps enabling him to urge an expanded role for Britain in Spain. Nonetheless, to ensure adequate cabinet strength, he still hoped to include George Canning as a voice in his favor. To bolster the British economy and make the financing of an enlarged subsidy easier, Wellesley planned to work for a commercial agreement with Spain. On the strength of Henry Wellesley's reports, prospects for such an agreement seemed better than usual. The political situation in Cádiz had stabilized, and Anglo-Spanish relations were good. Henry was prepared not only to negotiate a commercial agreement but also to oversee military and governmental reform. Unfortunately for all concerned, the favorable atmosphere did not last. The financial position of the regency deteriorated rapidly in June, and when Britain could not meet all of Spain's professed needs tensions grew between the allies. To make matters worse, colonial revolts in Caracas and Buenos Aires greatly complicated both Henry's negotiations and the regency's ability to govern. Once again Henry found himself preoccupied with reestablishing political order

134

and tranquillity in Cádiz. By the end of September Henry had accomplished little, while in London the Marquess had met a similar fate. Though successful in debate, Wellesley had been unable to strengthen the cabinet or to conclude a commercial agreement; as a result Perceval continued to refuse to expand Britain's role in the peninsula.

On June 8, 1810, Parliament began its inquiry into the government's handling of Spanish affairs.[1] Although the Spanish government was beginning to show some determination, ominous news had arrived from the peninsula. Marshal André Masséna, Duc de Rivoli, Prince de Essling, was laying siege to Ciudad Rodrigo.[2] "There can be little question, that the French are putting or about to put the finishing stroke to Spanish independence," explained the *Examiner*. "The Paris papers inform us that Masséna is marching towards this consumation with 75,000 men, so that we may soon look out for the return of my Lord Wellington—and then *Exeunt omnes,*—the farce is ended."[3] Such was not the atmosphere in which Wellesley had hoped the debates would be conducted.

The Marquis of Lansdowne opened the opposition's attack. Hoping to bring a vote of censure upon the government, he introduced two resolutions: first, "that it appears to this House, after the most attentive examination of the papers laid before them, relative to the late campaign in Spain, that the safety of the army was improvidently and uselessly risked, and every loss and calamity suffered, without ground on which to expect any good result, and that the whole did end in the retreat of the army"; second, "that, previous to entering on this campaign, ministers did not procure the necessary information of the state of Spain, or of its military resources—of the supplies that could be afforded, and as the most obvious policy required; and that the result of this rashness and ignorance was a result the most calamitous."[4] Although Lansdowne conceded that Wellesley had acted correctly while ambassador to Spain, he believed that the ministry had not learned from its past mistakes and that only through a censure of its policy could another disaster be averted.

The Marquess followed, presenting a detailed defense of the Battle of Talavera and of the government's continuing efforts in the peninsula. He reminded the opposition that when Wellington embarked on the Talavera campaign, the Supreme Junta was of a different composition from the one Sir John Moore found when he entered Spain in late 1808. The junta, in contrast to Moore's experience with it, "had given particular instances of zeal, activity and energy, in procuring supplies of every kind for their own armies" prior to Wellington's entering Spain. The British army had no reason to expect the logistical prob-

lems it encountered. Despite the junta's demonstration of incompetence, Britain was committed to the campaign. The Battle of Talavera
was waged, and although the results were not as significant as they
might have been, they were indeed considerable. Wellesley maintained
that the battle gave Portugal a "breathing spell," a chance to reorganize
her army and defenses. Further, southern Spain would have been
secure if the junta had not ordered the ill-advised autumn offensive.[5]

The heart of Lord Wellesley's defense was the premise that Spain and
Portugal offered the best hope for carrying on the war against France.
"The brightest prospect which had offered itself for several years of
reasserting the independence of Europe, and with it the security of this
country," Wellesley stated, "opened at the moment when Spain mag-
nanimously rose to maintain her legitimate monarchy, and to resist the
most unprincipled usurpation of which history affords an example."[6] If
the war in Spain gave Britain a front on which to operate directly against
France, it also provided the foreign secretary with an example which, if
successful, could elsewhere stimulate similar uprisings against Napoleon. He admitted that there were numerous obstacles to success—a
product of Spain's unique situation—but he saw them as removable.
Moreover, Spain was Britain's ally, and as long as she offered a spark of
resistance Britain was obliged to assist in the effort.[7]

When the Marquess relinquished the floor, the subsequent debate
revealed little support for Lansdowne's resolutions. He could not have
considered this surprising, for it had always been his contention that the
Spanish papers would reveal the government's Spanish policy as valid.
He could not have anticipated that the papers made him the object of
prodigious praise from both sides of the House. Lord Sidmouth commended his "sagacity and judgement" while ambassador to Spain, re-
gretting that "recourse had not been had earlier to the services of that
noble marquis."[8] The Earl of Rosslyn, an opponent of the ministry's
Spanish policy, also claimed to be "sorry the noble marquis had not been
employed sooner," speculating that if he had, "the contest would have
been much more favorable to the patriots."[9] Lord Holland followed with
similar compliments, and when a vote was taken the government found
itself with a majority of thirty-two votes.[10]

Despite the vote, the opposition had not lost its zest. It remained
vehemently opposed to the government's policies and continued to find
Wellesley a convenient target for its attacks. The *Examiner's* description
of his defense of the Spanish policy was illustrative: "Speaking of the
Spanish Government, he let drop two or three truisms, which appeared

to amuse the Whigs.—He said, 'When men, assuming the reins of Government, obtain power, they seldom are disposed to relinquish their situations (*Hear! from the opposition*). It is not natural to the human character to see its own defects, and there is no wonder the Sp. Gov't. should be insensible to its inefficiency. . . . for Noble Lords will be aware, from *experience*, that there is scarcely an instance in any country of a government reforming itself. It reminds me of a sect of philosophers, who always delayed their information to the subsequent day; and it ought not to incur extreme censure, if such was the character of the Gov't. of Spain.' "[11]

Similarly, Wellesley still believed the cabinet needed strengthening. As part of his overall peninsular policy, he hoped to reinforce Wellington's army and begin reforms in Spain's military system—plans which would require a considerable increase in expenditure. The Marquess believed that rapid reforms could be made in the Spanish army only by placing it under British officers and bringing it into Britain's pay, much in the same way Beresford was reorganizing the Portuguese army.[12] There were several reasons for this obsession with direct British involvement in army reform. First, the current conditions of the Spanish government and army gave little hope for rapid improvement. Second, a strong Spanish army was essential to the success of any military operation in Spain—the only way to create diversions powerful enough to disperse the numerically superior French. Third, Spaniards were potentially superior soldiers and certainly the cheapest Great Britain could employ.[13]

Under Wellesley's plan Great Britain would have complete control in forming a corps of 30,000 Spanish soldiers. They would be raised, armed, clothed, equipped, paid, fed, trained, and commanded by British authorities, and no interference on the part of the Spanish government would be tolerated. Wellesley estimated the cost of such control at nearly £3 million per year. But given the resulting benefits to Britain and comparing this cost with that of maintaining a comparable British contingent, he considered the expense to be reasonable.[14] In June 1810, however, the Marquess concluded that securing such funds would be virtually impossible because of the ministry's weakness and the lack of resolve among its members.

Not only would Wellesley be unable to effect this plan, but reinforcing Wellington's army would also be impossible. Liverpool in fact informed him that Britain would be unable to support Wellington's army even at its present strength. The secretary of war maintained that either Spain would aid in that project by supplying specie or the British army would be withdrawn.[15] Wellesley was thus forced into fighting to maintain the war effort at its current level rather than to expand it. In addition, Liverpool's notice presented him with what appeared to be an insoluble dilemma. It came at a time when Spain was again desperately seeking a loan, and although it was a legitimate request the Marquess could not respond. How then could Spain be expected to cooperate in the financing of British troops in Portugal when in fact she could not support herself and Britain was failing to grant her even minimal financial assistance? Wellesley's frustration must have been great. Besides being genuinely convinced that Britain had to enlarge her effort in the peninsula, he was still an autocrat, used to having his way. His response was to renew his efforts to strengthen the ministry through the introduction of Canning, Castlereagh, and Sidmouth.

On his own initiative Wellesley met with Sidmouth to discuss the proposal. To his surprise Sidmouth would have nothing to do with the project, apparently refusing to serve in a cabinet of which Canning was a part.[16] Realistically that left only Canning, for it seemed certain that Castlereagh would not agree to serve with Canning without Sidmouth's support. This conclusion met with Wellesley's approval since it was Canning's support that he had desired all along. Similarly Canning was anxious to regain a ministerial post, and he urged Wellesley to take steps toward effecting a new arrangement.[17] In so doing, Canning's penchant for deceit reappeared. He attempted to instill in the Marquess the notion that other arrangements were being made behind his back—most likely that Perceval was attempting to bring Castlereagh into the cabinet to the exclusion of Canning and in the hope that Wellesley would resign. "The rumors of other arrangements are so strong," warned Canning, "that I cannot help fearing that something is doing unknown to you, which will place you in an awkward situation."[18] Whether or not the Marquess believed Canning's speculation (and it appears to have been mere speculation) cannot be determined, but he did go to Perceval with the suggestion that Canning alone be brought into the ministry. Wellesley offered to take another post to facilitate this move or, if that were not possible, to remain in the cabinet without office. Perceval, who was hesitant to include Canning in his cabinet, refused to commit himself, much to Wellesley's consternation.[19]

In Cádiz, Henry Wellesley was also beset with problems. Although these were considerable, he reacted to them decisively, keeping the Anglo-Spanish alliance intact while his brother struggled with his colleagues in London. In early June, Henry was operating in an atmosphere of renewed Anglophobia. British newspapers suggesting the seizure of Ceuta to protect British commerce in the western Mediterranean had reached Cádiz,[20] causing a revival of Spanish suspicions of British intentions in Spain—and justifiably so. Irresponsible journalism thus prevented young Wellesley from starting discussions on a commercial agreement and on reinforcing the weakly defended Balearic Islands. Commercial interests in Cádiz were determined to oppose the granting of any trading concessions, convinced that such concessions would only promote what they considered a British conspiracy to destroy the economic power of Cádiz. Many believed also that Britain ultimately sought a complete take-over of the Balearic Islands under the guise of protecting them from French invasion.[21] Perceiving these sentiments, Henry wisely avoided the issues for the time being.

Wellesley was not, however, inhibited from responding to other problems, particularly Wellington's lack of specie. Sympathizing with his brother's problems, Henry investigated the feasibility of assisting in the procurement of specie. He determined that each month he could purchase up to $500,000 on the private market in Cádiz, thus avoiding any dealings with the regency. Without awaiting instructions he began purchasing what he could in Cádiz and urged Colin Campbell in Gibraltar to do the same. By the first week in July he was able to make an initial shipment of over $300,000.[22]

In mid-June, however, a more serious problem threatened the course of Anglo-Spanish relations. After a brief respite provided by the shipment of specie which arrived from Mexico in May, the regency had again found itself in financial trouble and besieged both Henry and the Marquess with solicitations for a loan of £2 million.[23] Henry was in a better position than Lord Wellesley and his colleagues to judge the urgency of the request and the dire consequences of its rejection. Yet on this issue Henry proceeded cautiously, wary of Perceval's preoccupation with fiscal responsibility.

With pronounced misgivings, Henry rejected Bardaxi's first request for the loan. He saw the loan as not only a way to alleviate Spain's most urgent needs but also as a boost toward discussions on British trade with Spanish America. Henry suggested to his brother that in return for the loan an attempt be made to secure a commercial agreement whereby Britain could ship cotton goods to South America by a circuitous route through Spain. Henry admitted that this was a small concession, but he

believed that once commercial communications were well established
with the American colonies they could not be severed and trade would
eventually burgeon.[24]

In desperate need of financial assistance, the regency continued to
harass Henry for the loan and not without effect. According to young
Wellesley, the government's financial position had deteriorated to such
an extent that unless Spain received immediate pecuniary assistance she
might be forced to terminate her military activities for the rest of the
summer.[25] After relaying the gloomy new analysis to the Marquess,
Henry could only wait for instructions. On June 29 Bardaxi made
another effort at persuading Henry to grant a loan, this time stating that
he was prepared to discuss a commercial convention in return. By
commercial convention, he did not mean the opening of direct South
American trade to Great Britain, and because Henry had instructions
not to bargain on less he rejected the solicitation.[26] Yet Bardaxi was
relentless. The next day, detailing the distress of his government, Bardaxi suggested that Henry issue bills of exchange to the amount of $1.5
million on the condition that if a loan was not granted in London the
amount could be paid from the first specie received from South
America. Wellesley, lacking the authority to grant such a request, again
declined. The appeal was renewed, with the same result, on July 2.[27]

Henry then began to give this latest proposal greater consideration.
He could see that if Spain's financial distress continued, it would not be
long before it would bring about the total disintegration of the Spanish
armies still in the field. The results would be particularly disastrous in the
case of the Marquis de la Romana's army, which, although not a potent
force, was occupying the attentions of General Jean Louis Reynier's 2d
Corps.[28] Reynier, according to Jean Jacques Pelet, Masséna's aide-de-
camp, "was engaged in scouring all the land between the Tagus and the
Guadiana to reconnoiter Badajoz and Olivenza," precisely the area occupied by Romana.[29] With Romana gone, Wellesley assumed that
Reynier would be at liberty to reinforce Masséna with the over 17,000
men under his command. Such reinforcements could have disastrous
effects on Wellington, so Henry, on his own authority, granted a short-
term loan of $1.5 million under the conditions Bardaxi had outlined on
June 30.[30]

This bold, independent act on the part of the young envoy horrified
Perceval, who feared, among other things, that the issuance of bills of
exchange to this amount would disrupt the money market in Cádiz to the
detriment of Wellington and his needs. "I tremble for the effect of it,"

exclaimed the prime minister, "as far as our exertions in Portugal & our Portuguese subsidy is concerned."[31] Perceval's reaction precipitated another quarrel with the Marquess. Perceval believed that the occasion called for a strong reprimand, but Wellesley, protective of his brother, disagreed. Instead, he merely advised Henry that in the future he should keep in mind the effects of such a loan on the ability to supply Wellington with specie. Henry was, however, ordered to inform the regency that the loan could not be granted and to demand repayment of the advance out of the first shipment of specie received from the American colonies.[32]

Meanwhile, Henry sought to capitalize on the improved state of Anglo-Spanish relations created by the $1.5 million advance. Wellesley was particularly anxious to negotiate some sort of commercial agreement, even if it meant proceeding on the assumption that direct trade between Britain and the colonies would never be granted. From his vantage point, Henry could see that one of the unfortunate consequences of the Spanish government's forced retirement to Cádiz was that it fell under the influence of the powerful merchant community which controlled the city.[33] This community was dependent upon its lucrative trading monopoly on the Spanish colonies and would not consider sharing it. To counteract such sentiment would take a government far stronger than the regency. Britain had long been aware of the power of the Cádiz merchants, but until the regency was established in that city it was generally assumed that their opposition to a trade agreement could be overcome in the name of national interest. Now, in a sense, Cádiz was the nation, and its interests prevailed.

The extent of the city's opposition to opening colonial trade to Great Britain and of its influence over the regency was best illustrated by an incident that occurred in late June. At that time an undersecretary in Spain's finance department, by birth a South American and closely tied to colonial interests, was plotting to open colonial trade to Great Britain because of the economic benefits such trade would bring to the colonies. Secretly he drew up an official edict granting such privileges to Great Britain and inserted it among many others awaiting the signature of the secretary of state for the Finance Department, the Marquis de las Hormazes. Hormazes signed all the documents without examining them. The edict was then removed, and several copies were printed for distribution in the colonies. Before they could be sent, the junta of Cádiz secured a copy. Unaware of the circumstances which had produced the edict, the junta protested vehemently to the regency. The regency truthfully disclaimed all knowledge of the edict. When its investigation into the matter revealed no complicity on the part of any of its members, the regency believed that the issue would soon be forgotten. Unfortunately, the junta's alarm and indignation over this episode persisted until the regents were forced to arrest all persons under suspicion, including the unsuspecting Hormazes, a key member of the government.[34]

Duly impressed, Henry determined that the demand for unrestricted trade with the colonies would create untold chaos in Cádiz. "I should be sorry to see them put to the test of resigning all the commercial advantages derived from their connection with South America," Henry explained. "I am apprehensive that any measure likely to prove injurious to their mercantile interests would contribute more towards the completion of the designs of the enemy upon Cádiz than all his own efforts and exertions of whatever descriptions they might be."[35] Wellesley had also come to believe, perhaps erroneously, that it would be advisable to conclude with the regency a moderate commercial agreement of some sort before the Cortes assembled. The Cortes, he thought, would be too much under the influence of Cádiz to grant any sort of trading concession. Therefore Wellesley presented Bardaxi with these proposals: the exportation through Spain to South America of cotton products manufactured in Britain or her colonies and of raw materials and certain other manufactured products of Great Britain and Ireland; an agreement to modify duties levied in Spain upon all British articles of trade and, further, to reduce these duties to a standard by which the arbitrary exactions and vexatious delays experienced by British merchants would be abolished; the eventual conclusion of a regular treaty of commerce between Spain and Great Britain when circumstances permitted; and permission to export specie from South America duty free for the duration of the war.[36]

The main feature of Henry's proposal was the establishment of British commercial contact in the Spanish colonies through a circuitous process instead of direct trade. Bardaxi agreed only in part, suggesting several additions and alterations. He demanded that British goods be transported from Spain to the colonies only on Spanish ships. More important, he sought the passage of Spanish produce, including that of her colonies, into Great Britain. In addition, he reminded Wellesley of Spain's desire to combine this trade agreement with an understanding on Britain's subsidy. "It becomes indispensable," wrote Bardaxi, "that under the same order, that the two allied nations unite their commercial interests with frankness & liberality by the Convention which is separately proposed, it should be, that is to say, an integral part of the same Convention, that His Britanic Majesty concedes to Spain the indispensable aid required, to insure its liberty & independence." Specifically, Spain wanted a loan of £10 million and the use of 40 naval transports and adequate escort to convey troops and military equipment to wherever the Spanish government deemed proper.[37]

The Spanish requests took Henry by surprise. He could see that allowing the importation of Spain's colonial produce would be prejudicial to British East and West Indian trade and would arouse the opposition of the many merchants involved in that trade. Yet his greatest concern was Spain's desire to combine the issues of subsidy and commerce, for he knew that the Marquess would not negotiate on this premise. Wellesley informed the regency that unless it agreed to separate negotiations on these subjects, he would forward nothing to London. Castaños agreed, and Henry forwarded to his brother the trade proposal and the loan request.[38] Henry was not completely satisfied with the results of these initial discussions, but he considered them a beginning. He was confident that once British commerce had made inroads into the Spanish trading monopoly, it would expand rapidly—beyond the control of the Spanish government.

As Henry relayed these ideas to London, Wellesley was sending his own to Cádiz. Not having received Henry's evaluation of public opinion in Cádiz concerning trading concessions, he wrote urging his brother to negotiate without delay an agreement opening direct trade between Spanish America and Great Britain.[39] The Marquess had sent this exhortation many times before, but only at Perceval's urging. The prime minister believed that Britain could not long continue her support for Spain unless trade was expanded, a goal contingent upon the relaxation of Spanish commercial laws. Now, however, British trade with Spain's colonies had become a central issue to Wellesley primarily because of the news of a successful revolt in one of Spain's colonies, Venezuela.

Led by the city of Caracas, Venezuela had declared its independence from any executive authority in Spain on April 19, 1810, shortly after receiving the news of the fall of Seville. Although she wisely declared a continuing allegiance to the person of Ferdinand VII, it was clear that Venezuela intended to govern herself.[40] In need of assistance, the revolutionary junta in Caracas promptly applied to Great Britain for support, turning first to the British military governor in Curaçao, General Layard. Venezuelan representative Joseph de las Llamosas requested muskets, ammunition, and naval protection. In return, Venezuela gave a

vague promise to cooperate with Britain in the war and to open her ports
to British commerce.[41] Enthusiastic over these events, Layard irrespon-
sibly agreed to the requests without first confirming the arrangements
with London. "The manner in which the chief authority has been constituted in the persons of your highnesses," he exclaimed to the junta of
Caracas, ". . . must and will be the admiration of future ages."[42]

Wellesley and Liverpool, whose offices were directly affected by the
events in Venezuela, were not surprised by the revolution, but they were
dismayed over Layard's conduct. For years Venezuelan revolutionary
Francisco de Miranda had been using London as a base of operation,
and he had often solicited British aid. In fact, it was in conjunction with
Miranda's schemes that Wellington was ordered to lead an army to South
America in 1808.[43] Only the outbreak of the conflict between Spain and
France forced Britain to terminate her subversive activities in Spanish
America and sever her connections with Miranda.[44] As Spain's ally
Britain was obliged to keep hands off her colonies. Obviously, Layard's
response to the revolt did not comply with the spirit of the alliance and
was sure to evoke a vigorous protest from Cádiz. Before a protest could
be formed, Liverpool sent a harsh reprimand to General Layard. Outlining the ministry's position on the revolution, the secretary explained that
Britain simply desired to mediate Venezuela's grievances in an effort to
bring her back into Spain's colonial system.[45] Wellesley, in turn, sent
copies of this communication to Admiral Apodaca and to the regency
(through Henry) in an effort to dispel Spain's fears.[46]

Britain found herself in a very difficult position. She was committed by
treaty to the support of Spain and her colonial empire. But her failure to
help the Venezuelan revolutionaries would probably cause them to turn
to France for aid. Even so, English commercial interests would never
tolerate government assistance in suppressing the revolt, for it would
jeopardize not only future dealings in America but also some existing
illegal arrangements.[47] It was clearly in Britain's interest that disputes
between Spain and her colonies be resolved.

But easy solutions would not be found. Spain's abusive colonial system
created fundamental discontent. Of the five ethnic groups populating
the colonies—native Spaniards, Creoles, Negroes, Indians, and qua-
droons—only native Spaniards were included in the governments. This
prejudicial political system, coupled with archaic economic policies, bred
resentment and hatred.[48] Conditions resulting from the war in Spain
ignited these dormant sentiments into support for revolution, a fact not
lost upon Wellesley. While he conceded that Spain's preoccupation with

the war had created the opportunity for revolution, he believed that the strongest push toward revolution came from the collapse of Spain's economy. Commercial intercourse between Spain and the colonies had nearly ceased. Colonists, including the dominant middle class, found themselves impoverished and destitute of manufactured goods, but, because of Spain's rigidly enforced trading monopoly, they had no legal recourse to another source, creating greater despair and frustration. Convinced that he was correct, Wellesley was confident that the spirit of revolution would proliferate if the situation did not alter.[49]

According to Wellesley's logic the best way to eliminate the direct cause of revolt, and thus prevent the further spread of revolutionary activity, was for Spain to open her colonial ports to British commerce. Such a move would not only improve economic conditions in the colonies and thus reduce popular discontent; it would also enhance Britain's ability to support Spain. The Marquess was not so naïve as to see economic conditions as the sole cause of colonial discontent, but he apparently believed that restoring favorable economic conditions would forestall further revolutionary activity, at least until the end of the war. Then Spain could deal with her colonial problems alone. Henry was therefore instructed to persuade the regency that the continuing existence of Spain's colonial empire depended on its granting to British merchants direct trading rights with Spanish America.[50]

Henry promptly attempted to carry out his brother's instructions, but unfortunately for him the Venezuelan revolt had not alarmed the Spanish government very much. The regency merely intended to send ships of war to blockade the ports of Venezuela; if that was not sufficient to subdue the revolt, troops would be dispatched from Cuba.[51] The regency saw the Venezuelan revolt as an isolated incident, and since it had received dispatches from the other colonies confirming its authority it had no reason to believe otherwise. Consequently the Spanish referred Henry to the arrangement he and Bardaxi had discussed earlier. The sentiments of the merchants in Cádiz dictated that Britain not be allowed direct trade with the Spanish colonies.[52]

At the same time, Wellesley's problems were multiplying. On July 11, 1810, two representatives from the junta of Caracas, Simón Bolívar and Luis Méndez, arrived in Britain to solicit British support for Venezuela.[53] Obviously the Marquess could not ignore them, but he was apprehensive about the Spanish embassy's reaction. In an effort to allay Spanish fears, Wellesley explained to the Duke of Albuquerque that he "considered the arrival of these deputies as a circumstance of great advantage, as it would enable H.M.'s Govt. to represent in the most expeditious manner to the authorities in the Province of Venezuela the erroneous view which they have taken of the state of Spain and to urge the expediency of reuniting that province to the authorities of the provisional Govt. established in the Mother Country."[54]

Bolívar and Méndez met with Wellesley on July 21 and presented him with a request similar to that made to General Layard. Venezuela desired British naval protection and arms and ammunition. She also requested British mediation of any issues arising between Spain and Venezuela. In return Britain would be granted free trade.[55] The Marquess was noncommittal. He agreed to protect Venezuela from French aggression but urged the revolutionary government to make an honest effort to reconcile its differences with Spain, offering British mediation "to establish an amicable adjustment . . . with that authority." In the interim Britain would do everything in her power to prevent the outbreak of war between Spain and Venezuela. Wellesley also hoped that Venezuela would continue her commercial intercourse with Spain for the duration of the war and cooperate in the effort against France.[56]

This conference could only have reinforced Wellesley's desire to prevent the spread of similar revolts throughout the Spanish colonies. He must have therefore been dismayed when he received word from Henry that the regency would grant nothing more than the circuitous trade agreement suggested by Bardaxi.[57] In response he promptly drew up a new set of instructions. Wellesley personally remained convinced that Spain should grant Britain direct trading rights with the colonies, worrying that anything less than direct trade would inhibit rather than expand trade between Britain and the colonies. He based this conviction on Britain's growing illicit trade with Spanish America through free ports in the West Indies. "If a formal convention were to be established," he explained, "limiting our intercourse with the Spanish colonies to the circuitous trade through the Port of Cádiz, it might be inferred, that His Majesty's Government might be bound by the obligation of good faith to prevent the commerce carried on."[58] This logic is difficult to understand. If Britain was already illegally superseding the colonial laws of an ally, what difference would the conclusion of a trade agreement make to Britain's moral sensibilities?

Regardless, Wellesley directed Henry to make another effort to reach an agreement opening direct trade if he judged conditions in Cádiz conducive to such bargaining. The Marquess wanted a commercial convention placing the trade of both countries on a most-favored-nation basis. The agreement would be applicable to all goods except sugar, coffee, cocoa, and logwood from the Spanish colonies, with all goods subject to a maximum duty of 15 percent. The exempted items would be allowed into British ports free of duty, for reexportation to Europe, with the understanding that Spain would reciprocate on any British goods which she might choose to exclude from the agreement.[59]

Wellesley was committed to the belief that this type of agreement was in the best interest of the alliance. But he was willing to accept a circuitous trade agreement if Spain insisted on maintaining her colonial laws because of "the delicate & difficult situation in which the Regency is placed with reference to this question, by the local interests and pre-judices of the city of Cádiz."[60] Still, the agreement he envisioned differed from that proposed by his brother. In particular, the Marquess wanted the circuitous trading to take place on British vessels: British ships would stop in Cádiz, present their invoices as a basis for the assignment of duties, pay the duty, and sail on to America. The only difference between this method and trading directly would be the payment of a larger duty and perhaps three weeks' longer passage.

Wellesley instructed Henry in negotiating such an agreement to re-mind the regency that Britain had already opened her ports to Spain. Because of the threat which the French posed to shipping in Cádiz, Britain had deemed it advisable to grant Spain the right to use British harbors and warehouses free of duty for the shipping of goods to foreign ports. Wellesley and his colleagues considered this a great concession, one deserving of reciprocity.[61] There was, however, a distinct difference between what Britain had granted and what she sought. Spanish goods allowed into British ports were destined for markets outside Britain's colonial interests, while British goods passing through Cádiz were des-tined for distinctly Spanish markets. It was hardly an even exchange. In fact, the entire British position was characterized by an absence of reciprocity: in essence she was demanding unilateral concessions on Spain's part. Then again, Spain could not meet the needs of her colonies in the current situation, and the British economy needed new markets to provide the revenue to increase the effort in the peninsula.

By the first week in August the Marquess had again modified his position. Originally he had hoped that both Spain and Britain would adopt the necessary commercial regulations without the conclusion of a formal convention. On August 4, however, he sent Henry a formal "Projet of a Commercial Arrangement."[62] This new proposal allowed the use of Spanish vessels in the circuitous trade if duties were lowered—a significant alteration. Several factors had influenced these changes. One was the inclusion in the proposal of a provision for the free exportation of specie from Spanish America, a commodity direly needed in Britain. Another was that many of Wellesley's colleagues were becoming impatient with the Spanish, especially when they learned that the regency would not grant direct trade. "When . . . they are in no possibility of supplying South America themselves they will not allow us to do so but upon terms utterly inadmissable," wrote George Rose, "one would almost be tempted to say, founded in idiotcy or madness—thus wantonly punishing their colonies and only ally, and compelling the former to break their ties with the parent country to obtain supplies which they cannot do with out. Mules as they are, it seems hardly credible that they cannot be made sensible of the perverse folly of their conduct."[63] Conversely the Spanish were becoming impatient with Britain's conduct, and this too influenced Wellesley's actions.

On August 1 Albuquerque and Apodaca protested the Marquess' meeting with Bolívar and Méndez as a bad precedent which would not be lost on the other colonies.[64] Once again reminded of his delicate position between Spain and Venezuela, Wellesley attempted to justify his actions in a meeting with the Spanish representatives. At the same time he moderated his demands for a commercial agreement. But the Spanish Embassy continued to bombard him with protests.[65] To these the Marquess issued an official response, explaining that while he had received the Venezuelan deputies amicably, all discussions with them would be strictly unofficial. If he had refused to meet with them, he feared that Venezuela might adopt a course of action that would "have estranged her from her legitimate Sovereign, and from the crown and monarchy of Spain." As it was, Britain hoped to mediate the differences between the two parties, ultimately seeking to bring Venezuela back into Spain's colonial system. Albuquerque accepted Wellesley's explanation, but the Spanish were clearly annoyed.[66]

In Cádiz, Henry had received Wellesley's dispatches of July 24 instructing him to commence negotiations on the commercial agreement. Although authorized to conclude an agreement offering either direct or circuitous trade, Henry was distressed by the fact that Britain was offering little in return. He respected his brother's desire to keep matters of subsidy and commerce separate, but he also realized that the small amount of aid which Britain offered for the remainder of the year was far below Spanish expectations and not likely to elicit cooperation on their part. In response to Spain's request for an advance of £2 million and a loan of £10 million, Britain was offering only £1 million in aid, including military stores. "If Perceval had taken a credit for six million instead of three," railed Henry, "he might have been enabled to assist the Spaniards effectually but the assistance they are prepared to give them will be of little or no use."[67]

Henry submitted Wellesley's proposal for direct British commerce with Spanish America on August 16, confident that the Regency would promptly reject it. Yet he hoped to use the rejection as a means to bargain for his brother's proposals for a circuitous trade arrangement.[68] Bardaxi responded as expected. In rejecting the British projet, he explained that Spain could not alter the basic principles of her colonial system for Britain's sake: "A nation that is fighting for the preservation of its liberty, and independence, ought never to depart from those principles, that constitute either of these privileges, and from the moment that it should do so, it would renounce for ever the glory of acquiring them."[69] But what bothered the Spaniards most was that Britain, by stating that further subsidies might be contingent upon Spain's granting commercial advantages, appeared to be blackmailing Spain into an agreement. Moreover, the regents believed that an agreement on subsidies should precede one on trade and pointed to the treaty of January 1809 to justify this position. The Spanish considered themselves a reliable ally, especially in light of Britain's previous experiences with continental alliances, and believed that they were deserving of better treatment. Bardaxi informed Henry that the regents would be willing to grant trading privileges only to the extent that had been proposed before. He explained that given the amount of aid Britain was presently supplying, she was not in need of a more extensive agreement: "since . . . the expenses which England incurs in assisting Spain, are not so exhorbitant as to render it impossible to continue them, there can be no reason why Spain should renounce the only resource that is left to her under the present circumstances, when on the other hand she can furnish means to her ally of extending her commerce without prejudice to herself."[70]

To a certain extent Henry agreed with Bardaxi's analysis. Writing to the Marquess, he explained: "Bardaxi is constantly endeavoring to point out the advantages of the convention which I have already submitted to you, and which certainly holds out great advantages to merchants who might be disposed to trade in Spanish ships and likewise furnishes an opening to our cotton trade. It strikes me that a convention of this kind ought not to operate as a prohibition to the contraband trade any more than any commercial treaty which may actually subsist between England

and Spain. This Convention holds out, besides other advantages which might be worth looking at, such as a reduction and regulation of duties on Spain, the importation of species from the colonies free of duty, etc.—it would also have the advantage of being well received here, and I am not at all clear, that it might not in a short time lead to the admission of British ships to the circuitous trade with the colonies."[71] Yet Henry took issue with the regency's complaint that Britain was not making a maximum effort to subsidize Spain. Consequently, he outlined for the regents Britain's total contribution to the Peninsular War. Further, Henry reminded the Spanish that Britain had relaxed her navigation laws to accommodate Spain's unique situation and, according to instructions, threatened to revoke these privileges if Spain did not reciprocate.[72]

Henry's exhortations and threats had little effect on the regents. Always suspicious of British intentions in South America, the Spanish suspected British complicity in the Venezuelan revolt or at least acquiescence in its occurrence. Initially Liverpool's stern reprimand to General Layard allayed many of these suspicions, but by the end of August these had returned in exaggerated form.[73] Wellesley's open dealings with Bolívar and Méndez and the public adulation accorded these men in London irritated the Spanish. They were further aggravated by an article in *El Español,* published in London but circulated in both Britain and Spain, calling for prompt British recognition of all colonial revolutions. When these sentiments were coupled with the news of a revolt in Buenos Aires, the regency openly attacked British motives. Because Henry tried in vain to defend Britain's conduct, he deemed it best not to initiate discussions on his brother's proposals for a circuitous trade agreement—at least until the Cortes had met. Henry believed that there was a remote possibility that events in Buenos Aires might convince the Cortes of the severity of their colonial problems and pressure it into trading concessions.[74]

The negotiations left Henry discouraged. Expressing his frustration to Wellington, he wrote: "Thus are petty British objects of commerce suffered to interfere with the great and interesting work of releasing this country from the yoke of France; and, unless the British Government takes the decided line of discouraging the spirit which has broken forth in the colonies, and that too in the most open manner, it will create such a jealousy here as never can be got under, and will probably be the ruin of the whole cause."[75] In his anger Henry forgot the dilemma confronting the Marquess. Britain was bound by treaty to maintain the Spanish empire as it existed in January 1809, but if she refused to deal with the new revolutionary governments they would turn to France for assistance. Britain could effectively prevent regular communications between France and South America, but doing so would necessitate increasing naval activity in the Caribbean at the expense of other vital areas. Similarly, suppressing the revolts would divert Spain's attentions from the peninsula. Britain could therefore steer only a middle course while an attempt was made to effect a reconciliation between the mother country and the rebellious colonies.

When discussions on trade and subsidy became less heated, Henry Wellesley's concern turned to the problems confronting the regency, which seemed unable to govern. Charges against the regents were numerous: they were blamed for Spain's wretched financial position, for the deteriorating military situation, and for attempting to open colonial trade to Great Britain. Yet what cut across Spain's political lines and attracted the attention and aroused the ire of the people were the circumstances surrounding the upcoming assembling of the Cortes and the sudden presence in Cádiz of the Duke of Orleans.

Young Wellesley was among those most surprised when the Duke of Orleans arrived in Cádiz on June 21, 1810, for, as instructed, he had previously warned Bardaxi that Britain would not look favorably upon the duke's employment in Spain.[76] Given no warning of the visit, Henry set about investigating the circumstances which prompted it and discovered that Orleans was in Cádiz at the invitation of the regency to take command of a Spanish army in Catalonia.[77] Hearing this report, the Spanish secretary of state quickly exonerated the regents of all responsibility for the invitation. Bardaxi explained that it had been issued much earlier by the junta on the recommendation of the British government and that the regents were in no position to revoke it. He assured Henry that, given the military situation, Orleans would be allowed to act only as a partisan on the French frontier.[78] Dubious of Bardaxi's response, Henry warned him: "If the command of the Spanish armies in Catalonia was conferred upon the Duke of Orleans it would not only be attended with the most fatal consequences in Spain, but would also produce very bad effects in England, that even at the time when the most intimate political connection subsisted between France & Spain the employment of a French Prince at the head of the Spanish army would have been viewed with a very jealous eye, but that now when the greatest animosity prevailed towards Frenchmen of every description, and when every motive of sound policy should induce the Government to endeavor to keep alive, and if possible to augment this feeling, to write a French Prince to command in one of the most important Provinces of the Kingdom and to select for that command one who (whatever his opinions might now be) had not only been brought up in revolutionary principles but whose military reputation had been acquired in revolutionary armies appeared to me to destroy the foundation upon which all hope of success must rest, and to defeat the grand object (so essential to the future of Spain) of an eternal separation between Spain and France."[79]

As Wellesley had predicted, Orleans' presence in Cádiz prompted numerous protests to the regency. Even more distressing than his presence was the widespread impression that the duke was there at the invitation of Great Britain. Henry saw at this early stage that the episode could cause Britain considerable embarrassment and the Spanish government great loss of credibility.[80] Yet Henry did not know how to react. His instructions dealt only with preventing Orleans from coming to Cádiz and contained none in the event this should fail. Henry was inclined to terminate British aid until the duke was ordered to leave, but he was uncertain of the actual circumstances surrounding Orleans' arrival in the city. Considering both Bardaxi's and the duke's claims that the idea originated in Britain, he hesitated. For various reasons Henry doubted the assertions of British responsibility. Orleans, for instance, pointedly avoided meeting Henry, which, if Britain was indeed responsible for his presence in Cádiz, was highly irregular behavior. Moreover, Henry had received no advance information from Lord Amherst, the British representative in Sicily, where Orleans officially resided. Certainly, if there had been British involvement, Amherst would have been a party to it. Thus Henry remained suspicious. He had no knowledge of the ultimate intentions of either the regency or Orleans—only that "there is something at the bottom of this transaction which has not come to light." Henry wrote to the Marquess for instructions.[81]

Orleans' unpopularity continued to grow, making Henry's position even more difficult. He was acutely aware of Great Britain's embarrassment, but he feared issuing an official denial of British involvement in the duke's presence in Cádiz, since he did not have all the facts. Nevertheless, public reaction was undermining the regency's authority, and Henry felt compelled to be cautious in affairs concerning Orleans until he had received instructions from his brother. He therefore urged the regents to ignore the duke and refrain from giving him employment. Realizing their mistake the regents complied.[82]

As the situation deteriorated, Henry became more decisive. To counteract the belief that Orleans was in Cádiz at Britain's request, Henry addressed an official note to the regency on June 27. It contained his communications on the subject and a denial that he personally had any knowledge of British complicity. At the same time he induced the regents to appoint Romana to command the Armies of Valencia and Catalonia and General Joseph Henry O'Donnell that of Murcia, thus precluding a military role for Orleans.[83]

These actions lessened the tension, but the duke remained in Cádiz and his mere presence fed the general discontent. Finally instructions arrived from Wellesley, giving Henry license to remove Orleans quietly from Cádiz.[84] Henry went to the duke without delay, advising him that his services in the peninsula would not aid the common cause and suggesting that he go to England to discuss his employment elsewhere. Noncommittal, Orleans replied that he would comply with anything consistent with his rank and dignity.[85] Actually, the duke was actively trying to obtain a command in the Spanish army. He presented the regents with an official request for such an appointment, only to be refused.[86] Still Henry believed that the duke would not leave Cádiz without an official request from the regency to do so. Strangely, this was not forthcoming. Writing to Wellington, Henry detailed the situation: "The Duke of Orleans is intriguing to a much greater extent than you are aware of. Castaños told me yesterday that he had given in plans for the defense of Catalonia and of the Isla de León, and was very angry at not being admitted to discuss them in the Council of Regency, or that the Ministers were not, at least, instructed to communicate with him upon them. In addition to this, he has applied for the command of the army in the Isla de León, and, upon that being refused, for the command in Galicia, which has likewise been refused. I told Castaños that, in one case, the English would not have served under him, and, in the other, all supplies would have been withheld by England from Galicia. It is wonderful that he does not feel the impossibility of his being employed here. I am persuaded that the first intelligence of his employment would occasion an insurrection. I fear it will require some strong measure to drive him from hence, for I have no hope of being able to get him away, excepting by an official application to the government."[87]

Henry was perplexed over the regency's failure to order Orleans out of the city. The reason became apparent, however, when Bardaxi explained on August 12 that the regents had in fact invited the duke to take command of an army in Catalonia but that the invitation had been issued at a time when conditions were favorable to such an event. In this light the regents believed that if they ordered Orleans to leave, he might expose their role in bringing him to Cádiz, which could lead to such a public uproar that they might be forced from office. For this reason, Bardaxi requested Henry's assistance in removing Orleans.[88] Although angered by the regency's deceit, Wellesley agreed, responding with a public statement declaring Britain's opposition to the duke's employment in Spain. The regents hoped that Orleans would now leave without exposing their role in the misadventure. To their dismay this was not to be; the duke countered by publishing the regency's letters inviting him to Spain.[89]

Public discontent with the government was now considerable. The regents were blamed for the duke's unfortunate presence, the static military situation, and the chaos in Spain's finances. This antagonism combined with the indignation created by Britain's acceptance of the colonial revolutionaries from Caracas and Buenos Aires made the political situation in Cádiz highly volatile. Spaniards began clamoring for the Cortes, originally scheduled to meet in March and then postponed to August, to assemble. A second postponement to September made many people feel that the regents were postponing the meeting because the Cortes's first act would be the removal of the regents.[90]

Its plans to meet were not the only problem the Cortes was causing the regency. Liberals, dissatisfied with the mode of electing deputies to the Cortes, were complaining bitterly. Elections, which had been held early in the year, were conducted through an indirect system, which established a progression of elections from the parish level, to the town, to the district, and, finally, to the province, where deputies to the Cortes were chosen. Such a system favored the established classes, and a large number of nobles and priests were elected. Liberals therefore looked to the regency to alter this situation.[91]

To the regency's dismay, even louder complaints were coming from conservatives, especially those from Castile. The Castilians maintained that the method of election to the Cortes, as drawn up by the junta and approved by the regency, was illegal. In particular, they opposed the provision establishing general representation according to population. Historically, the Cortes was composed in much the same manner as the old French Estates-General. Representation was divided among three groups, the clergy, the nobility, and the commoners, including peasants and bourgeoisie. The system ensured a conservative majority, which, Castilians maintained, was necessary, or a "revolutionary spirit would introduce itself into that assembly, which would produce all the evils which had desolated France." Conservatives argued that only the Cortes itself could alter the form of its representation and that any enabling decree by either the junta or the regency was invalid. The censure, though leveled primarily against the old junta, was evidently intended to fall as heavily on the council of regency.[92]

Besieged with complaints from all sides, it is little wonder that the regency could not come to a conclusion on other issues which were delaying assembling of the Cortes. In particular, the regents had to decide how to provide representation for those provinces whose deputies, due to French occupation, could not get to Cádiz, and for the American colonies. In late August the regents finally ruled that these areas would be represented by provisional deputies elected from natives of those provinces and colonies residing in Cádiz. This accomplished, the date of September 24, 1810, was set for the opening session of the Cortes.[93]

Despite these actions the regency continued to decline in popularity. Plots to overthrow the regents began to take form among those deputies already in Cádiz. In one case, the conspirators sought to involve Henry in their plot. On August 29 Henry's opinion was solicited on the prospect of calling the Princess of Brazil to the throne of Spain, if at the same time her son would marry a British princess. Wisely, Henry would have nothing to do with the plan, nor would he comment upon it—doing so would have implicated him as part of the conspiracy. On the other hand, he also refused to inform the regents of the plot, fearing that they would use it as a pretext to postpone the meeting of the Cortes even further.[94]

Henry began to feel that the political situation in Cádiz was becoming overly volatile. In addition to the party which supported Doña Carlotta as regent, there was also a small party favoring the Duke of Orleans. For this reason Orleans refused to leave Cádiz until the Cortes had assembled, resulting in more public outrage. Confident that the duke lacked the support to be seriously considered as a candidate for the regency, Henry feared the possibility that the duke might throw his support to the princess in return for his being appointed head of the armies.[95] This prospect caused Wellesley much concern. If the princess became regent, it would weaken British influence in the peninsula and "would place the Army of Portugal in some measure at the disposal of the Spanish Government, and would probably expose the Commander in Chief of the British Army to the interference of the Spanish Government in military points, from which he is now entirely free."[96]

Henry met with several influential delegates to the Cortes. He out-lined Britain's objections to either the princess or the Duke of Orleans becoming regent and suggested instead that if a new regency was to be formed it should be composed of men from the Cortes. Similarly, Henry acquainted the Portuguese representative in Cádiz with Britain's opposi-tion to the claims of the princess. Making public Britain's position low-ered the level of tension, and the Cortes assembled on September 24, 1810, in a calmer atmosphere.[97]

The Marquess Wellesley too was in a difficult political situation. In-creasingly frustrated in his efforts to meet Apodaca's requests for arms, money, and reinforcements, he became more insistent with his prime minister that he strengthen the government. This time he would not tolerate procrastination.[98] "Perceval came and passed two hours here," wrote Lord Sidmouth, "but I cannot say that our meeting was satisfac-tory: Lord Wellesley's difficulties were the beginning, middle and end of what he had to say."[99] Wellesley urged Perceval to extend an invitation to Canning to enter the cabinet as soon as possible, pointing out that he (or anyone else) would refuse to join once the government's policies for the coming year had been determined.[100] Perceval agreed to meet with Canning on July 25, but no offer was forthcoming.[101]

Wellesley, sick and irritable, besieged by the innumerable complaints and requests of the Spanish embassy, disillusioned over his colleagues' despair after the fall of the important fortress of Ciudad Rodrigo, and perplexed by the revolts in South America, now demanded that Perceval act decisively.[102] Wellesley insisted that Perceval extend an invitation to Canning to join the ministry. The prime minister agreed, provided Castlereagh could be persuaded to join as well. Wellesley could not object to this, so Perceval composed a letter to Castlereagh offering him a cabinet post along with Canning.[103] The draft was sent to the Marquess for comment. Approving the letter, Wellesley was optimistic that Castlereagh would agree to join the ministry. He suggested that some communication be made to Canning as well, but Perceval preferred to wait, pending a decision from Castlereagh.[104] The official offer was sent on August 22, 1810, and while Wellesley eagerly awaited the reply he kept Canning posted on all that was happening.[105]

To Wellesley's disappointment, Castlereagh declined the offer, ex-plaining that it was too soon after the duel for him to serve alongside Canning.[106] Without Castlereagh, Perceval would not agree to a new arrangement, and for the time being the issue was again dropped. A disappointed Canning, however, indignantly informed Perceval that while he would never serve with Castlereagh, he would consider taking the Foreign Office if Wellesley was given another post to his liking. Perceval naturally declined.[107]

It was a difficult time for Lord Wellesley, as he faced disappointment and trouble on all fronts. To compound the numerous problems that had accumulated that summer, the news of the fall of the fortress of Almeida left Wellesley's colleagues more dispirited than ever. He did manage to muster some reinforcements for Wellington, but they certainly fell far short of what he envisioned.[108] There is evidence that the Marquess considered resigning at this time, but military events in Portugal, the convocation of the Cortes in Cádiz, which held out new hope for Spain, and political events in Britain would shortly convince him to stay.

8

False Hope: Marquess Wellesley, Henry Wellesley, and the Blake Regency, September 1810–June 1811

Lord Wellesley's despondency, a result of the political situation in Great Britain, and Henry Wellesley's frustration, brought on by the Spanish government's continuing ineptness and failure to cooperate, were momentarily alleviated in the autumn of 1810. On September 24, the Spanish Cortes assembled for the first time in over twenty years, amid hopes that Spain would finally produce an effective government. Three days later the Duke of Wellington fought and won a significant battle against Marshal André Masséna on the heights of Serra de Bussaco, providing Britain with its first military victory since the Battle of Talavera fourteen months earlier. The renewed enthusiasm which these events brought to the Wellesley clan, however, would be short-lived. Political developments in both London and Cádiz combined to make the conduct of Anglo-Spanish diplomacy as difficult as ever.

The Battle of Bussaco was by no means a decisive British victory. Though Masséna lost 4,487 men to Wellington's 1,252, the French army remained formidable, superior in most ways to the allied army.[1] Nonetheless, Bussaco proved to be Masséna's last opportunity to do battle before the allies fell behind the nearly unassailable Lines of Torres Vedras, and it proved to Briton and Frenchman alike that the Portuguese army had become both a reliable and a valuable part of Wellington's forces. Of equal importance was the effect the battle had on morale in Lisbon, London, and Cádiz.[2]

The victory could not have come at a better time for Lord Wellesley. Many Britons believed the cause in Spain was hopeless, a sentiment which had become increasingly pervasive with the numerous French military successes of 1810 and which extended, as mentioned, even into the Perceval ministry. To Wellesley, confident of ultimate success, such opinions were discouraging. But Bussaco revived lagging enthusiasm. Wellesley responded characteristically to what he considered a favorable event, again displaying the energy of his first weeks in the Foreign Office. His mind turned to the future, envisioning a heightened British effort in Iberia and from there the spreading of the struggle to central Europe. "I entertain great confidence respecting Portugal," the Marquess exalted in a note to Perceval, "and if we should succeed, according to our real merits, in that quarter, a new & great scene may be expected to open in Europe."[3]

Wellesley's plans for extending the war against France reflected a comprehensive grasp of the importance of the conflict in the peninsula and the nature of the war against Napoleonic France. The Marquess believed that overall success could be achieved only when the people of Europe rose in national revolts against the power of France. One of the first British politicians to perceive the value of nationalism, he was realistic enough to see that such insurrections would not take place unless the potential for success was amply demonstrated. Therein Wellesley saw the value of the Peninsular War apart from the importance of freeing Portugal and Spain of French domination. "The wisdom of maintaining the war in Spain and Portugal," he wrote after Bussaco, "has been fully proved by the shade it has cast on the military and political character of Bonaparte."[4]

Not content with theorizing, Wellesley sent agents throughout Europe to encourage insurrection as a supplement to the war in the peninsula. He considered the Illyrian provinces, Tyrol, Switzerland, Austria, north Germany, and Denmark ripe for revolt. In each, Wellesley instructed his agents to play upon the hardships caused by the Continental System and the new optimism promoted by Wellington's success.[5] Politically, pursuing this policy involved a considerable risk. In the debate on the Corunna campaign, the opposition had made it clear that it considered immoral the undertaking of any operation which could not promise success, as failure would surely bring heavy retribution from Paris upon the continentals involved.[6] Yet Wellesley considered this a narrow view and unworthy of consideration. "It is said to be inhuman and impolitic to excite any people to a resistance, which must be finally overpowered, and to encrease their calamities, without procuring their freedom," he wrote to his brother-in-law, Culling Charles Smith. "But the interference of England presents the only means of facilitating the success of those, who resist, by combining their efforts, and therefore removes the principal objection; while it must be granted, that much partial suffering must be endured, in order to accomplish a general, or even a partial release from the Yoke of France."[7] Nevertheless, Wellesley hoped that his agents could discourage premature revolts.

Wellesley's colleagues apparently shared his enthusiasm. In the days following the announcement of the victory at Bussaco, generous shipments of military stores were sent to Spain.[8] Beyond the encouraging effects which the battle produced in the cabinet, optimism was promoted by subsequent news of Wellington's strong position behind the Lines of Torres Vedras and particularly by the first meeting of the Spanish Cortes. The opening session of the Cortes amidst elaborate ceremony on the Isla de León on September 24, 1810, was the culmination of months of concerted diplomatic effort. Both the Marquess and Henry Wellesley believed that given the necessity of an interim government to rule in Ferdinand's absence, a representative assembly would be necessary to overcome local jealousies and to give the government public support. In the absence of such support, both the Supreme Junta and the regency had found it difficult to control provincial authorities as well as their own generals, rendering coordination of the national effort impossible. It was hoped that a regency ruling with the Cortes would strengthen the central government's authority.[9]

The Marquess' desire to convene the Cortes was also motivated by the opposition's demand for a liberalization of Spain's political, economic, and social systems. He saw the gathering as a visible first step in this process. At the same time he advised Henry to use his influence to prevent the Cortes from initiating what might be interpreted as radical legislation. While the Marquess was intent upon silencing the liberal parliamentary opposition, he was not willing to do so at the risk of losing the support of the conservative majority.[10] Henry appreciated his brother's concern and remained acutely alert to the problem.

The opening session of the Cortes was taken up with formalities and the election of Don Ramada Fagaro de Don as its president and Pérez de Castra as its secretary. As attention turned to more important matters, the Cortes, as hoped, expressed concern for the country's financial state and the army's afflictions, while the members revealed a willingness to come to terms with the American colonies.[11] Most observers, including Henry Wellesley, were satisfied with the proceedings. The Cortes, how-

ever, before embarking on protracted discussions or coming to any sort
of conclusions, turned its attentions to defining its own position and
powers in relation to the regency's. In an arrogant and jealous assertion
of power, the Cortes declared itself the sovereign authority in the absence of Ferdinand VII. Although the Council of Regency was entrusted
with executive responsibilities, it in turn was ultimately responsible to the
Cortes and was always under its jealous scrutiny.[12] Instead of sharing
power and responsibility equally with the Cortes, the regents had merely
become ministers, a fact which would inhibit the decisive executive
action that was essential in time of war. Thus the specter of Spanish
indecisiveness and inefficiency still loomed.

Henry, for the time being, was unconcerned. He believed that the
problem of sovereignty would resolve itself and saw in the Cortes a
promise for improvement in Spanish politics. Writing to Lord Wellesley,
he explained: "Upon the whole, with the exception of the decree by
which the rank of the executive power is placed below that of the Cortes,
their proceedings are extremely creditable to them, and justify a confident expectation that the most important consequences will be derived
from this meeting. It has certainly already produced more men of talent,
energy, and usefull knowledge than the country was generally supposed
to possess; and it is to be recollected that the Deputies of those provinces
which were principally relied upon for men of capacity are not yet
arrived. In justice, likewise, to the motives of those who proposed the
decree relative to the title of Majesty being conferred upon the Cortes,
and that of Highness on the Council of Regency, I must express my firm
conviction that this does not proceed from any revolutionary feeling
among the Deputies, many of whom declare both titles to be in conformity to ancient usage."[13] Henry's excitement was shared by other En-
glishmen, Whigs and Tories alike. Most reports on the Cortes sent from
Cádiz to London were favorable.[14] Clearly, for the first time since its
outbreak in 1808, the Peninsular War was given some semblance of
bipartisan support.

Regrettably the cabinet had little time to enjoy this new state of affairs
or to capitalize on the opportunity it presented. On October 15, 1810, it
was announced that George III was ill. What was first reported as a cold
quickly developed into a far more serious malady.[15] The king, a weary
seventy-two, was attempting to deal with the prospect of the death of his
favorite daughter, Princess Amelia. Weakened by illness, distraught with
grief, he succumbed to something which resembled a fit of insanity,
similar to that which he had experienced years earlier.[16]

The Privy Council was summoned to Windsor at once to analyze and discuss the situation. The king's illness presented a unique problem. In the event he was judged incompetent to rule, it would become necessary to establish a regency, with the Prince of Wales as regent. For the Perceval ministry this was an ominous possibility. Politically the prince was inclined toward the Whigs, and it was generally assumed that if he became regent he would turn out the Perceval cabinet. In its place would be a Whig ministry led by Grenville and Grey, who would, in all likelihood, withdraw Britain from the war. The prospect struck alarm throughout the Tory party. It was especially disturbing to Wellesley, as it ran counter to both his political philosophy and the family fortunes.[17]

Instead of turning immediately to a regency, Perceval delayed, hoping the king would recover. Through the first days of the king's illness, every effort was made to keep the malady a secret. The Privy Council came and went from Windsor as inconspicuously as possible.[18] Finally, the monarch's condition deteriorated so rapidly and drastically that it could no longer be concealed, as Wellesley himself had observed: "When his Lordship entered the apartment in which the royal sufferer was confined he found the man whom he had been accustomed to see surrounded with the insignia of power, and all the heraldic pomp of state ceremonial, sitting in a condition of complete nakedness on his bed, sunk apparently in hopeless oblivion. Lord Wellesley was so deeply affected that he could not refrain from tears and in after life never adverted to the subject without emotion."[19] The king's illness was made public, and when Parliament convened on November 1, 1810, Perceval asked for and was granted a two-week prorogation while prospects for the king's recovery were reviewed.[20] The monarch's health did not improve in the intervening days, and two more such prorogations followed. When Parliament assembled again on December 13, 1810, Perceval confronted the facts and announced that discussions on a regency would begin.[21]

Perceval, with the unanimous consent of his colleagues, decided to base the new Regency Bill on the one drawn up by William Pitt in 1788. The bill was characterized by the limitations placed on the regent for a period of one year, preventing him from making any basic alterations in the character of Parliament as left by the king. Such a bill was justifiable, given the possibility of the king's recovering; in such a case it would be improper for the regent to make ineradicable changes which the king might deem abhorrent. Advocating such a bill, however, presented basic problems for the ministry. Foremost among them was the fact that it was bound to alienate the regent. Because the regent could not be denied the right to change ministers, many believed that arousing the anger of the already Whiggish Prince of Wales ensured the dismissal of the Perceval cabinet. Aware that this was more than mere speculation, the cabinet became cautious in its policies, unwilling to commit itself on new issues or programs until the political situation stabilized. This prudence was especially evident in foreign affairs, where a change in ministries would be felt most drastically.

Thus the political advantages gained by Wellington's success at Bussaco and the favorable opinions created by the assembling of the Cortes quickly faded. Yet while Wellesley prudently abstained from pressing for an extension of the effort in Spain, neither did he see fit to contract Britain's involvement.[22] British diplomacy became static in the months that followed. No new promises were made to Spain; Wellesley sought only to keep relations functioning smoothly.

Certainly this sudden turn in events disappointed the Marquess, yet in some ways it was fortunate. While the opposition was neatly distracted by the regency question, two events occurred which in normal circumstances would have caused the government much distress—indeed they might have forced an alteration in policy to the detriment of the peninsular effort. First, Wellington decided to remain on the defensive behind the Lines of Torres Vedras, transforming the Battle of Bussaco into another apparent exercise in futility. Second and simultaneously there appeared what was known as the Bullion Report.

Wellington based his decision on the knowledge that Masséna, at his present strength, could not attack and that a dearth of subsistence would ultimately force the French to withdraw. "This time last year," wrote Wellington to Liverpool, "I was obliged to remove the British Cavalry only from the district which they now occupy with their whole army, because it could not be subsisted."[23] In essence Wellington believed he could force the French out of Portugal, under trying conditions, without risking his army in pitched battle. His was a wise policy, but it was one which required time and patience, the latter a mood distinctly lacking among critics at home. Wellington was reexposing himself to the charge leveled against him after Talavera—that he had fought a useless battle—only this time he had retreated to the extremity of Portugal. Such charges did in fact appear but generally were minimized by public and parliamentary interest over the regency question and, to a certain degree, by the enthusiasm generated by the Cortes.[24] As a result the ministry gave Wellington its unqualified support and encouraged him to persevere in his plans. "I am anxious to assure you," Liverpool wrote, "that we are most fully and completely satisfied with all that you have done, and all that you are doing."[25]

The Bullion Report might have presented more serious problems for the ministry. As pointed out earlier, Britain's economy had been totally disrupted by the Continental System and the war effort. Forced to revert to a paper currency, Britain used her specie reserves for subsidies to various continental allies, particularly Spain and Portugal. When these reserves ran short, specie was purchased in South America through the issuance of bills of exchange. The system resulted in a drastic rise in the price of gold and silver. Devaluation of the paper currency followed, causing considerable inflation. Britain's deteriorating economic situation in the early months of 1810 led to the appointment of a committee to investigate the situation. The report of the committee that autumn called for resumption of payments in specie and the abolition of paper currency.[26] While these moves would have helped relieve Britain's economic distress, they would also have crippled the war effort. Had the report been presented for discussion at this time, when, even after Bussaco, there seemed little chance for success in the peninsula, it is likely that the recommendations would have been given serious consideration by Parliament. Fortunately, because of the regency question, the debate did not take place until Wellington was once again prepared to take the offensive and success seemed within reach.[27] Nonetheless, it should be understood that the report had a chastening effect on Perceval and further discouraged Wellesley from pressing for increased expenditures in Spain. William Hamilton, permanent undersecretary in the Foreign Office, writing to Charles Vaughan, reflected Wellesley's despair: ". . . 30,000 men more would ensure success—but unluckily men are scarce, & money still more so. The distress in the city (individually) is very great, & foreign (European) trade is at a very low ebb, & as if B. Parte [Napoleon] had the Devil's own luck, this bullion report has gone well nigh to convince him of the final efficacy of the measures w^h he has long been taking to destroy our commerce."[28]

Meanwhile, the Foreign Office functioned as usual, with the continuing embarrassments of being unable to explain the revolts in the Spanish colonies and unable to meet the Spanish government's requests for subsidy. Throughout November and December, Spain was the recipient of the usual shipments of military stores directed to Cádiz, Galicia, Catalonia, and Valencia. But Spain considered these shipments insufficient and persisted in her requests for more aid, particularly in the form of a loan.[29] Wellesley could not comply, and either responded with an outright refusal or, as was often his inclination, did not respond at all. Failing to perceive the importance of the regency question and the effect it might have upon the war, the Spanish became perplexed and offended by Wellesley's uncooperativeness.[30]

Moreover, the Spanish were still outraged over Wellesley's conduct toward their rebellious colonies. The Marquess had continued to meet with representatives from Buenos Aires and Caracas in an unofficial capacity.[31] Discomforted by the situation and alarmed over reports of revolts in other colonies, he repeatedly urged the Spanish to come to terms with the rebels, offering himself as mediator. But the Spanish solution to colonial problems was suppression, while Wellesley, who was familiar with the rebellious colonies' complaints, saw accommodation as the only chance for a reasonable solution.[32]

The Spanish were inflexible. Their agreement to the principle of reconciliation and discussion of grievances carried with it certain conditions. The colonies, then in a state of revolt, would have to concede publicly that their actions were a mistake and subsequently place themselves under the authority of the regency.[33] Realizing that this was completely unacceptable to the colonies, Wellesley attempted to moderate Spain's position. He supplied the Spanish embassy with proof that both France and the United States were effectively aiding the rebels in an effort to make the revolutions permanent. He further warned that Britain would not condone or assist any attempt to subdue the colonies by force.[34] At the same time the Marquess began considering the form a mediation council might assume and how it would proceed.

Thus during a time of anxiety over the domestic political situation, the alliance with Spain became strained again, a situation which Wellesley could do little to alter. Accordingly, during the last months of 1810 he sent few dispatches to Cádiz, trusting Henry to act on his own judgment. Although this annoyed Henry, he came to understand his brother's position and was gratified to receive on December 9 Lord Wellesley's warm congratulations for a job well done and encouragement for the future: "I will not send this short note, without my most cordial congratulations on the character, which you have established by your very judicious conduct at Cádiz, in circumstances of the utmost delicacy and difficulty. This will be amply expressed to you, as soon as possible, in a formal dispatch. In the meanwhile, let me assure you, that even the opposition render you justice. . . . Whatever may be the result of the present melancholy condition of our good King's health, and whatever

may be the fate of those now in office, your honor will stand un-
blemished."[35]

It was a well-timed note, for Henry too had been under considerable
stress. Contrary to his prediction of October, the Cortes had proved itself
less than enlightened, and Wellesley still found himself perpetually
occupied with Spain's internal politics. The first serious problem arose
from the Cortes's decree which assumed the executive powers of the
regency. In response, the regents had petitioned the Cortes for a clarification of their powers. The simple reply was that they possessed the
same powers as the king but were responsible to the laws of Spain for
their acts and did not possess the inviolability of the sovereign. In other
words, they could be removed at the discretion of the Cortes.[36]

The regents' dissatisfaction with this situation came to a head only
after the Cortes repeatedly asked the Council of Regency to account for
its actions. Frustrated by this intervention, the regents considered resignation but first turned to Henry for advice. He suggested negotiations
with the Cortes and advised them to emphasize that governing would
become impossible unless the Cortes manifested greater confidence in
them.[37] Wellesley's advice went unheeded. Instead of opening discussions, the regents simply submitted their resignations outright. The
Cortes, in reply, ordered them to remain at their posts until suitable
replacements could be found.[38]

Concern over the unknown character and nature of a new regency
created additional problems for Henry. Fortunately, the Duke of Orleans was no longer one of them. Much to Henry's delight the Cortes had
ordered Orleans out of Spain. After a desperate but futile appeal, he had
sailed for Palermo on October 3, 1810, aboard the Spanish frigate
Emerald.[39] But Henry still had to combat the intrigues of the Princess of
Brazil. To the Portuguese representative in Cádiz, he reiterated Britain's
unqualified opposition to her becoming regent. Subsequently he expressed the same opinion to some of the Cortes's most influential members and persuaded them to maintain the extant format for a Council of
Regency.[40] With this accomplished the problem became one of finding
new, suitable regents. "It may perhaps appear extraordinary," Henry
wrote to the Marquess, "that after my repeated expressions of regret at
the want of energy and activity in the present members of the Regency, I
should, in my conversation with M. de Bardaxi relative to their sending
in their resignations, have suggested anything calculated to prolong
their continuance in power; but such is the extreme difficulty of supplying their places, that if the appointment of a new government were to be

left to me, I should feel great embarrassment upon whom to fix my choice."[41]

For this reason, and realizing that his influence would be discredited if a regency he had suggested failed to be effective, Henry initially abstained from showing too much interest in the formation of a new regency. He decided to intervene, however, when he heard of the Cortes's determination to appoint several nonentities to the new regency. Meeting with several members of the Cortes, Henry explained that "the appointment to the government of persons of obscure birth, and who in the course of the contest had done nothing to distinguish themselves," would demonstrate to Great Britain and to the rest of Europe that Spain was following the path of the French Revolution. He suggested, instead, that the Cortes nominate prominent nobles and generals and the most capable members of the present regency.[42]

Wellesley's appeal had little effect. In the ensuing days the Cortes passed a resolution prohibiting anyone who had signed Napoleon's Constitutional Act at Bayonne from serving on the Council of Regency. Because nearly all Spanish aristocrats had signed the act, the resolution served to eliminate several capable nobles even though they were now staunch opponents of the Bonaparte regime. Shortly after the ruling the Cortes also determined that it would not appoint anyone who had been a member of the Supreme Junta. Some of the most able and respected men in Spain were thus ineligible for an active role in Spain's government. Consequently Henry found little solace in the assurance that every effort was being made to appoint prominent Spanish citizens to the regency.[43]

After extensive deliberations the Cortes elected a new regency of three men in place of the former five-man council. The new regents were General Joaquin Blake, Don Gabriel Ciscar, and Don Pedro Agar. Henry, less than satisfied with the new regency, believed it to be no better than the earlier one. Nevertheless, because it was the direct choice of the Cortes and thus could probably count on its support, he hoped it would act more decisively.[44]

The meeting of the Cortes and the appointment of a new regency did not initially alter the course of Anglo-Spanish relations. Henry continued to encounter the familiar problems of Spanish inefficiency and dilatoriness. While he anxiously promoted reforms in Spain's army and bureaucracy, the Spanish concerned themselves with constitutional issues. Freedom of the press and provisions establishing length of terms and ethics for members of the Cortes were frequent topics for debate.[45]

Henry found some satisfaction in the Cortes's deliberations when colonial problems were brought up, but here, confronted with difficult and controversial problems, it avoided any decisions. The debate centered on the all-important issue of whether the colonies and native Americans should enjoy political rights similar to those in the mother country and among her citizens. The Cortes concluded that colonists of all classes would be granted political rights but deferred action on how the colonies would be represented in the Cortes. It was apparent that if equal representation was granted to the colonies they would hold a majority in the Cortes and this its members were not yet willing to grant.[46]

Despite the somewhat disappointing performance of the newly assembled Cortes, Henry detected a cooperative spirit within the assembly. So he risked the introduction of a proposal for the formation of a new Spanish army under British command. The previous August, Major General Samuel Ford Whittingham had suggested to Henry that he be allowed to undertake the raising and training of a Spanish corps of 10,000 men. The corps (8,000 infantry, 1,600 cavalry, and 400 artillery) would be paid by Spain but armed and clothed by Great Britain. Whittingham proposed to draw the troops from the provinces of Murcia, Valencia, Aragon, and Catalonia and to train them on the island of Majorca. Each battalion would, in its final form, have at least two British officers.[47]

Henry's views coincided with Whittingham's, for the proposal represented an opportunity to begin the reorganization of the Spanish army. Specifically, he saw three basic advantages to the plan: the new corps would effectually provide for the defense of the Balearic Islands; British officers would be introduced into the Spanish army; and, under British direction, a well-disciplined corps could be formed which would serve as a model to the rest of the Spanish army. Henry therefore sent Whittingham's proposal along with the embassy's recommendation to the Council of Regency and to Lord Wellesley in London for approval.[48]

Henry was confident of a quick sanction by both parties. While approval from London was forthcoming, he was shocked to find the Spanish uncooperative. The regents explained that the proposal had been temporarily set aside because it involved basic changes in Spain's military system and would entail a lengthy discussion. Henry, however, detected another reason for the decision. "I have reason to believe," he explained to the Marquess, "that the real motive for relinquishing this plan which has promised to be attended with so many advantages is pique at the reception which the Deputies from the Caracas have met with in England and at the expectations of our merchants to have colonial trade opened to them."[49] Henry's conclusion was based on conversations with Castaños and from communications Whittingham had had on the subject. Whatever the reason for Spain's reluctance to adopt the proposal, the issue was temporarily dropped; Wellesley decided to wait for a more opportune time to reintroduce it.

Accordingly, Henry reintroduced the proposal for military reform in late October. The new regents were installed, the news of Wellington's victory at Bussaco had arrived in Cádiz, Spain was again in need of financial assistance, and the Cortes was showing a renewed interest in military reform. Henry presented the regents with Whittingham's proposal along with another from Colonel Philip Roche, suggesting that he be entrusted with the training of an infantry corps of 5,000 troops to be employed at Cartagena.[50] This time the Spanish cooperated. Whittingham received the government's consent to proceed with his project, and by November 26, 1810, Henry was able to report significant progress in the corps's formation.[51] In an uncommon display of cooperation, the regency also granted Colonel Roche permission to train an army and commissioned Whittingham to extend his corps gradually to 30,000 when feasible.[52]

The spirit of cooperation was brief. Henry soon found the Cortes ineffective and the regents, particularly General Blake, antagonistic. The Cortes engaged itself in endless debates on military and fiscal problems but failed to decide on any remedies. Henry came to view the Cortes as timid, irresolute, and suspicious, but he knew it was Spain's only hope for rejuvenation. "I am apprehensive that what I have felt it my duty to state in this dispatch will impress His Majesty's Government with no very favorable opinion of the Cortes," Henry wrote gloomily to Wellesley. "I must observe however that whatever defects may exist in the Cortes, we can look to no other source for the salvation of the country, and it is therefore necessary that every possible degree of support should be given to them."[53]

Henry's frustration turned to despair when the Cortes announced it would begin discussions on a new constitution. Recognizing that the immediate problems were those of war and finance, Henry questioned the wisdom of the decision, knowing that the regency would not take the radical, remedial steps which those problems necessitated. He realized, moreover, that discussions on a constitution at this juncture would expose the Cortes to British charges of republicanism, accusations the Wellesleys hoped to avoid.[54] Acquainting various Spanish politicians with his sentiments, Henry was pointedly informed that "it was in vain to call to the people to enlist into their armies until they are assured, that after they had risked their lives to secure the independence of their country, they shall return to live under a government the abuse of which had been corrected."[55] Henry could not agree and went so far as to suggest that aid be terminated until the Cortes decided to address more practical problems.[56]

Fortunately, as Henry rarely gave way to his emotions, he continued to cooperate with the Spanish. On December 21, His Majesty's ship *Bulwark* arrived in Cádiz with specie from Mexico. The *Bulwark* had been commissioned to bring back $5 million for the Spanish government, and from this sum Spain was to repay the short-term loan of $1.5 million advanced by Henry the previous July. Unfortunately, the *Bulwark* returned with only $1.5 million: a recent fire in the mint and the scarcity of quicksilver had inhibited the production of specie. Because the Spanish government was destitute of funds, Henry asked for only one-third of the payment of the loan until more specie arrived. Bardaxi, emphasizing his government's distress, requested that the payment be lowered even further to $300,000. Henry agreed, promptly sending that sum to Wellington in Portugal.[57]

Henry's concession was unreciprocated; instead of improving, Anglo-Spanish relations grew worse. Since taking office as president of the new Council of Regency, General Blake had demonstrated a marked dislike of all things British. While feigning cooperation, he attempted to undermine British influence in Cádiz. Under his guidance a profound mistrust of Britain's role in the colonial revolts had again been fostered in Cádiz. In a sense this was a continuation of the old regency's policy, but Blake's vigorous pursuit of it was unprecedented. The immediate result of his Anglophobia was a cessation of all discussions on trade, and soon it became the cause of bitter disagreement between the two allies over military reform.[58]

General Whittingham's plans were proceeding smoothly; in a matter of weeks he had assembled an effective cavalry force. The more difficult task of assembling and training the infantry lay ahead.[59] Whittingham believed that success was contingent upon his employing officers of his own choosing—both Spanish and British. To this the regency had agreed on November 28, but a month later Whittingham was facing obstructions in his efforts to recruit both men and officers. He protested to the minister of war, Don José de Heredia, who responded with a promise of speedy action to clear the way.[60] Accordingly Whittingham presented his choice of officers to serve in the new corps. To his surprise Heredia rejected the list on the grounds that the chosen officers could not be spared from active service in the peninsula, and he advised Whittingham to make his selection from a list of officers then unemployed.[61]

Since the onset of the war, the Spanish army had been plagued with an overabundance of officers. As the war proceeded on its disastrous course and desertion from the ranks became a chronic problem, the rolls of unemployed officers increased. As early as October 10, 1809, Colonel Roche reported that there were "an infinite number of generals, without any destination or employment, they merely follow the headquarters with the aid de camps . . . consume forage and provisions and fill up the quarters."[62] By December 1810 the group included officers of all ranks and, as might be expected, men of generally inferior ability. Whittingham therefore chose to ignore them, while the regency, which saw the officers only as a drain on the treasury, decided to send them as skeleton battalions or *cuadros* to Majorca.[63] Whittingham was outraged and promptly sent an appeal to Henry, threatening to resign his commission if the Spanish did not comply with the original agreement. Wellesley subsequently sent a similar threat to Bardaxi, warning that British aid might cease if Spain did not become more cooperative.[64]

As usual the Spanish refused to succumb to coercion, and relations between the regency and the British embassy became more acrimonious. Heredia maintained that no agreement on recruiting procedure had ever been concluded and expressed annoyance at Wellesley's intervention in the dispute.[65] Whittingham retorted: "The basis of everything I have hitherto had the honour to propose to the Council of Regency, relative to the organization of 10,000 men in the Island of Majorca, has been the exclusive selection of officers by me."[66] An impasse was avoided through a compromise whereby Whittingham alone would choose his staff officers and aid in the selection of the rest. Henry, however, took the opportunity to issue a stinging censure to the regency. "I must take the liberty of observing," he wrote to Bardaxi, "that if this transaction is to interrupt the good understanding which has hitherto so happily subsisted between the Spanish Government and His Majesty's Minister, it is not to be imputed to those who are anxious to maintain conditions formally agreed to, but to those who break them."[67] The episode left a legacy of mistrust from which neither party would ever fully recover. Henry would be on his guard in any future dealings with the regents.

Meanwhile, Perceval's Regency Bill had been given its first reading on

December 27, 1810. The most important debate was to take place in the House of Lords, where the bill faced opposition not only from the Whigs but also from the regent's brothers and other princes of the blood. The cabinet decided that Liverpool would make the introductory statements, with the chancellor, Lord Eldon, and Lord Wellesley prepared to enter the debate. As expected, a vigorous debate ensued but, strangely, Wellesley sat silent.[68] Although the first reading passed by a considerable majority, there was much controversy over Wellesley's failure to enter the debate. His colleagues felt deserted, and his enemies conjectured that he had sold his support to the Prince of Wales for a seat in a new government. The Marquess never offered an explanation, but it is highly unlikely that he had struck a deal with the prince. Lord Holland offered perhaps the most plausible explanation, remarking that such behavior was not at all unusual for Wellesley: "He was, indeed, a most uncertain speaker in every sense of the word. After studiously announcing his intentions of speaking, and repeating his views and arguments and illustrations in private to friend and foe, he not unfrequently sat silent."[69]

Regardless of the reasons, the occasion of Wellesley's silence was not so significant as some historians have suggested. Debates on the specifics of the Regency Bill continued throughout the month of January, and in these Wellesley took an active part. A final vote was taken and carried on February 5, 1811.[70] When the Prince of Wales took his oath as regent the following day, many assumed that the Perceval cabinet would be promptly dismissed. Yet, disillusioned by the divisiveness within his party and the arrogance of some of its members, the prince hesitated to make such a drastic decision. Soon word came from Windsor that the king was sufficiently coherent to perceive significant changes in policy and that there was a remote chance for his recovery. In these circumstances, the regent chose temporarily to retain Perceval. Wellesley would remain in the Foreign Office, and the Peninsular War would continue. There was, however, little reason for exuberance. The regent was known for his unpredictability, and the old problems of conducting a war with a weak government persisted.[71]

Meanwhile Henry Wellesley's negotiations with the Spanish government over military reform were not proceeding smoothly. Already upset over Whittingham's problems, Wellesley became disillusioned with the Spanish army's poor performance. He sent numerous complaints to the regency, but, as usual, Bardaxi, echoing Blake's sentiments, flatly denied accusations of Spanish incompetency.[72] Blake now opposed everything in which Britain was involved, much to Henry's resentment. Never had

Anglo-Spanish relations been worse. Nonetheless, Wellesley persisted in his complaints, pointing to the inactivity, inefficiency, and lack of discipline in the Spanish armies. Bardaxi, in turn, attributed all problems to a lack of funds, a problem, he maintained, only Britain could alleviate. Spain's fiscal distress was obviously great, and Henry saw in it an opportunity to force the Spanish into greater activity. He conjectured that if a loan of sufficient magnitude was promised, the Cortes would be forced to implement Britain's suggestions for reform, even without the consent of the regents. This was, however, for the moment mere speculation; a new loan would be decided on in London, where the political situation was still uncertain.[73]

The Spanish armies continued to perform poorly. In January the city of Tortosa fell, making Catalonia's collapse imminent.[74] Additional requests for arms, supplies, and money were Spain's only action. Faced with uncertainty in London, negligence, obstinacy, and belligerence in Cádiz, Henry's frustrations grew. When word arrived that the Spanish had again failed at Maida, he lamented: "The situation of Spain is unfortunately such, that she must depend on her military force alone for her deliverance from the usurpation of France. There is nothing desperate in this situation if the most were made of those qualities requisite to form good soldiers which the people of Spain possess in an eminent degree—their undaunted spirit, their patience under hardship and fatigue, their temperate habits, and above all, their unconquerable hatred of a foreign yoke, are qualities which require only to be properly directed to produce an army unequalled perhaps by any in Europe. If I am correct in my conception of the character of the Spanish people, one would naturally ask, to what circumstances it is to be attributed that such a people have not produced an army capable of driving the enemy from the Peninsula! It would not become me to state the causes which have checked the valour of the people, and have led to the ill success of the Spanish armies—but they are so obvious as to require no explanation."[75]

On January 23, 1811, Spain suffered the loss of its most able general, the Marquis de la Romana, behind the Lines of Torres Vedras, leaving the Spanish military in an even weaker state.[76] As a result Wellesley's concern grew more pronounced, not to be abated by Bardaxi's response to the above note. Writing on February 4, Bardaxi again claimed that all Spain's problems were attributable to the scarcity of money, but he promised that the regency would see to the alteration of the military system.[77] This was not the answer Henry had anticipated. He had no confidence in the regency's determination to make significant changes, which he believed would have to come directly from the Cortes. To Bardaxi, Henry wrote: "I continue therefore to be of the opinion, that it is absolutely necessary that the Executive Power [the regency] should of itself submit to the consideration of the Cortes, the whole question relative to the military system of Spain, pointing out its defects & the disastrous consequences that have hitherto resulted from them, & calling upon the assembly to adopt the regulations necessary for its improvement."[78] Similarly, Henry believed that the Cortes was well disposed to taking British officers into the service of Spain and eventually conferring a command upon Wellington, but he preferred that matters dealing with clothing, feeding, and paying of troops be considered first.[79]

In the course of these negotiations, British troops took part in a cooperative military adventure with the Spanish. The results confirmed Henry's opinion that military reform would have to be prompt and comprehensive. In late February the Spanish suggested an expedition to raise the siege of Cádiz. Because such an expedition, if successful, would serve also to relieve Wellington and give impetus to local uprisings in Andalusia, and because the allied armies could easily disembark if it became necessary, the British commander in Cádiz, Lieutenant General Thomas Graham, agreed to cooperate. In so doing, Graham exceeded his orders but, considering the reduced state of the French forces before Cádiz, he saw a reasonable prospect for success.[80]

In the initial discussions of the operations, Graham assumed that he would have full command. Once again, however, Blake's prejudices and jealousies came into play. He demanded that the Spanish general, Tomás Lapeña, be given overall command. But Graham's orders specifically stated that British troops could not be placed under the command of Spanish officers. A compromise was reached which established a loose chain of command. Graham was given direct command of British forces and Lapeña of Spanish troops, with the latter also assuming a strictly ceremonial authority over the whole operation.[81] Both armies were then assembled and readied in Tarifa, from which they embarked. Following a sixteen-hour march by night, Graham's troops were the first to be engaged by French troops, led by Marshal Claude Perrin Victor. Fighting from a strong position at Barrosa, Graham held the advantage throughout the day. Lapeña, however, failed to engage his troops, and what might have been a decisive allied victory became a significant but costly repulse. With his army decimated by the day's fighting, Graham could not follow up his success. He withdrew from the field of battle, enraged over Lapeña's conduct.[82]

The next day, with the French on the defensive, and his troops fresh and unscathed, Lapeña suggested a pursuit. Graham refused to cooperate. Lapeña protested, claiming that the British had deserted him, and boldly took credit for the success of the previous day.[83] Graham kept a cool head, stating simply that he could do no more. Henry was not so even-tempered; he condemned Lapeña and wholeheartedly supported Graham's decision to withdraw. Writing to Lord Wellesley, he vividly revealed his feelings: "Your Lordship will perceive a great similarity between the conduct of the Spaniards in this action, and in that of Talavera. In both, the British troops were left to sustain unsupported the whole weight of the enemy's force. Upon both occasions, the Spaniards have attempted to assume to themselves much of the credit of the victory; have boasted of their exploits; and have expressed their readiness to advance, if supported by the British; when they knew that the British could no longer confide in them, and indeed when they had exhibited indisputable proofs of want of confidence in themselves."[84] So distressed was Henry that three days after the battle he demanded an inquiry by the Cortes into the proceedings of the Spanish army from the time it left Tarifa to the night of March 5, 1811. The Cortes agreed to the demand but only because a refusal would cast a doubt on the Spanish claims.[85] At the same time, the Cortes sought to mollify British anger by conferring on General Graham the titles of duke and grandee for his services. Graham politely refused, asking only for a vote of thanks.[86]

The inquiry was not the only result of the Battle of Barrosa. Having received word that Masséna was withdrawing from Portugal, Henry realized that Wellington would soon be operating in Spain. The prospect revived the question of coordinating allied operations. Henry believed that the action at Barrosa proved that the Spanish, acting independently, still could not be depended upon. He believed that Britain should have direct control of all military affairs in the areas of Spain in which British armies would be campaigning. On March 15 Henry formally asked the regents to place Wellington in temporary command of the provinces contingent to Portugal. He pointed out that this move, combined with a complete reorganization of the military system and the appointment of new officers to command the armies, held out the only hope of Spain's making a successful effort against France.[87]

The regents were slow to respond to the request, and Henry believed that Blake was working to prevent the government's concurrence. His suspicion proved correct, as Bardaxi's response of March 25, 1811, bore the mark of Blake's xenophobia: "As the war in which Spain is engaged had from the beginning a national character, so decisive, as that there is scarcely an example in history of another war declared by the unanimous consent of a whole population, abandoned to themselves; and the free will of the said people, being its principal foundation, who aspire to independence, this will, must necessarily suffer a very sensible change, upon the fact of seeing, that the command, although it should be temporary, of some Provinces, is confided to a foreign General."[88] Bardaxi added, however, that Henry's request, along with the regency's reply, would be submitted to the Cortes for its opinion.

Wellesley was livid. He saw the regency's action as both irrational and detrimental to the cause. Moreover, Blake's motive in seeking the opinion of the Cortes was transparent. Although the Cortes was beginning to show some interest in military reform, it was obvious that it would not overrule a public decision by the regency. As Henry suggested, if the regents had truly wanted an unbiased opinion from the Cortes, they would have sought it prior to coming to a decision, or at least before that decision had been made public.[89]

Before discussions on Henry's request began in the Cortes, Blake began a concerted effort to discredit the British position. Although the Cortes's concurrence with the regent's decision was certain, rumors were circulated that Britain sought to replace all Spanish officers with their own. Spanish soldiers, it was alleged, would be subjected to corporal punishment, and Britain would seek to retain permanent possession of the provinces in question.[90] Having attempted to arouse Spanish pride, Blake delivered a stirring speech before the Cortes: "They had begun the war with no other support than their partriotism and. . . ought to look to nothing else to carry them through it." All things considered, the Cortes had no other choice but to veto Wellesley's request. It confirmed the regency's right to appoint and dismiss generals but pointedly warned the regents that they should always consider the great importance of maintaining good relations with Great Britain.[91]

The episode confirmed for Henry the fact that with Blake he was dealing with a cunning and pernicious politician. Henceforth, while Wellesley's major concern would remain that of military reform, he would take every opportunity to secure a change in regents. To do so would require considerable diplomatic leverage, obtainable only through the promise of increased subsidies. And there was little prospect of such a promise.

The situation in London had changed little. Though the ministry now had the support of the prince regent, fiscal distress remained a problem, and as a result Perceval was still reluctant to commit himself to an increase in war expenditures. The adverse effects of the Continental System on commerce and the failure of Britain's main source of specie—Veracruz—to meet demands were the primary causes of this distress. There was little Lord Wellesley could do about the former, but in the latter he saw a problem which could be controlled if not remedied. Wellesley realized that the precipitous decline in the production of specie was due to a dearth of quicksilver.[92] To alleviate the situation he induced the Spanish to abolish the royal monopoly on quicksilver as an incentive to increased production; to provide immediate relief quantities of quicksilver were sent from London to Veracruz free of charge. In the meantime, he applied for a license to purchase specie in Lima, known to be a lucrative, if distant, source of gold and silver.[93]

One result of Britain's economic situation was that Lord Wellesley was unable to comply with Spain's numerous requests for a loan. Instead he informed the Spanish they would have to content themselves with aid in kind, which would continue in a steady flow.[94] There were, however, other factors inhibiting Wellesley's desire to increase British aid to Spain. Public opinion in Britain was turning against Spain. Various reports had reached London of the Cortes's nebulous debates on constitutional issues, annoying many Britons who felt that its attentions would be better directed toward military and fiscal reform. More annoying still was Spain's refusal to grant trading privileges. Henry had reported that the Cortes would not risk losing the support of Cádiz's merchant community for the sake of British commerce; even if it would, trading concessions would be contingent on Britain's granting a loan.[95] The failure to achieve a trade agreement brought numerous complaints to Wellesley's office, primarily sentiments of British merchants and manufacturers with strong influence in Parliament.[96]

Another significant factor was Britain's predilection toward Portugal, where Wellington was about to assume the offensive. The prince regent's message to Parliament called for continued support for the Peninsular War in general but specifically asked for increased support for Portugal. In addition to the £1 million granted for 1810, the government wanted an additional £1 million for 1811. Perceval introduced the formal motion in the Commons on March 18, 1811, contending that the Portuguese had proved themselves effective and reliable and that the Portuguese government was doing everything in its power to support the resistance.[97]

In response the opposition did not question the valor or determination of the Portuguese. Instead, it questioned whether the allies were in as advantageous a position to pursue the French as they suspected. This doubt, coupled with the dire economic situation in Britain and Portugal's inability to support herself, led the opposition to question the wisdom of an increased subsidy, and even the decision to stay in the war at all.[98] The opposition's strongest appeal came from Mr. Freemantle, who believed the cause was hopeless. The British experience, as he perceived it, had been characterized solely by setbacks. With Napoleon's strong position in Europe, he saw no reason for this trend to change. "I must ever lament that what is done," he concluded, "can never, from the nature of its policy, be beneficial either to our allies or to this country."[99]

Robert Peel answered admirably for the ministry. "Under what circumstances then did his Majesty now call upon the House to renew the grant of aid to Portugal," he asked. "What last year was expectation, now was proof: what then was doubt, was now become certainty: what then was apprehension, was now confidence." Peel maintained that Wellington held the advantage in Portugal, and therefore all requests for aid should be granted. The motion was subsequently brought to a vote and carried with little opposition.[100]

In the House of Lords, Wellesley represented the government's case. In a comprehensive speech praising his brother's accomplishment in Portugal, the Marquess, like Perceval, argued that conditions necessitated an increase in subsidy. Besides, the Portuguese had proved themselves worthy of British support.[101] Lord Grenville answered, basing his opposition on Britain's poor financial state and his belief that the Peninsular War had reached a point of diminishing returns. Success in the Peninsula could come only when another front was opened in Europe, as Napoleon's resources were far too great for Britain to combat alone. Grenville's argument convinced no one; the motion carried easily.[102]

Parliamentary generosity toward Portugal went further. On April 8, 1811, in accordance with the regent's wishes, Wellesley moved in the Lords for a £100,000 grant for the relief of those Portuguese made destitute by the French invasion. The Marquess pointed out that the Portuguese had suffered greatly in preparing for the French invasion and were experiencing even more hardships in the retreat. They had demonstrated a determined willingness to resist, he continued, and helping them at this juncture would only make them stronger.[103]

The request was extraordinary, a fact which some members of Parliament detected. Those who opposed the motion maintained that Britain was doing all she could afford at the present and that freedom from

French domination was ample reward for their sacrifice. But the enthusiasm over Masséna's retreat and the humanistic nature of the motion appealed to members of both parties in each house. The motion passed with little discussion.[104]

Though Lord Wellesley must have been pleased with the increased subsidy for Portugal, he was still concerned with Spain's financial plight. Parliament granted the government an extraordinary budget, from which aid for Spain came, similar to that of 1810. Wellesley wanted more, of course, but Perceval was unwilling to make such a request, considering the disillusionment in Parliament over events in Spain. At one point, in fact, Lord Boringdon threatened an investigation of the Spanish army, and deferred only when Liverpool explained before the House that the alliance would suffer irreparably from such an inquiry.[105] Wellesley too was discouraged over Spain's performance. Consequently he ordered Henry to request that Wellington be given command of the provinces contiguous to Portugal and that British officers be incorporated into the Spanish army for the purpose of reorganization and reform. The Marquess was unaware that Henry had already made and been denied this request. Yet in this case Henry was authorized to negotiate on the premise that Britain would undertake to arm, clothe, and supply a force of 30,000 men in return for Spanish concessions.[106]

Lord Wellesley's dispatches reveal that he considered the Spanish army's dilapidated state of the utmost importance and wanted Henry to apply considerable pressure to secure improvements. Nonetheless he demonstrated a remarkable understanding of the Spanish character and its relation to the conflict. "You will avoid topics which might wound the national pride," he explained to Henry: "that sentiment (although partially injurious in its operation on some branches of the affairs of Spain) must be considered with esteem & respect as one of the sources of the independent spirit of the Spanish people and of their steadfast resistance to the designs of France."[107]

In the meantime, Parliament's attention remained centered on Wellington and Portugal. As reports of Masséna's retreat and Wellington's consequent advance reached London, enthusiasm grew. On April 26 another debate opened on a new motion of Thanks to Wellington. Lacking opposition, the debate was uneventful, except when Canning took the opportunity to attack the opposition for its position on the war and to justify his own policies as foreign secretary. The opposition chose to ignore Canning's tirade, and the motion passed unanimously in both houses.[108] Even the *Examiner* found itself, embarrassingly, in agreement:

"And though it is somewhat droll, not to say disgusting, to hear Ministers, on this occasion, calling to mind the purity of their political lives, and boasting of their systemic philanthropy and love of freedom, yet it is very gratifying to find them producing proofs that Lord Wellington foresaw the whole of the late proceedings in Portugal, and had laid his plans accordingly. Let such of us, then, as have doubted the prudence and ability of that General, do justice at once to him and to ourselves, and shew him that we have not withheld our praise because he deserved it, but because we were ignorant of that desert."[109]

Still there was no money for Spain, and the financial situation there was growing desperate. In this situation the convenient relationship between the foreign secretary and the minister plenipotentiary in Cádiz again proved invaluable. As had become his policy, Henry, although refusing to grant Spain the large sums she requested, subsidized the government with small amounts of cash for specific occasions or when he sought favor in return. Such had been the case in February when he advanced $25,000 for the removal of naval stores from Cartagena, and again on April 12, 1811, when he advanced $60,000 so that Blake might take an army to aid General William Carr Beresford, who was planning a siege of Badajoz in the wake of the French retreat.[110] In return for this grant, Henry obtained a license to purchase specie in Lima.

Spain's needs, however, extended beyond these specific grants, and on April 13 Bardaxi asked for a loan of $500,000.[111] Having already exceeded the limits of his authority, Henry did not feel that he could comply with the request. Yet the following day he granted the loan. Writing to the Marquess, he clarified his actions: "I have frequently had occasion to mention in my dispatches the pecuniary distress of the Sp. Gov't. It is now arrived at its full height, the treasury is entirely empty, the Gov't. has not credit sufficient to raise a dollar in the town, nor is there any prospect of their soon receiving a supply from the colonies."[112]

Already holding notes for over $1 million, Henry hedged this new loan with several conditions. First, he stipulated that it be repaid in specie, preferably in Lima. If this condition could not be met, then security was to be provided by receipts from the customhouse in Cádiz or from sums received from South America. Second, he demanded a new license for the exportation from Mexico, free of duty, of $5 million in specie. And finally, realizing that the Spanish were not receptive to his suggestions for military reform, he sought a guarantee that the money would be applied solely to the Spanish armies operating in Estremadura, Murcia, and Cádiz.[113] Henry considered Spanish acquiescence to these

conditions a major accomplishment and was confident that Lord Wellesley would support his decision to advance the money. On April 21, 1811,
he dispatched Captain George Cockburn to London with the details of
the transaction along with the license on Veracruz. He also sent an
urgent appeal for permission to advance funds to Whittingham and
Roche, who were suffering from Spain's troubled finances.[114]

With the knowledge that Portugal would soon be free of French
occupation and that the struggle would divert to Spain, the Marquess
realized he would have to make a realistic appraisal of how best to
employ his limited resources. The Cortes, he knew, continued to ignore
its most pressing problems, busying itself instead with discussion on
judicial reforms and the abolition of seignorial rights. The regents too
remained adamant in their refusal to confer command upon Wellington
or to employ British officers in the Spanish army. Whittingham and
Roche were making the only perceptible progress in Spanish military
reform. Consequently Wellesley gave Henry the authority to provide
these men with the pecuniary assistance they required. At the same time
he was instructed not to "give the Spanish Gov't. to understand that you
have received such authority; but you will state to them that you are
induced, by their urgent representations of their pecuniary distress, to
make advances for their relief."[115] The motive for such an approach was
to give Henry diplomatic leverage to force the Spanish to institute
necessary reforms.

The plan was sound, but again Henry faced Blake's opposition, made
even more pronounced by recent events. On May 16, 1811, allied forces
under the command of Lieutenant General Beresford met a French
corps commanded by Marshal Nicolas Soult at Albuera. The allies won a
costly and debatable victory, but the importance of the battle for Anglo-
Spanish relations lay in the behavior of the Spanish troops, led by Blake
and Castaños. At Albuera, although unable to maneuver, the Spanish
stood and fought, an event which even Wellington was forced to commend.[116] Encouraged by the regency, Spanish pride rose considerably in
Cádiz. The battle was portrayed as a Spanish victory, illustrative of
Spain's ability to handle her military affairs without British interference.[117]

This was unfortunate, for Henry was again about to seek a command
for Wellington. Because of public opinion, however, Henry decided it
would be better "to continue as we now are than to risk the chance of
offending those at the head of the armies by proposing a measure which
would put an end to their influence, and which, if it were rejected, might

place us in a worse situation than we are at present, inasmuch as it might destroy the cordiality actually subsisting between the British and Spanish commanders, by the jealousy it would occasion to the latter."[118] Moreover, General Castaños was endeavoring to cooperate with Wellington in Estremadura, as were Spanish forces operating in Galicia. Henry did not therefore consider the situation as desperate as it might have been. Wellington concurred: "I have no doubt whatever, that the Spanish Government will not comply with this requisition; and from all that I can see and hear, I am convinced that the demand will tend to interrupt much of the harmony and good will which exist amongst us at present."[119]

In London the Marquess also was increasingly frustrated. He was convinced that the cabinet had not made—and was not making—an adequate effort in Spain, in either manpower or money. Now, with the army's recent successes offering new opportunity, he called for greater determination on the part of his colleagues. From the beginning of the Peninsular War, the Marquess had seen the effort not as a means alone to destroy the power of France but, instead, only as a part of a broader effort. The placement of French power within acceptable limits, he hypothesized, "could be accomplished only by creating so powerful a diversion in the Peninsula as might enable the powers on the Continent to oppose the views of France, according to their respective means, so that France might be reduced to the alternative, either of relinquishing her designs in the Peninsula or elsewhere, or of making an imperfect effort in two quarters."[120] Spain and Portugal were showing that France was not irresistible—a fact which, in the case of Russia, was about to have significant influence.

Wellesley had been secretly negotiating with the Russians for weeks, and it now appeared that with guarantees of British aid they would break with Napoleon.[121] The Marquess realized that Britain could spare neither men nor money. Thus he saw the best assistance to be an escalation of the effort in Spain. In addition continued success in Spain, coupled with effective resistance by Russia, would, Wellesley believed, give rise to national movements in Austria, Prussia, and Denmark.[122] These reasons, plus the great opportunity presented in Spain alone, caused Wellesley to press his colleagues for greater subsidies.

Beyond these immediate rewards for Britain's efforts, he foresaw long-lasting effects: "With respect to the ultimate result of the proposed system, the advantages which it holds forth to England, if successful, are equally manifest and important. It will rescue the Peninsula and its colonies from the dominion of France; it will place the Peninsula and its colonies, from a natural union of interest, under the influence of Great Britain; it will relieve an extensive country, full of resource, military, naval, and commercial, possessing the richest and most extensive colonies in the world, from an oppressive Government, and establish in its room a Government of well-tempered liberty, formed upon the model of our own constitution; it will secure to us a great and efficient ally on the very border of France, and will enable us to impose a stronger restraint upon France than was ever before in our power. Such are the probable results of the system, if it be admitted that it be carried into effect."[123] Unfortunately, no significant increase in expenditure was forthcoming. Disappointed, Wellesley responded by treating his colleagues with scorn and by withdrawing from regular dealings with them. Seldom attending cabinet meetings, he conducted the business of the Foreign Office as he saw fit.

The period from September 1810 to June 1811 was a frustrating time for the Marquess and his brother Henry. It began optimistically with the convening of the Cortes and Wellington's victory at Bussaco, but political events in both countries quickly changed the atmosphere. The regency question in London, with all its uncertainties, inhibited decisive action by the Marquess, and the election to the regency in Cádiz of the nationalistic General Blake increased the incidence of Spanish obstruction to Henry's programs for reform. To compound matters, the events in London and Cádiz preyed on one another. Spain resented Britain's failure to provide what she considered to be adequate support. At the same time, Spanish obstinacy and inefficiency led many Britons to conclude that Spain was undeserving of such support. Thus it would be the Wellesleys' goal in the upcoming months to change these feelings of mutual hostility.

9

Wellesley Diplomacy, the Last Phase: Negotiations with the Blake Regency, June 1811– February 1812

In the remaining months of 1811, there was reason to believe that Spain might soon be liberated. Although the French were still strongly entrenched, they were not secure. Wellington was advancing cautiously but steadily into the province of Estremadura, Spanish guerrilla activity remained devastatingly effective, and there were rumors of an impending split between Napoleon and Alexander I of Russia. Such conditions would have seemed conducive to harmonious Anglo-Spanish relations. Yet, strangely, disagreements between the allies became more common, more acrimonious, and potentially more damaging to the alliance. Responding to the perplexing situation, Lord Wellesley and his brother Henry became unusually aggressive in their negotiations, exerting considerable pressures in an effort to resolve the problems of colonial revolt and military reform and to establish a more cooperative government in Cádiz.

Spain's rebellious American colonies were the most bewildering problem confronting the Wellesleys. Aside from the disruptive effect which the revolts had on Spain's economy, much of General Blake's success in spreading his Anglophobia around Cádiz was due to the belief that Britain was encouraging the revolutionary activity.[1] Spaniards remembered that General Layard had initially furnished arms, money, and military stores to the junta of Caracas. Now, annoyed by Britain's refusal to respect a blockade of the colonies, Spain's latent mistrust of her ally

184

reemerged. "The irritation and discontent excited by these suspicions," explained Henry, "tend considerably to weaken the influence of Great Britain here; to retard the conclusion of any commercial arrangement, and to impede the adoption even of those measures, which I have recommended as necessary to the successful prosecution of the War in the Peninsula."[2]

To combat this sentiment, Lord Wellesley made an official denial of Britain's encouraging the revolts in any way.[3] Yet he, more than anyone, knew that mere protestations of good faith would not solve the colonial problem. In fact the failure to offer tangible solutions to the principal issues had caused the revolts to spread. Chile and New Granada (Colombia) had declared their independence. Mexico was in a state of turmoil, held within the Spanish sphere only through the decisive action of General Venegas, its governor.[4] The colonies still looked to Britain for support. They appealed for money, arms, naval support, public recognition, and, in return, offered liberal trading concessions to British merchants.[5] Regrettably, Wellesley's options were few. If he openly sided with the colonies, he risked alienating the Spanish. If he stood by Spain's desire to suppress the revolts, the colonies would turn to France or the United States for support. The Marquess would then face the wrath of Britain's commercial community.[6] The dilemma seemed insoluble, but an attempt would have to be made to accommodate both sides.

Wellesley knew that accommodation—or reconciliation, as he called it—would be a difficult task. The Cortes had already declined one colonial demand—the right to equal representation in the governmental process—out of a sense of self-preservation. "The proposition cannot be admitted," Henry explained, "without placing the Peninsula completely at the mercy of the colonies, and I doubt whether the preservation of the Peninsula would be considered by the American Deputies to be of much importance, unless the welfare of the colonies were thought to be connected with it: on the other hand the rejection of the proposition cannot fail to increase the discontent already prevailing in the Colonies."[7] In an effort at compromise, the Cortes subsequently voted to allow equal representation in future meetings after a constitution had been completed. At the same time, however, the Cortes declared as rebels all those involved in the insurrections. Moreover, Henry informed his brother that before Spain would submit to mediation, she would probably want Britain's guarantee to "break off all communications with the colonies, & moreover assist Spain with her forces, in order to reduce them to their duty" if the mediation failed.[8]

Britain could never agree to such a condition, but Lord Wellesley sent to Spain his own plan for mediation, containing ten major points: there would be a cessation of all hostilities, including blockades and every other act of mutual injury between parties; a general amnesty would be granted to all Spanish Americans involved in the revolts; the Cortes would confirm colonial admission to a full, fair, and free representation in the Cortes and elections would take place immediately; free trade would be granted with a proper degree of preference to old Spain and her colonies; native Americans would be granted an equal voice in the governmental process; Spanish America would acknowledge allegiance to Ferdinand VII and his heirs; Spanish America would recognize the authority of the Cortes; the colonies would provide Spain with assistance during the course of the war; the colonies would cooperate in the war against France; finally, all articles would be guaranteed by Great Britain. Receiving Wellesley's proposals on May 27, 1811, Henry delivered them to Bardaxi without delay.[9]

Henry soon met with Bardaxi to discuss mediation, only to discover that Spain's position still differed significantly from Britain's. Spain refused to grant the rebellious colonies equal representation in the present Cortes or to issue a comprehensive redress of grievances. When queried on the reasons, Bardaxi answered that it would be unjust to grant concessions to the rebellious colonies which had not been granted to others. Henry, amazed by the narrowness of this view, quickly pointed out that although the colonies in revolt were the subject of the mediation, concessions must be extended to all colonies. Otherwise the revolutions would spread.[10]

Henry's opinions apparently made only a limited impression. Spain's counterproposals for mediation contained little with which he could agree. Beginning with a denunciation of British conduct toward the colonies, the project ended with a provision which Britain considered totally inadmissible. In what was to be a secret provision, Britain, if reconciliation was not accomplished in fifteen months, would agree to "suspend all communications with the said provinces, and moreover . . . assist the Mother Country with her forces in order to reduce them to their duty."[11] Wellesley argued vehemently against the article, informing Bardaxi that London would never agree to Spain's plan even if it remained a part only as a secret provision. He explained that the mediating power had to maintain an appearance of strict impartiality. If such a demand was justified, it would have to be made after the negotiations had failed. In the present situation, "it could have no other effect than that of indisposing those persons to a reconciliation, and inclining them to listen to the enemy." Bardaxi, however, defended the article as "perfectly just" and demanded that it remain a part of any overall plan for mediation.[12]

Already discouraged, Henry then had to confront what he considered a systematic attempt to undermine his influence in Cádiz. The regency had made it known that it considered Britain's conduct toward the colonies contrary to the spirit of the alliance. Rumors that Britain was concerned only with the defense of Portugal were circulated. Britain was supposedly allowing Spain to ruin herself in her own defense so that when Napoleon completed the conquest the country would be completely despoiled.[13] More serious was a resolution introduced in the Cortes prohibiting members of the government from communicating with foreign representatives for fear the latter might exert undue influence. Fortunately Henry was able to organize a successful protest to this motion, but he could do little to counteract public sentiment.[14]

Obstructions of this sort convinced Henry that the Spanish, beyond their unwillingness to compromise with the colonies, were not likely to undertake the military reforms he had repeatedly suggested. Speculating on the future, he saw that the only hope for reform lay in Britain's assuming the obligation of financing the Spanish troops. Considering Lord Wellesley's plan for Wellington to employ 30,000 Spanish troops under his command, Henry believed that it could not be refused if, in addition to arming and supplying the army, Britain also agreed to provide for paying the troops. The corps, coupled with those of Whittingham and Roche, would produce an army of 50,000 upon which Britain could depend. The project, Henry estimated, would cost nearly £6 million, but he considered it worthwhile, as he explained to the Marquess: "Since the commencement of the War in the Peninsula there never has been a moment when pecuniary assistance has been so much required, or promised to be attended with such advantageous effects, as the present. If, by a great pecuniary effort on the part of Great Britain, the war in the Peninsula is shortened by one campaign only, it will repay the whole sum, which I have ventured to recommend should be advanced to the Spaniards; and supposing it to be true that Bonaparte is likely to be engaged in a war with the Northern Powers, we never again can have so favorable an opportunity of bringing the War in the Peninsula to a successful issue."[15]

As the Spanish already knew, there was to be little help from London. On June 11, 1811, Lord Wellesley received an urgent appeal from

Admiral Don Ruiz de Apodaca for a loan of £2 million.[16] Apodaca apparently thought the time propitious for such a request—Parliament had just passed unanimous votes of Thanks for the Battle of Albuera, singling out the activity of the Spanish army. This was the first time the Spanish military had been commended in Parliament since the Battle of Baylen.[17] That Spencer Perceval still did not consider an increase in expenditures feasible should have become apparent to Apodaca when the prime minister opposed a motion in the Commons requiring the government to make greater exertions in Spain.[18] Nonetheless, Wellesley referred Apodaca's request to Perceval, who replied tartly: "The amount of 2,000,000 is totally out of the question and impossible."[19] Given the desperate state of Spain's finances, Perceval's decision increased tensions between the allies as well as between Wellesley and himself. Supplies and military stores continued their steady flow, but all available pecuniary assistance was directed to Roche and Whittingham.[20]

Henry's position, as a result, did not improve. With the Marquess paralyzed by Perceval's intransigence, Henry was forced to reject even a minor request of $250,000 for use by Blake's army.[21] This latest British rejection might have caused even more discomfort for Henry if it had not been for the opportune arrival of $1.5 million from Veracruz. Henry took the opportunity to waive Britain's right to $250,000 as partial payment for the loan of the previous July.[22] Although momentary good will resulted, Henry was clearly groping for a way to increase his influence and promote good will within the alliance. "I think, between ourselves," he wrote to Wellington, "that there is a very bad spirit prevailing here, and that it is increasing daily, and I am sure I know not what to do to correct it. I do not see how things are to go on here unless England furnishes some pecuniary assistance."[23]

Wellington sympathized with his brother but not with Spain: "Great Britain did not bring Spain into the contest. On the contrary, the war, in its commencement, and throughout its progress, has been carried on by the Spaniards without reference to our opinions, and generally in direct contradiction to our recommendation; and then we are to be blamed and abused, because, contrary to our own judgements and the plain dictates of military expediency, we don't choose to enter upon wild and visionary schemes which we have not the means of accomplishing. . . . Are we to blame if the Spanish armies are not in such a state as that they can be opposed to the Enemy? or if the Cortes have neglected their duty, have usurped the powers of the executive Gov't. & have misspent their time in fruitless debates? Are we in fault because by the mismanagement of the

American Colonies the world has been deprived of its usual supply of specie, & G. Britain in particular cannot find money to carry on her own operations, or aid the allies?"[24]

To Wellesley's dismay, British popularity continued to decline in Cádiz. The newest rumor was that Britain was sending more troops, under the pretext of a French threat, in an effort to seize Cádiz as she had Gibraltar.[25] Henry's patience was now exhausted. Writing to Bardaxi, he protested the allegations running rampant concerning British intentions: "In the name of the British Government and the whole British Nation, I most solemnly and distinctly disclaim all views of aggrandizement, of acquisition of territory or of property either in Europe or America, at the expense of the Spanish nation." He demanded the immediate publication of this statement along with letters favorable to Britain's conduct and a proclamation by the regency in favor of Great Britain. If the regents refused, Wellesley threatened to make public all the government's disastrous mistakes resulting from its failure to follow Britain's advice.[26] Reluctantly Bardaxi agreed, and within two weeks Henry was able to report that public abuse of Great Britain had ceased.[27]

While criticism of Great Britain subsided, public discontent with the Spanish government increased, making the conduct of diplomacy no easier. As discussions on a constitution were about to begin, the Cortes found itself confronted by a full-scale revolt by colonial deputies. On August 24 the deputies from Santafé petitioned the Cortes to be excused from the constitutional debate on the grounds of having neither proper representation nor adequate instructions from their province.[28] The Cortes, hoping to display the new constitution as a reflection of the views of both the mother country and the colonies, denied the request.[29] The American delegates, speaking as a group, agreed to obey the order to attend the discussions, but "that on that account they shall not be esteemed parties to depriving their constituents of the powers belonging to the latter in this particular, indeed so far from it that, while they immediately obey Y.M. order, they likewise enter the most solemn protest; that they ever leave untouched the right of their native provinces to remonstrate, at the proper season, against every circumstance in which they think themselves aggrieved."[30]

The Cortes now had a new problem. If it accepted this representation, the American delegates would be on record as cooperating only under protest. Consequently, the petition was returned without comment. Realizing the Cortes's motive, the Americans resubmitted their protest, hoping to force official action. Again it was refused and returned without comment. The delegates were then ordered to attend the sessions.[31]

Once this tactic had failed, the delegates attempted to resign individually as representatives to the Cortes. Again the Cortes proved obdurate, refusing to accept the resignations. Instead the delegates were once again ordered to attend the sessions and make no other acts of protest or resignation. Here the affair ended, but subsequently it had a profound effect on the Cortes's prestige. The Americans consistently defamed the work of the government and blamed it for the continuing problems in the colonies.[32]

Similarly, the Cortes drew considerable criticism from Spanish nobles residing in Cádiz by beginning discussions on the abolition of seignorial rights. Thus by the end of August Henry reported that defeatism and despondency were being spread in Cádiz by several groups: the pro-French hoped to sap Spanish morale; the Spanish grandees believed that they were being unjustly and illegally deprived of their favored economic and political status; the Americans resented the actions of the Cortes and in some cases viewed the cause of Spain as lost.[33] In addition, there were the merchants and lower classes, who remained implacable foes of the French. The merchant community was fiercely independent and wary of British intent, and the lower classes generally considered the regents to be inept. All things considered, Cádiz was not an ideal place in which to conduct the affairs of government or important diplomatic negotiations.[34]

In this atmosphere the Spanish failed to respond to the exigencies of the time. Consequently, his greatest concern being the state of the Spanish army, Henry decided to support military enterprises in which the Spanish had a minimal part. Besides supplying Whittingham and Roche with money, arms, military stores, and encouragement, Henry decided to pursue his brother's suggestion to establish a depot in Cádiz for the training of Spanish troops by British officers, and submitted a detailed proposal on August 29, 1811. Similar to the concept behind Whittingham's operation, the purpose of this new depot, to be commanded by Brigadier General William Doyle, was to train Spanish officers and soldiers to replace field casualties. The depot was to maintain a constant strength of 2,000 to 3,000 recruits, for whom Britain would assume the responsibility of supplying, arming, and clothing.[35] The Spanish quickly accepted the proposal because it offered several advantages to them. Britain would be bearing the bulk of the expense, but, more important, the recruits would go into the field wholly under

Spanish leadership.[36] The system was an acceptable compromise. Britain would provide the Spanish with proper training, while the Spanish army would retain its national identity.

Obviously most of Henry's problems remained. There was still the need to give Wellington some control over the armies with which he would be cooperating. The logistical problems so evident in the Talavera campaign also had to be resolved. The Spanish government had to do something to increase its revenues, and steps had to be taken to settle the colonial problem. Yet none of these issues could be dealt with effectively until Spain had a more efficient and resolute government. Henry believed this could not be achieved without constant diplomatic pressure from Great Britain, and the only pressure which Spain understood was pecuniary.[37] Quite simply Henry needed money for diplomatic leverage, and it would be up to Lord Wellesley to provide it.

Throughout the spring and summer of 1811, the cabinet's failure to respond to what the Marquess considered an obvious need for an expanded involvement in Spain in the form of men, money, and supplies further alienated him from his colleagues, most of whom he considered to be of inferior talent. Wellesley's absence from cabinet meetings became more frequent and his conduct of foreign affairs more independent. He maintained constant communication with Perceval, but their vast personal differences frequently led to disagreement. Perceval's timidity toward the war's financing so outraged the Marquess at times that he became insulting and sarcastic in his dealings with the prime minister. In one instance, Perceval sent to Wellesley for comment a draft of a speech he had composed for the prince regent to deliver at the closing session of Parliament in July 1811. Wellesley responded: "As you wish for free observation upon it, you will not be offended when I tell you that I object to the whole plan of it which in my opinion is totally inadequate to the occasion. The great feature of the present session (with respect to the very existence of this Empire) is the effort which Parliament has made to support the war in the Peninsula. And the principles from which that effort proceeded are, in my judgement, essentially necessary to be stated in the opening of the speech, quite distinctly from the success of our operation. . . . I really think that the general plan of the speech is far below the magnitude of the occasion."[38]

Lord Wellesley's conduct during these months was not surprising. As a visionary, he could perceive a change in momentum in Europe, a change which was placing Napoleon on the defensive. He had his own ideas on how to take advantage of this change but was powerless to implement them. It was this powerlessness, contrasting so drastically with his situation as governor-general in India, that created so many personal problems for Lord Wellesley. Arrogant by nature, he simply could not cope with his position in the cabinet. What was surprising about his behavior was that he did not succumb to despondency, as he was likely to do when disappointed.

Unable to persuade Perceval to place more money at Spain's disposal, the Marquess decided to work through the prince regent.[39] The two men were long-time acquaintances but not close friends. Realizing, however, that they had much in common philosophically, Wellesley set out to change the relationship in the summer of 1811. What Wellesley's precise motives were at this time can only be conjectured, but certainly he must have hoped to persuade the prince to apply pressure on Perceval to change his policy. By August the Marquess had become a member of the regent's circle of close friends.[40]

At the same time Wellesley was active on the diplomatic front, preparing the ground for an all-out European uprising against Napoleonic power. In constant communication with Russian representatives in an effort to alienate Alexander I from Napoleon, he had assurances that a split was imminent and that Russian trade would shortly be opened to Great Britain. Similarly, he cautiously wooed Sweden's favor, ignoring numerous encounters between British and Swedish vessels on the high seas.[41] From the volume of his dispatches, personal correspondence, and accounts of his contemporaries, Wellesley's activity was unprecedented in his term as foreign secretary. He worked long hours at his desk at Apsley House, his home on Hyde Park Corner.[42]

At the same time, he was active in Spanish affairs. Apodaca and the new Spanish ambassador, the Duke of Infantado, issued persistent complaints over Britain's failure to provide a loan and about her suspected activities in the American colonies.[43] Accustomed to such abuse, Wellesley was more concerned about his inability to secure additional money and the Spanish government's failure to respond to its colonial, military, and economic problems. He came to agree with Henry that Britain should work for a favorable change in government and give full support to the military projects of Whittingham, Roche, and Doyle.[44]

Since these men could take care of themselves, he directed his attentions toward bringing about a change of regents. On July 8, 1811, the Marquess met with Don Andres Angel de la Vega, who was about to depart London for Cádiz to assume a seat in the Cortes.[45] At the outset of the Spanish revolt in 1808, Vega was among the first Spanish representatives to travel to London to solicit aid. A known Anglophile, he had remained in London representing the interests of Galicia. What was discussed between Wellesley and Vega is not recorded, but it seems certain from subsequent events that the Marquess urged the Spaniard to use his influence to bring in a new regency.

On September 4, 1811, shortly after arriving in Cádiz, Vega initiated discussions with Henry Wellesley on governmental reform. "The Cortes should take without loss of a moment," he wrote, "the resolution of constituting a Regency, with competent and independent faculties to act, without being constrained in its operations, however, liable to be called to an account in due time."[46] For Henry this was like a voice from the wilderness, and he quickly replied. Agreeing that the regency had to be changed, Henry made several suggestions: the regents must be invested with unlimited powers for an agreed period of time; the government should be moved from Cádiz to a place where communications with the interior could exist; Wellington should be consulted on all military operations; the government should direct its attentions solely to military reform.[47] Although Vega could not comment on all of Henry's suggestions, he believed that the Cortes was well disposed to a change in regents and asked Henry's opinion of individuals he would prefer in the new government. Henry recommended the Duke of Infantado as the man best qualified to be regent and Henry O'Donnell as secretary of war. He also advised the employment of Pedro Cevallos, Padre Gil, and M. Cuesta. The main purpose of any new government, Wellesley explained, would be to establish closer cooperation with Britain. Vega accepted Henry's recommendations and a week later reported that a change was being negotiated and might take place within seven to ten days.[48]

Vega was overoptimistic. Opposition to his manueverings quickly mounted. In addition, sensing imminent change, the Princess of Brazil was again promoting her claims to the regency; this time her intrigues had a pernicious effect on Anglo-Spanish relations.[49] While her vocal supporters had worked persistently to influence members of the Cortes, Henry had never considered her a serious threat until September, when he realized the extent of her activities. For months she had been actively involved in events in Buenos Aires, giving military support to the governor of Montevideo, who was attempting to suppress the revolt.[50] Originally the British had viewed this as merely an effort at aggrandizement. In the summer months, however, she used the Braganzas' strategic position in America to undermine British influence in Spain, knowing that Britain opposed her claims to the regency. Writing to

Cádiz, the princess claimed that the British were acting against the interests of Spain in their conduct toward the colonies. To Lord Strangford, the British representative to the Portuguese court in Brazil, she attributed numerous schemes to assist the revolution in Buenos Aires. In one particularly hostile note, she reminded the Spanish "that there is no degree of baseness of which the English are not capable when their interests are concerned."[51]

The effect on the Spanish public of these accusations, coupled with opposition to Britain's terms for colonial mediation, gave the regents a reason to send troops to the rebellious colonies—an event which gave rise to an acrimonious debate between Wellesley and Bardaxi. Early in September 1811 the commercial interests of Cádiz offered $400,000 to finance an expedition of 4,000 men to Mexico, 2,000 to Caracas, and 2,000 to Buenos Aires.[52] Because it does not appear that the British embassy took the offer seriously, Wellesley must have been shocked when on September 19 Bardaxi informed him of the government's intention to send troops to America. Protesting, Wellesley pointed out that such action contravened the proposal for mediation, which called for cessation of hostilities, and violated the method and conduct of the war in the peninsula.[53] The protest had little effect. Bardaxi justified the proposed expedition, explaining that the regency, entrusted with responsibility for both internal and external affairs, was duty-bound to protect the loyalists in America. He pointed out that mediation had not yet been agreed upon; that Spain could not continue the war without the unqualified support of America; that men were not in short supply— only equipment; and that the expedition would be financed privately. "Moreover," Bardaxi remarked sardonically, "it is notorious that the succour hitherto granted by England to Spain, have not been so extensive as to admit of their being applied to other objects than those for which they were immediately solicited."[54]

Highly agitated, Henry tried another approach, maintaining that sending troops to America would be useless—only concessions could restore peace. Once 6,000 troops were sent, he explained, more would surely follow. The original detachment could not possibly be successful, and Spain would be embarking on a policy which would steadily drain her armed forces—men desperately needed in the peninsula.[55] Unmoved, Bardaxi informed Wellesley that the *Algeciras* and the *Mincho* were already sailing to Corunna to transport troops to America. To Henry the information proved extremely galling. The two ships had recently been refitted in London at Britain's expense, and the troops from Galicia, to be employed in the operation, had been outfitted and supplied wholly by Britain since the outset of the war.[56]

Learning of Spain's intentions, Lord Wellesley, in London, intensified his efforts at mediation. To this point, Spain had essentially rejected Britain's conditions for mediation, as Britain had rejected Spain's counterproposals. Believing his proposals were the acceptable minimum for the colonies and that mediation was the only practical solution to the problem, the Marquess planned to prevail upon the Spanish to accept his terms. To this end, he decided to appoint three British commissioners of mediation and send them to Cádiz, presenting the Spanish with a fait accompli. Either the Spanish would agree to sail to America to begin mediation on British terms or they would be held responsible for the failure of the mediation. Either decision would be to Britain's advantage. If the Spanish refused to cooperate, Britain could accuse them of obstruction, thus retaining some flexibility for her actions. Wellesley appointed Charles Stuart, George Cockburn, and Philip Morier as tentative commissioners.[57]

Events moved slowly. The commissioners needed time to prepare themselves, and proper transportation had to be secured. Moreover, Wellesley, who had lately been enjoying a favorable press, found some segments of British public opinion decidedly against mediation. The *Morning Chronicle* wrote: "What can be effected by Commissioners in South America, it is very difficult to conjecture, and we cannot but consider it impolitic to intermeddle in any way between Spain and her colonies, or rather perhaps, it may be said, after the events that have taken place, what were her colonies. A mission of this kind we think much better let alone than undertaken. The true policy of this country with respect to South America, is to let events take their course. The very attempt on our part to interfere, will impress the people of America with an idea that our Commissioners go there not as friends, but as being allied with the Spanish Government, at home against their interests."[58] Obviously the prospect of increased trade in South America was foremost in the minds of many Britons.

In Cádiz, Henry, now advanced to the rank of ambassador extraordinary and minister plenipotentiary, continued to watch over a deteriorating situation. The Spanish government was in total disrepute, failing either to come up with any remedy for military problems or to cooperate with Great Britain.[59] Moreover, Vega had encountered additional problems in his effort to effect a change of regents. Through his urgings the three major parties of the Cortes, which the British embassy labeled simply the liberal, antiliberal, and American parties, met to discuss the problem. No agreement could be reached. "After this period Mr. Vega seems to have made but little progress in his plans," Vaughan noted. "The choice of Regents brought into action private interests & personal animosities in such a manner that some weeks elapsed without any communication being made to Mr. W. [Wellesley] on the part of Mr. Vega."[60] The real obstacle lay with those who were trying to maintain Blake in his present position. Undoubtedly frustrated with the turn of events, Henry saw British interference in the management of the war as the only means of making the Spanish army respectable. Realizing that Spain was now destitute of funds, he proposed that Britain provide for the clothing, feeding, and arming of 100,000 Spanish soldiers, on condition that Wellington would be given overall command of these troops and that aid would be issued only when a soldier was prepared to enter the field. Henry estimated the cost of this enterprise to be over $4.5 million a year, but the proposal did have the advantage of requiring no specie.[61]

At the same time Henry suggested that the junta of Cádiz be granted a loan of £530,000 to help support the national government and the allied army in Cádiz. The loan would be granted in monthly payments of not more than $200,000, one-half to come in the form of provisions. Henry conceded the additional demand on the money market that supplied Wellington but felt that the results would make the hardship worthwhile.[62] The junta would assume responsibility for the maintenance of an army of 20,000 men, funds could be easily directed to Doyle, and British influence in Cádiz might increase. A softening in the attitude of the Cádiz merchants toward opening trade with the colonies might also result. If the loan was not granted, he explained, discontent with the government and within the army might lead to disastrous results.

The regents, meanwhile, remained obdurate, proceeding with their plans to send troops to America and doing their best to discredit Britain. Outraged, Henry determined to oppose the election of regents of whom he did not approve and to control more tightly the distribution of British subsidies. On November 18, 1811, Vega presented Henry with a list of prospective regents and asked him to comment on them. The list contained the names of General Blake, Admiral Villa Vicencio, M. Rodrigo, M. Bodego, and M. Valésques de León.[63] With straightforward and unmistakable clarity, Wellesley informed Vega that if Rodrigo and Blake, men he considered inimical to Anglo-Spanish harmony, were appointed to the new regency, he would withdraw from Cádiz. Of the remaining three, Henry could approve of only Villa Vicencio; the other two resided in Mexico and were of little note. Henry also lamented that the Duke of Infantado was not included on the list.[64]

Vega explained that the latest plan was to form a regency of three men—Blake, Vicencio, and Bodega—and to change some of the ministers. Henry, who had already adequately expressed his opinion of Blake, explained that the plan would produce little change and thus should be avoided. Moreover, he expressed disappointment that complete revamping of the ministerial system had not been planned. Vega then put two questions to Henry: "Whether, in the formation of a new Regency, the exclusion of Gen'l Blake was indispensable," and "Whether, in the event of his removal being impracticable, it would be expedient to defer for the present any attempt to affect a change in Gov't." Rather than going on record as opposing any individual, Wellesley stated only that the new government should be based on harmony and cooperation between Britain and Spain but, given the ambassador's well-known opinion of General Blake, he had made his position quite clear.[65]

Although Henry now realized that Vega lacked the power to effect what he had originally proposed, he would not stand idly by and let matters take their own course. The regents were continuing their obstructive behavior. They had failed to cooperate with Whittingham, Roche, and Doyle, who were achieving success in their respective projects. Consequently Henry decided to dispatch Charles Vaughan to London to confer with Lord Wellesley on negotiations for a change in government.[66] Before Vaughan departed, however, Henry learned of a well-conceived plan to destroy British credibility and his own efforts to bring about a change in regents. On December 17, 1811, Blake's adherents secured passage of a motion in the Cortes stating that some direct trade would be granted to Great Britain if a treaty of subsidy was concluded: "The General and Extraordinary Cortes anxious to avail themselves of all means to supply the present wants; have authorized the Council of Regency immediately to proceed to treat with the British Government, concerning the assistance, which it may think proper to afford to Spain, offering it a participation with the commerce of America upon the following basis. That it shall be for a certain and limited time. That the Ports through which the trade shall be carried on, shall be specified. That the number of vessels to be admitted, and the merchandise they convey shall be determined; and His Majesty orders, that he may be previously informed of whatever convention may be entered into, in order that he may approve of it, if He should think it advisable."[67]

Henry soon learned that the real object of this measure was to discredit him. It was alleged that he had coerced the government into making this concession by promising to drop his demand for a new government if it passed. Henry therefore refused to accept the offer. Fortunately, he possessed a letter he had written prior to this latest action in the Cortes. The letter, which was his response to a query on whether Britain would conclude an agreement on subsidies in return for trade concessions, stated: "The question of commerce is one upon which I should wish to decline giving any opinion at this moment, and I have avoided mixing it with the question relative to the change of the Gov't., in order that there may be no ground for supposing that in urging the necessity of changing the Gov't., Great Britain has any interest unconnected with the immediate welfare & interest of the Spanish nation."[68]

Henry had inadvertently upstaged the Cortes and now held the diplomatic advantage. Sending Vaughan to London made the Cortes uneasy because Vaughan, more than anyone else in the British embassy, knew the Spanish and their motives. Because Vaughan was capable of producing a negative report on conditions in Cádiz, greater consideration was subsequently given to a change in regents.[69] In addition the Cortes had now committed itself to trade concessions in return for a subsidy agreement. Thus, if more money was procured, Britain would suddenly find herself with a trade agreement, a favorable change in government, better conditions for mediating the colonial disputes, and perhaps even Wellington in command of a Spanish army. Vaughan was instructed to explain these developments to Lord Wellesley and to emphasize that the cabinet must make a decision before the money arrived in Cádiz from Mexico or Lima, altering Henry's bargaining position.[70]

Vaughan arrived in London on December 28, 1811, to find Wellesley alienated from the cabinet. That autumn he and Perceval had been in constant disagreement. Embittered over what he undoubtedly felt was Perceval's total lack of resolve, the Marquess ignored the prime minister entirely, making appointments, granting rewards, and forming policy without consultation. Perceval justifiably considered such behavior insulting and unwise. The two talented but stubborn men bickered, each ignoring the other's advice.[71] The proper course for Wellesley, given his sentiments toward the cabinet, would have been resignation, but he remained at his post, believing he would shortly assume the premiership himself.

As mentioned, Wellesley had become a member of the regent's intimate circle of friends, hoping the prince would promote his views. This hope had proved to be in vain, owing to Perceval's independence, but now with the Regency Bill about to expire, Wellesley apparently believed the regent could be induced to make a change in ministries. Since he had been working his way into closer confidence with the regent, Wellesley's views came to dominate the prince, as a letter addressed to Lord Buckingham indicates: "I presume it must be that, as the Prince is determined to make an administration, of which he is determined to be himself the framer, and to carry on the war in Spain on principles known to be adverse from those of Lords Grenville and Grey; and as Perceval will not go to the lengths, which, according to Lord Wellesley, are necessary to carry on the war with effect; and that Lord Wellesley, on whom everything turns, will not serve any longer with Perceval; therefore he, Lord Wellesley, will be the only person eligible to that high situation."[72]

In addition to the issue of the war in Spain, Wellesley also appealed to the regent's sentiments on Ireland. Ever since his initiation into politics, the Marquess had favored Catholic emancipation as the best solution to the Irish problem. George III had been implacably opposed to emancipation and had declared that he would tolerate no ministry unless it agreed not to discuss the issue. When the Perceval ministry assembled on this understanding, Wellesley considered the war an issue of greater importance than Catholic emancipation. But he had not abandoned his original belief, and he now considered the two issues related. At a time when the government refused to give what he considered proper support for the peninsula, he was annoyed to find that 17,375 soldiers were being employed in Ireland to maintain a peace that he believed could be achieved by merely granting emancipation.[73] Knowing that Perceval's fierce opposition to emancipation was in contrast to the prince regent's favorable attitude, Wellesley did not hesitate to express his opinion. Moreover, he could see that a liberal position on this controversial issue could form the basis for a coalition with the Whigs—if that proved necessary.[74]

Thus Wellesley's course was determined. When discussion in the cabinet began on the permanent regency settlement, Wellesley took the opportunity to champion the interests of the Prince of Wales. Discussions centered on the allowance for the regent's civil list, maintenance of the royal household, and payment of the regent's personal debt. In every case the tightfisted Perceval refused to grant what the prince requested, and in every case Wellesley voiced the cabinet's only objections. Being a minority of one, he could do little to alter the course of the discussions, but he could demand that his objections be made public, which he did on December 24, 1811.[75]

Such was the situation when Vaughan arrived in London. As might be expected, he and Wellesley met with little success regarding the subsidies for Spain. Wellesley secured the cabinet's concurrence on Henry's suggestion to arm and clothe 100,000 soldiers and to provide the £500,000 loan for the junta of Cádiz—but there could be no treaty of aid because of the scarcity of specie. Vaughan was bitterly disappointed, but did not blame the Marquess. "I am afraid that there is no hope . . . of obtaining larger succours," he wrote to Henry, "notwithstanding the liberal views of Lord Wellesley—and I have therefore ventured to state, that from such limited supplies and from the manner in which it is thought proper to grant them, no great expectation ought to be entertained by the Govern't at home of a material and permanent improvement in the temper of the Government of Spain."[76] Even after Vaughan explained that if Britain could guarantee a certain amount of aid, then Spain would open her trade, change her government, and reform her army, the cabinet refused to change its policy. Henry was instructed to negotiate by threatening to withdraw aid, not by promising more.[77]

As for other matters, Lord Wellesley ordered Henry to desist from becoming directly involved with the Cortes in securing a change of government. To do so, Wellesley warned, would create jealousy and involve Britain directly in all errors which a new government would commit. Henry was instead to retain control of all aid supplied, determining how and when it would be applied, as a means of influencing the Spanish government. If the Spanish refused to comply with his demand for a new government or to confer partial command on Wellington, Henry was to protest strongly, suspend communications, and await instructions.[78]

Henry was given license to supply monetary assistance to the Spanish as he saw fit. The amount of the grant would be £600,000 to be distributed £100,000 at a time at two-month intervals. The only condition was that the British government would not allow its aid to be used in prosecuting hostilities against Spanish America. Henry was "to require positive assurance that no similar misapplication of the British supplies shall again be attempted." And if possible he was to secure the recall of the Galician troops from Mexico.[79]

Actually, what was occurring in London meant little, for events in Cádiz were proceeding on their own course. On December 29, 1811,

Bardaxi notified Henry of what Spain had in mind in return for trade concessions. Spain first wanted a loan of £10 million within 18 months. For security, Britain would receive two-thirds of the duty levied on British goods entering Spanish America as part of the trade agreement. Second, Spain demanded a formal treaty of subsidy, pointing to the treaty of 1809 and her past performance in the war as justification: "It may well be said, and with great truth," explained Bardaxi, "that England has never yet found in any Power, a more sure guarantee for the employing well those subsidies, than she has in the well known sentiments . . . which animate the Spanish people." Specifically, Spain wanted Britain to guarantee that she would maintain on a war basis 100,000 Spaniards, fully armed, clothed, and appointed.[80]

Henry knew that the request was too extravagant. Yet what annoyed him most was Spain's assumption of the right to British aid and her assertion that Britain had not lived up to the treaty of 1809. Outlining the amount of aid in both material and specie, Henry asked: "Can any assurance be given to the Ministers of His Royal Highness the Prince Regent which shall enable them to state to Parliament, that, nowithstanding [sic] the disasters of the last year, a system has been formed from which better things may be expected in future? Whenever these assurances are given, and can be depended upon, the calls upon Great Britain for increased sacrifices may be made with better grace." Further, he reiterated that he had never demanded the grant of free trade as the price of a subsidy treaty. Finally, he informed Bardaxi that all discussions would be forwarded to London.[81]

After disappointing the Spaniards on this point, Henry had little reason to expect any action on a change in government. But the uncertainty created in Spanish circles by Vaughan's mission and the disappointing performance of the Blake regency stirred the Cortes to action. On January 12, 1812, a decree was passed calling for a change in government with the hope that Britain would be satisfied with the new regents. The Cortes also agreed that no royal personage would for the present be placed at the head of the Spanish government, a pledge that eliminated the threat of the Princess of Brazil. Henry was subsequently informed that at least two of the regents would be of his choosing. Henry's despair quickly turned to optimism. Even without an enormous increase of support from London, he could count on a greater degree of cooperation from the Spanish government on military matters and the problem of colonial mediation.[82]

In contrast to his brother, Lord Wellesley had no reason to be cheer-

ful. Political events in London were not developing as he had predicted.
With Parliament reconvened and the prince regent about to assume
unrestricted authority, there appeared to be a good prospect that the
prince would call together a coalition cabinet based on strong support
for the war and Catholic emancipation. The Marquess busily prepared
himself for this eventuality, again opening discussions with Canning.[83]

After the opening session of Parliament, however, prospects for a
coalition government must have seemed less appealing to Wellesley. He
had undoubtedly hoped that Wellington's progress in the peninsula
would modify the Whigs' stand on the war, making coalition less difficult. This proved wishful thinking, as Lord Grenville made a bristling
antiwar speech in the opening session.[84] This blow to Wellesley's plans
was followed by an even greater setback when the ministry announced
that there would be no compromise on the question of Catholic rights.[85]
His position in the cabinet now became untenable. On January 16, 1812,
he told the prince regent of his intention to resign, hoping that the
prince would soon dismiss Perceval.[86] The following day Wellesley met
with one of his few friends in the cabinet, Lord Bathurst. He explained
that his resignation was not a sudden decision but rather one which he
had been contemplating since October 1810 and postponed only because of the instability created by the regency question. His primary
reason for retiring, Wellesley explained, was his being denied the leading role in the cabinet that he had been led to assume would be his when
he accepted office in 1809. Instead he found himself "frequently executing the suggestions and opinions of others, not his own." He conceded that the habits he had developed as governor general had made
him less receptive to discussion, but he honestly believed that the
grounds on which he strongly disagreed with his colleagues—Spain and
the Catholic question—there was only one valid point of view.[87] Writing
to Perceval, the Marquess announced his intentions to the prime minister with the cordial but wholly untrue assurance "that my sentiments and
my determination are entirely unconnected with any feelings of un-
kindness or disrespect."[88]

The prince regent refused to accept Wellesley's resignation, asking
him to stay at his post until further arrangements could be made. To
Perceval, this meant until a successor could be found; to Wellesley, it
meant until the Regency Bill expired and the prince assumed full control. There would be no decision until the Regency Bill expired in
February, but Wellesley's fate was sealed. With Grenville's and Grey's
continued opposition to the war, there was little hope that they would

cooperate with Wellesley. As for a realignment of the Tory cabinet, here old problems also remained. Canning and Castlereagh would not serve together. Wellesley would not serve without Canning; Sidmouth would not serve with Canning; the regent would not tolerate Sidmouth; Canning and Wellesley would not serve unless there was a liberalization on the Catholic question; Wellesley would not serve unless Perceval stepped down as prime minister. Amid these complexities the cabinet decided on February 17, 1812, to accept Wellesley's resignation and to replace him with Castlereagh.[89] The prince, on the other hand, was not prepared to accept the resignation until he had received an answer to an offer which had been made to Grey and Grenville. As expected, however, they refused to cooperate.[90]

The prince regent has generally and justifiably been described as unpredictable, unreliable, and irresolute, but in Wellesley's case there was little he could do. He was not turning away from his friend because of any of these weaknesses but, rather, because it was the only choice open to him. On February 15, 1812, Lord Wellesley was informed that Perceval would be retained as prime minister. Four days later, shocked at the sudden turn of events, he gave up the seals of office.[91] Even the *Examiner*, never fond of the Marquess, expressed regret: "The Marquis Wellesley has not only resigned, but is to be succeeded by Lord Castlereagh.—Another Walcheren Expedition may therefore be expected."[92] The editor, like many Britons, realized that Wellesley, for all his faults, had demonstrated in his brief tenure as foreign secretary a comprehensive grasp of foreign policy. He was the first minister to see that Britain's resources could be efficiently applied in only one place and that only through the example of success would the rest of Europe respond against French expansion.

10

Into the Wilderness

The prince regent's decision to retain Perceval was a staggering blow to Lord Wellesley, who found himself in a position in which he had the support of neither the Tories nor the Whigs. Yet Wellesley's career did not come to an end in February 1812. After recovering from his disappointment, the Marquess spent the spring of 1812 attempting to gain the premiership. Only when he failed in this last bid for political preeminence did his influence as a leader in British politics begin to wane.

Wellesley could not have timed his resignation more poorly. While he had been maneuvering for the premiership, important changes took place in Spain which could have had a positive effect on his career if he had remained as foreign secretary. On January 19, 1812, in what was considered the first step in the liberation of Spain, Wellington had forced the French to surrender Ciudad Rodrigo.[1] The city's capture resulted in a sudden surge of British prestige in Cádiz, which Wellington enhanced when, in an uncommon display of tact and diplomacy, he passed control of the city to General Castaños.[2] Three days later the Cortes announced the appointment of a new regency, consisting of the Duke of Infantado, General Henry O'Donnell, Admiral Villa Vicencio, Don Joaquin Mosquera, and Don Ignacia Ribas. Henry Wellesley, delighted with the change of regents, wrote that the new regency "promises to afford to Great Britain the influence which she ought to possess in the Councils of

204

Spain, and to be productive of that change of system without which it is in vain to hope for a successful issue to the contest in which we are engaged."[3]

These events hac inestimable effects in Great Britain. Perceval promptly moved and carried Thanks to Wellington and his army in both Houses of Parliament, and several days later Parliament agreed also to increase the general's annuity.[4] The import of the parliamentary debates, which were characterized by relatively little debate, was that they illustrated a fundamental change in the way many Britons perceived the war in the peninsula. It was now believed that there was hope for success. Wellesley could have received much of the credit for these positive changes abroad and at home had he remained as foreign secretary. Instead, he watched as the praise fell to Perceval.

Still the Marquess was not yet a forgotten man. Writing from Spain, Wellington expressed regret over the resignation.[5] Others followed suit. In Lisbon, Charles Stuart was particularly concerned. "I am greatly distressed by the intelligence, conveyed in your's of the 2nd March, of Lord Wellesley's retirement, and the unfortunate state of affairs, which has followed the assumption of unrestricted authority on the part of the Prince Regent," he wrote. "I am at a loss to conceive how at the very moment, when the effects of the system Lord Wellesley has pursued during the last two years began to be evident in almost every part of Europe, that any motive should induce the Prince to part with a minister, who I really believe to be the only man in the country, who is equal to manage an Administration, of which the leading principle must be (if we are to continue an independent nation) the maintenance of the contest on a scale, corresponding with the objects, which it is intended to obtain."[6]

More important, Wellesley was also considered an important factor in British politics. The Perceval cabinet sought his support despite past disagreements, realizing that its own position in Parliament was anything but secure. For his part the Marquess agreed to cooperate in debate, but all parties realized that this assurance was equivocal at best.[7] Bathurst, in an effort to prevent complete alienation, kept Wellesley well informed on peninsular affairs and the progress of the war.[8] At the same time, however, Perceval sought to take advantage of the increased enthusiasm for the war. Debates were launched and carried in Parliament for the maintenance of the Portuguese subsidy. So confident of his position was Perceval at the conclusion of these debates that he ventured to increase the Spanish pecuniary subsidy by £400,000, two-thirds more than he had been willing to grant in January.[9]

Perceval's decision on the subsidy both pleased and annoyed Lord Wellesley. Naturally the Marquess believed it was the correct course of action, but for nearly two and a half years he had listened to Perceval refuse his recommendations for increased expenditures on the grounds that they were not economically feasible. Now, with Perceval increasing aid when the state of Britain's economy was unchanged, it appeared that his earlier policy had been governed more by politics than economics. Wellesley consequently determined to abandon the government entirely to pursue a more self-seeking course. He opened an almost daily correspondence with Canning, who was more than willing to work for Perceval's downfall.[10] As a first step Canning, along with Lord Boringdon, urged the Marquess to state before the House of Lords his reasons for resigning. It was hoped that such a revelation would deprive Perceval of the prestige he was acquiring from Wellington's successes and would transfer it to Wellesley.

In a motion put before the House of Lords calling for a more efficient administration, Boringdon asked Lord Wellesley if he "would in the course of this debate explain the reasons which had enduced him to resign, at a moment when his services, with a view to the war in the Peninsula, were so very essential."[11] In the subsequent debate Wellesley remained silent, to the consternation of his friends. His failure to speak, attributed by some to nervousness and by others to the fact that the speaker, Lord Eldon, had refused to call on him, left Perceval unscathed.[12] Further, the prime minister later made good use of another British success, the fall of Badajoz. On April 27 Thanks to Wellington were again easily passed by both houses, leaving Perceval more entrenched than ever.[13]

In light of these events Wellesley began work on a memorandum, intended for public consumption, outlining the reasons for his resignation. The Marquess could of course say nothing that would surprise the Perceval cabinet, but his account of Perceval's opposition to increased subsidies for Spain could affect public opinion. Before the memorandum could be published, however, on May 11, 1812, Perceval was assassinated as he entered the House of Commons.[14] Suddenly the already uncertain state of British politics became chaotic. Liverpool took over temporarily as prime minister pending new arrangements.

The cabinet met on May 13 to decide its course of action. The members concluded that the government could survive only if Wellesley and Canning were included. Subsequent negotiations proved complicated. First, the discussion proceeded on the premise that Liverpool would be prime minister, and neither Wellesley nor Canning had a high opinion of his abilities. Second, Castlereagh was already a member of the ministry, giving rise to old jealousies. Finally, there were problems of principle. Would the new ministry pledge itself to an increased effort in the peninsula? Would it favor Catholic emancipation? Would members of the opposition be asked to join? Liverpool replied in the negative, causing Wellesley and Canning to decline his offer.[15] Clearly, however, it was Liverpool's reluctance to increase that effort in Spain that disturbed the Marquess most:

> It was always stated to me, that it was *impracticable to enlarge* that system. I thought that it *was perfectly practicable* to extend the plan in the Peninsula and that it was neither safe nor honest towards this country or the allies to continue the present inadequate scheme.
>
> From Ld. Liverpool's statement on this point, it is evident, that since my resignation, it has been found practicable to make some extension of the system in the Peninsula; but it is still intimated that my views are more extensive than the resources of the country can enable the government to reduce to practice.[16]

Beyond these issues it was apparent that both Wellesley and Canning saw an opportunity to break Liverpool's efforts, thrusting themselves to the forefront in the formation of a new ministry. It was as clear to them as it was to Liverpool that a Tory ministry would have a difficult time standing without their support. Their reasoning proved correct. On May 21 Stuart-Wortley, a Tory, carried a parliamentary address to the prince regent, asking him to take the necessary steps to secure an efficient administration.[17] Liverpool subsequently resigned on May 22, 1812. Wellesley became the obvious candidate to assume the task of putting together a new government.

The Marquess had, however, prejudiced his chances with two ill-conceived publications. On the morning of May 21, 1812, the *Times* published Wellesley's correspondence with Liverpool relative to his returning to the cabinet along with Canning.[18] Although intended to show Liverpool's inflexibility on basic issues, the correspondence appeared before Wellesley had notified the acting prime minister of his intentions. The indiscretion embittered the cabinet, which blamed Wellesley to a certain extent for the success of Stuart-Wortley's address. To compound matters there appeared at the same time Wellesley's statement containing his reasons for resigning from the Foreign Office.[19] His motives for

resignation were by now well known, and so this revelation shocked no
one. Rather its significance lay in several deprecating remarks directed at
the late prime minister, Spencer Perceval. Wellesley claimed, among
other things, that Perceval was incompetent and incapable of filling the
office of prime minister.[20] Obviously Perceval could not answer the
charges, a fact which alienated both the cabinet and the British public.

It seems unlikely that Wellesley personally submitted the statement for
publication. Instead, it was probably the work of his friends Benjamin
and Thomas Sydenham.[21] For days, the *Morning Post* and the *Morning
Chronicle* had been embroiled in a debate over Perceval's merits and his
decision to accept Lord Wellesley's resignation. The controversy, which
actually centered on Wellesley's reputation, coupled with the opportunity to strike a blow at Liverpool and his colleagues, must have been an
irresistible inducement to Wellesley's coterie. This explanation for the
appearance of the statement was accepted even by the *Morning Post,* a
confirmed admirer of Perceval: "We have scarce a doubt, that on duly
reconsidering the various topics, the Noble Marquis will not feel much
indebted to his overofficious friends, who have forced into public notice,
at such a time a statement, which alas! Mr. Perceval cannot himself now
answer, and the publication of which, under such circumstances, we are
persuaded, no man will more sincerely regret than the Noble Marquis
himself."[22]

Regardless of the conditions leading to the two publications, their
appearance so alienated Liverpool and his friends from Wellesley that
the cabinet resolved "to have no further communication" with him.[23]
Thus a Tory ministry under Wellesley's leadership was totally out of the
question. Consequently the Marquess, with Canning's support, explored
the possibility of a coalition cabinet based on Catholic emancipation and
strong support for the Peninsular War. Wellesley spent the next week in
extensive communications with the prince regent, Canning, and various
members of the opposition.[24] Although Wellesley's stand on the Catholic
question and the continuing success in the peninsula had endeared him
to some Whigs, others still viewed him with suspicion or even hostility.
Creevey writes: "My jokes about Wellesley are in great request. Lady
Holland said to me on Sunday in the drawing room after dinner—
'Come here and sit by me, you *mischievous toad,* and promise that you
won't begin upon the new Government with your jokes. When you do,
begin with those Grenvilles.' I dined at old Tankerville's yesterday, who
said— 'Creevey, never desert Wellesley! give it him well, I beg of you.'
Sefton asked me to dine there today, evidently with the same view."[25]

On June 1, 1812, the prince regent commissioned Wellesley to form a ministry. The Marquess subsequently extended to Lords Grey and Grenville official invitations to join him in a coalition government. Though he promised four seats to their party, they hesitated, asking for more time to consider the proposal.[26] When Wellesley reported their reply to the regent, he took it as an outright refusal. Presuming that the Marquess could do no better, the prince asked Lord Moira to put together a new government, ending Wellesley's last chance at becoming prime minister.[27] The *Morning Chronicle,* sensing inevitability in his failure, nonetheless expressed disappointment:

> The termination of Lord Wellesley's commission to form a Ministry was a severe disappointment to the wishes of the country; but it was, we are convinced, in the judgement of all impartial men, a necessary consequence of the limited and conditional authority with which he was invested.
>
> We do not dispair, because we are confident, that Lord Wellesley, and Lord Grenville, Lord Moira and Lord Grey, are all animated by the same spirit of the occasion—all earnestly zealous to promote the welfare and wishes of the Country, and all equally disposed to sacrifice every consideration but that of character and honour (in the maintenance of which the public is scarcely less interested than themselves) to the attainment of an end, which is become indispensible to the safety of the Crown, and essential to the happiness of the Empire.[28]

Lord Moira had no more success than Wellesley, and on June 8 Liverpool assembled a government which would remain in power with minor changes for the next fifteen years.[29]

Lord Wellesley would never again be considered for a high cabinet post, and as a result his contribution to British diplomacy has been largely forgotten. Yet in two and a half years, his direction of foreign policy, in both practical and theoretical terms, changed the course of the war against France and was decisive for success in the peninsula.

Until the year 1808 British foreign and military policy had been characterized by the granting of pecuniary assistance to any country willing to confront France, by small diversionary expeditions to the continent, and by a systematic effort to seize French colonial possessions throughout the world. The first two were totally unsuccessful, while the last made little difference to the situation in Europe. The French invasion of Portugal and the Spanish revolt, however, gave new opportunity

to Great Britain. To take advantage of the opportunity, British troops
were sent to Iberia. Still, while England had committed herself to the
peninsula, so too was she committed to Pitt's policy of military diversions.
Failing to conceive any clear-cut policy for the peninsula, the Portland
ministry embarked on an effort to open a second front with the ill-fated
Walcheren expedition.

Aside from the fact that the Walcheren expedition was doomed to
failure from the beginning, Lord Wellesley knew that it drew valuable
resources from the peninsula. For this reason, the Marquess had opposed the expedition. He was among the first to realize that Britain could
be successful in the war against France only through a vast and concerted
effort in one area rather than through lesser and more numerous
exertions. Moreover, he saw the Iberian Peninsula as an ideal place for
such an effort. George Canning, the foreign secretary, shared this belief
with the Marquess and began efforts to introduce him into the cabinet.
Wellesley was, during the interim, appointed ambassador to Spain.

While ambassador, Wellesley guided the Anglo-Spanish alliance, always fragile at best, through a period of mutual mistrust and suspicion.
Arrogant, independent, autocratic, and efficient, he smothered his personal inclinations in an effort to deal with the Spanish firmly and fairly
when he undoubtedly would have preferred to leave Spain to her own
fate. More important, perhaps, his four months as ambassador proved
an invaluable experience which served him well as foreign secretary. He
saw that Spain's military and bureaucratic inefficiency retarded ultimate
success in the peninsula. Consequently as foreign secretary his goals
were simply to induce Spain to institute military and governmental
reforms and to maintain harmonious relations between the two countries. Wellesley faced enormous obstacles—weaknesses in the Spanish
military, political, and social structures, the colonial revolts, the lack of
specie, and the distressed state of the British economy—but he handled
them deftly. He was particularly responsive to the Spanish character,
which was uniquely stubborn, formal, and independent. While this
character was the source of many of Spain's problems, he could see that it
was also the source of Spain's strength, something that Canning in
particular never realized. Wellesley's understanding was probably a result of the fact that he himself possessed many Spanish characteristics.
The Prince of Wales was not greatly mistaken when he described the
Marquess as a Spanish grandee grafted on an Irish potato.

Ultimately Wellesley met with only moderate success in his Spanish
policy, but it was not because his policy was ill conceived or poorly

executed. He used a maximum of diplomatic leverage without withdrawing British support. Henry Wellesley's appointment to the embassy in Cádiz was in fact a part of this effort in that it gave him extraordinary influence in Spanish affairs. Yet despite Henry's power and Spain's dependence on Britain, the Spanish, contrary to accepted opinion, remained remarkably independent. Although they changed governments three times at Britain's insistence, they were obdurate on such key issues as military reform and trading concessions. Nonetheless, the Wellesley brothers were persistent, and much of the credit for Spain's maintaining her resistance belongs to them.

As foreign secretary, Wellesley showed remarkable insight in his overall foreign policy. Among his contemporaries he was seemingly the first to perceive the value of nationalism. Napoleon, he knew, sustained his power in France through the exploitation of nationalism but expanded it throughout Europe through suppression of the same sentiment. The Marquess also knew that the spasmodic and ineffectual resistance posed by Austria and Prussia was the response of jealous monarchs, not enraged nations. The reaction in the Iberian Peninsula, on the other hand, was a revolt on the part of the citizenry, and the fact that it continued despite the repeated failures of Spain's armies demonstrated to Wellesley—as it should have to others—the value of a nationalistic response.

Wellesley realized as early as 1809 that success could come elsewhere in Europe if similar national uprisings could be promoted. This, he believed, could be accomplished only through the example of success. He therefore perceived the value of the Peninsular War in two ways: that victory would be a significant blow to French expansion and that success would stimulate revolt elsewhere. Thus, while the war in the peninsula continued, he carried on secret negotiation with, and sent agents to, the nations of northern and eastern Europe. What made Wellesley's foreign policy unique was that, in his negotiations with these countries (and those with Russia are particularly illustrative), Spain and Portugal were always declared the focal point of British exertions. He dismissed pleas for British military involvement in northern Europe and explained that Britain's resources were best directed toward the common end of limiting French power by maintaining or expanding the effort in Iberia. His efforts were a departure from past policy, for which Wellesley has been given little credit.

Regrettably, Lord Wellesley's term as foreign secretary was marred by constant conflict with the prime minister, Spencer Perceval, and the rest of the cabinet. Although his foreign policy was ultimately revealed as sound, Wellesley rarely received from his colleagues the support he desired. To them the brilliance of his ideas and the prospects for success were not apparent in the period 1809–12. Led by Perceval, they considered immediate problems more important. Britain's economic situation was perilous at best. Napoleon posed a constant threat of leading an enormous army across the Pyrenees to subdue the peninsula and confront Wellington. The army had to be maintained in case Napoleon, victorious in Europe, again planned a cross-channel invasion. To Perceval, these situations justified caution. Only with Wellington's increasing success and Napoleon's retreat from Russia did the risks of total commitment become small enough to secure the near unanimous support of public and Parliament. It was this basic change in conditions which provided the luster to Castlereagh's early years as foreign secretary, but it was Wellesley's persistent support for the Peninsular War in the crucial years of 1810 and 1811 which helped make success possible.

Nevertheless, Wellesley's impatience and failure to appreciate Perceval's position led to his downfall and were the reasons his legacy to British policy was at first ignored and then forgotten. To most of his contemporaries the Marquess' autocratic and haughty bearing overshadowed his brilliance. He did not work well with others and found it nearly impossible to work under another's authority. It becomes obvious to anyone studying the career of Wellesley that he neither understood nor fitted into British politics. He would not have been a good prime minister, nor would he have lasted long in that position. George Canning, the only man to whom Wellesley deferred, might have provided the type of leadership under which the Marquess could have served. It is not difficult to imagine Wellesley as foreign secretary or minister without portfolio in a Canning cabinet. But without the controlling influence of a personality like Canning's, Wellesley could never have succeeded in British politics. The *Examiner,* commenting on Lord Wellesley in May 1812, realized this:"The Marquis Wellesley is very far from satisfying, as at all coming up, to one's ideas of a desirable Minister:—his private habits, his aristocratic pride, on the one hand, and courtliness on the other, his wasteful and Eastern notions of what is efficient as well as magnanimous in matters of policy, all give him an aspect very much the reverse of what is English, and very distinct from those great and simple qualities which have ever been esteemed the best security as well as ornament of this nation."[30]

After Wellesley's resignation, Anglo-Spanish relations remained a challenge even though the war had clearly shifted to the allies' advantage, especially when Wellington defeated Marshal Auguste Marmont at the Battle of Salamanca on July 22, 1812. Castlereagh, the new foreign secretary, was unable to mediate the colonial disputes.[31] Moreover, Spain persisted in her extravagant requests for a loan, denied Great Britain a trade agreement, and refused to institute military reforms.[32] For his part, Henry Wellesley sorely missed his brother. Bitter over the circumstances of Wellesley's resignation and his inability to form a ministry, Henry also found Castlereagh less trusting than the Marquess. Writing to Arbuthnot in September 1812, Henry explained: "With respect to public business I naturally feel less confidence in myself, & act with less than I did when Lord W[ellesley] was in office, and (between ourselves) I do not believe that our Minister for Foreign Affairs has the same confidence in me that he, Ld. W. had."[33] Henry nonetheless remained in Spain as ambassador until 1822, gaining a reputation as an outstanding diplomat. Later he was ambassador to Vienna from 1823 to 1831 and to Paris from 1841 to 1846.[34]

Following his resignation, Wellesley remained active in the House of Lords, taking particular interest in the debates on Ireland and Catholic rights. As the years passed, he and Wellington drew further apart because of political and personal differences. While the Marquess became more liberal, Wellington became identified with archconservativism. They quarreled first over a postwar solution on France, Wellesley favoring an arrangement which would have left Napoleon on the throne of a France reduced to her pre-1789 boundaries.[35] The most violent disagreements between the brothers were, however, over the Irish question. The Marquess wanted Catholic emancipation; Wellington adamantly opposed it. It is ironic, and somewhat characteristic of Wellesley's life, that Wellington would ultimately be the one given credit for emancipation, since it occurred in 1828 while he was prime minister.

Wellesley held one more governmental post in his long political career—that of lord lieutenant of Ireland. He served from 1821 to 1827 and again from 1833 to 1834. He displayed considerable talent in Dublin, but the position of lord lieutenant was a thankless job; he could never hope to please all parties.[36] Wellesley married for a second time, on October 29, 1825. The new marchioness was an American named Marianne Patterson, whose deceased husband, Robert Patterson, was the brother of Jerome Bonaparte's first wife. The second marriage proved far more successful than the first, Marianne being more under-standing and responsive than Hyacinthe to her husband's tempera-ment.[37]

Wellesley lived out his life quietly. In his declining years, he reconciled his differences with Wellington and became closer to his own family. His only discomfort came from financial distress, an ever present plague throughout his life. He died on September 26, 1842, at the age of eighty-three.[38] A man of obvious weaknesses, he has never been popular as a subject among historians, and his reputation has suffered from neglect as a result. Yet, his brilliance has never been denied. Though impractical and ill suited to the place and times in which he lived, his contribution to British foreign policy, in its most critical period, was indeed considerable. For three difficult years Wellesley worked hard to maintain and improve the Anglo-Spanish alliance, while conceiving and directing a foreign policy which would ultimately lead to victory over Napoleonic France.

Notes

Chapter 1

1. British Museum, Wellesley Papers, Additional MSS. 13,914. This document is the pedigree of the families Wellesley, Cusack, and Colley, drawn up in 1770; the origins of the Wellesleys can be found here. The details of the lives of the early Wellesleys are, however, difficult to trace. Most of Richard Wellesley's biographers differ on several points, as do the numerous biographers of Arthur Wellesley, the first Duke of Wellington. Probably the most accurate accounts can be found in recent biographies of the two brothers: Elizabeth Longford, *Wellington: The Years of the Sword,* and Iris Butler, *The Eldest Brother: The Marquess Wellesley, the Duke of Wellington's Eldest Brother.*

2. Butler, *The Eldest Brother,* p. 26; G. B. Malleson, *The Life of the Marquess Wellesley, K.G.,* pp. 2–4; W. M. Torrens, *The Marquess Wellesley, Architect of Empire,* pp. 3–7; Robert Rouiere Pearce, *Memoirs and Correspondence of the Most Noble Richard Marquess Wellesley, K.P.,* I:15.

3. *The Dictionary of National Biography,* ed. Sir Leslie Stephen and Sir Sidney Lee, XX:1134.

4. Wellesley Papers, Add. MSS. 37,416. The information that appears here was gathered by Wellesley himself; in his old age he seems to have contemplated an autobiography and had thus sent questionnaires to his surviving friends who had been associated with him in his youth.

5. Ibid.; Malleson, *The Life of Marquess Wellesley, K. G.,* p. 3; Pearce, *Memoirs and Correspondence of Marquess Wellesley,* I:17–19; Butler, *The Eldest Brother,* pp. 32–34. William Wyndham Grenville came from a prominent English family. He served as home secretary and foreign secretary in William Pitt's first administration (1783–1801). He joined the opposition in 1801 over Catholic rights, and there he remained until he became prime minister in 1806 in the Ministry of All

215

the Talents. The fall of the ministry a year later left him in opposition for the remainder of his political career.

6. Wellesley Papers, Add. MSS. 37,416; Malleson, *Life of Marquess Wellesley,* p. 3; Pearce, *Memoirs and Correspondence of Marquess Wellesley,* 1:20. Henry Addington, who later became Viscount Sidmouth, was prime minister from 1801 to 1804. He became lord president in Pitt's 1804–6 ministry and retained the position in Grenville's Ministry of All the Talents. He served also in the Perceval and Liverpool cabinets.

7. Pearce, *Memoirs and Correspondence of Marquess Wellesley,* I:15; Malleson, *Life of Marquess Wellesley,* pp. 2–5; Longford, *Years of the Sword,* pp. 10–15.

8. Butler, *The Eldest Brother,* p. 42; Malleson, *Life of Marquess Wellesley,* p. 4; Great Britain, Historical Manuscripts Commission, *Report on the Manuscripts of J. B. Fortescue, Esq., Preserved at Dropmore* (hereafter cited as *Dropmore Papers*), Richard Wellesley to William Grenville, Oct. 9, 1783, I:223.

9. Butler, *The Eldest Brother,* pp. 46–47; Malleson, *Life of Marquess Wellesley,* p. 5.

10. Butler, *The Eldest Brother,* pp. 47–49; *Dropmore Papers,* Richard Wellesley to William Grenville, Nov. 7, 1784, I:241; Pearce, *Memoirs and Correspondence of Marquess Wellesley,* I:32.

11. Longford, *Years of the Sword,* p. 18; Butler, *The Eldest Brother,* pp. 43–50. Butler is the only source for the family and personal affairs of Richard Wellesley and is the first historian to examine the private correspondence of Richard Wellesley and his wife, Hyacinthe, and the private family papers, all in the possession of Field Marshal Michael Carver.

12. Marquess Curzon of Kedleston, *British Government in India,* II:174.

13. Butler, *The Eldest Brother,* p. 25.

14. Lord Beverly, who controlled Bere Alston, claimed that Wellesley neglected his political claims; ibid., p. 51.

15. Torrens, *The Marquess Wellesley,* p. 123.

16. Great Britain, *Cobbett's Parliamentary History of England from the Earliest Period to the year 1803,* XXVII:675–1122. *Cobbett's Parliamentary History* precedes the *Parliamentary Debates.* The debates are divided into five series: one, 1803–20; two, 1820–30; three, 1830–91; four, 1892–1908; five, 1909 to the present. Each series is numbered separately. The debates were privately reported up to 1907, when verbatim reports began. Only the fifth series is official. The name of the early reporter and printer, Hansard, is often applied to the whole series.

17. Butler, *The Eldest Brother,* pp. 58–60; the *Dropmore Papers* contain some letters from Wellesley to William Grenville while the former was in Europe.

18. Great Britain, Public Record Office, Cowley Papers, F.O. 519/60. This is a diary kept by Henry Wellesley, which gives details of the author's early life.

19. *Cobbett's Parliamentary History,* XXX:849–78; Malleson, *Life of Marquess Wellesley,* p. 6; Butler, *The Eldest Brother,* pp. 44, 73.

20. *Cobbett's Parliamentary History,* XXX:1009–74; Richard Marquess Wellesley, *The Dispatches and Correspondence of the Marquess Wellesley, K.G. during His Lordship's Mission to Spain as Ambassador Extraordinary to the Supreme Junta in 1809,* pp. v–lxix.

21. Butler, *The Eldest Brother,* p. 77.

22. *Cobbett's Parliamentary History,* XXXI:474.

23. Wellesley Papers, Add. MSS. 37,416, William Ramsey to R. Wellesley, Oct. 4, 1797; Lord Rosebery, *Pitt*, p. 204.

24. Butler, *The Eldest Brother*, pp. 94–100.

25. Cowley Papers, P.R.O., F.O. 519/60; Henry Wellesley, First Lord Cowley, *The Diary and Correspondence of Henry Wellesley, First Lord Cowley, 1790–1846*, p. 31; Longford, *Years of the Sword*, p. 53; Wellesley Papers, Add. MSS. 37,284, detailed notes on India taken by R. Wellesley.

26. Sir Alfred Lyall, *The Rise and Expansion of the British Dominion in India*, pp. 217, 234; Vincent A. Smith, *The Oxford History of India*, p. 548.

27. P.E. Roberts, *India under Wellesley*, pp. 22–33; Fortescue, *Wellington*, p. 23; Lyall, *British Dominion in India*, pp. 225–36; Smith, *Oxford History of India*, p. 548.

28. Butler, *The Eldest Brother*, p. 116.

29. Wellesley Papers, Add. MSS. 37,284; Henry Dundas and Richard Colley Wellesley, *Two Views of British India: The Private Correspondence of Mr. Dundas and Lord Wellesley, 1798–1801*, Wellesley to Dundas, Feb. 23, 1798, pp. 18–24.

30. Butler, *The Eldest Brother*, p. 147.

31. Smith, *Oxford History of India*, p. 552; Roberts, *India under Wellesley*, pp. 34–40.

32. Depending on weather conditions, the trip by sea from Britain to India took from four to six months. Thus any instructions or communications sent to Wellesley in India were long delayed and often did not arrive at all. Moreover, once arrived they were frequently out of date because of changing political situations, and were thus rendered irrelevant. Consequently Wellesley had a great deal of independence in India—certainly more than the India Company would willingly grant under normal circumstances.

33. Fortescue, *Wellington*, pp. 26–31; Smith, *Oxford History of India*, p. 553; Lyall, *British Dominion in India*, pp. 242–45; Roberts, *India under Wellesley*, pp. 41–84; Dundas and Wellesley, *Two Views of British India*, Wellesley to Dundas, Oct. 11, 1798, pp. 90–100.

34. Roberts, *India under Wellesley*, pp. 137–40; Smith, *Oxford History of India*, pp. 553–54.

35. Cowley Papers, P.R.O., F.O. 519/60. Henry was sent to England in 1800 to relate Lord Wellesley's problems and accomplishments to the Court of Directors and to the government. Writing to the Marquess, he stated: "Both the Government and the Court of Directors were loud in their commendations of Lord Wellesley's proceedings in India, though I had then the opportunity of remarking what further observation has abundantly confirmed, that military successes, and indeed proceedings of all kinds in India, however important and advantageous, produce but little effect in England . . . though their results, as is usually the case, may be more important to the Mother Country than those of her negociations in Europe."

36. Butler, *The Eldest Brother*, pp. 205–6.

37. Ibid., pp. 212–18, 224–30. Using the private correspondence between the Marquess and Hyacinthe, heretofore unexamined, Iris Butler has constructed an interesting account of the relationship and the effects it had on Lord Wellesley.

38. Rosebery, *Pitt*, p. 211. Rosebery deals with this topic in great detail.

39. Dundas and Wellesley, *Two Views of British India*, Wellesley to Dundas,

April 29, 1800, pp. 257–61. "Being sensible that the public opinion here will be, and indeed is, that the title granted to me in Ireland is a proof that his Maj[esty] does not deem *me* a proper object of those honours which are appropriate to such services, I feel my new dignity as a mark rather of deprecation than of honour, and I know that it will be so felt throughout India, where the scale of British and Irish honours is well understood."

40. Ibid. "I am satisfied that upon reflection you will perceive, that my acceptance of such a grant w[oul]d place me in a very invidious and humiliating situation with respect to the army. The army w[oul]d feel that I had been rewarded at their expense: and they w[oul]d view the transaction with perhaps aggravated jealousy and contempt for my character when they recollected the effort, which I made in the face of the prejudices and popularity, to reserve these very stores for the ostensible purpose of saving the rights of the Crown."

41. Wellesley eventually accepted a twenty-year pension of £5,000 a year in place of the £100,000. This grant came from the company's revenues and not from the booty taken at Seringapatam, which rightfully belonged to the army. Butler, *The Eldest Brother*, p. 257.

42. Ibid., pp. 255–60. Regarding Wellesley's physical appearance, Butler quotes his son-in-law, Edward Hatherton: "He was about five feet seven inches high; of rather small bone and at the same time spare in his person. His head was a perfect model, very bald and with fine grey hair about the ears and at the back part of it. . . . Though seen a thousand times the eye always remarked the beauty of his head. His face was a fine oval of a natural and healthy colouring; his forehead high; his eyebrows large, finely arched, and what was extraordinary, quite black. Beneath them his penetrating and enquiring eye seemed to investigate and look through the person he addressed. . . . His attire was always studied, costly and of the most perfect taste." Ibid., p. 573.

43. Ibid., pp. 256–59.

44. Torrens, *The Marquess Wellesley*, p. 242; Butler, *The Eldest Brother*, pp. 231–41. For a detailed account of the conduct of Britons in India, see Percival Spear, *The Nabobs: A Study of the Social Life of the English in 18th Century India*.

45. Marquess Wellesley, *The Despatches, Minutes and Correspondence of the Marquess Wellesley, K.G., during the Administration in India*, III:116.

46. Ibid., IV:204–5; Roberts, *India under Wellesley*, pp. 236–55; Smith, *Oxford History of India*, pp. 556–57.

47. Butler, *The Eldest Brother*, pp. 349–56.

48. *Dropmore Papers*, Thomas Grenville to Lord W. Grenville, Jan. 5, 1805, VII:248. "I have this moment been *confidentially* informed from the *best* authority, that Pitt has found it impossible that L[ord] Wellesley can go on in his warfare with the Directors and that L.W. is believed to be now actually at sea on his return."

49. Butler, *The Eldest Brother*, p. 370.

50. *Dropmore Papers*, Wellesley to Grenville, Jan. 23, 1806, VII:332.

51. Ibid., Wellesley to Grenville, Jan. 25, 1806, VII:336–37.

52. Ibid., Wellesley to Grenville, June 11, 1806, VIII:184. "My anxious desire is to support you in every way steadfastly and openly. But in my present situation, standing accused of every crime which man can commit, and that accusation having been admitted on the table of the House of Commons without a word of defense from those who lead that House, I really think that it would be indelicate

in me to take any part in the House of Lords." Paull's vendetta stemmed from Wellesley's having expelled him from India for shady business practices.

53. Ibid., William Windham to Grenville, Feb. 17, 1806, VIII:34; ibid., Grenville to Windham, June 4, 1806, VIII:174.

54. Wellesley Papers, Add. MSS. 37,295, R. Wellesley to Portland, April 22, 1807; *Dropmore Papers*, Wellesley to Grenville, March 19, 1807, IX:120. The "delicacy" involved both the investigation in Parliament and his friendship with Lord Grenville.

55. Butler, *The Eldest Brother*, p. 377.

56. Great Britain, *The Parliamentary Debates from the Year 1803 to the Present Time*, 1st ser. XI:947.

57. Ibid., p. 1037. Paull committed suicide on April 15, 1808; The *Times*, April 18, 1808. The *Times* carried a detailed account of the debates on Wellesley's policies throughout the spring of 1808, having, on Feb. 22, 1808, declared strong support for his policies.

58. Butler, *The Eldest Brother*, p. 381.

59. *Dropmore Papers*, Lord Auckland to Grenville, June 15, 1806, VIII:188.

60. Arthur Wellesley, 1st Duke of Wellington, *Some Letters of the Duke of Wellington to His Brother, William Wellesley-Pole*, A. Wellesley to Pole, Aug. 19, 1808, p. 4.

61. Wellesley Papers, Add. MSS. 37,416, "An Independent Englishman" to Wellesley, Oct. 1808.

Chapter 2

1. An excellent discussion of British foreign policy during this period appears in Sir John William Fortescue, *British Statesmen of the Great War, 1793–1814*; for a detailed explanation of the Continental System see Eli Filip Heckscher, *The Continental System: An Economic Interpretation*.

2. Granville Leveson-Gower, *Private Correspondence of Granville Leveson-Gower*, Lady Bessborough to Gower, Dec. 20, 1807, II:315; George Jackson, *The Diaries and Letters of Sir George Jackson*, F. J. Jackson to George Jackson, Sept. 26, 1807, II:218; *Dropmore Papers*, Thomas Grenville to Lord Grenville, Nov. 15, 1807, IX:144–45; Wendy Hinde, *George Canning*, pp. 175–77.

3. *Dropmore Papers*, See vol. IX for numerous letters between Lord Grenville and Wellesley during this period.

4. *Parliamentary Debates*, X:342–50. The *Times*, Feb. 9, 1808; Sir Charles Alexander Petrie, *George Canning*, p. 80.

5. Butler, *The Eldest Brother*, p. 386; Malleson, *Life of Marquess Wellesley*, pp. 156–57.

6. Arthur Bryant, *Years of Victory, 1802–1812*, pp. 217–18; Louis Antoine Fauvelet de Bourrienne, *Memoirs of Napoleon Bonaparte*, III:123–24; Fortescue, *British Statesmen*, pp. 214–16; John Sherwig, *Guineas and Gunpowder: British Foreign Aid in the Wars with France*, p. 191.

7. Sherwig, *Guineas and Gunpowder*, p. 196; Public Record Office, F.O. 72/89. This volume contains the correspondence between Venezuelan patriot General Miranda and the British government, showing British involvement in his revolutionary schemes. British troops were actually sent to Buenos Aires in

1806, and Arthur Wellesley was preparing to lead a force to South America before he was diverted to the peninsula.

8. William F. P. Napier, *History of the War in the Peninsula and in the South of France, from the Year 1807 to the Year 1814*, I:78; Charles W. C. Oman, *A History of the Peninsular War*, I:199; J. W. Fortescue, *A History of the British Army*, VI:166.

9. Napier, *War in the Peninsula*, I:19; Spain, Archivo Histórico Nacional (hereafter A. H. N.), Sección de Estado, Legajo 70. This legajo contains correspondence of the local juntas throughout Spain, some relating to the formation of a central junta. For a detailed account of the Spanish uprising and the formation of the juntas, see Morton Goldstein, "Great Britain in Spain, 1807– 1809" (dissertation). The Battle of Baylen was reported in the *Times* on July 11, 1808.

10. The *Times*, March 4, 1808.

11. Ibid., May 23, 1808. Articles on the events in Spain appeared almost daily from March 7 to May 23, 1808.

12. Ibid., June 1, 1808.

13. *Parliamentary Debates*, XI:890– 91.

14. Henry Lord Brougham, *The Life and Times of Henry Lord Brougham*, Henry Brougham to Earl Grey, July 21, 1808, I:283: "It must be admitted, however, that things are looking very well in Spain, and great things may follow if they go on in the same way; but I am no believer in the *duration* and steadiness of popular feelings, and a great believer in regular armies and well-bread officers." (Brougham and Grey were staunch Whigs.) Elizabeth Holland, *The Journal of Elizabeth, Lady Holland*, II:246; the traditionally Whig-oriented *Edinburgh Review*, *Morning Chronicle*, and *Political Register* voiced strong support for Spain.

15. The *Times*, June 9, 1808; A.H.N., Sección de Estado, Legajo 71, Materosa and Vega to Canning, June 6, 1808.

16. A.H.N., Sección de Estado, Legajo 71, Canning to Materosa and Vega, June 12, 1808. Canning promised support, but in future correspondence he urged the Spanish to form a central Spanish authority so that aid could be more effectively rendered. See Goldstein, "Great Britain in Spain"; P.R.O., F.O. 72/89, Miranda Correspondence; the *Times*, June 11, 1808.

17. The *Times*, July 16, 1808.

18. Arthur Wellesley, 1st Duke of Wellington, *Supplementary Dispatches, Correspondence, and Memoranda of Field Marshal Arthur, Duke of Wellington*, Arthur Wellesley to Viscount Castlereagh, Aug. 23, 1808, VI:122; Sherwig, *Guineas and Gunpowder*, pp. 197– 98; Longford, *Years of the Sword*, pp. 154– 56. Dalrymple was placed in command because Sir John Moore had become suddenly available; Dalrymple superseded Arthur Wellesley, and, as the cabinet mistrusted Moore because of his close ties to the opposition, Burrard and Dalrymple were placed in command. It has been suggested that the cabinet hoped that Moore would resign in disgust.

19. The *Times*, September 19, 1808.

20. Sherwig, *Guineas and Gunpowder*, p. 199; Arthur Wellesley, Duke of Wellington, *Wellington at War, 1794–1815: A Selection of Wartime Letters*, Arthur Wellesley to R. Wellesley, Oct. 5, 1808, p. 150: "I have arrived here this day, & I don't know whether I am to be hanged drawn & quartered; or roasted alive." Brougham, *Life and Times of Henry Brougham*, Grey to Brougham, Sept. 29, 1808, I:285– 88. The opposition complained about the convention for two reasons: the government had not given A. Wellesley sufficient troop strength to follow up the

victory, and the command was confused and in the wrong place. Sir John Moore should have been in command.

21. The *Times*, August 26, 1808.

22. Wellington, *Dispatches*, A. Wellesley to Castlereagh, Oct. 4, 1808, III:126–27; Oman, *The Peninsular War*, I:291; Napier, *War in the Peninsula*, I:172; Fortescue, *History of the British Army*, VI:249.

23. Wellesley Papers, Add. MSS. 37,286. Major Campbell was in constant correspondence with Wellesley and kept him well informed on peninsular activities.

24. Thomas Creevey, *The Creevey Papers: A Selection from the Correspondence and Diaries of the Late Thomas Creevey, M.P.*, Samuel Whitbread to Thomas Creevey, Sept. 25, 1808, I:89.

25. Ibid., William Cobbett to Lord Folkestone, Oct. 9, 1808, I:89.

26. Wellington, *Supplementary Dispatches*, W. W. Pole to A. Wellesley, Oct. 19, 1808, VI:164.

27. Fortescue, *British Statesmen*, pp. 222–23; C. J. Bartlett, *Castlereagh*, p. 75; Hinde, *Canning*, pp. 201–3.

28. Denis Gray, *Spencer Perceval: The Evangelical Prime Minister, 1762–1812*, p. 183.

29. Spencer Walpole, *Life of Spencer Perceval*, Castlereagh to Perceval, Sept. 27, 1808, I:300–301; Hinde, *Canning*, p. 204; Bartlett, *Castlereagh*, p. 75.

30. Longford, *Years of the Sword*, p. 163.

31. Wellington, *Supplementary Dispatches*, W. W. Pole to A. Wellesley, Oct. 27, 1808, VI:170–73.

32. Great Britain, Parliament, House of Commons, Board of General Officers Appointed to Inquire into the . . . Convention etc. in Portugal, A Copy of the Proceedings upon the Inquiry Relative to the Armistice and Convention etc., Made and Concluded in Portugal, in August, 1808, between the Commanders of the British and French Armies. . . .

33. Sir John Moore, *Diary of Sir John Moore*, II:272–73 (hereafter Moore, *Diary*); James Carrick Moore, *A Narrative of the Campaign of the British Army in Spain, Commanded by His Excellency Lieut. General Sir John Moore* (hereafter Moore, *Narrative of the Campaign in Spain*), Castlereagh to Moore, Sept. 25, 1808, pp. 237–40.

34. Moore, *Diary*, II:373–74; Moore, *Narrative of the Campaign in Spain*, Frere to Moore, Nov. 13, 1808, pp. 29–30, Nov. 25, 1808, pp. 53–55, Nov. 30, 1808, pp. 79–80, Dec. 3, 1808, pp. 89–90, Dec. 8, 1808, pp. 93–94, Dec. 14, 1808, pp. 149–53.

35. Moore, *Narrative of the Campaign in Spain*, Moore to Frere, Dec. 23, 1808, pp. 160–61; Moore, *Diary*, II:374.

36. *Parliamentary Debates*, XII:1083–84; Napier, *War in the Peninsula*, I:295; Oman, *The Peninsular War*, I:513-22; Fortescue, *History of the British Army*, VI:327.

37. Carola Mary Anima Oman Lenanton, *Sir John Moore*, p. 599; Oman, *The Peninsular War*, I:596; Lewis William George Butler, *Wellington's Operations in the Peninsula*, I:129–30.

38. Sherwig, *Guineas and Gunpower*, p. 203; Fortescue, *British Statesmen*, p. 224.

39. Bryant, *Years of Victory*, p. 294. Moore's soldiers failed to tell of their disgraceful behavior during the retreat when they were guilty of numerous crimes against the Spanish; see Moore, *Diary*, II:374–85.

40. *Parliamentary Debates,* XII:106–7.
41. Ibid., p. 133.
42. Ibid., pp. 134–35.
43. Ibid., pp. 131–33.
44. Ibid., pp. 138–44, 144–58.
45. Ibid., pp. 133–38.
46. Ibid., pp. 208–10.
47. Ibid., pp. 1057–62.
48. Ibid., p. 1063; Brougham, *Life of Brougham,* Brougham to Grey, July 22, 1808, I:284. From this early date the Whigs felt the Church was playing too great a role in the Spanish insurrection.
49. *Parliamentary Debates,* XII:1064–75.
50. Ibid., pp. 1075–84.
51. Ibid., pp. 1080–84.
52. Ibid., p. 1095.
53. Ibid., pp. 1096–1105.
54. Ibid., p. 1119.
55. Moore, *Narrative of the Campaign in Spain,* Frere to Moore, Nov. 30, 1808, pp. 29–30, Dec. 3, 1808, pp. 88–90, Dec. 8, 1808, pp. 138–40, Dec. 14, 1808, pp. 149–53, Dec. 16, 1808, p. 154; Lenanton, *Sir John Moore,* p. 586; Oman, *The Peninsular War,* I:523; Frere was envoy extraordinary and minister plenipotentiary from November 1808 to August 1809.
56. *Parliamentary Debates,* XIII:640–41; Brougham, *Life of Brougham,* I:302: "The object of Lord Grey's motion was to represent to the Crown the disgrace which the proceedings of the Government had brought upon England, and the injury which the British nation had suffered from the rashness and mismanagement of ministers."
57. *Parliamentary Debates,* XIII:641.
58. The *Times,* March 24, 1809; *Parliamentary Debates,* XIII:796–97.
59. *Parliamentary Debates,* XIII:798.
60. Ibid., pp. 799–800.
61. Ibid., p. 800.
62. Ibid., p. 807.
63. Moore, *Narrative of the Campaign in Spain,* Prince of Neufchatel to Duke of Dalmatia, Dec. 10, 1808, pp. 314–16; Moore, *Diary,* pp. 399–400. Moore decided to advance when he learned the French thought he was in retreat.
64. *Parliamentary Debate,* XIV:70. Lord Auckland and Earl Darnley were also vehement in their denunciations of Frere.
65. Ibid., pp. 70–71.
66. Ibid., pp. 121–50.
67. Ibid., p. 151.
68. Ibid., pp. 69–70, 150–64.
69. Ibid., p. 170. Erskine was supported by Viscount Sidmouth.
70. Ibid., p. 172. The vote was 92 yes, 145 no.
71. Ibid., p. 173.
72. Hinde, *Canning,* pp. 209–12; *Parliamentary Debates,* XIV:69–70; Wellesley Papers, Add. MSS. 37,286, Earl Camden to R. Wellesley, Nov. 29, 1804. Frere handled himself creditably while representative to Spain in 1804.
73. *Parliamentary Debates,* XIV:107.

74. Ibid., pp. 262–64.

75. Butler, *The Eldest Brother*, p. 401; Hinde, *Canning*, p. 210. On April 24 Liverpool informed the Lords that the ministry had concluded that Frere had conducted himself improperly in his relationship with John Moore.

76. Wellesley Papers, Add. MSS. 37,286, A. Wellesley to Castlereagh, Sept. 5, 1808; Robert Stewart Londonderry, *Correspondence, Despatches, and Other Papers of Viscount Castlereagh*, Memorandum on the Defense of Portugal, March 7, 1809, VII:38–42.

77. Londonderry, *Correspondence of Castlereagh*, Castlereagh to George III, March 26, 1809, VII:43–44.

78. Wellington, *Supplementary Dispatches*, Castlereagh to A. Wellesley, April 2, 1809, VI:210.

79. Ibid.; P.R.O., F.O. 72/75, Canning to R. Wellesley, June 27, 1809.

80. Butler, *The Eldest Brother*, pp. 392–401. The relationship between Wellesley and his wife had deteriorated to the point of complete estrangement.

81. British Museum, Bathurst Papers, loan no. 57, vol. 4, no. 324, Bathurst's full explanation of the events leading to the breakup of the Portland ministry; Hinde, *Canning*, pp. 217–20; Fortescue, *British Statesmen*, p. 236.

82. *Dropmore Papers*, vol. IX. This volume contains much correspondence between Canning, Grenville, and Wellesley from 1807 to 1809. Canning and Wellesley became especially close friends when the Marquess approached the former on behalf of Grenville for a seat in his ministry.

83. Butler, *The Eldest Brother*, p. 400; Bathurst Papers, loan no. 57, vol. 4, no. 324; Hinde, *Canning*, p. 219.

84. Bathurst Papers, loan no. 57, vol. 4, no. 324; Butler, *The Eldest Brother*, p. 400; Hinde, *Canning*, p. 219; Torrens, *The Marquess Wellesley*, p. 348; Gray, *Spencer Perceval*, p. 222.

85. The *Times*, May 1, 1809. For Spain's acknowledgment of the appointment, see A.H.N., Sección de Estado, Legajo 5459, Don Martín de Garay to Don Ruiz de Apodaca, May 25, 1809; Wellesley Papers, Add. MSS. 37,309, Marquis of Buckingham to R. Wellesley, April 30, 1809.

86. Butler, *The Eldest Brother*, pp. 402–3. From Wellesley's private personal papers, Iris Butler has carefully constructed this episode which had been told in so many ways.

87. Torrens, *The Marquess Wellesley*, p. 351; Butler, *The Eldest Brother*, p. 404.

88. Bathurst Papers, loan no. 57, vol. 4, no. 324; Hinde, *Canning*, pp. 219–20.

89. George III, *The Later Correspondence of George III*, pp. xxiv, 310–11; Hinde, *Canning*, p. 221; Butler, *The Eldest Brother*, pp. 403–4.

90. P.R.O., F.O. 72/90, Cooke to Hammond, May 22 1809; and Notice to George Canning, April 3, 1809 (these are but two of several letters in this volume representing the issues noted); P.R.O., F.O. 72/84, Apodaca to Canning, July 22, 1809; A.H.N., Sección de Estado, Legajo 5459, Apodaca to Garay, March 29, July 10, 1809.

91. Wellesley Papers, Add. MSS. 37, 286, Garay to Canning, March 12, 1809; A.H.N., Sección de Estado, Legajo 5459, Apodaca to Garay, March 29, 1809; *Parliamentary Debates*, XII:1119. The fact that the Spanish refused to allow the British into Cádiz played into the hands of the opposition as they maintained that the Spanish were not so desirous of British aid as the government maintained.

92. P.R.O., F.O. 93/99–6.

93. Sherwig, *Guineas and Gunpowder*, p. 205; P.R.O., F.O. 72/88, Woodford to Dundas, May 1, 1809. Canning refused to negotiate on subsidies despite the fact that there was a great deal of pressure in Britain to obtain a trade agreement with Spain.

94. P.R.O., F.O. 72/86, 90. Numerous letters between Canning and Apodaca, the Spanish representative in London, and Canning and Perceval on this issue are contained in these volumes. Specie was essential to Britain since it was the only way foreign aid could be paid. To secure it in the absence of trade, Britain issued bills of exchange at 5 percent interest on the treasury, the principal to be redeemed two years after the conclusion of peace. See British Museum, Huskisson Papers, Add. MSS. 38,759, Huskisson Memorandum, April 1809.

95. P.R.O., F.O. 72/86, 88. These volumes contain letters between Canning and Apodaca in the months of March through June dealing with Spain's request for material and monetary aid—and Canning's inability to meet them. See also A.H.N., Sección de Estado, Legajo 5459, Apodaca to Garay, March 29, 1809.

96. P.R.O., F.O. 185/16. The Embassy Archives of this period show that Frere did little to alleviate Spanish suspicions of Britain.

97. P.R.O., F.O. 72/75, Canning to R. Wellesley, June 27, 1809 (there are four separate letters bearing this date); P.R.O., F.O. 72/84, Canning to Apodaca, July 17, 1809.

98. P.R.O., F.O. 72/75, Canning to R. Wellesley, June 27, 1809; P.R.O., F.O. 72/84, Canning to Apodaca, July 17, 1809; A.H.N., Sección de Estado, Legajo 5459, Apodaca to Garay, June 9, 1809.

99. P.R.O., F.O. 72/84, Canning to R. Wellesley, July 8, 1809; P.R.O., F.O. 72/75, Canning to R. Wellesley, June 27, 1809; H. Wellesley, *Diary and Correspondence*, p. 47.

100. P.R.O., F.O. 72/84, Canning to R. Wellesley, June 27, 1809.

Chapter 3

1. Wellesley Papers, Add. MSS. 37,286, R. Wellesley to J. H. Frere, July 31, 1809, to Canning, Aug. 11, 1809, Garay to R. Wellesley, Aug. 5, 1809; P.R.O., F.O. 72/76, R. Wellesley to Canning, Aug. 11, 1809; P.R.O., F.O. 72/80, Duff to Canning, Aug. 14, 1809; U.S., National Archives, Dept. of State, no. 59, vol. 11, George Erving to Robert Smith, Aug. 3, 1809. Erving, the United States' representative in Seville, attributed the lavish reception to the celebration for the Battle of Talavera.

2. P.R.O., F.O. 72/76, R. Wellesley to Canning, Aug. 11, 1809; Wellesley Papers, Add. MSS. 37,286, R. Wellesley to Canning, Aug. 11, 1809.

3. A.H.N., Sección de Estado, Legajo 5459, Apodaca to Garay, May 1, 19, 1809.

4. P.R.O., F.O. 72/84, Garay to Apodaca, May 25, 1809, Apodaca to Canning, July 1, 1809; A.H.N., Sección de Estado, Legajo 5459, Garay to Apodaca, May 25, 1809; P.R.O., F.O. 72/86, Cevallos to Canning, June 2, 1809.

5. Wellesley Papers, Add. MSS. 37,286, R. Wellesley to Canning, Aug. 11, 1809; P.R.O., F.O. 72/76, R. Wellesley to Canning, Aug. 11, 1809.

6. Napier, *War in the Peninsula*, II:100–105; Oman, *The Peninsular War*, II:340–41.

7. A.H.N., Sección de Estado, Legajo 5459, Canning to Apodaca, June 8,

1809, Apodaca to Garay, June 9, 1809; Wellington, *Supplementary Dispatches*, A. Wellesley to Castlereagh, June 11, 1809, VI:281; A. Wellesley, *Letters to William Wellesley-Pole*, A. Wellesley to Pole, July 1, 1809, pp. 13–14.

8. Wellesley Papers, Add. MSS. 37,286, A. Wellesley to J. H. Frere, July 13, 1809. At this meeting, Cuesta refused to speak French, in which both he and Arthur were fluent, so the discussions were conducted through an interpreter.

9. Wellington, *Dispatches*, A. Wellesley to R. Wellesley, Aug. 8, 1809, III:404–5. Many of Sir Arthur's general orders from this period reflect concern for his commissariat.

10. Wellington, *Supplementary Dispatches*, Notes of Bartholomew Frere, VI:317, General Order, July 15, 1809, VI:315, Additional General Order, July 9, 1809, VI:301; A. Wellesley, *Letters to William Wellesley-Pole*, A. Wellesley to Pole, July 25, 1809, pp. 16–17; Wellesley Papers, Add. MSS. 37,286, A. Wellesley to J. H. Frere, July 24, 1809.

11. Wellesley Papers, Add. MSS. 37,286, A. Wellesley to J. H. Frere, July 24, 1809, to Maj. Gen. O'Donoghe, July 16, 1809.

12. Napier, *War in the Peninsula*, II:157; Oman, *The Peninsular War*, II:500; Wellesley Papers, Add. MSS. 37,288, An account of the Talavera Campaign.

13. Wellesley Papers, Add. MSS. 37,286, A. Wellesley to J. H. Frere, July 24, 1809.

14. Fortescue, *History of the British Army*, VII:256; Napier, *War in the Peninsula*, II:177–78; Oman, *The Peninsular War*, II:555–56; Wellesley Papers, Add. MSS. 37,288, An account of the Talavera Campaign; Wellington, *Supplementary Dispatches*, General Order, July 29, 1809, VI:360.

15. Wellesley Papers, Add. MSS. 37,286, Cuesta to Venegas, July 31, 1809; ibid., Add. MSS. 37,288, An account of the Talavera Campaign.

16. Napier, *War in the Peninsula*, II:181; Oman, *The Peninsular War*, II:573; Fortescue, *History of the British Army*, VII:266; Wellington, *Dispatches*, A. Wellesley to J. H. Frere, July 31, 1809, III:384.

17. Londonderry, *Correspondence of Castlereagh*, A. Wellesley to Castlereagh, Aug. 1, 1809, VII:100–101; Wellington, *Dispatches*, A. Wellesley to J. H. Frere, July 24, 1809, III:382.

18. Wellington, *Dispatches*, A. Wellesley to J. H. Frere, July 31, 1809, III: 383–84.

19. Wellesley Papers, Add. MSS. 37,286, A. Wellesley to J.H. Frere, July 31, Aug. 5, 1809, to Castlereagh, Sept. 5, 1808 (the Spanish, in an effort to appease Arthur Wellesley, offered him the rank of Captain General in the Spanish Army for his services at Talavera; he politely refused), R. Wellesley to Canning, Aug. 11, 1809.

20. P.R.O., F.O. 72/76, R. Wellesley to Canning, Aug. 11, 1809; Wellesley Papers, Add. MSS. 37,286, R. Wellesley to Canning, Aug. 11, 1809.

21. Wellington, *Dispatches*, A. Wellesley to R. Wellesley, August, 8, 1809, III:403–4; Wellesley Papers, Add. MSS. 37,286, R. Wellesley to Canning, Aug. 15, 1809; P.R.O., F.O. 72/76, R. Wellesley to Canning, Aug. 15, 1809; Wellesley Papers, Add. MSS. 37,315, R. Wellesley (son) to R. Wellesley, Aug. 5, 1809. Seville was vastly overcrowded due to the advance of French troops, making housing difficult to obtain, so Wellesley sent his son to secure a residence.

22. Wellesley Papers, Add. MSS. 37,286, Cuesta to Cornel, Aug. 1, 1809, A. Wellesley to J. H. Frere, Aug. 5, 1809, J. H. Frere to R. Wellesley, Aug. 9, 1809;

ibid., Add. MSS. 37,287, Roche to R. Wellesley, Sept. 2, 1809. Actually the British wounded received better treatment once they were in French hands.

23. Wellington, *Dispatches,* A. Wellesley to R. Wellesley, Aug. 8, 1809, III:401–3.

24. P.R.O., F.O. 72/76, R. Wellesley to Canning, Aug. 15, 1809; Wellesley Papers, Add. MSS. 37,286, R. Wellesley to Canning, Aug. 15, 1809; Wellington, *Dispatches,* A. Wellesley to R. Wellesley, Aug. 8, 1809, III:403–4.

25. Wellesley Papers, Add. MSS. 37,286, R. Wellesley to Canning, Aug. 15, 1809; P.R.O., F.O. 72/76, R. Wellesley to Canning, Aug. 15, 1809, to A. Wellesley, July 31, 1809.

26. P.R.O., F.O. 72/76, A. Wellesley to R. Wellesley, Aug. 8, 1809.

27. Ibid.; Wellington, *Supplementary Dispatches,* General Order, Aug. 9, 1809, VI:327.

28. Wellesley Papers, Add. MSS. 37,315, R. Wellesley (son) to R. Wellesley, Aug. 10, 1809; ibid., Add. MSS. 37,286, R. Wellesley to Canning, Aug. 15, 1809; P.R.O., F.O. 72/76, R. Wellesley to Canning, Aug. 15, 1809.

29. P.R.O., F.O. 72/76, Cuesta to A. Wellesley, Aug. 10, 1809.

30. Ibid., A. Wellesley to Cuesta, Aug. 11, 1809, to R. Wellesley, Aug. 12, 1809. Arthur Wellesley's concern about looting is apparent from his general orders: Wellington, *Supplementary Dispatches,* VI:318–19, 324.

31. P.R.O., F.O. 72/76, A. Wellesley to R. Wellesley, Aug. 12, 1809.

32. Ibid., R. Wellesley to Garay, Aug. 12, 1809.

33. Wellesley Papers, Add. MSS. 37,286, R. Wellesley to Canning, Aug. 15, 1809; P.R.O., F.O. 72/76, R. Wellesley to Canning, Aug. 15, 1809.

34. P.R.O., F.O. 72/76, Garay to R. Wellesley, Aug. 12, 1809.

35. Wellesley Papers, Add. MSS. 37,315, R. Wellesley (son) to R. Wellesley, Aug. 13, 1809.

36. P.R.O., F.O. 72/76, R. Wellesley to A. Wellesley, Aug. 13, 1809.

37. Wellesley Papers, Add. MSS. 37,286, R. Wellesley to Canning, Aug. 15, 1809; ibid., Add. MSS. 37,287, Armstrong to R. Wellesley, Aug. 16, 1809; P.R.O., F.O. 72/76, R. Wellesley to Canning, Aug. 15, 1809.

38. Wellington, *Dispatches,* A. Wellesley to R. Wellesley, Aug. 13, 1809, III:417–18.

39. Wellesley Papers, Add. MSS. 37,286, R. Wellesley to A. Wellesley, Aug. 15, 1809; P.R.O., F.O. 72/76, R. Wellesley to A. Wellesley, Aug. 15, 1809.

40. R. Wellesley, *Dispatches and Correspondence,* Cuesta to A. Wellesley, Aug. 11, 1809, pp. 13–14; P.R.O., F.O. 72/76, A. Wellesley to Cuesta, Aug. 13, 1809.

41. Wellington, *Dispatches,* A. Wellesley to R. Wellesley, Aug. 13, 1809, III:417–18; P.R.O., F.O. 72/76, A. Wellesley to Cuesta, Aug. 13, 1809.

42. Wellesley Papers, Add. MSS. 37,286, R. Wellesley to Canning, Aug. 15, 1809; P.R.O., F.O. 72/76, R. Wellesley to Canning, Aug. 15, 1809.

43. National Archives, Dept. of State, no. 59, vol. 11, Erving to Madison, March 14, 1809.

44. Ibid., Erving to Robert Smith, Aug. 3, 1809.

45. Wellington, *Supplementary Dispatches,* R. Wellesley to A. Wellesley, Aug. 13, 1809, VI:329–30; P.R.O., F.O. 72/76, R. Wellesley to A. Wellesley, Aug. 13, 1809.

46. Wellesley Papers, Add. MSS. 37,286, J. H. Frere to R. Wellesley, Aug. 10, 1809.

47. P.R.O., F.O. 72/76, R. Wellesley to A. Wellesley, Aug. 13, 1809.

48. Wellesley Papers, Add. MSS. 37,286, R. Wellesley to Canning, Aug. 15, 21, 1809; P.R.O., F.O. 72/76, R. Wellesley to Canning, Aug. 15, 1809, A. Wellesley to R. Wellesley, Aug. 14, 1809, Garay to R. Wellesley, Aug. 21, 1809. The official announcement of Cuesta's resignation came on August 21, 1809.

49. P.R.O., F.O. 72/76, R. Wellesley to Canning, Aug. 15, 1809.

50. Ibid., A. Wellesley to Eguia, Aug. 14, 1809; R. Wellesley, *Dispatches and Correspondence,* A. Wellesley to R. Wellesley, Aug. 14, 1809, pp. 15–16.

51. Wellington, *Dispatches,* A. Wellesley to Eguia, Aug. 15, 1809, III:423.

52. Wellesley Papers, Add. MSS. 37,286, R. Wellesley to Canning, Aug. 15, 1809; P.R.O., F.O. 72/76, R. Wellesley to Canning, Aug. 15, 1809.

53. Ibid.

54. P.R.O., F.O. 72/78, Colonel Roche to R. Wellesley, Aug. 18, 1809.

55. Wellesley Papers, Add. MSS. 37,287, Garay to R. Wellesley, Aug. 17, 1809; P.R.O., F.O. 72/76, Garay to R. Wellesley, Aug. 17, 1809.

56. P.R.O., F.O. 72/76, R. Wellesley to Canning, Aug. 24, 1809; Wellesley Papers, Add. MSS. 37,287, R. Wellesley to Canning, Aug. 24, 1809.

57. P.R.O., F.O. 72/76, Garay to R. Wellesley, Aug. 17, 1809; Wellesley Papers, Add. MSS. 37,287, Garay to R. Wellesley, Aug. 17, 1809, Eguia to A. Wellesley, Aug. 16, 1809.

58. Wellesley Papers, Add. MSS. 37,287, Garay to R. Wellesley, Aug. 18, 1809.

59. Ibid., Venegas to Cornel, Aug. 18, 1809.

60. Ibid., R. Wellesley to Garay, Aug. 17, 1809; P.R.O., F.O. 72/76, A. Wellesley to R. Wellesley, Aug. 18, 1809.

61. Wellesley Papers, Add. MSS. 37,287, Garay to R. Wellesley, Aug. 18, 1809; P.R.O., F.O. 72/76, Garay to R. Wellesley, Aug. 18, 1809.

62. P.R.O., F.O. 72/76, A. Wellesley to R. Wellesley, Aug. 18, 1809, Hill to A. Wellesley, Aug. 16, 1809.

63. Wellesley Papers, Add. MSS. 37,287, R. Wellesley to Canning, Aug. 24, 1809; P.R.O., F.O. 72/76, R. Wellesley to Canning, Aug. 24, 1809, to Garay, Aug. 21, 1809.

64. P.R.O., F.O. 72/76, R. Wellesley to Canning, Aug. 24, 1809; Wellesley Papers, Add. MSS. 37,287, R. Wellesley to Canning, Aug. 24, 1809.

65. Wellington, *Dispatches,* A. Wellesley to Eguia, Aug. 18, 1809, III:427.

66. P.R.O., F.O. 72/78, Roche to R. Wellesley, Aug. 19, 1809.

67. P.R.O., F.O. 72/76, Eguia to A. Wellesley, Aug. 19, 1809.

68. National Archives, Dept. of State, no. 59, vol. 11, Erving to Smith, Aug. 26, 1809.

69. Ibid., Erving to Smith, August 25, 1809. Erving felt it was fortunate that the British were going to withdraw because the Allies were not capable of cooperating.

70. Jonathan Leach, *Rough Sketches of the Life an Old Soldier,* p. 95.

71. P.R.O., F.O. 72/78, Roche to R. Wellesley, Aug. 19, 1809.

72. Longford, *Years of the Sword,* p. 202.

73. P.R.O., F.O. 72/76, A. Wellesley to R. Wellesley, Aug. 21, 1809.

74. Ibid., R. Wellesley to Canning, Aug. 24, 1809; Wellesley Papers, Add. MSS. 37,287, R. Wellesley to Canning, Aug. 24, 1809.

75. P.R.O., F.O. 72/76, R. Wellesley to Garay, Aug. 21, 1809; Wellesley Papers, Add. MSS. 37,287, Plan of Supply, Aug. 21, 1809.

76. P.R.O., F.O. 72/76, R. Wellesley to Garay, Aug. 21, 1809.

77. Ibid.; Wellesley Papers, Add. MSS. 37,287, Plan of Supply, Aug. 21, 1809.
78. Ibid.
79. Ibid.
80. Ibid.
81. Ibid.
82. P.R.O., F.O. 72/76, R. Wellesley to Canning, Aug. 24, 1809; Wellesley Papers, Add. MSS. 37,287, R. Wellesley to Canning, Aug. 24, 1809.
83. P.R.O., F.O. 72/76, R. Wellesley to A. Wellesley, Aug. 22, 1809; Wellesley Papers, Add. MSS. 37,287, R. Wellesley to A. Wellesley, Aug. 22, 1809.
84. Wellesley Papers, Add. MSS. 37,287, R. Wellesley to Canning, Aug. 24, 1809; P.R.O., F.O. 72/76, R. Wellesley to Canning, Aug. 24, 1809.
85. P.R.O., F.O. 72/76, R. Wellesley to Garay, Aug. 23, 1809.
86. Wellesley Papers, Add. MSS. 37,287, Garay to R. Wellesley, Aug. 23, 1809.
87. P.R.O., F.O. 72/76, A. Wellesley to R. Wellesley, Aug. 24, 1809.
88. Ibid.
89. Ibid.; A. Wellesley, *Letters to William Wellesley-Pole*, A. Wellesley to Pole, Aug. 29, 1809, pp. 165−66: "Since I have separated from the Spaniards, I have received a letter from Lord Wellesley in which he desires that I will remain in Spain; & connect myself again with the Spanish Army in a plan to defend the Guadiana. I consider it however a question of a very different description, & one to be decided on grounds entirely different, whether I shall again enter into cooperation with the Spaniards having separated from them; or being with them I should separate from them. . . . My opinion is that in the existing state of their affairs we (the army I mean) ought to have nothing to say to the Spaniards."
90. P.R.O., F.O. 72/76, R. Wellesley to A. Wellesley, Aug. 30, 1809.
91. Wellesley Papers, Add. MSS. 37,287, R. Wellesley to Canning, Sept. 2, 1809; P.R.O., F.O. 72/76, R. Wellesley to Canning, Sept. 2, 1809.
92. P.R.O., F.O. 72/76, Calvo to A. Wellesley, Aug. 19, 1809, A. Wellesley to R. Wellesley, Aug. 22, 28,1809; Londonderry, *Correspondence of Castlereagh*, A. Wellesley to Castlereagh, Aug. 25, 1809, VII:108−17; Wellesley Papers, Add. MSS. 37,287, R. Wellesley to Canning, Aug. 24, 1809; P.R.O., F.O. 72/78, Roche to R. Wellesley, Aug. 23, 1809. Wellesley had information that the Spanish army was in miserable shape: "Nothing can exceed the degree of irritation of General Eguia and all this army at the separation of the British, who wholly forgetful of the sacrifices we have made, endulge themselves now in the most violent invectives against us. . . . The melancholy truth is, my Lord, it is impossible to conceive an army in a worse state."
93. P.R.O., F.O. 72/76, Garay to R. Wellesley, Aug. 25, 1809; Wellesley Papers, Add. MSS. 37,287, Garay to R. Wellesley, Aug. 25, 1809.
94. Wellesley Papers, Add. MSS. 37,287, Garay to R. Wellesley, Aug. 25, 1809; P.R.O., F.O. 72/76, Garay to R. Wellesley, August 25, 1809, R. Wellesley to Canning, Sept. 2, 1809.
95. Wellesley Papers, Add. MSS. 37,287, R. Wellesley to Canning, Aug. 24, 1809; P.R.O., F.O. 72/76, R. Wellesley to Canning, Aug. 24, 1809.
96. P.R.O., F.O. 72/76, R. Wellesley to Garay, Aug. 28, 1809.
97. Ibid., R. Wellesley to Garay, August 30, 1809.
98. Wellington, *Supplementary Dispatches*, R. Wellesley to A. Wellesley, Aug. 29, 1809, VI:337; Londonderry, *Correspondence of Castlereagh*, Castlereagh to A.

Wellesley, Aug. 26, 1809, VII:117. In this last dispatch, Castlereagh informed Arthur that he had been made Baron Douro of Wellesley in the county of Somerset and Viscount Wellington of Talavera.

99. Wellesley Papers, Add. MSS. 37,287, R. Wellesley to Canning, Sept. 2, 1809; P.R.O., F.O. 72/76, R. Wellesley to Canning, Sept. 2, 1809.

100. P.R.O., F.O. 72/76, Garay to R. Wellesley, Aug. 30, 1809; Wellesley Papers, Add. MSS. 37,289, Garay to R. Wellesley, Aug. 30, 1809.

101. P.R.O., F.O. 72/76, A. Wellesley to R. Wellesley, Aug. 31, 1809.

102. Ibid., Garay to R. Wellesley, Aug. 30, 1809; Wellesley Papers, Add. MSS. 37,289, Garay to R. Wellesley, Aug. 30, 1809.

103. P.R.O., F.O. 72/76, R. Wellesley to Garay, Sept. 1, 1809; Wellesley Papers, Add. MSS. 37, 287, R. Wellesley to Canning, Sept. 2, 1809.

104. Wellesley Papers, Add. MSS. 37,286, Canning to R. Wellesley, Aug. 12, 1809; P.R.O., F.O. 185/17, Canning to R. Wellesley, Aug. 12, 1809; Londonderry, *Correspondence of Castlereagh*, Castlereagh to A. Wellesley, Aug. 12, 1809, VII: 101.

105. Wellesley Papers, Add. MSS. 37,286, Canning to R. Wellesley, Aug. 12, 1809.

106. Ibid.

107. Ibid., Canning to R. Wellesley (Official Instructions), Aug. 12, 1809.

108. Ibid., Add. MSS. 37,289, R. Wellesley to Canning, Sept. 15, 1809; P.R.O., F.O. 72/76, R. Wellesley to Canning, Sept. 15, 1809.

109. Wellesley Papers, Add. MSS. 37,289, R. Wellesley to Canning, Sept. 15, 1809; P.R.O., F.O. 72/76, R. Wellesley to Canning, Sept. 15, 1809; Napoléon I, *Correspondance de Napoléon Ier publiée par ordre de l'Empereur Napoléon III*, No. 15340, Napoleon to Clarke, June 12, 1809, XIX: 116–17. Napoleon ordered a cessation of military operations toward Portugal until reinforcements arrived in Spain.

110. Wellesley Papers, Add. MSS. 37,287, Brig. Gen. Whittingham to R. Wellesley, Sept. 4, 1809.

111. P.R.O., F.O. 72/76, R. Wellesley to Canning, Sept. 15, 1809; Wellesley Papers, Add. MSS. 37,289, R. Wellesley to Canning, Sept. 15, 1809; ibid., Add. MSS. 37,287, Lord Collingwood to Rear Admiral Purvis, March 26, 1809.

112. Wellesley Papers, Add. MSS. 37,287, R. Wellesley to Garay, Sept. 8, 1809; P.R.O., F.O. 72/76, R. Wellesley to Garay, Sept. 8, 1809.

113. Ibid.

Chapter 4

1. P.R.O., F.O. 72/76, R. Wellesley to Canning, Sept. 2, 1809; Wellesley Papers, Add. MSS. 37,287, R. Wellesley to Canning, Sept. 2, 1809.

2. P.R.O., F.O. 72/76, R. Wellesley to Canning, Sept. 15, 1809; Wellesley Papers, Add. MSS. 37,287, R. Wellesley to Canning, Sept. 15, 1809.

3. A.H.N., Sección de Estado, Legajo 70, documents relative to the formation of the Supreme Junta; Wellesley Papers, Add. MSS. 37,287, R. Wellesley to Canning, Sept. 15, 1809; P.R.O., F.O. 72/76, R. Wellesley to Canning, Sept. 15, 1809; Count José María Quiepo de Llano Ruiz Saravía Toreno, *Historia del levantamiento, querra y revolución de España*, p. 130; A.H.N., Legajo 71, Canning to

Matarosa, Vega and Sangro, August 20, 1808. Canning warned the representatives from Asturias and Galicia that he would terminate British aid if Spain did not form a central authority.

4. Toreno, *Historia de España*, pp. 129–30; A.H.N., Sección de Estado, Legajos 70, 71, documents relative to the formation of the Supreme Junta; Lovett, *Napoleon in Spain*, p. 292; the *Times*, Aug. 20, 1808. Representatives were sent by the Juntas of Aragon, Asturias, Canary Islands, Old Castile, Catalonia, Cordoba, Estremadura, Galicia, Granada, Jaen, León, Madrid, Mallorca, Murcia, Navarra, Seville, Toledo, and Valencia.

5. P.R.O., F.O. 72/76, R. Wellesley to Canning, Sept. 15, 1809; Wellesley Papers, Add. MSS. 37,289, R. Wellesley to Canning, Sept. 15, 1809; Toreno, *Historia de España*, p. 175.

6. A.H.N., Sección de Estado, Legajos 9, 60.

7. P.R.O., F.O. 72/76, R. Wellesley to Canning, Sept. 15, 1809; Wellesley Papers, Add. MSS. 37,289, R. Wellesley to Canning Sept. 15, 1809; Toreno, *Historia de España*, p. 198–99.

8. A.H.N., Sección de Estado, Legajos 52, 60. These contain letters of complaint to the Supreme Junta.

9. William Jacob, *Travels in the South of Spain*, p. 60.

10. P.R.O., F.O. 72/76, R. Wellesley to Canning, Sept. 15, 1809; Wellesley Papers, Add. MSS. 37, 289, R. Wellesley to Canning, Sept. 15, 1809.

11. National Archives, Dept. of State, no. 59, vol. 11, Erving to Madison, April 14, 1809. Canning had similar information; see P.R.O., F.O. 72/80, Lt. Col. William Parker Carroll to Canning, March 22, 1809.

12. Wellesley Papers, Add. MSS. 37,286, Decree of Don Martín de Garay, May 25, 1809; Toreno, *Historia de España*, p. 199.

13. Henry Richard (Lord) Holland, *Foreign Reminiscences*, 99.

14. Wellesley Papers, Add. MSS. 37,286, Johnstone to R. Wellesley, May 22, 1809; Brougham, *Life of Brougham*, John Wishaw to Brougham, Aug. 19, 1809, I:313. Wishaw, traveling in Spain, said of the junta: "The Junta appears to be feebleness itself, too numerous for an effective or strong government, and too few for any purposes of popular representation; for indeed they are in other respects altogether unfit. . . . With respect to military talents, the want of them is sufficiently apparent in the whole scheme of their campaign, and almost in every battle that has taken place."

15. Holland, *Foreign Reminiscences*, p. 99.

16. Jacob, *Travels in Spain*, pp. 62–65. Jacob provides many colorful descriptions of several members of the junta. Of the president, Marquis de Astorga, he writes: "He has the physiognomy of a baboon and is said to possess little more intellect than that mimic of man"; of the Marquis de Villel: "his stupidity, his frivolous turn of mind, and his ignorance, unfit him for any office requiring mental exertion"; of Count Tilly: "was known there only from his ill-gotten wealth, and his generally profligate character." Jacob did find exceptions: he describes Don Martín de Garay as a "man of plain good sense, without finesse, and tolerably assiduous in business." Lord Holland felt there were several capable men in the junta, including among them Jovellanos, Saavedra, Hermida, and Garay (*Foreign Reminiscenses*, pp. 99–100). Lovett, *Napoleon in Spain*, pp. 334–36, provides several good portraits of the junta's members.

17. In addition to reports sent to him from Spain by British agents and friends (Wellesley Papers, Add. MSS. 37,286) there were also numerous accounts on Spain printed in the *Times.*

18. P.R.O., F.O. 72/75, Canning to R. Wellesley, June 27, 1809.

19. Wellesley Papers, Add. MSS. 37, 287, Plan of Supply, Aug. 21, 1809, R. Wellesley to Canning, Sept. 15, 1809; P.R.O., F.O. 72/76, R. Wellesley to Garay, Aug. 21, 1809.

20. P.R.O., F.O. 72/76, R. Wellesley to Canning, Sept. 15, 1809; Wellesley Papers, Add. MSS. 37,287, R. Wellesley to Canning, Sept. 15, 1809.

21. P.R.O., F.O. 72/76, R. Wellesley to Canning, Sept. 15, 1809; Wellesley Papers, Add. MSS. 37,287, R. Wellesley to Canning, Sept. 15, 1809; Wellington, *Dispatches,* Wellington to R. Wellesley, Sept. 22, 1809, III: 514. Wellington did not agree with his brother on this point: "I acknowledge that I have a great dislike to a new popular assembly. Even our own ancient one would be quite unmanageable, and, in these days, would ruin us, if the present generation had not before its eyes the example of the French Revolution; and if there were not certain rules and orders for its guidance and government, the knowledge and use of which render safe, and successfully direct its proceedings."

22. Wellesley Papers, Add. MSS. 37,287, R. Wellesley to Canning, Sept. 15, 1809; P.R.O., F.O. 72/76, R. Wellesley to Canning, Sept. 15, 1809.

23. Ibid.

24. National Archives, Dept. of State, no. 59, vol. 11, Erving to Smith, Aug. 25, 1809.

25. Toreno, *Historia de España,* p. 198.

26. Wellesley Papers, Add. MSS. 37,287, Plans for the future of the Peninsula, end of August–early September 1809. This is one of several memoranda which Wellesley wrote to himself.

27. P.R.O., F.O. 72/76, R. Wellesley to Canning, Sept. 15, 1809; Wellesley Papers, Add. MSS. 37,287, R. Wellesley to Canning, Sept. 15, 1809.

28. Wellesley Papers, Add. MSS. 37,287, R. Wellesley to Garay, Sept. 8, 1809, to Canning, Aug. 24, Sept. 15, 1809; P.R.O., F.O. 72/76, R. Wellesley to Canning, Aug. 24, 1809.

29. Wellesley Papers, Add. MSS. 37,287, R. Wellesley to Garay, Sept. 8, 1809.

30. P.R.O., F.O. 72/76, R. Wellesley to Canning, Sept. 15, 1809; Wellesley Papers, Add. MSS. 37,287, R. Wellesley to Canning, Sept. 15, 1809. At this time, Wellesley was annoyed by the fact that Spanish soldiers when forced to retreat, were throwing away the arms and ammunition supplied by Great Britain.

31. Wellesley Papers, Add. MSS. 37,314, R. Wellesley to Earl Bathurst, Sept. 19, 1809.

32. A.H.N., Sección de Estado, Legajo 5460, Apodaca to Garay, Aug. 4, 1809.

33. Wellington, *Dispatches,* A. Wellesley to R. Wellesley, Sept. 1, 1809, III:463; P.R.O., F.O. 72/76, R. Wellesley to Canning, Sept. 15, 1809; Wellesley Papers, Add. MSS. 37,287, R. Wellesley to Canning, Sept. 15, 1809.

34. P.R.O., F.O. 72/76, R. Wellesley to Canning, Sept. 15, 1809; Wellesley Papers, Add. MSS. 37,287, R. Wellesley to Canning, Sept. 15, 1809.

35. Wellington, *Dispatches,* A. Wellesley to R. Wellesley, Sept. 1, 1809, III:463.

36. P.R.O., F.O. 72/78, Roche to R. Wellesley, Sept. 14, 1809; Wellington, *Supplementary Dispatches,* R. Wellesley to A. Wellesley, Sept. 19, 1809, VI:372,

Albuquerque to Cornel, Sept. 22, 1809, VI:378; Wellington, *Dispatches,* A. Wellesley to R. Wellesley, Sept. 21, 1809, III:512.

37. Wellesley Papers, Add. MSS. 37,288, R. Wellesley to Canning, Sept. 19, 1809; P.R.O., F.O. 72/76, R. Wellesley to Canning, Sept. 19, 1809; Wellington, . *Dispatches,* A. Wellesley to R. Wellesley, Sept. 22, 1809, III:514.

38. P.R.O., F.O. 72/90, Huskisson to Hammond, July 19, 1809; P.R.O., F.O. 72/75, Canning to R. Wellesley, July 20, 1809; Wellesley Papers, Add. MSS. 37,287, R. Wellesley to Garay, Sept. 3, 1809.

39. P.R.O., F.O. 72/90, Harrison to Pole, March 17, 1809, to Johnstone, March 17, 1809, Huskisson to Hammond, May 23, 1809; P.R.O., F.O. 72/75, Canning to R. Wellesley, Aug. 24, 1809.

40. P.R.O., F.O. 72/86, Johnstone to Saavedra, April 14, 1809: "I will give bills on the English treasury for the amount of three millions of dollars in return for an order for the like sum payable to me at Mexico."

41. P.R.O., F.O. 72/90, Huskisson to Hammond, May 23, 1809.

42. P.R.O., F.O. 72/86, Saavedra to Frere, April 20, 1809, Cevallos to Canning, May 13, 1809, Johnstone to Garay, May 23, 1809; P.R.O., F.O. 72/90, Worswick to Dent, Aug. 4, 1809; Wellesley Papers, Add. MSS. 37,287, Canning to R. Wellesley, Aug. 27, 1809.

43. P.R.O., F.O. 72/90, Huskisson to Hammond, May 23, 1809, to Johnstone, June 6, 1809 (the latter is a letter of censure); P.R.O., F.O. 72/89, Arbuthnot to Hammond, July 11, 1809; P.R.O., F.O. 72/75, Canning to R. Wellesley, Aug. 24, 1809.

44. P.R.O., F.O. 72/95, Canning to R. Wellesley, Aug. 24, 1809; P.R.O., F.O. 72/90, Huskisson to Hammond, May 23, 1809; Wellesley Papers, Add. MSS. 37,287, Garay to R. Wellesley, Aug. 18, 1809.

45. P.R.O., F.O. 72/75, Canning to R. Wellesley, June 27, 1809; P.R.O., F.O. 72/90, Treasury Memorandum, June 29, 1809.

46. P.R.O., F.O. 72/75, Canning to R. Wellesley, June 29, 1809.

47. Wellesley Papers, Add. MSS. 37,287, Garay to R. Wellesley, Sept. 14, 1809, R. Wellesley to Canning, Sept. 15, 1809; P.R.O., F.O. 72/76, R. Wellesley to Canning, Sept. 15, 1809.

48. Wellesley Papers, Add. MSS. 37,287, R. Wellesley to Garay, Sept. 13, 1809, Garay to R. Wellesley, Sept. 13, 1809.

49. Wellesley Papers, Add. MSS. 37,289, R. Wellesley to Canning, Sept. 19, 1809; ibid., Add. MSS. 37,288, Garay to R. Wellesley, Sept. 21, 23, Oct. 2, 1809; Wellington, *Supplementary Dispatches,* R. Wellesley to A. Wellesley, Sept. 24, 1809, VI:376; Wellington, *Dispatches,* A. Wellesley to R. Wellesley, Sept. 28, 1809, III:527–28; P.R.O., F.O. 72/78, Roche to R. Wellesley, Oct. 6, 1809.

50. Wellington, *Supplementary Dispatches,* Albuquerque to Cornel, Sept. 22, 1809, VI:378; Wellesley Papers, Add. MSS. 37,288, Duff to R. Wellesley, Sept. 26, 1809; P.R.O., F.O. 72/78, Roche to R. Wellesley, Oct. 17, 1809. Wellesley speculated that the junta left Albuquerque with so few men and in such a terrible state in order to draw Wellington back into Spain.

51. Wellesley Papers, Add. MSS. 37,287, R. Wellesley to Canning (Private and Confidential), Sept. 15, 1809; ibid., Add. MSS. 37,288, R. Wellesley to Garay, Sept. 30, 1809. Wellesley was also upset over the fact that the junta was still not providing Wellington with adequate supplies.

52. R. Wellesley, *Dispatches and Correspondence,* p. 160; Napier, *War in the Peninsula,* II:254; Wellington, *Supplementary Dispatches,* R. Wellesley to A. Wellesley, Sept. 19, 1809, VI:372–73.

53. Wellesley Papers, Add. MSS. 37,287, R. Wellesley to Wellington, Oct. 17, 1809.

54. Wellington, *Supplementary Dispatches,* R. Wellesley to A. Wellesley, Sept. 19, 1809, VI:372–73.

55. P.R.O., F.O. 72/77, Garay to R. Wellesley, Oct. 3, 1809.

56. P.R.O., F.O. 93/99–6.

57. P.R.O., F.O. 72/86, Cevallos to Canning, March 23, 1809.

58. Ibid., Canning to Cevallos, April 19, 1809.

59. National Archives, Dept. of State, no. 59, vol. 11, Erving to Smith, Aug. 26, 1809; Sherwig, *Guineas and Gunpowder,* p. 218; Wellesley Papers, Add. MSS. 37,416, Huskisson to Canning, Aug. 18, 1809.

60. P.R.O., F.O. 72/85, Apodaca to Canning, July 31, 1809; A.H.N., Sección de Estado, Legajo 5460, Apodaca to Garay, Aug. 1, 1809.

61. P.R.O., F.O. 185/17, Apodaca to Canning, Aug. 7, 1809; P.R.O., F.O. 72/85, Apodaca to Canning, Aug. 7, 1809.

62. P.R.O., F.O. 185/17, Canning to R. Wellesley, Sept. 16, 1809; Wellesley Papers, Add. MSS. 37,288, Canning to R. Wellesley, Sept. 16, 1809.

63. Wellesley Papers, Add. MSS. 37,288, Canning to R. Wellesley, Sept. 16, 1809; P.R.O., F.O. 185/17, Canning to R. Wellesley, Sept. 16, 1809; P.R.O., F.O. 72/85, Canning to Apodaca, Sept. 19, 1809.

64. P.R.O., F.O. 72/76, R. Wellesley to Canning, Oct. 8, 1809.

65. Numerous articles were appearing in the British press. The *Edinburgh Review,* vol. XV, no. 29, p. 235, provided some of the harshest commentaries; the *Morning Post* and the *Examiner* followed suit. See also A.H.N., Sección de Estado, Legajo 5460, Apodaca to Garay, Sept. 22, 1809; Wellington, *Supplementary Dispatches,* Castlereagh to Wellington, Sept. 9, 1809, VI:359; P.R.O, F.O. 72/78, Roche to R. Wellesley, Oct. 10, 1809; National Archives, Dept. of State, no. 59, vol. 11, Erving to Smith, Oct. 12, 1809. George Erving hailed the junta's unwillingness to institute Wellesley's reforms: ". . . the Junta in the midst of its misfortunes has preserved the dignity of its own character, and its country from a disgraceful vassalage to Great Britain; resisting with equal firmness her preposterous pretensions, and the intrigues and divisions with which it has been menaced here."

66. Wellesley Papers, Add. MSS. 37,288, R. Wellesley to Canning, Oct. 8, 1809, to Admiral Purvis, Oct. 13, 1809, to Captain Breaton, Oct. 17, 1809.

67. A.H.N., Sección de Estado, Legajo 5460, Apodaca to Garay, Sept. 22, 1809.

68. Wellesley Papers, Add. MSS. 37,288, R. Wellesley to Garay, Oct. 24, 1809.

69. Ibid; A.H.N., Sección de Estado, Legajo 2, Proceedings of the Supreme Junta.

70. Wellesley Papers, Add. MSS. 37,288, R. Wellesley to Garay, Oct. 24, 1809.

71. Toreno, *Historia de España,* p. 228; Don José Gómez de Arteche y Moro, *Guerra de la Independencia,* VII:32; Napier, *War in the Peninsula,* II:256; P.R.O., F.O. 72/78, Romana to Supreme Junta, Oct. 14, 1809. Romana presented a logical explanation for the necessity of reform, stressing the unconstitutionality

of the Supreme Junta. For a detailed account of his role in this affair, see Winslow Copley Goodwin, "The Political and Military Career of Don Pedro Caro y Sureda, Marquess de la Romana" (dissertation), pp. 212–22.

72. P.R.O., F.O. 185/17, Garay to R. Wellesley, Oct. 31, 1809. This is a full response to all of Wellesley's comments on the junta's plans, along with a notification that it would proceed to institute them.

73. Toreno, *Historia de España*, p. 228; Miguel Artola, *Los orígenes de la España contemporánea*, I:235–36; P.R.O., F.O. 72/78, Romana to Supreme Junta, Oct. 14, 1809; A.H.N., Sección de Estado, Legajo 2.

74. Wellesley Papers, Add. MSS. 37,288, R. Wellesley to Garay, Oct. 26, 1809.

75. Ibid., R. Wellesley to Garay, Oct. 29, 1809; P.R.O., F.O. 72/78, R. Wellesley to Garay, Oct. 29, 1809.

76. Wellesley Papers, Add. MSS. 37,288, R. Wellesley to Garay, Oct. 31, 1809; P.R.O., F.O. 185/17, R. Wellesley to Garay, Oct. 31, 1809.

77. Wellesley Papers, Add. MSS. 37,288, R. Wellesley to Saavedra, Nov. 3, 1809; ibid., Add. MSS. 37,314, R. Wellesley to Bathurst, Nov. 3, 1809.

78. Ibid., Add. MSS. 37,288, Memorandum by R. Wellesley, Nov. 4, 1809.

79. Ibid., Add. MSS. 37,314, R. Wellesley to Bathurst, Nov. 3, 1809; ibid., Add. MSS. 37,288, R. Wellesley to Saavedra, Nov. 7, 1809.

80. Ibid., Add. MSS. 37,288, R. Wellesley to Saavedra, Nov. 3, 8, 1809, to Romana, Nov. 8, 1809.

81. Ibid., R. Wellesley to B. Frere, Nov. 10, 1809; P.R.O., F.O. 72/78, R. Wellesley to B. Frere, Nov. 10, 1809. For questions on policy, Wellesley referred Frere to Canning's dispatches.

82. Wellesley Papers, Add. MSS. 37,288, R. Wellesley to Saavedra, Nov. 10, 1809, to Duff, Nov. 10, 1809; P.R.O., F.O. 72/78, R. Wellesley to Saavedra, Nov. 10, 1809; P.R.O., F.O. 72/85, Bathurst to Apodaca, Oct. 28, 1809. Apodaca had been similarly informed in London.

83. Arthur Wellesley, 1st Duke of Wellington, *Wellington at War, 1794–1815: A Selection of Wartime Letters*, Wellington to Pole, Nov. 16, 1809, p. 175; P.R.O., F.O. 72/79, Saavedra to R. Wellesley, Nov. 11, 1809. Most letters of thanks are in Wellesley Papers, Add. MSS. 37, 288.

84. Napier, *War in the Peninsula*, II:283.

85. The lines were constructed in utmost secrecy while Wellington's army was at Badajoz. See Sir John Thomas Jones, *Memoranda Relative to the Lines Thrown up to Cover Lisbon in 1810*.

86. P.R.O., F.O. 72/78, Wellington to R. Wellesley, Oct. 30, 1809. Wellesley carried all his dispatches home with him along with several of Sir Arthur's. Some dispatches he apparently had written specifically for this purpose, such as the one from Wellington written on Oct. 30, shortly before his departure, which certainly would have served him no purpose in Spain.

87. P.R.O., F.O. 72/89, An account of Wellesley's expenses in Spain. The Marquess overspent to the amount of £2,301 but this was covered by the sale of several items from the embassy when he left Seville.

88. Wellesley Papers, Add. MSS. 37,309, Bathurst to R. Wellesley, Oct. 21, 1809; ibid., Add. MSS. 37, 288, Villiers to R. Wellesley, Sept. 27, 1809. Mr. Villiers, the British representative in Lisbon, wrote: ". . . let me thank you for the lesson which your dispatches have afforded me of political energy and wisdom recommended by clear, captivating, and impressive language."

89. Pearce, *Memoirs and Correspondence of Marquess Wellesley*, III:55.

Chapter 5

1. See chap. 2.
2. Bathurst Papers, loan no. 57, vol. 4, no. 324, Bathurst's full explanation of the events leading to the resignation of the Duke of Portland, Canning and Castlereagh, and the subsequent break-up of the ministry; British Museum, Liverpool Papers, Add. MSS. 38,243, Liverpool to Wallace, Sept. 23, 1809 (Liverpool's account of the dissolution of the Portland Ministry).
3. British Museum, Perceval Papers, Add. MSS. 49,188. This volume contains correspondence between Canning and Perceval on the subject of ministerial reorganization.
4. Ibid.; Liverpool Papers, Add. MSS. 38,243, Liverpool to Wallace, Sept. 23, 1809; Bathurst Papers, loan no. 57, vol. 4, no. 324, Bathurst's account of the dissolution of the Portland Ministry.
5. Bathurst Papers, loan no, 57, vol. 4, no. 324, Bathurst's account of the dissolution of the Portland Ministry; Liverpool Papers, Add. MSS. 38,243, Liverpool to Wallace, Sept. 23, 1809; Perceval Papers, Add. MSS. 49,188.
6. Liverpool Papers, Add. MSS. 38,243, Liverpool to Wallace, Sept. 23, 1809; Bathurst Papers, loan no. 57, vol. 4, no. 324, Bathurst's account of the dissolution of the Portland Ministry; Perceval Papers, Add. MSS. 49,188, Perceval to Lord Arden, Sept. 9, 1809.
7. Wellesley Papers, Add. MSS. 37,309, W. W. Pole to R. Wellesley, Sept. 3, 1809.
8. Ibid., Add. MSS. 37,295, Sydenham to R. Wellesley, Sept. 5, 1809.
9. Liverpool Papers, Add. MSS. 38,243, Liverpool to Wallace, Sept. 23, 1809; Bathurst Papers, loan no. 57, vol. 4, no. 324, Bathurst's account of the dissolution of the Portland Ministry.
10. Bathurst Papers, loan no. 57, vol. 4, no. 371, Camden to Bathurst, Sept. [?], 1809; Perceval Papers, Add. MSS. 49,188, Perceval to Lord Arden, Sept. 9, 1809.
11. Wellesley Papers, Add. MSS. 37,295, Sydenham to R. Wellesley, Sept. 19, 1809; Liverpool Papers, Add. MSS. 38,243, Liverpool to Wallace, Sept. 23, 1809; Bathurst Papers, loan no. 57, vol. 4, no. 324, Bathurst's account of the dissolution of the Portland Ministry.
12. Liverpool Papers, Add. MSS. 38,243, Liverpool to Wallace, Sept. 23, 1809; Bathurst Papers, loan no. 57, vol. 4, no. 324, Bathurst's account of the dissolution of the Portland Ministry; Perceval Papers, Add. MSS. 49,188, Perceval to Lord Arden, Sept. 9, 1809; Wellesley Papers, Add. MSS. 37,295, Sydenham to R. Wellesley, Sept. 19, 1809; Huskisson Papers, Add. MSS. 38,737, Arbuthnot to Huskisson, Nov. 11, 1809; Wellesley Papers, Add. MSS. 37,315, Hyacinthe Wellesley to R. Wellesley, Sept. 23, 1809. Rumors abounded in London of Wellesley's being appointed prime minister. His daughter, Hyacinthe, wrote to him: "I hear from all quarters that you are coming home immediately to be Prime Minister; I hope it may be true but I fear you will prefer remaining in Spain."
13. Liverpool Papers, Add. MSS. 38,243, Liverpool to Wallace, Sept. 23, 1809; Bathurst Papers, loan no. 57, vol. 4, no. 324, Bathurst's account of the dissolution of the Portland Ministry.
14. Ibid.

15. Cowley Papers, P.R.O., F.O. 519/67, Henry Wellesley's Memoir; Liverpool Papers, Add. MSS. 38,243, Liverpool to Wallace, Sept. 23, 1809.

16. Liverpool Papers, Add. MSS. 38,243, Liverpool to Wallace, Sept. 23, 1809; Cowley Papers, P.R.O., F.O. 519/67, Henry Wellesley's Memoir; Wellesley Papers, Add. MSS. 37,295, H. Wellesley to R. Wellesley, Sept. 22, 1809.

17. Huskisson Papers, Add. MSS. 37,737, Arbuthnot to Huskisson, Sept. 14, 1809. Pole did inform Perceval that he could not answer for Wellesley.

18. Castlereagh had taken a strong line in favor of Sir Arthur regarding his role in the signing of the Convention of Cintra. See chap. 2.

19. Wellesley had left both Pole and Benjamin Sydenham in charge of his business affairs while he was in Seville. Many historians confuse the person of Benjamin Sydenham with his brother, Thomas, but it was the former who was Wellesley's closest confidant.

20. Wellesley Papers, Add. MSS. 37,295, Sydenham to R. Wellesley, Sept. 16, 1809.

21. Bathurst Papers, loan no. 57, vol. 4, no. 324, Bathurst's account of the dissolution of the Portland Ministry; Liverpool Papers, Add. MSS. 38,243, Liverpool to Wallace, Sept. 23, 1809.

22. Wellesley Papers, Add. MSS. 37,295, Sydenham to R. Wellesley, Sept. 19, 1809.

23. Liverpool Papers, Add. MSS. 38,243, Liverpool to Wallace, Sept. 23, 1809; Bathurst Papers, loan no. 57, vol. 4, no. 324, Bathurst's account of the dissolution of the Portland Ministry.

24. Cowley Papers, P.R.O., F.O. 519/67.

25. Liverpool Papers, Add. MSS. 38,243, Liverpool to Wallace, Sept. 23, 1809; Bathurst Papers, loan no. 57. vol. 4, no. 324, Bathurst's account of the dissolution of the Portland Ministry.

26. Liverpool Papers, Add. MSS. 38,243, Liverpool to Wallace, Sept. 23, 1809; Bathurst Papers, loan no. 57, vol. 4, no. 324, Bathurst's account of the dissolution of the Portland Ministry; Huskisson Papers, Add. MSS. 38,737, Canning to Huskisson, Oct. 13, 1809; British Museum, Canning Papers, Add. MSS. 46, 841, Canning to Booth, Dec. 19, 1809. The king asked Canning for a detailed description of the duel and his wound. Canning, never one to lose his sense of humor, later commented to Mr. Booth: "It used to be difficult to get *in* [to a ministry]—at all times; but I never knew that getting out again was a matter of so much difficulty."

27. Liverpool Papers, Add. MSS. 38,243, Perceval to Grey, Sept. 23, 1809, Liverpool to Wallace, Sept. 23, 1809; Bathurst Papers, loan no. 57. vol. 4, no. 324, Bathurst's account of the dissolution of the Portland Ministry.

28. Liverpool Papers, Add. MSS. 38,243, Grenville to Perceval, Sept. 23, 1809, Grey to Perceval, Sept. 23, 1809.

29. Francis Horner, *Memoirs and Correspondence of Francis Horner, M.P.,* Horner to John Allen, Sept. 30, 1809, I:469.

30. Perceval Papers, Add. MSS. 49,188, Perceval to Lord Arden, Oct. 2, 1809; Wellesley Papers, Add. MSS. 37,295, Perceval to R. Wellesley, Oct. 5, 1809; Huskisson Papers, Add. MSS. 38,737, Canning to Huskisson, Oct. 13, 1809; Bathurst Papers, loan no. 57, vol. 4, no. 324, Bathurst's account of the dissolution of the Portland Ministry; A.H.N., Sección de Estado, Legajo 5460, Apodaca to

Garay, Oct. 3, 1809. Bathurst served as foreign secretary ad interim with the understanding that he would resign if Wellesley accepted the post.

31. Wellesley Papers, Add. MSS. 37,415, Wellington to R. Wellesley, Oct. 5, 1809.

32. A. Wellesley, *Letters to William Wellesley-Pole*, Wellington to Pole, Oct. 6, 1809, p. 26.

33. Wellesley Papers, Add. MSS. 37,295, R. Wellesley to W. W. Pole, Oct. 8, 1809.

34. Ibid., Canning to R. Wellesley, Oct. 20, 1809.

35. Ibid., R. Wellesley to Liverpool, Oct. 30, 1809, to H. Wellesley, Oct. 30, 1809. To Henry Wellesley the Marquess wrote: "Is Canning insane, or determined from the first to join opposition? I cannot understand any part of his conduct, except his jealousy of my pretensions."

36. *Morning Chronicle*, Sept. 29, 1809.

37. Ibid., Oct. 4, 1809.

38. *Morning Post*, Oct. 5, 1809.

39. *Morning Chronicle*, Oct. 27, 1809.

40. Ibid., Nov. 15, 25, 1809; the *Examiner*, October 8, 1809, made the following comment: "The meek-spirited Lord Wellesley is leaving Spain for England, for the purpose, it is said, of occupying one of those golden and glorious niches in the temple of British fame! Lord Melville's Son is talked of as coming in also!— Napoleon, beware now of your proceeding: these *well known* and exalted Statesmen, with the religious Mr. Perceval at their head, who has *modestly* accepted the highly responsible and dignified office of Prime Minister, will cut you out of plenty of work!—Beware!"

41. George Pellew, *The Life and Correspondence of the Right Honourable Henry Addington, lst Viscount Sidmouth*, Powis to Addington, Nov. 25, 1809, III:13–14.

42. Bathurst Papers, loan no. 57, vol. 4, no. 331, Malmesbury to Bathurst, Oct. 12, 1809; A.H.N., Sección de Estado, Legajo 5460, Apodaca to Garay, Nov. 28, 1809.

43. The *Times*, Nov. 25, 1809.

44. Bathurst Papers, loan no. 57, vol. 4, no. 328, Pembroke to Bathurst, Oct. 10, 1809; *Morning Chronicle*, Oct. 25, 1809.

45. Wellesley Papers, Add. MSS. 37,314, R. Wellesley to Bathurst, Nov. 26, 1809. Wellesley landed at Portsmouth on Nov. 26 and arrived in London on November 29, 1809.

46. Ibid., Add. MSS. 37,295, Perceval to George III, Nov. 30, 1809, George III to Perceval, Dec. 1, 1809.

47. George III had planned to confer the Garter on the Duke of Richmond, Lord Lieutenant of Ireland.

48. Ibid., George III to Perceval, Dec. 1, 1809, R. Wellesley to Perceval, Dec. 2, 1809. The investiture took place on March 10, 1810.

49. P.R.O., F.O. 185/16, Circular announcing Wellesley's acceptance of the seals of office, Dec. 6, 1809.

50. Cowley Papers, P.R.O., F.O. 519/67; A.H.N., Sección de Estado, Legajo 5460, Regency to Apodaca, Feb. 10, 1810. The Spanish knew there would be both advantages and disadvantages to having the foreign secretary's brother at the embassy in Cádiz.

51. Wellesley Papers, Add. MSS. 37,295, R. Wellesley to H. Wellesley, Oct. 30, 1809.

52. Ibid., Add. MSS. 37,288, R. Wellesley to George III, Dec. 11, 1809.

53. Ibid., R. Wellesley to George III, Dec. 17, 1809; A.H.N.., Sección de Estado, Legajo 5460, Apodaca to Saavedra, Dec. 25, 1809. Mr. Vaughan had been Lord Bathurst's secretary. He had traveled in Spain extensively, knew the language well, and was popular with Spanish leaders.

54. Cowley Papers, P.R.O., F.O. 519/67, Henry Wellesley's Memoir.

55. Ibid.

56. Ibid.

57. Ibid.

58. Ibid.; George Charles Henry Victor Paget, 7th Marquess of Anglessy, *One Leg: The Life and Letters of Henry William Paget, First Marquess of Anglessy, K.G.,* pp. 89–92, 96–97.

59. Huskisson Papers, Add. MSS. 38,737, H. Wellesley to Huskisson, March 21, 1809.

60. Cowley Papers, P.R.O., F.O. 519/67.

61. Wellington, *Supplementary Dispatches,* Wellington to Beresford, Oct. 20, 1809, VI:408–10; Wellesley Papers, Add. MSS. 37,288, Roche to R. Wellesley, October 24, 1809; Napier, *War in the Peninsula,* II, 257; Charles William Vane, 3d Marquis of Londonderry,*Narrative of the Peninsular War from 1808 to 1813,* I:438; Oman, *The Peninsular War,* III:69, 74–75.

62. Wellesley Papers, Add. MSS. 37,288, Roche to R. Wellesley, Oct. 28, 1809; P.R.O., F.O. 72/80, Carroll to Canning, Oct. 28, 1809; Toreno,*Historia de España,* pp. 225–30.

63. P.R.O., F.O. 72/79, B. Frere to Bathurst, Nov. 17, 1809, Saavedra to B. Frere, Nov. 16, 1809.

64. Ibid.

65. Wellesley Papers, Add. MSS. 49, 981, B. Frere to Bathurst, Nov. 21, 1809; P.R.O., F.O. 72/79, Saavedra to Frere, Nov. 17, 1809.

66. P.R.O., F.O. 72/79, B. Frere to Saavedra, Nov. 23, 1809, Wellington to B. Frere, Nov. 19, 1809; Wellesley Papers, Add. MSS. 49,981, B. Frere to Bathurst, Nov. 28, 1809.

67. Toreno, *Historia de España,* pp. 230–32; P.R.O., F.O. 72/79, Areizagas to Cornel, Nov. 19, 20, 1809; Wellesley Papers, Add. MSS. 49,981, B. Frere to Bathurst, Nov. 23, 1809; P.R.O., F.O. 72/78, Roche to R. Wellesley, Nov. 27, 1809.

68. P.R.O., F.O. 72/78, Roche to R. Wellesley, Nov. 27, 1809.

69. National Archives, Dept. of State, no. 59, vol. 11, Erving to Smith, Nov. 28, 1809; Arteche y Moro, *Guerra de la Independencia,* VII:47.

70. P.R.O., F.O. 72/80, Hamlet to Bathurst, Nov. 27, 1809; P.R.O., F.O. 72/89, Purvis to Croker, Nov. 19, 1809.

71. P.R.O., F.O. 72/79, B. Frere to Bathurst, Nov. 29, 1809.

72. Oman, *The Peninsular War,* III:95; P.R.O., F.O. 72/79, Parque to Cornel, Dec. 5, 1809, B. Frere to Bathurst, Dec. 10, 1809; Wellesley Papers, Add. MSS. 49,981, B. Frere to Bathurst, Dec. 10, 1809; Toreno,*Historia de España,* p. 233.

73. Wellington,*Dispatches,* Wellington to B. Frere, Dec. 6, 1809, III:622, Dec. 9, 1809, III:630.

74. Ibid.

75. P.R.O., F.O. 72/85, Apodaca to R. Wellesley, Dec. 13, 1809; Wellesley Papers, Add. MSS. 49,979, R. Wellesley to B. Frere, Dec. 7, 1809.

76. Wellesley Papers, Add. MSS. 49,981, B. Frere to Bathurst, Dec. 15, 1809; P.R.O., F.O. 72/79, B. Frere to Bathurst, Dec. 15, 1809.

77. P.R.O., F.O. 72/78, B. Frere to Bathurst, Dec. 25, 1809; Wellesley Papers, Add. MSS. 49,981, B. Frere to Bathurst, Dec. 25, 1809.

78. P.R.O., F.O. 72/79, Representation made by the Junta of Seville to the Central Junta, Dec. 19, 1809.

79. Wellesley Papers, Add. MSS. 32,288, J. H. Frere to R. Wellesley, Dec. 26, 1809, B. Frere to R. Wellesley, Dec. 26, 1809; ibid., Add. MSS. 37,315, R. Wellesley (son) to R. Wellesley, Jan. 14, 1810.

80. P.R.O., F.O. 185/19, Notes of R. Wellesley, Jan. 25, 1810; Wellesley Papers, Add. MSS. 37,291, Notes of R. Wellesley, Jan. 25, 1810; ibid., Add. MSS. 49,985, R. Wellesley to Villiers, Jan. 5, 1810. "In Spain the assembly of the Cortes is the only remedy to which that country can resort for the purpose of investing the government with a regular form or national spirit."

81. Wellesley Papers, Add. MSS. 37,291, Notes of R. Wellesley, Jan. 25, 1810; P.R.O., F.O. 185/19, Notes of R. Wellesley, Jan. 25, 1810.

82. Ibid.

83. Ibid., Add. MSS. 37,295, Perceval to R. Wellesley, Dec. 1, 1809, R. Wellesley to Perceval, Dec. 2, 1809; Huskisson Papers, Add. MSS. 38,759, Report on expenditure.

84. P.R.O., F.O. 72/93, R. Wellesley to H. Wellesley, Jan. 4, 1810; Wellesley Papers, Add. MSS. 49,979, R. Wellesley to H. Wellesley, Jan. 4, 1810.

85. Wellesley Papers, Add. MSS. 49,979, R. Wellesley to H. Wellesley, Jan. 27, 1810; P.R.O., F.O. 72/93, R. Wellesley to H. Wellesley, Jan. 27, 1810; P.R.O., F.O. 72/90, Barrow to Hamilton, Dec. 22, 1809; P.R.O., F.O. 72/85, Apodaca to R. Wellesley, Dec. 27, 1809; Wellesley Papers, Add. MSS. 37,291, Notes of R. Wellesley, Jan. 25, 1810.

86. P.R.O., F.O. 72/92, B. Frere to R. Wellesley, Jan. 6, 1810; Wellesley Papers, Add. MSS. 49,981, B. Frere to R. Wellesley, Jan. 6, 1810. The Salic Law had in fact been abolished in Spain.

87. Wellesley Papers, Add. MSS. 37,291, Notes from R. Wellesley, Jan. 25, 1810; P.R.O., F.O. 185/19, Notes from R. Wellesley, Jan. 25, 1810.

88. Ibid.

89. Wellesley Papers, Add. MSS. 37,286, Canning to R. Wellesley, July 20, 1809.

90. P.R.O., F.O. 185/19, Notes from R. Wellesley, Jan. 25, 1810; Wellesley Papers, Add. MSS. 37,291, Notes from R. Wellesley, Jan. 25, 1810.

91. P.R.O., F.O. 72/78, R. Wellesley to Purvis, Nov. 10, 1809.

92. A.H.N., Sección de Estado, Legajo 5461, Apodaca to Saavedra, Feb. 12, 1810.

93. P.R.O., F.O. 72/92, B. Frere to R. Wellesley, Jan. 20, 1810, to Saavedra, Jan. 10, 1810, Saavedra to B. Frere, Jan. 9, 1810.

94. Wellesley Papers, Add. MSS. 37,291, B. Frere to R. Wellesley, Jan. 8, 1810; P.R.O., F.O. 72/92, B. Frere to R. Wellesley, Jan. 7, 1810; Wellesley Papers, Add. MSS. 49,981, B. Frere to R. Wellesley, Jan. 7, 1810. The junta blamed the British for the military situation: "That the loss of Galicia might be attributed to the want

of concert between Sir John Moore and the Spanish Generals, especially the Marquis of Romana—the invasion of Asturias to the having neglected to follow up the pursuit of M1. Soult—the disasters in Castile to the passage of the Tagus by the British troops after the battle of Talavera, and the want of cooperation in that quarter."

Chapter 6

1. Liverpool Papers, Add. MSS. 38,244, Liverpool to Wellington, Dec. 15, 1809; Wellington, *Supplementary Dispatches,* Liverpool to Wellington, Dec. 15, 1809, VI: 441.
2. Wellesley Papers, Add. MSS. 37,295, Perceval to R. Wellesley, Dec. 1, 1809.
3. Ibid., R. Wellesley to Perceval, Dec. 2, 1809.
4. Ibid., Add. MSS. 37,291, An explanation of the purposes of the Walcheren Campaign.
5. Ibid., Add. MSS. 37,288, Villiers to R. Wellesley, Dec. 24, 1809; *Examiner,* Dec. 17, 1809.
6. *Examiner,* Dec. 31, 1809. On Dec. 17, it commented: "It must be repeated for the hundredth time, that the whole affair of Spanish resistance is nothing but a pompous jest. The Inquisition will not do: the slavery of the press will not do: the reign of the Priests will not do: and for all these reasons, the new French government *will do.*"
7. A.H.N., Sección de Estado, Legajo 5460, Apodaca to Saavedra, Dec. 13, 1809; ibid., Legajo 5461, Castaños to George III, Jan. 3, 1810; P.R.O., F.O. 72/85, Apodaca to R. Wellesley, Dec. 23, 1809; P.R.O., F.O. 72/89, Spanish proclamation, Sept. 5, 1809; P.R.O., F.O. 72/117, Apodaca to R. Wellesley, Jan. 3, 1810; P.R.O., F.O. 72/100, Apodaca to R. Wellesley, Jan. 16, 1810 (much of the communication between Apodaca and R. Wellesley in this volume deals with seizure of Spanish ships by British ships).
8. *Creevey Papers,* Lord Milton to Creevey, Jan. 8, 1810, I:118.
9. Ibid., p. 113. Creevey comments: "I met Abercromby in my walk. He is as artificial as the devil—will scarcely touch politicks—thinks, however, the Wellesleys will now be beat if they are attacked properly; upon which I fire into our leaders for their meanness in not having attacked them long ago."
10. *Parliamentary Debates,* XV:25; A.H.N., Sección de Estado, Legajo 5461, Apodaca to Saavedra, Jan. 24, 1810. Apodaca was quite impressed with the speech, which was drafted in part by Lord Wellesley.
11. Ibid.
12. *Creevey Papers,* Jan. 24, 1810 I:123. Creevey himself was exacerbated: "The Opposition found themselves in a still more disorganized plight, so as to be quite unready to . . . gain any advantage from the confusion of their enemies. And the Opposition, as is commonly to be seen under similar circumstances, took to quarreling among themselves, mistrusting each other, unable to decide upon the choice of a leader."
13. *Parliamentary Debates,* XV:106–7.
14. Ibid., p. 107.
15. Ibid., pp. 107–9.
16. Ibid., pp. 131–36.

17. Ibid., pp. 136–38.

18. Ibid., p. 138.

19. Ibid., pp. 145–52.

20. Ibid., pp. 140–45, 152–54.

21. Lady Holland, *Journal of Lady Holland*, II:254.

22. *Parliamentary Debates*, XV:277–80.

23. Ibid., pp. 280–81 (speech by Milton), pp. 282–84 (speech by Vernon), pp. 286–88 (speech by Tarleton), pp. 295–98 (speech by Whitbread).

24. Ibid., pp. 288–95.

25. *Creevey Papers*, Feb. 1, 1810, I:127; *Parliamentary Debates*, XV:302. The debate on Thanks was followed by one granting a pension to Wellington; it passed with difficulty. The debate in the Lords appears on pp. 357–58, in the Commons, pp. 440–67.

26. Wellesley Papers, Add. MSS. 37,295, R. Wellesley to Perceval, Feb. 12, 1810.

27. *Parliamentary Debates*, vol. XVI, The Walcheren debates.

28. Wellesley Papers, Add. MSS. 37,295, R. Wellesley to Perceval, Feb. 12, 1810.

29. P.R.O., F.O. 72/85, Apodaca to Bathurst, Dec. 1, 1809; A.H.N., Sección de Estado, Legajo 5460, Regency to Apodaca, Jan. 3, 1810, ibid., Legajo 5461, Apodaca to Saavedra, Feb. 7, 1810.

30. Neither Perceval nor Liverpool commented on the matter, and it was not brought up in Parliament.

31. Wellesley Papers, Add. MSS. 37,309, Arbuthnot to R. Wellesley, December 12, 1809; ibid., Add. MSS. 37,291, Plans of Baron de Kolli for the escape of Ferdinand VII; Léonce Grasilier, *Adventuriers politiques sous le Consulat et l'Empire. Le baron de Kolli. Le comte Pagowski*, p. 11; Charles Leopold, Baron de Kolli, *Mémoires du baron de Kolli et de la reine d'Éturie*, p. 30.

32. Wellesley Papers, Add. MSS. 37,291, R. Wellesley to Mulgrave, Jan. 29, 1810 (Cockburn was a close friend of the Wellesleys and thus his confidence could be trusted), Croker to Hamilton, Jan. 29, 1810; Grasilier, *Baron de Kolli*, pp. 42, 60; Kolli, *Mémoires du baron de Kolli*, p. 50.

33. Wesllesley Papers, Add. MSS. 37,291, R. Wellesley to Cockburn, Feb. 2, 1810.

34. Grasilier, *Baron de Kolli*, p. 61; Wellesley Papers, Add. MSS. 37,291, R. Wellesley to Cockburn, Feb. 27 (labeled "very secret"), March 1, 1810.

35. Kolli, *Mémoires du baron de Kolli*, p. 52; Grasilier *Baron de Kolli*, pp. 64, 72; Wellesley Papers, Add. MSS. 37,291, Cockburn to R. Wellesley, March 2, 15, 1810, to Shawe, March 2, 1810.

36. Wellesley Papers, Add. MSS. 37,291, Cockburn to R. Wellesley, March 2, 15, 1810, to Shawe, March 2, 1810; Kolli, *Mémories du baron de Kolli*, p. 52; Grasilier, *Baron de Kolli*, pp. 64, 72, 100–121, 128; Wellesley Papers, Add. MSS. 37,294, Extract from a diary of Rear Admiral Sir George Cockburn, with particular reference to General Napoleon Bonaparte, on passage from England to St. Helena in 1815, on board H.M.S. *Northumberland*, then bearing the Rear Admiral's Flag, Aug. 12, 1815.

37. Le *Moniteur*, April 26, 1810; Kolli, *Mémoires du baron de Kolli*, p. 55; Grasilier, *Baron de Kolli*, pp. 100–121, 128; Wellesley Papers, Add. MSS. 37,294, Extract from a diary of Rear Admiral Sir George Cockburn, Aug. 12, 1815.

Napoleon assured Cockburn "that until Kolly [*sic*] was discovered at Paris the French government had no idea of our attempting to carry off Ferdinand." He also denied that Kolli had betrayed the mission.

38. Wellesley Papers, Add. MSS. 37,292, Cockburn to R. Wellesley, May 25, 1810, to Shawe, June 7, 1810. Cockburn states that Kolli's accomplices were not guilty of betraying the mission. Instead, they were completely dedicated to what they were undertaking and, though to some degree indiscreet, their intentions were always noble.

39. A.H.N., Sección de Estado, Legajo 5461, Apodaca to Bardaxi, May 9, 1810; Oxford, All Souls College, Vaughan Papers, C:48:5, Hamilton to Vaughan, May 7, 1810; ibid., C:104:8, Stuart to Vaughan, May 26, 1810: "I say my dear Vaughan who the Devil is Baron Kolly [*sic*] & how much of the negotiation with which he was charged are we to credit. I never heard such a mess in my life. If I had been aware of the proposition I should have strongly advised it not to be listened to because I am sure Ferdinand will not come away if he can." Cowley Papers, P.R.O., F.O. 519/36, H. Wellesley to R. Wellesley, June 12, 1810: "People hardly know what to think of the Baron de Kolli's business. It does not appear to have created much sensation here."

40. Wellesley Papers, Add. MSS. 49,981, H. Wellesley to R. Wellesley, March 10, 1810, B. Frere to R. Wellesley, Jan 29, Feb. 2, 1810; P.R.O., F.O. 72/94, H. Wellesley to R. Wellesley, March 10, 1810; Oman, *The Peninsular War*, III: 130–31; Napier, *War in the Peninsula*, II: 292; Toreno, *Historia de España*, pp. 230, 236–39. Spanish resistance in the Sierra Morena lasted only a few hours, as Colonel Roche predicted.

41. P.R.O., F.O. 72/92, B. Frere to Saavedra, Jan. 18, 1810; Wellesley Papers, Add. MSS. 49,981, B. Frere to R. Wellesley, Jan. 20, 1810.

42. P.R.O., F.O. 72/92, B. Frere to R. Wellesley, Jan. 29, 1819, to Colin Campbell, Jan. 28, 1810; Wellesley Papers, Add. MSS. 49,981, B. Frere to R. Wellesley, Jan. 29, 1810.

43. P.R.O., F.O. 72/92, B. Frere to R. Wellesley, Jan. 29, 1810; Wellesley Papers, Add. MSS. 49,981, B. Frere to R. Wellesley, Jan. 29, 1810; Toreno, *Historia de España*, p. 193, 238–42; Arteche y Moro, *Guerra de la Independencia*, VII:47; Jacob, *Travels in the South of Spain*, p. 367; A.H.N., Sección de Estado, Legajo 9, Circulares, reglamentos proclamares, y manifestos de la Regencia, January 1810. Frere seemingly played a more important role during these chaotic days in Seville than he is generally given credit for.

44. Wellesley Papers, Add. MSS. 49,981, B. Frere to R. Wellesley, Jan. 29, 1810; P.R.O., F.O. 72/92, B. Frere to R. Wellesley, Jan. 29, 1810.

45. P.R.O., F.O. 72/92, Don Pedro Rivero to B. Frere, Jan. 29, 1810; A.H.N., Sección de Estado, Legajo 9, Circulares, reglamentos, proclamares, y manifestos de la Regencia, January 1810; Toreno, *Historia de España*, p. 193; Wellesley Papers, Add. MSS. 49,981, B. Frere to R. Wellesley, Feb. 1, 2, 1810. M. de León resigned his seat on the Council of Regency and was replaced by Miguel de Lardizabal y Uribe. Castaños was elected head of the regency.

46. Wellesley Papers, Add. MSS. 49,981, B. Frere to R. Wellesley, Feb. 2, 1810; Liverpool Papers, Add. MSS. 38,244, Purvis to Croker, Feb. 2, 1810; Oman, *The Peninsular War*, III: 145; Napier, *War in the Peninsula*, II:294.

47. Wellesley Papers, Add. MSS. 49, 981, B. Frere to R. Wellesley, Feb. 2, 11, 1810; Liverpool Papers, Add. MSS. 38,244, Purvis to Croker, Feb. 2, 1810;

Oman, *The Penisular War*, III:145–52; Napier, *War in the Peninsula*, II: 295; National Archives, Dept. of State, no. 195, vol. 11, Erving to Smith, Feb. 9, 1810. Actually the Andalusian campaign was ill conceived; the only real danger in the peninsula after the autumn campaign was the British army then in Portugal. The conquest of Andalusia was not only needless, but its occupation committed more French troops to the task of supervising the hostile Spanish populace. When the Spanish safely occupied Cádiz, before the arrival of Marshal Victor, even more troops were required to watch the Anglo-Spanish force that garrisoned the harbor city. In total, the Andalusian campaign resulted in the pinning down of 70,000 French troops for the duration of the war.

48. Wellesley Papers, Add. MSS. 49,981, B. Frere to R. Wellesley, Feb. 11, 1810; P.R.O., F.O. 72/92, Campbell to B. Frere, Feb. 1, 1810, B. Frere to R. Wellesley, Feb. 10, 1810; Vaughan Papers, E:1:5, Ideas concerning the means to prevent the English from taking Cádiz found in O'Farrel's portfolio, February 1810. "In fine the love for my Country, and especially for Cadiz, induces me to set forth all the ideas that may prove necessary to prevent this fine city from becoming a prey to the English, and divided from the whole nation as Gibraltar."

49. Wellesley Papers, Add. MSS. 49,981, B. Frere to R. Wellesley, Feb. 11, 1810; P.R.O., F.O. 72/92, B. Frere to R. Wellesley, Feb. 11, 1810; Wellington, *Dispatches*, Wellington to B. Frere, Feb. 5, 1810, III: 726.

50. P.R.O., F.O. 72/92, B. Frere to R. Wellesley, Feb. 16, 1810; Wellesley Papers, Add. MSS. 49,981, B. Frere to R. Wellesley, Feb. 16, 1810.

51. Wellesley Papers, Add. MSS. 49,981, B. Frere to R. Wellesley, Feb. 15, 23, 1810; P.R.O., F.O. 72/92, B. Frere to R. Wellesley, Feb. 10, 1810; P.R.O., F.O. 72/94, H. Wellesley to R. Wellesley, March 8, 1810. "The Junta of Cádiz was annoyed at Albuquerque's appointment to the governor of Cádiz as it did not believe he would have time to attend to the affairs of the city."

52. P.R.O., F.O. 72/94, H. Wellesley to R. Wellesley, March 7, 1810; P.R.O., F.O. 72/92, B. Frere to R. Wellesley, March 2, 1810; Wellesley Papers, Add. MSS. 49,979, R. Wellesley to B. Frere, Jan. 27, 1810; A.H.N., Sección de Estado, Legajo 5461, Apodaca to Bardaxi, April 11, 1810.

53. P.R.O., F.O. 72/92, B. Frere to R. Wellesley, March 2, 1810; Wellesley Papers, Add. MSS. 49,981, B. Frere to R. Wellesley, March 2, 1810. Frere had not dared press these questions before; see P.R.O., F.O. 72/92, Campbell to B. Frere, Feb. 7, 1810, B. Frere to Campbell, Feb. 15, 1810. For a British opinion of the value of Ceuta, see P.R.O., F.O. 72/89, Swetland to Gill, Sept. 5, 1809.

54. Liverpool Papers, Add. MSS. 38,244, Liverpool to Wellington, Feb. 13, 1810.

55. *Parliamentary Debates*, XVI: 11; *Creevey Papers*, Feb. 22, 1810, I:130: "I heard Wellesley open his plan of taking the 30,000 Portuguese into our pay, and the most sanguine expectations I have ever formed respecting him were more than realized. His speech (tho' he had shammed ill for the purpose of preparing it) was an absolute and unqualified failure."

56. *Parliamentary Debates*, XVI:16.

57. Ibid., pp. 10–11.

58. Ibid., pp. 9, 11–15, 16.

59. Wellesley Papers, Add. MSS. 49,981, H. Wellesley to R. Wellesley, March 10, 1810; Cowley Papers, P.R.O., F.O. 519/34, H. Wellesley to Wellington, March 9, 1810.

60. P.R.O., F.O. 72/94, Stewart to H. Wellesley, March 8, 1810, Purvis to Wellesley, March 8, 1810; Wellesley Papers, Add. MSS. 49,981, H. Wellesley to R. Wellesley, March 10, 1810.

61. P.R.O., F.O. 72/94, Stewart to H. Wellesley, March 8, 1810.

62. Wellesley Papers, Add. MSS. 49,981, H. Wellesley to R. Wellesley, March 10, 1810; P.R.O., F.O. 72/94, Collingwood to Purvis, March 5, 1810, Marquis de las Hormazas to H. Wellesley, March 6, 1810.

63. Wellesley Papers, Add. MSS. 49,981, H. Wellesley to R. Wellesley, March 10, 1810; Cowley Papers, P.R.O., F.O. 519/34, H. Wellesley to Wellington, March 16, 1810. Britain did not want responsibility for such a large number of French prisoners.

64. Cowley Papers, P.R.O., F.O. 519/34, H. Wellesley to Wellington, April 2, 1810; Vaughan Papers, C:48:2, Hamilton to Vaughan, March 29, 1810. Hamilton was confident Wellesley would approve of Henry's actions: "I do not believe that your measures about French prisoners will be at all disapproved of here. If indeed they could be drowned in their passage, there would be no great harm, but we shall not grudge the pittence they will cost." Canning suggested the same idea the previous August (Wellesley Papers, Add. MSS. 37,287, Canning to R. Wellesley, Aug. 27, 1809). Perceval thought Henry had acted incorrectly, but Wellesley ignored his opinion. .

65. Cowley Papers, P.R.O., F.O. 519/34, H. Wellesley to Wellington, March 9, 1810; Wellesley Papers, Add. MSS. 49,981, H. Wellesley to R. Wellesley, March 12, 1810.

66. Cowley Papers, P.R.O., F.O. 519/34, H. Wellesley to Wellington, March 9, 1810.

67. Wellesley Papers, Add. MSS. 37,291, H. Wellesley to R. Wellesley, March 12, 1810.

68. P.R.O., F.O. 72/94, H. Wellesley to R. Wellesley, March 20, 1810; Wellesley Papers, Add. MSS. 49,981, H. Wellesley to R. Wellesley, March 20, 1810.

69. P.R.O., F.O. 72/94, Address of the Duke of Albuquerque, Captain General of the four Kingdoms of Andalusia, and commander of the Army to the Supreme Council of Regency.

70. Wellesley Papers, Add. MSS. 49,981, H. Wellesley to R. Wellesley, March 20, 1810; P.R.O., F.O. 72/94, H. Wellesley to R. Wellesley, March 20, 1810.

71. P.R.O., F.O. 72/94, Junta of Cádiz to Albuquerque, March 16, 1810.

72. Wellesley Papers, Add. MSS. 49,981, H. Wellesley to R. Wellesley, March 20, 1810; P.R.O., F.O. 72/94, H. Wellesley to R. Wellesley, March 20, 1810.

73. P.R.O., F.O. 72/94, H. Wellesley to R. Wellesley, March 21, 1810; Wellesley Papers, Add. MSS. 37,291, H. Wellesley to R. Wellesley, March 21, 1810.

74. P.R.O., F.O. 72/94, H. Wellesley to Castaños, March 20, 1810, Bardaxi to H. Wellesley, March 22, 1810.

75. Cowley Papers, P.R.O., F.O. 519/34, H. Wellesley to Wellington, March 27, 1810; Wellesley Papers, Add. MSS. 49, 981, H. Wellesley to R. Wellesley, March 30, 1810; P.R.O., F.O. 72/94, H. Wellesley to R. Wellesley, March 30, 1810, Bardaxi to H. Wellesley, March 27, 1810.

76. Cowley Papers, P.R.O., F.O. 519/34, H. Wellesley to Wellington, March 27, 1810; P.R.O., F.O. 72/93, R. Wellesley to H. Wellesley, March 12, 1810; National Archives, Dept. of State, no. 59, vol. 11, Hormazes to Erving, March 10, 1810;

Wellesley Papers, Add. MSS. 49,981, H. Wellesley to R. Wellesley, March 30, 1810.

77. Wellesley Papers, Add. MSS. 37,291, H. Wellesley to R. Wellesley, March 12, 1810.

78. Ibid., H. Wellesley to R. Wellesley, March 21, 1810; ibid., Add. MSS. 49,981, H. Wellesley to R. Wellesley, March 12, 1810; P.R.O., F.O. 72/94, H. Wellesley to R. Wellesley, March 21, 1810; Wellington, *Dispatches*, Wellington to H. Wellesley, March 27, 1810, III:800.

79. Wellesley Papers, Add. MSS. 37,291, H. Wellesley to R. Wellesley, March 21, 1810; Cowley Papers, P.R.O., F.O. 519/34, H. Wellesley to Wellington, April 23, 1810.

80. P.R.O., F.O. 72/94, H. Wellesley to Hormazes, March 11, 14, 1810, Hormazes to H. Wellesley, March 13, 1810.

81. P.R.O., F.O. 72/93, R. Wellesley to H. Wellesley, March 13, 1810.

82. P.R.O., F.O. 72/94, Bardaxi to H. Wellesley, March 28, 31, 1810; Vaughan Papers, E:2:5, Report on duties (7 percent on silver from America to Spain, 4 percent from Spain to England, a total of 11 percent); Wellesley Papers, Add. MSS. 49,981, H. Wellesley to R. Wellesley, March 31, 1810; A.H.N., Sección de Estado, Legajo 5461, Apodaca to Bardaxi, May 14, 1810.

83. Wellington, *Supplementary Dispatches*, Liverpool to Wellington, March 13, 1810, VI, 493; Vaughan Papers, C:48:2, Hamilton to Vaughan, March 29, 1810.

84. Wellesley Papers, Add. MSS. 37,295, Perceval to R. Wellesley, March 4, 1810; Perceval Papers, Add. MSS. 49,188, Perceval to Arden, January 22, 1810. Perceval was not sanguine of success in the peninsula or the war in general. Writing to Lord Arden, he explained: "The most probable means of overturning the extended power of France are those which the resistance of the oppressed people on the continent, taking advantage of some favorable circumstances which may stimulate & facilitate a combination amongst themselves, may some-day produce. Yet I cannot flatter myself that the minds and condition of those people are so far ripe for an exertion of this description."

85. P.R.O., F.O. 72/93, R. Wellesley to H. Wellesley, March 13, 1810.

86. Wellesley Papers, Add. MSS. 37,295, Memorandum, March 13, 1810: "My opinion has long been decided that no strong or permanent government can be formed on the present basis unless it shall comprehend all or at least a very large portion of the parties now denominated Canning's, Lord Castlereagh's and Lord Sidmouth's. I am aware of the difficulties of bringing these persons to act together, and also of the obstacles which might impede a cordial union between some of them and the leading members of the present Cabinet. But unless a sacrifice can be made of some portion of the personal animosities and prejudices of the hour by those who concur in general political principles, the Administration must not only pass into the hands of the opposite party, but must remain there." Canning and Wellesley were again on good terms: Huskisson Papers, Add. MSS. 38,737, Arbuthnot to Huskisson, November 29, 1809.

87. Wellesley would broach the subject intermittently throughout his term as foreign secretary.

88. *Parliamentary Debates*, XVI: 305–6, 373–79.

89. Ibid., pp. 379–84.

90. Ibid.

91. Ibid.

92. Ibid., p. 388; Vaughan Papers, C:48:3, Hamilton to Vaughan, March 31, 1810.

93. Wellesley Papers, Add. MSS. 49,981, H. Wellesley to R. Wellesley, April 5, 1810; P.R.O., F.O. 72/94, H. Wellesley to R. Wellesley, April 5, 7, 1810; Cowley Papers, P.R.O., F.O. 519/34, H. Wellesley to Wellington, April 2, 1810.

94. Cowley Papers, P.R.O., F.O. 519/34, H. Wellesley to Wellington, April 2, 1810.

95. P.R.O., F.O. 72/94, Bardaxi to H. Wellesley, April 4, 1810, H. Wellesley to R. Wellesley, April 7, 1810, H. Wellesley, April 7, 1810; Wellesley Papers, Add. MSS. 49,981, H. Wellesley to R. Wellesley, April 7, 1810.

96. Wellesley Papers, Add. MSS. 49,981, H. Wellesley to R. Wellesley, April 7, 1810; P.R.O., F.O. 72/94, H. Wellesley to R. Wellesley, April 7, 1810.

97. Ibid.

98. Ibid.

99. A.H.N., Sección de Estado, Legajo 5461, Apodaca to Saavedra, Feb. 14, 1810, to Bardaxi, May 15, 1810, Saavedra to Apodaca, April 15, 1810; P.R.O., F.O. 72/100, Apodaca to R. Wellesley, April 16, 1810; Wellesley Papers, Add. MSS. 37,295, Apodaca's proposal for a loan of £2 million: (1) the loan is to be repaid in six years after the conclusion of peace at a rate of $1.5 million per year; (2) the rate of exchange should be $6.00 to the pound paid in London; (3) some of the bills to be drawn for the purpose of executing the loan be at a short date because of Spain's present necessities.

100. Wellesley Papers, Add. MSS. 37,295, Perceval's observation on Apodaca's request for a loan.

101. P.R.O., F.O. 185/19, Notes of R. Wellesley, Jan. 25, 1810; Wellesley Papers, Add. MSS. 37,291, Notes of R. Wellesley, Jan. 25, 1810.

102. Wellesley Papers, Add. MSS. 37,288, R. Wellesley to Apodaca, no date.

103. Ibid., Add. MSS. 37,295, Perceval to R. Wellesley, April 29, 1810.

104. Ibid., Add. MSS. 37,292, H. Wellesley to R. Wellesley, April 16, 1810.

105. Ibid., H. Wellesley to R. Wellesley, April 16, 23, 1810.

106. Ibid., Add. MSS. 49,981, H. Wellesley to R. Wellesley, April 16, 1810.

107. P.R.O., F.O. 72/94, H. Wellesley to R. Wellesley, April 22, 1810, to Bardaxi, April 19, 1810; Wellesley Papers, Add. MSS. 49,981, H. Wellesley to R. Wellesley, April 22, 1810.

108. Wellesley Papers, Add. MSS. 49,981, H. Wellesley to R. Wellesley, May 30, 1810; P.R.O., F.O. 72/95, H. Wellesley to R. Wellesley, May 30, 1810; Cowley Papers, P.R.O., F.O. 519/34, H. Wellesley to Wellington, May 18, 1810.

109. P.R.O., F.O. 72/95, H. Wellesley to Campbell, May 8, 1810, to Burgman, May 9, 1810, to John Stewart, May 9, 1810, to Bardaxi, May 22, 1810, to R. Wellesley, May 30, 1810; Wellesley Papers, Add. MSS. 49,981, H. Wellesley to R. Wellesley, May 30, 1810.

110. Wellesley Papers, Add. MSS. 49,981, H. Wellesley to R. Wellesley, May 8, 1810; P.R.O., F.O. 72/95, H. Wellesley to R. Wellesley, May 8, 1810; Cowley Papers, P.R.O., F.O. 519/34, H. Wellesley to Wellington, May 4, 1810.

111. P.R.O., F.O. 72/94, H. Wellesley to R. Wellesley, April 23, 1810.

112. P.R.O., F.O. 72/95, Bardaxi to H. Wellesley, April 24, 26 (2 letters of that date), H. Wellesley to Bardaxi, April 25, 1810.

113. Wellesley Papers, Add. MSS. 49,981, H. Wellesley to R. Wellesley, May 5, 1810; P.R.O., F.O. 72/95, H. Wellesley to R. Wellesley, May 8, June 10, 1810.

114. P.R.O., F.O. 72/95, H. Wellesley to R. Wellesley, May 30, 1810; Wellesley Papers, Add. MSS. 49,981, H. Wellesley to R. Wellesley, May 30, 1810. The prisoners escaped when the anchor cables on one of the barges were cut and the barge drifted up on the opposite shore.

115. P.R.O., F.O. 72/95, H. Wellesley to Bardaxi, May 27, 28, 1810, Bardaxi to H. Wellesley, May 27, 1810.

116. Ibid., H. Wellesley to R. Wellesley, May 30, 31, 1810; Wellesley Papers, Add. MSS. 49,981, H. Wellesley to R. Wellesley, May 30, 31, 1810.

117. *Quarterly Review* (May 1810), III:338; *Edinburgh Review* (April 1810), XVI: 4, 23–35.

118. Liverpool Papers, Add. MSS. 38,323, Liverpool to Craig, April 4, 1810; ibid., Add. MSS. 38,244, Wellington to Liverpool, April 2, 11, 1810; Add. MSS. 38,245, Wellington to Liverpool, May 23, 1810; P.R.O., F.O. 72/94, H. Wellesley to R. Wellesley, April 3, 1810.

119. Huskisson Papers, Add. MSS. 38,738, Wellington to Huskisson, April 26, 1810.

120. Wellesley Papers, Add. MSS. 37,295, R. Wellesley to Perceval, May 3, 1810.

121. Ibid., Perceval to R. Wellesley, May 4, 1810.

122. A. Wellesley, *Letters to William Wellesley-Pole,* Wellington to Pole, April 6, 1810, pp. 31–32.

123. Butler, *The Eldest Brother,* pp. 428–48, 487–90.

Chapter 7

1. *Parliamentary Debates,* XVII: 472.

2. Napoléon I, *Correspondance de Napoléon,* N. 16385, Decree, April 17, 1810, XX: 338; A.H.N., Sección de Estado, Legajo 3072, Herrasti to Romana, April 28, 1810; Jean Jacques Pelet, *The French Campaign in Portugal, 1810–1811: An Account by Jean Jacques Pelet,* pp. 49–87.

3. *Examiner,* June 3, 1810.

4. *Parliamentary Debates,* XVII: 472–84.

5. Ibid. pp. 484–97.

6. Ibid.

7. Ibid.

8. Ibid., p. 499.

9. Ibid., p. 500.

10. Ibid., pp. 502–3.

11. *Examiner,* June 10, 1810.

12. Wellington, *Supplementary Dispatches,* Memorandum by Marquess Wellesley on a Spanish Army, June 1810, VI: 550–52; for details, see Samuel Edison Vichness, "The Military Career of William Carr Beresford" (dissertation), chap. 9.

13. Wellington, *Supplementary Dispatches,* Memorandum by Marquess Wellesley on a Spanish Army, June 1810, VI: 550–52; National Archives, Dept. of

State, no. 59, vol. 11, Erving to Smith, Aug. 3, 1809: "The Spaniard has far more bodily strength and activity, is more temperate, hardy, and enduring, more resolute and persevering; and added to these advantages, in the actual war enter moral causes which augment the vigor of his physical qualities; so that it may well be believed that a regiment of well disciplined Spaniards, cannot be equalled by any troops in Europe."

14. Wellington, *Supplementary Dispatches,* Memorandum by Marquess Wellesley on a Spanish Army, June 1810, VI: 550–52.

15. Wellesley Papers, Add. MSS. 37,295, Liverpool to R. Wellesley, June 15, 1810; ibid., Add. MSS. 37,415, Wellington to [?], June 4, 1810. Wellington was bitter over the lack of support: "If *there was any Gov't.* or publick sentiment in England, if we thought of any thing excepting the saving of our shillings and six penses, if I could expect any thing but the gallows for making an exertion in which five lives should be lost, and which should not be followed by an immediate evacuation of the Peninsula by the French, I should say that we should yet make Boney repent his invasion of Spain. But alas! what can be done *for such a gov't.* and such a people?"

16. Ibid., Add. MSS. 37,295, R. Wellesley to Perceval, June 12, 1810.

17. Ibid., Canning to R. Wellesley, June 13, 1810.

18. Ibid., and Canning to R. Wellesley, June 14, July 9, 1810.

19. Ibid., R. Wellesley to Perceval, June 14, 1810, Perceval to R. Wellesley, June 15, 1810.

20. Cowley Papers, P.R.O., F.O. 519/35, H. Wellesley to Wellington, June 9, 1810.

21. Wellesley Papers, Add. MSS. 37,292, H. Wellesley to R. Wellesley, June 12, 1810.

22. P.R.O., F.O. 72/95, H. Wellesley to R. Wellesley, June 12, 1810; Wellesley Papers, Add. MSS. 49,981, H. Wellesley to R. Wellesley, June 12, 1810; Cowley Papers, P.R.O., F.O. 519/35, H. Wellesley to Wellington, June 9, 1810; Wellington, *Supplementary Dispatches,* H. Wellesley to Wellington, June 19, 1810, VI: 535–36.

23. P.R.O., F.O. 72/95, H. Wellesley to R. Wellesley, June 12, 1810; A.H.N., Sección de Estado, Legajo 5461, Apodaca to R. Wellesley, June 17, 1810; ibid., Legajo 5462, Apodaca to R. Wellesley, July 16, 1810.

24. Wellesley Papers, Add. MSS. 49,981, H. Wellesley to R. Wellesley, June 12, 1810; P.R.O., F.O. 72/95, H. Wellesley to R. Wellesley, June 12, 1810.

25. P.R.O., F.O. 72/95, Bardaxi to H. Wellesley, June 19, 1810, H. Wellesley to R. Wellesley, June 23, 1810.

26. Wellesley Papers, Add. MSS. 49,981, H. Wellesley to R. Wellesley, June 29, 1810; P.R.O., F.O. 72/95, H. Wellesley to R. Wellesley, June 29, 1810; A.H.N., Sección de Estado, Legajo 5462, Bardaxi to Albuquerque, July 11, 1810.

27. P.R.O., F.O. 72/95, H. Wellesley to R. Wellesley, June 30, 1810; Wellesley Papers, Add. MSS. 49,981, H. Wellesley to R. Wellesley, June 30, 1810; P.R.O., F.O. 72/96, Bardaxi to R. Wellesley, July 2, 1810.

28. Fortescue, *History of the British Army,* VII: 410; Oman, *The Peninsular War,* III: 215. For a detailed account of Romana's activities at this time, see Goodwin, "The Political and Military Career of the Marquis de la Romana," pp. 228–39.

29. Pelet, *The French Campaign in Portugal,* p. 23.

30. P.R.O., F.O. 72/96, H. Wellesley to Bardaxi, July 5, 1810, to R. Wellesley, July 11, 1810; Wellesley Papers, Add. MSS. 49,981, H. Wellesley to R. Wellesley, June 11, 1810.

31. Wellesley Papers, Add. MSS. 37,295, Perceval to R. Wellesley, July 14, 1810.

32. Ibid., Perceval to R. Wellesley, July 23, 1810; ibid., Add. MSS. 49,979, R. Wellesley to H. Wellesley, July 24, 1810.

33. National Archives, Dept. of State, no. 59, vol. 11, Erving to Madison, Jan. 1, 1809. Erving became aware of this sentiment in Cádiz several months before when he visited his consul in that city. He wrote to Madison, "I have perceived also since my arrival here, what I was not before so sensible of, that considerable inconvenience attends Mr. Izznardis . . . this inconvenience results not only from the great importance of this port as a place of commerce, but from the peculiar character of the commercial people here, opposing more than ordinary difficulties to, & requiring therefore the peculiar vigilance and attention of a consul. Mr. Izznardis is himself sensible of this. . . ."

34. Wellesley Papers, Add. MSS. 49,981, H. Wellesley to R. Wellesley, July 11, 1810; P.R.O., F.O. 72/96, H. Wellesley to R. Wellesley, July 11, 1810.

35. P.R.O., F.O. 72/96, H. Wellesley to R. Wellesley, July 13, 1810.

36. Wellesley Papers, Add. MSS. 49,981, H. Wellesley to R. Wellesley, July 13, 1810; P.R.O., F.O. 72/96, H. Wellesley to R. Wellesley, July 13, 1810.

37. P.R.O., F.O. 72/96, H. Wellesley to R. Wellesley, July 15, 1810, Bardaxi to H. Wellesley, July 15, 1810.

38. Wellesley Papers, Add. MSS. 49,981, H. Wellesley to R. Wellesley, July 15, 1810; P.R.O., F.O. 72/96, H. Wellesley to R. Wellesley, July 15, 1810.

39. P.R.O., F.O. 72/93, R. Wellesley to H. Wellesley, July 13, 1810; Wellesley Papers, Add. MSS. 49,979, R. Wellesley to H. Wellesley, July 13, 1810.

40. P.R.O., F.O. 72/106, R. Wellesley's notes on the Venezuelan revolt, July 1810; A.H.N., Sección de Estado, Legajo 5462, Apodaca to Bardaxi, July 11, 1810.

41. P.R.O., F.O. 185/18, Lamosas to Layard, May 4, 1810.

42. Ibid., Layard to Junta of Caracas, May 14, 1810.

43. P.R.O., F.O. 72/89, Miranda to Marquis del Toso, July 20, 1808; P.R.O., F.O. 72/88, Cockburn to Rowley, March 27, 1809; P.R.O., F.O. 72/90, Communications from Charles Stuart on the Spanish colonies, May 15, 1809, Cooke to Hammond, May 22, 1809.

44. P.R.O., F.O. 72/90, Cooke to Hammond, May 22, 1809.

45. P.R.O., F.O. 185/18, Liverpool to Layard, July, 1810; A.H.N., Sección de Estado, Legajo 5462, Albuquerque to Bardaxi, July 4, 1810.

46. A.H.N., Sección de Estado, Legajo 5462, R. Wellesley to Albuquerque, June 21, 1810; P.R.O., F.O. 185/18, R. Wellesley to H. Wellesley, July 13, 1810.

47. P.R.O., F.O. 72/106, Notes on the revolt in Venezuela by R. Wellesley, July 21, 1810; Wellesley Papers, Add. MSS. 37,315, R. Wellesley (son) to R. Wellesley, July 14, 1810.

48. Wellesley Papers, Add. MSS. 37,315, R. Wellesley (son) to R. Wellesley, July 14, 1810; P.R.O., F.O. 72/106, Notes on the revolt in Venezuela by R. Wellesley, July 21, 1810; Liverpool Papers, Add. MSS. 38,360, Memorandum of Lord Harrowby, May, 1810.

49. Wellesley Papers, Add. MSS. 49,979, R. Wellesley to H. Wellesley, July 13, 1810; P.R.O., F.O. 72/106, R. Wellesley's note on the revolt in Venezuela, July, 1810.

50. Wellesley Papers, Add. MSS. 49,979, R. Wellesley to H. Wellesley, July 13, 1810.

51. P.R.O., F.O. 72/96, H. Wellesley to R. Wellesley, July 11, 1810; Wellesley Papers, Add. MSS. 49,981, H. Wellesley to R. Wellesley, July 11, 1810; A.H.N., Sección de Estado, Legajo 5461, Apodaca to Bardaxi, July 20, 1810.

52. Wellesley Papers, Add. MSS. 49,981, H. Wellesley to R. Wellesley, July 16, 30, 1810; P.R.O., F.O. 72/96, H. Wellesley to R. Wellesley, July 16, 30, 1810; Wellesley Papers, Add. MSS. 37, 292, H. Wellesley to R. Wellesley, Aug. 1, 1810; A.H.N., Sección de Estado, Legajo 5462, Apodaca to Bardaxi, August 1, 1810.

53. P.R.O., F.O. 72/106, Bolívar and Méndez to R. Wellesley, July 11, 1810.

54. Wellesley Papers, Add. MSS. 49,979, R. Wellesley to H. Wellesley, July 13, 1810; A.H.N., Sección de Estado, Legajo 5462, R. Wellesley to Albuquerque, July 14, 1810, Albuquerque to R. Wellesley, July 16, 1810, Albuquerque to Bardaxi, July 18, 1810, Apodaca to Bardaxi, July 20, 1810; P.R.O., F.O. 72/93, R. Wellesley to H. Wellesley, July 13, 1810.

55. P.R.O., F.O. 72/106, Bolívar and Méndez to R. Wellesley, July 21, 1810, Views and objects of the Junta of Caracas, July 21, 1810.

56. Ibid., Note in reply to the propositions from the Commissioners of Venezuela, July 1810; Cowley Papers, P.R.O., F.O. 519/35, H. Wellesley to Wellington, July 28, 1810.

57. P.R.O., F.O. 72/96, H. Wellesley to R. Wellesley, July 15, 1810.

58. P.R.O., F.O. 72/93, R. Wellesley to H. Wellesley, July 24, 1810; Wellesley Papers, Add. MSS. 49,979, R. Wellesley to H. Wellesley, July 24, 1810.

59. Ibid.

60. Ibid.

61. Wellesley Papers, Add. MSS. 37,310, Bathurst to R. Wellesley, July 14, 1810; P.R.O., F.O. 72/93, R. Wellesley to H. Wellesley, July 24, Aug. 4, 1810; Wellesley Papers, Add. MSS. 49,979, R. Wellesley to H. Wellesley, July 24, Aug. 4, 1810.

62. P.R.O, F.O. 72/93, R. Wellesley to H. Wellesley, Aug. 4, 1810; Wellesley Papers, Add. MSS. 49,979, R. Wellesley to H. Wellesley, Aug. 4, 1810.

63. Bathurst Papers, loan no. 57, vol. 95, no. 83, Rose to Bathurst, Aug. 8, 1810; Wellesley Papers, Add. MSS. 37,295, Perceval to R. Wellesley, Aug. 6, 1810: "What can be a greater absurdity than the idea of the Spanish Regency determining not to relax the law of the colonial trade under these circumstances, but to preserve the old monopoly not only to Spain generally, but to the priviledged ports in Spain. If they persevere in that determination they will necessarily lose that connection with her colonies, and if we join them and countenance them in so doing we shall lose it too."

64. A.H.N., Sección de Estado, Legajo 5462, Albuquerque to Bardaxi, Aug. 1, 1810.

65. Ibid., Albuquerque to Bardaxi, Aug. 13, 1810.

66. P.R.O., F.O. 72/106, Memorandum of the communications between the Marquess Wellesley & the commissioners from Venezuela, delivered to the Spanish Ministers on Aug. 9, 1810; A.H.N., Sección de Estado, Legajo 5462, Apodaca to Bardaxi, Aug. 10, 1810.

67. Cowley Papers, P.R.O., F.O. 519/35, H. Wellesley to Wellington, Aug. 16, 1810.

68. P.R.O., F.O. 72/96, H. Wellesley to Bardaxi, Aug. 16, 1810; Wellesley Papers, Add. MSS. 49,981, H. Wellesley to R. Wellesley, Aug. 22, 1810; ibid., Add. MSS. 37,292, H. Wellesley to R. Wellesley, Aug. 23, 1810.

69. P.R.O., F.O. 72/97, Bardaxi to H. Wellesley, Aug. 24, 1810.

70. Ibid.

71. Cowley Papers, P.R.O., F.O. 519/36, H. Wellesley to R. Wellesley, Aug. 25, 1810; Wellesley Papers, Add. MSS. 49,981, H. Wellesley to R. Wellesley, Aug. 25, 1810.

72. P.R.O., F.O. 72/97, H. Wellesley to Bardaxi, Aug. 28, 1810; Bathurst Papers, loan no. 57, vol. 95, no. 91, Rose to Bathurst, Aug. 16, 1810, no. 96, Rose to Bathurst, August 24, 1810.

73. P.R.O., F.O. 72/96, H. Wellesley to Bardaxi, July 30, 1810, to R. Wellesley, July 31, 1810, Bardaxi to H. Wellesley, July 30, Aug. 4, 1810; Wellesley Papers, Add. MSS. 49,981, H. Wellesley to R. Wellesley, Aug. 22, 1810.

74. Wellesley Papers, Add. MSS. 49,981, H. Wellesley to R. Wellesley, Aug. 29, 1810; P.R.O., F.O. 72/97, H. Wellesley to R. Wellesley, Aug. 29, 1810. Buenos Aires declared its independence on May 22, 1810. Details of the events in this colony are contained in the dispatches of a British merchant residing there, Mr. Alex MacKinnon, found in P.R.O., F.O. 72/107. Other accounts can be found in the dispatches of Lord Strangford, the representative in Brazil, the précis of which can be found in the Wellesley Collection, Add. MSS. 49,987.

75. Cowley Papers, P.R.O., F.O. 519/35, H. Wellesley to Wellington, Aug. 31, 1810; Wellington, *Supplementary Dispatches,* H. Wellesley to Wellington, Aug. 31, 1810, VI:583–84.

76. P.R.O., F.O. 72/95, H. Wellesley to R. Wellesley, June 10, 1810. Britain was providing Orleans with £4,800 a year for his support. For an account of the allowances given to all French emigrant princes, see Wellesley Papers, Add. MSS. 37,295.

77. Wellesley Papers, Add. MSS. 49,981, H. Wellesley to R. Wellesley, June 24, 1810 (two dispatches); P.R.O., F.O. 72/95, H. Wellesley to R. Wellesley, June 24, 1810 (two dispatches).

78. P.R.O., F.O. 72/95, H. Wellesley to R. Wellesley, June 24, 1810 (two dispatches); Wellesley Papers, Add. MSS. 49,981, H. Wellesley to R. Wellesley, June 24, 1810 (two dispatches); A.H.N., Sección de Estado, Legajo 5462, Apodaca to Bardaxi, Aug. 14, 1810.

79. P.R.O., F.O. 72/95, H. Wellesley to R. Wellesley, June 24, 1810 (two dispatches); Wellesley Papers, Add. MSS. 49,981, H. Wellesley to R. Wellesley, June 24, 1810 (two dispatches).

80. Ibid.

81. P.R.O., F.O. 72/95, H. Wellesley to R. Wellesley, June 24, 1810 (two dispatches); Wellesley Papers, Add. MSS. 49,981, H. Wellesley to R. Wellesley, June 24, 1810 (two dispatches); Cowley Papers, P.R.O., F.O. 519/35, H. Wellesley to Wellington, June 26, 1810, Wellington, *Supplementary Dispatches,* H. Wellesley to Wellington, June 26, 1810, VI: 548–49.

82. Wellington, *Supplementary Dispatches,* H. Wellesley to Wellington, June 26, 1810, VI: 548–49; Cowley Papers, P.R.O., F.O. 519/35, H. Wellesley to Wellington, June 26, 1810.

83. P.R.O., F.O. 72/95, H. Wellesley to Bardaxi, June 27, 1810; Wellesley Papers, Add. MSS. 49,981, H. Wellesley to R. Wellesley, June 28, 1810; P.R.O., F.O. 72/96, H. Wellesley to R. Wellesley, June 12, 1810.

84. Wellington, *Supplementary Dispatches*, H. Wellesley to Charles Stuart, July 9, 1810, VI: 556, to Wellington, July 9, 1810, VI: 555–56, to Wellington, July 28, 1810, VI: 560–61.

85. P.R.O., F.O. 72/96, H. Wellesley to Duke of Orleans, July 29, 1810; Wellesley Papers, Add. MSS. 49,981, H. Wellesley to R. Wellesley, July 31, 1810.

86. P.R.O., F.O. 72/96, Duke of Orleans to Regency, July 28, 1810; Wellesley Papers, Add. MSS. 37,292, H. Wellesley to R. Wellesley, Aug. 1, 1810.

87. Wellington, *Supplementary Dispatches*, H. Wellesley to R. Wellesley, Aug. 1, 1810, VI: 566.

88. P.R.O., F.O. 72/96, Bardaxi to H. Wellesley, Aug. 12, 1810.

89. Ibid., H. Wellesley to Bardaxi, Aug. 12, 1810; Wellesley Papers, Add. MSS. 49,981, H. Wellesley to R. Wellesley, Aug. 12, 29, 1810; ibid., Add. MSS. 37,292, H. Wellesley to R. Wellesley, Aug. 23, 1810.

90. P.R.O., F.O. 72/97, H. Wellesley to R. Wellesley, Sept. 7, 1810; Wellesley Papers, Add. MSS. 49,981, H. Wellesley to R. Wellesley, Aug. 29, 1810.

91. Wellesley Papers, Add. MSS. 49,981, B. Frere to R. Wellesley, Jan. 5, 1810 (regulations for the election to the Cortes), H. Wellesley to R. Wellesley, June 23, 1810; P.R.O., F.O. 72/92, B. Frere to R. Wellesley, Jan. 5, 1810; P.R.O., F.O. 72/95, H. Wellesley to R. Wellesley, June 24, 1810.

92. P.R.O., F.O. 72/96, H. Wellesley to R. Wellesley, July 11, 1810; Wellesley Papers, Add. MSS. 49,981, H. Wellesley to R. Wellesley, July 11, 1810.

93. P.R.O., F.O. 72/96, H. Wellesley to R. Wellesley, Aug. 12, 1810; Wellesley Papers, Add. MSS. 37,292, H. Wellesley to R. Wellesley, Aug. 23, 1810.

94. P.R.O., F.O. 72/97, Moreno to H. Wellesley, Aug. 29, 1810, H. Wellesley to R. Wellesley, Aug. 30, Sept. 12, 1810; Wellesley Papers, Add. MSS. 49,981, H. Wellesley to R. Wellesley, Aug. 30, 1810.

95. Wellesley Papers, Add. MSS. 49,981, H. Wellesley to R. Wellesley, Sept. 7, 1810; P.R.O., F.O. 72/97, H. Wellesley to R. Wellesley, Sept. 7, 1810.

96. P.R.O., F.O. 72/97, H. Wellesley to R. Wellesley, Sept. 17, 1810; Wellesley Papers, Add. MSS. 49,981, H. Wellesley to R. Wellesley, Sept. 17, 1810.

97. Ibid.

98. A.H.N., Sección de Estado, Legajo 5462, Apodaca to Bardaxi, Aug. 13, 14, 1810, to R. Wellesley, Aug. 13, 1810; P.R.O., F.O. 72/100, Apodaca to R. Wellesley, July 17, 24, 1810.

99. Pellew, *Correspondence of Sidmouth*, Sidmouth to Bathurst, July 17, 1810, p. 27.

100. Wellesley Papers, Add. MSS. 37,295, R. Wellesley to Perceval, July 23, 1810.

101. Ibid., Canning to R. Wellesley, July 23, Aug. 25, 1810.

102. *Morning Post*, Aug. 22, 29, 1810; P.R.O., F.O. 72/100, Apodaca to R. Wellesley, July 24, 1810; P.R.O., F.O. 72/101, Apodaca to R. Wellesley, Aug. 9, 13, 1810; Liverpool Papers, Add. MSS. 38,245, Dundas to Liverpool, July 12, 1810; A.H.N., Sección de Estado, Legajo 5462, Apodaca to Bardaxi, Aug. 29, 1810.

103. Wellesley Papers, Add. MSS. 37,295, Perceval to R. Wellesley, Aug. 17, 1810.

104. Ibid., R. Wellesley to Perceval, Aug. 17, 1810, Perceval to R. Wellesley, Aug. 19, 1810.

105. Ibid., Perceval to Castlereagh, Aug. 22, 1810, Canning to R. Wellesley, Aug. 30, Sept. 1, 1810.

106. Ibid., Castlereagh to Perceval, Sept. 4, 1810.
107. Ibid., Canning to Perceval, Sept. 26. 1810; Wellington, *Supplementary Dispatches,* Wellington to Arbuthnot, Oct. 5, 1810, VI: 611–12. Wellington agreed with Perceval.
108. Liverpool Papers, Add. MSS. 38,323, Liverpool to Craigg, Sept. 11, 1810; Wellesley Papers, Add. MSS. 37,295, Mulgrave to Perceval, Sept. 11, 1810.

Chapter 8

1. Donald D. Horward, *The Battle of Bussaco: Masséna vs. Wellington,* pp. 172–75; Pelet, *The French Campaign in Portugal,* p. 189.
2. Napier, *War in the Peninsula,* II: 397–99; Wellington, *Supplementary Dispatches,* Wellington to Pole, Oct. 4, 1810, VI: 606–7; P.R.O., F.O. 72/101, Apodaca to R. Wellesley, Oct. 2, 1810, Albuquerque to R. Wellesley, Oct. 15, 1810; A.H.N., Sección de Estado, Legajo 5462, Apodaca to Bardaxi, Oct. 24, 1810.
3. Wellesley Papers, Add. MSS. 37,295, R. Wellesley to Perceval, Oct. 9, 1810; ibid., Add. MSS. 37,310, Buckingham to R. Wellesley, Oct. 9, 1810.
4. Ibid., Add. MSS. 37,292, R. Wellesley to Smith, Oct. 12, 1810; P.R.O., F.O. 185/18, R. Wellesley to H. Wellesley, Dec. 8, 1810.
5. Wellesley Papers, Add. MSS. 37,292, King to R. Wellesley, Oct. 21, 1810, R. Wellesley to Smith, Oct. 12, 1810.
6. See chap. 2.
7. Wellesley Papers, Add. MSS. 37,292, R. Wellesley to Smith, Oct. 12, 1810.
8. P.R.O., F.O. 72/93, Hamilton to H. Wellesley, Oct. 13, 1810; Wellesley Papers, Add. MSS. 49,979, Hamilton to H. Wellesley, Oct. 13, 1810.
9. See chap. 5.
10. Wellesley Papers, Add. MSS. 37,291, Notes of R. Wellesley, Jan. 25, 1810; P.R.O., F.O. 185/19, Notes of R. Wellesley, Jan. 25, 1810.
11. Wellesley Papers, Add. MSS. 49,981, H. Wellesley to R. Wellesley, Sept. 26, 1810; A.H.N., Sección de Estado, Legajo 5462, Apodaca to Bardaxi, Oct. 23, 1810; P.R.O., F.O. 72/101, Apodaca to R. Wellesley, Oct. 22, 1810.
12. Wellesley Papers, Add. MSS. 49,981, H. Wellesley to R. Wellesley, Sept. 26, 1810; ibid., Add. MSS. 49,982, H. Wellesley to R. Wellesley, Sept. 27, 1810.
13. Wellesley Papers, Add. MSS. 49,981, H. Wellesley to R. Wellesley, Sept. 26, 1810.
14. Holland, *Journal of Lady Holland,* Campbell to Holland, Sept. 26, 1810, II: 297–300; Vaughan Papers, C:56:8, Lord Holland to Vaughan, Oct. 13, 1810; Holland, *Foreign Reminiscences,* pp. 105–7; *Morning Post,* Nov. 19, 1810.
15. Wellesley Papers, Add. MSS. 37,295, Ryder to R. Wellesley, Oct. 15, 1810.
16. Bathurst Papers, loan no. 57, vol. 4, no. 387, Liverpool to Bathurst, Oct. 27, 1810; A.H.N., Sección de Estado, Legajo 5462, Apodaca to Bardaxi, Oct. 11, Nov. 3, 1810, John Brooke, *King George III: A Biography of America's Last Monarch,* p. 382.
17. Wellington, *Supplementary Dispatches,* Wellington to H. Wellesley, Dec. 31, 1810, VII: 11–12; P.R.O., F.O. 185/18, R. Wellesley to H. Wellesley, Dec. 8, 1810; Butler, *The Eldest Brother,* pp. 451–52; John Wilson Croker, *The Correspondence and Diaries of John Wilson Croker, Secretary to the Admiralty from 1809 to 1830,* I:30; Bryant, *Years of Victory,* pp. 393–94.

18. Brooke, *King George III*, p. 382; Gray, *Spencer Perceval*, p. 399; A.H.N., Sección de Estado, Legajo 5462, Apodaca to Bardaxi, November 21, 1810.

19. Pearce, *Memoires and Correspondence of Marquess Wellesley,* III:167.

20. *Parliamentary Debates*, XVIII:6; Gray, *Spencer Perceval*, p. 402; *Times*, Nov. 2, 1810; A.H.N., Sección de Estado, Legajo 5462, Apodaca to Bardaxi, Dec. 5, 1810.

21. Torrens, *The Marquess Wellesley,* p. 455; Gray, *Spencer Perceval*, p. 403; *Parliamentary Debates*, XVIII:75, 188; A.H.N., Sección de Estado, Legajo 5462, Apodaca to Bardaxi, Dec. 26, 1810.

22. Wellesley Papers, Add. MSS. 37,292, Notes on Spain, Nov. 30, 1810; P.R.O., F.O. 72/101, Apodaca to R. Wellesley, Nov. 20, 1810; Wellesley Papers, Add. MSS. 49,979, R. Wellesley to H. Wellesley, Nov. 30, 1810; P.R.O., F.O. 72/93, R. Wellesley to H. Wellesley, Nov. 30, 1810; *Morning Post*, Jan. 1, 1811; A.H.N., Sección de Estado, Legajo 5463, Apodaca to Bardaxi, Jan. 8, 1811.

23. Wellesley Papers, Add. MSS. 37,292, Wellington to Liverpool, Nov. 3, 1810; British Museum, Herries Papers, Add. MSS. 57,375, Drummond to Herries, Oct. 27, 1810; Wellington, *Supplementary Dispatches,* Wellington to Pole, Dec. 8, 1810, VII: 1–2; Liverpool Papers, Add. MSS. 38,245, Wellington to Liverpool, Dec. 21, 1810.

24. Wellington, *Supplementary Dispatches,* Wellington to Pole, Oct. 4, 1810, VI: 606–7; Brougham, *Life of Brougham,* Brougham to Grey, Oct. 23, 1810, I:351; Holland, *Journal of Lady Holland,* Campbell to Lady Holland, Dec. 20, 1810, II: 304–5; Vaughan Papers, C:55:8, Lady Holland to Vaughan, Nov. 26, 1810.

25. Liverpool Papers, Add. MSS. 38,245, Liverpool to Wellington, Nov. 19, 1810.

26. Perceval Papers, Add. MSS. 49,177, Perceval's notes on the Bullion Report, n.d.

27. *Parliamentary Debates*, XIX: 798–1169; Oman, *The Peninsular War*, III:465; Napier, *War in the Peninsula*, III:59; Pelet, *The French Campaign in Portugal*, p. 423. Masséna began his retreat on March 5, 1811.

28. Vaughan Papers, C:49:6, Hamilton to Vaughan, Dec. 8, 1810; Wellesley Papers, Add. MSS. 37,310, Liverpool to R. Wellesley, late December 1810 or early January 1811: "Our expense in Spain and Portugal has been nearly threefold this last year, what it was in 1809, and is increasing every month, I fear it will be quite impossible to continue our exertions upon the present scale for many months longer and certainly quite impracticable to increase it."

29. P.R.O., F.O. 72/93, R. Wellesley to H. Wellesley, Nov. 30, 1810; Wellesley Papers, Add. MSS. 49,979, R. Wellesley to H. Wellesley, Nov. 30, 1810; P.R.O., F.O. 72/101, Apodaca to R. Wellesley, Oct. 22, Nov. 19, 20, 1810; A.H.N., Sección de Estado, Legajo 5462, Apodaca to Bardaxi, Sept. 26, Oct. 8, 1810, to R. Wellesley, Nov. 19, 1810; ibid., Legajo 3002, Decree of the Cortes to Council of Regency, Dec. 8, 1810.

30. P.R.O., F.O. 72/117, R. Wellesley to Apodaca, Jan. 12, 1811; A.H.N., Sección de Estado, Legajo 3002, Apodaca to Secretary of the Cortes, Dec. 18, 1810. The dispatches from London relative to the regency question, contained in A.H.N., Sección de Estado, Legajos 5462, 5463, are remarkable for the almost total absence of political analysis.

31. A.H.N., Sección de Estado, Legajo 5462, Abella to Bardaxi, Sept. 18,

1810; P.R.O., F.O. 72/107, Trigoyen to R. Wellesley, Sept. 27, 1810; P.R.O., F.O. 72/101, Apodaca to R. Wellesley, Oct. 8, 1810; A.H.N., Sección de Estado, Legajo 5462, Apodaca to Bardaxi, Oct. 10, Nov. 26, 1810, Abella to Bardaxi, Oct. 23, 1810; Wellesley Papers, Add. MSS. 49,987, R. Wellesley to Strangford, Oct. 12, 1810.

32. Wellesley Papers, Add. MSS. 37,292, Notes on Spain, Nov. 30, 1810; P.R.O., F.O. 72/98, H. Wellesley to R. Wellesley, Dec. 21, 1810; A.H.N., Sección de Estado, Legajo 5462, Apodaca to Bardaxi, Sept. 26, Nov. 3, 1810; Vaughan Papers, C:56:3, Holland to Vaughan, Oct. 1810.

33. P.R.O., F.O. 72/101, Apodaca to R. Wellesley, Oct. 8, 1810; A.H.N., Sección de Estado, Legajo 5462, Bardaxi to Apodaca, Oct. 18, 1810.

34. P.R.O., F.O. 72/101, R. Wellesley to Apodaca, Sept. 27, Oct. 27, 1810; A.H.N., Sección de Estado, Legajo 5462, Apodaca to Bardaxi, Sept. 22, Dec. 19, 1810.

35. P.R.O., F.O. 185/24, R. Wellesley to H. Wellesley, Dec. 9, 1810; Wellington, *Supplementary Dispatches*, H. Wellesley to Wellington, Nov. 10, 1810, VI:639; Vaughan Papers, C:49:7, Hamilton to Vaughan, Jan. 20, 1811.

36. Wellesley Papers, Add. MSS. 49,982, H. Wellesley to R. Wellesley, Oct. 6, 1810; Wellington, *Supplementary Dispatches*, H. Wellesley to R. Wellesley, Sept. 1810, VI:589.

37. Wellesley Papers, Add. MSS. 49,982, H. Wellesley to R. Wellesley, Oct. 6, 1810.

38. P.R.O., F.O. 72/97, Regency to Cortes, Oct. 7, 1810; Wellesley Papers, Add. MSS. 49,982, H. Wellesley to R. Wellesley, Oct. 24, 1810; Wellington, *Supplementary Dispatches*, H. Wellesley to Wellington, Oct. 22, 1810, VI:619.

39. Wellesley Papers, Add. MSS. 37,292, H. Wellesley to R. Wellesley, Sept. 28 Oct. 6, 1810; ibid., Add. MSS. 49,982, H. Wellesley to R. Wellesley, Oct. 4, 1810; P.R.O., F.O. 72/97, H. Wellesley to R. Wellesley, Oct. 4, 1810.

40. P.R.O., F.O. 72/97, H. Wellesley to R. Wellesley, Oct. 24, 1810; Wellesley Papers, Add. MSS. 49,982, H. Wellesley to R. Wellesley, Oct. 24, 1810; ibid., Add. MSS. 37,292, R. Wellesley's notes on Spain, Nov. 30, 1810.

41. Wellesley Papers, Add. MSS. 49,982, H. Wellesley to R. Wellesley, Oct. 24, 1810; P.R.O., F.O. 72/97, H. Wellesley to R. Wellesley, Oct. 24, 1810.

42. Ibid.

43. Ibid.

44. P.R.O., F.O. 72/98, H. Wellesley to R. Wellesley, Nov. 2, 1810; Wellesley Papers, Add. MSS. 49,982, H. Wellesley to R. Wellesley, Nov. 2, 1810; P.R.O., F.O. 72/100, Apodaca to R. Wellesley, Nov. 19, 1810; A.H.N., Sección de Estado, Legajo 5462, Apodaca to Bardaxi, Nov. 21, 1810; Wellington, *Supplementary Dispatches*, H. Wellesley to Wellington, Nov. 1, 1810, VI:628.

45. Wellesley Papers, Add. MSS. 37,292, H. Wellesley to R. Wellesley, Sept. 28, 1810; A.H.N., Sección de Estado, Legajo 3002, Decrees of the Cortes to the Regency, Oct. 10, 1810; Wellesley Papers, Add. MSS. 49,982, H. Wellesley to R. Wellesley, Oct. 5, 24, Nov. 10, 1810.

46. Wellesley Papers, Add. MSS. 37,292, H. Wellesley to R. Wellesley, Sept. 28, 1810; A.H.N., Sección de Estado, Legajo 3002, Decrees of the Cortes to the Regency, Oct. 10, 1810; Wellesley Papers, Add. MSS. 49,982, H. Wellesley to R. Wellesley, Oct. 5, 24, Nov. 10, Dec. 10, 1810.

47. P.R.O., F.O. 72/97, Whittingham to the Regency, Aug. 13, 1810, H. Wellesley to R. Wellesley, Aug. 22, 1810; Wellesley Papers, Add. MSS. 49,981, H. Wellesley to R. Wellesley, Aug. 22, 1810.

48. Wellesley Papers, Add. MSS. 49,981, H. Wellesley to R. Wellesley, Aug. 22, 1810; P.R.O., F.O. 72/97, H. Wellesley to R. Wellesley, Aug. 22, 1810.

49. P.R.O., F.O. 185/19, H. Wellesley to R. Wellesley, Sept. 1810; Wellesley Papers, Add. MSS. 37,295, Liverpool to R. Wellesley, Sept. 21, 1810; P.R.O., F.O. 72/93, R. Wellesley to H. Wellesley, Sept. 24, 1810; Wellesley Papers, Add. MSS. 49,979, R. Wellesley to H. Wellesley, Sept. 24, 1810.

50. Wellesley Papers, Add. MSS. 49,982, H. Wellesley to R. Wellesley, Oct. 24, 1810; P.R.O., F.O. 72/98, Bardaxi to H. Wellesley, Oct. 24, 1810, H. Wellesley to R. Wellesley, Oct. 24, 1810.

51. Wellesley Papers, Add. MSS. 49,982, H. Wellesley to R. Wellesley, Nov. 10, 1810; P.R.O., F.O. 72/98, H. Wellesley to R. Wellesley, Nov. 10, 26, 1810, Heredia to Whittingham, Nov. 26, 1810.

52. P.R.O., F.O. 72/98, H. Wellesley to R. Wellesley, December 11, 1810, Heredia to Whittingham, Nov. 28, 1810.

53. P.R.O., F.O. 72/98, H. Wellesley to R. Wellesley, Nov. 10, Dec. 10, 20, 1810; Vaughan Papers, C:106:1, Stuart to Vaughan, Nov. 2, 1810; Wellesley Papers, Add. MSS 49,982, H. Wellesley to R. Wellesley, Dec. 20, 1810.

54. Wellesley Papers, Add. MSS. 49,982, H. Wellesley to R. Wellesley, Dec. 16, 1810 (2 letters of that date); P.R.O., F.O. 72/98, H. Wellesley to R. Wellesley, Dec. 16, 1810.

55. P.R.O., F.O., 72/98, H. Wellesley to R. Wellesley, Dec. 16, 1810. The members of the Cortes believed that the Spanish people sought more out of the war with France than the mere assertion of national independence. Of equal importance, in their eyes, was the need to correct the weaknesses which led to Spain's succumbing to French coercion. Thus, the constitution which they completed in 1812 established constitutional monarchy for Spain, greatly limiting the traditional powers of the Spanish king. It proved to be one of the most important documents of the nineteenth century, when it served as a basis for nearly all the early revolutionary movements in Europe. Patterned after the British system, the constitution should not have been a cause for alarm amongst the English. Yet, the Wellesleys considered the political situation at home so delicate and the military situation in the Peninsula so threatening, that they viewed the Cortes's preoccupation with a constitution an example of misplaced priorities. While in a sense this judgement was correct, it too was a case of overreaction. The Spanish had enough time to consider problems of governmental and military administration as well as the constitution, and it is to their credit that they persevered in their plans. Nonetheless, this does not hide the fact that this issue was a sore spot in Anglo-Spanish relations.

56. Ibid., H. Wellesley to R. Wellesley, Dec. 16, 1810; Wellington, *Supplementary Dispatches,* H. Wellesley to R. Wellesley, Dec. 31, 1810, VII:13–17; Cowley Papers, P.R.O., F.O. 519/36, H. Wellesley to R. Wellesley, Jan. 1811.

57. P.R.O., F.O. 72/109, Bardaxi to H. Wellesley, Dec. 22, 1810, H. Wellesley to Bardaxi, Dec. 24, 1810; Wellesley Papers, Add. MSS. 49,982, H. Wellesley to R. Wellesley, Dec. 21, 1810; ibid., Add. MSS. 49,983, H. Wellesley to R. Wellesley, Jan. 3, 1811; P.R.O., F.O. 72/116, Duff to R. Wellesley, Jan. 4, 1811.

58. P.R.O., F.O. 72/98, H. Wellesley to Bardaxi, Nov. 11, Dec. 19, 1810, to R. Wellesley, Nov. 15, 1810, Instructions to the Commissioner General deputed to Caracas, n.d.

59. P.R.O., F.O. 72/109, Whittingham to Heredia, Dec. 24, 1810.

60. Ibid., Whittingham to H. Wellesley, Jan. 2, 1811, to Heredia, Dec. 24, 1810, Heredia to Whittingham, Dec. 25, 1810; P.R.O., F.O. 72/98, Heredia to Whittingham, Nov. 28, 1810. These documents are also contained in A.H.N., Sección de Estado, Legajo 5610.

61. P.R.O., F.O. 72/109, Heredia to Whittingham, Dec. 30, 1810; A.H.N., Sección de Estado, Legajo 5610, Heredia to Whittingham, Dec. 30, 1810.

62. P.R.O., F.O. 72/78, Roche to R. Wellesley, Oct. 10, 1809.

63. P.R.O., F.O. 72/109, Heredia to Whittingham, Dec. 30, 1810, Whittingham to H. Wellesley, Jan. 12, 1811; A.H.N., Sección de Estado, Legajo 5610, Heredia to Whittingham, Dec. 30, 1810.

64. P.R.O., F.O. 72/109, Whittingham to H. Wellesley, Jan. 2, 1811, H. Wellesley to Bardaxi, Jan. 2, 1811.

65. A.H.N., Sección de Estado, Legajo 5610, Heredia to Bardaxi, Jan. 5, 1811.

66. P.R.O., F.O. 72/109, Whittingham to H. Wellesley, Jan. 12, 1811.

67. Ibid., H. Wellesley to Bardaxi, Jan. 14, 1811, Whittingham to H. Wellesley, Jan. 12, 1811, H. Wellesley to R. Wellesley, Feb. 7, 1811. "The enclosed correspondence, which has passed between me and the Minister for Foreign Affairs, relative to General Whittingham's Corps, will enable Your Lordship to form some judgement of the difficulty of introducing any improvement into the military system of Spain."

68. *Parliamentary Debates*, XVIII:387–460; Malleson, *Life of Marquess Wellesley*, p. 176; Pearce, *Memoirs and Correspondence of Marquess Wellesley*, III:171; Liverpool Papers, Add. MSS. 38,323, Liverpool to Beauchamp, Dec. 29, 1810; A.H.N., Sección de Estado, Legajo 5463, Apodaca to Bardaxi, Jan. 17, 1811; Torrens, *The Marquess Wellesley*, p. 447. Torrens claims Wellesley was well prepared for the speech.

69. Holland, *Memoirs of the Whig Party*, pp. 115–16.

70. *Parliamentary Debates*, XVIII:1123–44; Liverpool Papers, Add. MSS. 38,323, Liverpool to Rockford, Jan. 21, 1811; ibid., Add. MSS. 38,246, Perceval to Dundas, Jan. 13, 1811.

71. Torrens, *The Marquess Wellesley*, p. 448; Pearce, *Memoirs and Correspondence of Marquess Wellesley*, III:179; Butler, *The Eldest Brother*, p. 453; Gray, *Spencer Perceval*, pp. 410–12; A.H.N., Sección de Estado, Legajo 5463, Apodaca to Bardaxi, Feb. 1811; Wellington, *Supplementary Dispatches*, Wellington to Pole, Jan. 11, 1811, VII:40–43; Bathurst Papers, loan no. 57, vol. 4, no. 405, Richmond to Bathurst, Feb. 5, 1811.

72. P.R.O., F.O. 72/109, H. Wellesley to Bardaxi, Dec. 31, 1810, Bardaxi to H. Wellesley, Jan. 8, 1811.

73. Wellesley Papers, Add. MSS. 37,292, H. Wellesley to R. Wellesley, Jan. 12, 1811; P.R.O., F.O. 72/109, H. Wellesley to R. Wellesley, Jan. 12, 1811.

74. Wellesley Papers, Add. MSS. 49,983, H. Wellesley to R. Wellesley, Jan. 21, 1811.

75. P.R.O., F.O. 72/109, H. Wellesley to Bardaxi, Jan. 24, 1811; P.R.O., F.O. 72/117, Apodaca to R. Wellesley, Jan. 24, 1811.

76. Wellesley Papers, Add. MSS. 37,292, Carrol to R. Wellesley, Jan. 27, 1811; Wellington, *Supplementary Dispatches,* H. Wellesley to Wellington, Feb. 4, 1811, VII:56. Castaños was given Romana's command.

77. P.R.O., F.O. 72/109, Bardaxi to H. Wellesley, Feb. 4, 1811.

78. Ibid., H. Wellesley to Bardaxi, Feb. 7, 1811.

79. Wellesley Papers, Add. MSS. 49,983, H. Wellesley to R. Wellesley, Feb. 17, 1811; Wellington, *Supplementary Dispatches,* H. Wellesley to Wellington, Jan. 25, 1811, VII:47; Herries Papers, Add. MSS. 57,375, Drummond to Herries, March 8, 1811.

80. P.R.O., F.O. 72/109, H. Wellesley to R. Wellesley, Feb. 27, 1811; Leveson-Gower, *Private Correspondence,* Ponsonby to his mother, March 7, 1811, II: 382–84 (an account of the Battle of Barrosa).

81. Wellesley Papers, Add. MSS. 49,983, H. Wellesley to R. Wellesley, March 10, 1811; P.R.O., F.O. 72/110, H. Wellesley to R. Wellesley, March 10, 1811. See chap. 6 for Graham's instructions.

82. P.R.O., F.O. 72/110, H. Wellesley to R. Wellesley, March 10, 1811; Wellesley Papers, Add. MSS. 49,983, H. Wellesley to R. Wellesley, March 10, 1811; Leveson-Gower, *Private Correspondence,* Ponsonby to his mother, March 7, 1811, II: 382–84; Wellington, *Supplementary Dispatches,* H. Wellesley to Wellington, March 11, 1811, VII: 80.

83. P.R.O., F.O. 72/110, Lapeña to Graham, March 6, 1811, Bardaxi to H. Wellesley, March 6, 1811, Graham to Lapeña, March 6, 1811.

84. Wellesley Papers, Add. MSS. 49,983, H. Wellesley to R. Wellesley, March 10, 1811; P.R.O., F.O. 72/110, H. Wellesley to R. Wellesley, March 10, 1811, to Bardaxi, March 6, 1811, Graham to Lapeña, March 6, 1811.

85. P.R.O., F.O. 72/110, H. Wellesley to Bardaxi, March 9, 1811, to R. Wellesley, March 10, 1811; Wellesley Papers, Add. MSS. 49,983, H. Wellesley to R. Wellesley, March 10, 1811.

86. Wellington, *Supplementary Dispatches,* H. Wellesley to Wellington, March 11, 1811, VII:80, March 13, 1811, VII:81; P.R.O., F.O. 72/110, Graham to H. Wellesley, March 11, 1811; *Parliamentary Debates,* XIX: 538–48 (Thanks to Graham); Vaughan Papers, C:56:10, Holland to Vaughan, March, 1811.

87. P.R.O., F.O. 72/110, H. Wellesley to Bardaxi, March 15, 1811; A.H.N., Sección de Estado, Legajo 5613, H. Wellesley to Bardaxi, March 15, 1811; Wellington, *Supplementary Dispatches,* H. Wellesley to Wellington, March 11, 1811, VII:80; Wellesley Papers, Add. MSS. 49,983, H. Wellesley to R. Wellesley, March 25, 1811.

88. P.R.O., F.O. 72/110, Bardaxi to H. Wellesley, March 25, 1811; Wellesley Papers, Add. MSS. 49,983, H. Wellesley to R. Wellesley, March 25, 1811; A.H.N., Sección de Estado, Legajo 5613, Bardaxi to H. Wellesley, March 25, 1811.

89. Wellesley Papers, Add. MSS. 49,983, H. Wellesley to R. Wellesley, March 26, 30 (two letters of same date), 1811; P.R.O., F.O. 72/110, H. Wellesley to R. Wellesley, March 26, 1811; A.H.N., Sección de Estado, Legajo 5613, H. Wellesley to Bardaxi, April 8, 1811.

90. P.R.O., F.O. 72/110, H. Wellesley to Bardaxi, April 8, 1811; A.H.N., Sección de Estado, Legajo 5613, H. Wellesley to Bardaxi, April 8, 1811; Wellesley Papers, Add. MSS. 49,983, H. Wellesley to R. Wellesley, March 25, 1811.

91. Wellesley Papers, Add. MSS. 49,983, H. Wellesley to R. Wellesley, April 5, 13, 1811; P.R.O., F.O. 72/110, H. Wellesley to Bardaxi, April 8, 1811.

92. P.R.O., F.O. 72/97, H. Wellesley to R. Wellesley, Sept. 12, 1810; Wellesley Papers, Add. MSS. 49,981, H. Wellesley to R. Wellesley, Sept. 12, 1810; P.R.O., F.O. 72/109, Fleming to H. Wellesley, Dec. 1810; Wellesley Papers, Add. MSS. 49,979, R. Wellesley to H. Wellesley, Dec. 11, 1810; P.R.O., F.O. 72/93, R. Wellesley to H. Wellesley, Dec. 11, 1810; A.H.N., Sección de Etado, Legajo 5462, Apodaca to Bardaxi, Dec. 12, 1810; Vaughan Papers, G:49:9, Hamilton to Vaughan, April 1, 1811.

93. Wellesley Papers, Add. MSS. 49,983, H. Wellesley to R. Wellesley, Feb. 10, 1811; ibid., Add. MSS. 49,980, R. Wellesley to H. Wellesley, March 2, 1811; A.H.N., Sección de Estado, Legajo 5463, Apodaca to Bardaxi, Jan. 16, 1811.

94. P.R.O., F.O. 72/117, R. Wellesley to Apodaca, Jan. 12, 1811, Apodaca to R. Wellesley, March 14, 1811; Wellesley Papers, Add. MSS. 49,980, Hamilton to H. Wellesley, Jan. 15, 1811; A.H.N., Sección de Estado, Legajo 5463, Apodaca to R. Wellesley, Jan. 16, 1811, to Bardaxi, Feb. 4, 9, 1811; P.R.O., F.O. 72/109, Bardaxi to H. Wellesley, Feb. 7, 1811; Wellesley Papers, Add. MSS. 49,983, H. Wellesley to R. Wellesley, Feb. 9, 1811.

95. Vaughan Papers, C:57:1, Holland to Vaughan, Feb. 8, 1811; ibid., C:49:7, Hamilton to Vaughan, Jan. 20, 1811; P.R.O., F.O. 72/109, H. Wellesley to R. Wellesley, Jan. 12, 1811; Wellesley Papers, Add. MSS. 49,983, H. Wellesley to R. Wellesley, Jan. 12, 1811.

96. P.R.O., F.O. 83/20, Manufacturers of Scotland to R. Wellesley, Feb. 8, 1811; P.R.O., F.O. 72/117, Apodaca to R. Wellesley, Feb. 19, 1811; the *Times*, Feb. 19, 1811; *Morning Post*, Feb. 21, 1811. The Spanish Ambassador, the Duke of Albuquerque, died Feb. 18, 1811.

97. *Parliamentary Debates*, XIX: 356, 387–94; Wellesley Papers, Add. MSS. 37,415, Wellington to R. Wellesley, March 16, 1811; A.H.N., Sección de Estado, Legajo 5463, Apodaca to Bardaxi, Feb. 19, 1811.

98. *Parliamentary Debates*, XIX: 394–98.

99. Ibid., pp. 398–410.

100. Ibid., pp. 410–14.

101. Ibid., pp. 447–50; *Morning Post*, March 22, 1811 (called Wellesley's speech "spirited, emphatic, forcefull").

102. *Parliamentary Debates*, XIX: 450–57, 461; P.R.O., F.O. 72/117, Apodaca to R. Wellesley, April 24, 1811; A.H.N., Sección de Estado, Legajo 5463, Bardaxi to Apodaca, March 29, 1811.

103. *Parliamentary Debates*, XIX: 735–38, 746–47.

104. Ibid., pp. 747–49 (in the Commons, Perceval handled the debate, pp. 755–59); Liverpool Papers, Add. MSS. 38,246, Liverpool to Wellington, April 11, 1811; A.H.N., Sección de Estado, Legajo 5463, Apodaca to Bardaxi, May 1, 1811.

105. Sherwig, *Guineas and Gunpowder*, p. 236; *Parliamentary Debates*, XIX: 754–55, 1169; A.H.N., Sección de Estado, Legajo 5463, Apodaca to Bardaxi, April 17, 1811.

106. Wellesley Papers, Add. MSS. 49,980, R. Wellesley to H. Wellesley, April 18, 1811.

107. Ibid.

108. *Parliamentary Debates*, XIX:762–76; Wellington, *Supplementary Dispatches*, Speakers of Parliament to Wellington, April 26, 29, 1811, VII:136–38; A.H.N., Sección de Estado, Legajo 5463, Apodaca to Bardaxi, April 9, 1811.

109. *Examiner,* April 28, 1811; the *Morning Post* of April 27, 1811, commented: "The speeches delivered on this occasion were worthy of the subject, and did equal honour to the heads and hearts of distinguished persons by whom they were spoken."

110. Wellesley Papers, Add. MSS. 49,983, H. Wellesley to R. Wellesley, Feb. 10, 1811; P.R.O., F.O. 72/110, Bardaxi to H. Wellesley, April 12, 1811, H. Wellesley to Bardaxi, April 12 1811.

111. P.R.O., F.O. 72/110, Bardaxi to H. Wellesley, April 13, 1811.

112. Ibid., H. Wellesley to R. Wellesley April 15, 1811, to Bardaxi, April 14, 1811; Wellesley Papers, Add. MSS. 49,983, H. Wellesley to R. Wellesley, April 15, 1811.

113. Wellesley Papers, Add. MSS. 49,983, H.Wellesley to R. Wellesley, April 12, 18, 1811.

114. P.R.O., F.O. 72/110, H. Wellesley to R. Wellesley, April 21, May 2, 1811; Wellesley Papers, Add. MSS. 49,983, H. Wellesley to R. Wellesley, April 21, 23, 1811; A.H.N., Sección de Estado, Legajo 5614, License for export of specie.

115. Wellesley Papers, Add. MSS. 49,980, R. Wellesley to H. Wellesley, May 3, 1811; P.R.O., F.O. 72/108, R. Wellesley to H. Wellesley, May 3, 1811; Wellesley Papers, Add. MSS. 49,983, H.Wellesley to R. Wellesley, May 2, 1811; P.R.O., F.O. 72/93, Hamilton to H. Wellesley, May 24, 1810. The British again showed concern for the Cortes' activities regarding the constitution, but the problem was a reluctance to institute military and administrative changes, not a lack of time.

116. Wellington, *Dispatches,* Wellington to H. Wellesley, May 22, 1811, V:30–31; Wellesley Papers, Add. MSS. 49,983, H. Wellesley to R. Wellesley, May 29, 1811 (2 letters of same date).

117. Wellington, *Supplementary Dispatches,* H. Wellesley to Wellington, May 28, 1811, VII:143–44; A.H.N., Sección de Estado, Legajo 5463, Apodaca to Bardaxi, May 29, 1811, to R. Wellesley, June 14, 1811. Actually, though the Spanish troops behaved better than usual at Albuera, their lack of discipline and inability to maneuver inhibited British operations. Nonetheless, the Spanish saw their action as a great contribution to the battle.

118. P.R.O., F.O. 72/111, H. Wellesley to R. Wellesley, May 29, 1811; Wellington, *Supplementary Dispatches,* H. Wellesley to Wellington, May 25, 1811, VII:140.

119. P.R.O., F.O. 72/111, Wellington to H. Wellesley, May 29, 1811.

120. Wellesley Papers, Add. MSS. 37,292, Notes on the State of Europe by R. Wellesley, May 15, 1811; Wellington, *Supplementary Dispatches* Wellington to Pole, May 15, 1811, VII:123–24.

121. A.H.N., Sección de Estado, Legajo 5463, Apodaca to Bardaxi, April 17,30, May 15, 29, 1811; Wellesley Papers, Add. MSS. 37,292, Notes on the State of Europe by R. Wellesley, May 15, 1811.

122. Wellesley Papers, Add. MSS. 37,292, Notes on the State of Europe by R. Wellesley, May 15, 1811.

123. Ibid.

Chapter 9

1. P.R.O., F.O. 72/110, H. Wellesley to R. Wellesley, March 30, 1811; Wellesley Papers, Add. MSS. 49,983, H. Wellesley to R. Wellesley, April 24, 1811.

2. P.R.O., F.O. 72/110, H. Wellesley to R. Wellesley, March 30, 1811; Wellesley Papers, Add. MSS. 49,983, H. Wellesley to R. Wellesley, April 24, 1811; A.H.N., Sección de Estado, Legajo 5463, Apodaca to Bardaxi, April 30, June 25, 1811, Bardaxi to Apodaca, May 17, 1811.

3. P.R.O., F.O. 72/117, R. Wellesley to Apodaca, April 1811; Liverpool Papers, Add. MSS. 38,246, Liverpool to R. Wellesley, April 19, 1811; P.R.O., F.O. 72/108, R. Wellesley to H. Wellesley, April 19, 1811; Wellesley Papers, Add. MSS. 49,980, R. Wellesley to H. Wellesley, April 26, 1811. Richard explained that Layard's recall had been delayed because of the confusion arising out of the regency question.

4. Wellesley Papers, Add. MSS. 49,980, R. Wellesley to H. Wellesley, May 12, 1811 (abstract of events in the colonies, 1810–11); ibid., Add. MSS. 49,983, H. Wellesley to R. Wellesley, Jan. 12, 1811; P.R.O., F.O. 72/126, MacKinnon to R. Wellesley, Jan. 21, 1811; P.R.O., F.O. 72/156, A Sketch of the disturbances in Mexico since July 1808, Dec. 21, 1811; A.H.N., Sección de Estado, Legajo 5463, Apodaca to Bardaxi, March 7, April 2, 17, 1811, Regency to Apodaca, June 27, 1811.

5. P.R.O., F.O. 72/125, Miranda to R. Wellesley, Jan. 7, 1811; P.R.O., F.O. 72/126, Padilla to R. Wellesley, Jan. 7, Feb. 12, 1811; MacKinnon to R. Wellesley, Jan. 10, 1811, Junta of Buenos Aires to R. Wellesley, Sept. 9, 1810, Guido to R. Wellesley, May 10, 1811.

6. P.R.O., F.O. 72/126, Junta of Buenos Aires to R. Wellesley, March 9, 1811; P.R.O., F.O. 72/117, Apodaca to R. Wellesley, March 14, 19, 1811, to Bardaxi, April 17, 1811; Wellesley Papers, Add. MSS. 49,980, R. Wellesley to H. Wellesley, May 4, 1811; *Examiner,* Sept. 1, 1811.

7. P.R.O., F.O. 72/109, H. Wellesley to R. Wellesley, Jan. 21, 1811; Wellesley Papers, Add. MSS. 49,983, H. Wellesley to R. Wellesley, Jan. 21, 1811.

8. Wellesley Papers, Add. MSS. 49,983, H. Wellesley to R. Wellesley, February 10, April 24, 1811.

9. Wellesley Papers, Add. MSS. 49,980, R. Wellesley to H. Wellesley, May 12, 1811, Present state of the colonies, May 12, 1811; P.R.O., F.O. 72/108, R. Wellesley to H. Wellesley, May 12, 1811, Present state of the colonies, May 12, 1811; A.H.N., Sección de Estado, Legajo 5463, Apodaca to Bardaxi, August 20, 1811; P.R.O., F.O. 72/111, H. Wellesley to Bardaxi, May 27, 1811; Wellesley Papers, Add. MSS. 49,983, H. Wellesley to R. Wellesley, May 29, 1811.

10. Wellesley Papers, Add. MSS. 49,983, H. Wellesley to R. Wellesley, June 14, 1811; P.R.O., F.O. 72/111, H. Wellesley to R. Wellesley, June 14, 1811, Bardaxi to H. Wellesley, June 15, 1811; Wellington, *Supplementary Dispatches,* H. Wellesley to Wellington, June 26, 1811, VII:171. The Duke of Infantado was at this time appointed ambassador to London.

11. P.R.O., F.O. 72/112, Bardaxi to H. Wellesley, June 29, 1811.

12. Wellesley Papers, Add. MSS. 49,983, H. Wellesley to R. Wellesley, June 30, 1811; Wellington, *Supplementary Dispatches,* H. Wellesley to Wellington, July 8, 1811, VII:178–79; P.R.O., F.O. 72/112, H. Wellesley to R. Wellesley, June 30, 1811; Wellington, *Dispatches,* Wellington to H. Wellesley, July 5, 1811, V, 139.

13. Vaughan Papers, E:2:8, Vaughan memorandum, July 23, 1811; P.R.O., F.O. 72/112, H. Wellesley to R. Wellesley, July 26, 1811.

14. P.R.O., F.O. 72/112, H. Wellesley to R. Wellesley, June 30, 1811.

15. Wellesley Papers, Add. MSS. 49,983, H. Wellesley to R. Wellesley, June 15, 1811; P.R.O., F.O. 72/111, H. Wellesley to R. Wellesley, June 15, 1811.

16. P.R.O., F.O. 72/117, Apodaca to R. Wellesley, June 11, 1811; A.H.N. Sección de Estado, Legajo 5463, Apodaca to R. Wellesley, June 11, 1811.

17. *Parliamentary Debates*, XX:511–17, 519–32; A.H.N. Sección de Estado, Legajo 5463, Apodaca to Bardaxi, May 29, June 12, 14, 1811.

18. *Parliamentary Debates*, XX:532–48.

19. This comment is scrawled on the back of Apodaca's written request: P.R.O., F.O. 72/117, Apodaca to R. Wellesley, June 11, 1811.

20. Wellesley Papers, Add. MSS. 49,983, H. Wellesley to R. Wellesley, July 17, 1811; A.H.N., Sección de Estado, Legajo 5463, Apodaca to Bardaxi, August 6, 1811.

21. P.R.O., F.O. 72/112, Bardaxi to H. Wellesley, July 18, 19, 1811, H. Wellesley to Bardaxi, July 19, 1811; Wellington, *Supplementary Dispatches*, H. Wellesley to Wellington, July 18, 1811, VII: 183.

22. P.R.O., F.O. 72/112, Bardaxi to H. Wellesley, July 22, 1811; Wellesley Papers, Add. MSS. 49,983, H. Wellesley to R. Wellesley, July 26, 1811; P.R.O., F.O. 72/116, Duff to R. Wellesley, July 27, 1811.

23. Wellington, *Supplementary Dispatches*, H. Wellesley to Wellington, July 26, 1811, VII: 187.

24. Wellington, *Dispatches*, Wellington to H. Wellesley, August 2, 1811, V: 197.

25. Wellesley Papers, Add. MSS. 37,293, H. Wellesley to R. Wellesley, July 27, 1811; Wellington, *Supplementary Dispatches*, H. Wellesley to Wellington, Aug. 3, 1811, VII: 194.

26. P.R.O., F.O. 72/112, H. Wellesley to Bardaxi, Aug. 5, 1811.

27. Ibid., Bardaxi to H. Wellesley, August 7, 1811; Wellington, *Supplementary Dispatches*, H. Wellesley to Wellington, Aug. 21, 1811, VII: 208.

28. P.R.O., F.O. 72/125, Deputies of Santa Fé to Cortes, August 24, 1811; Wellington, *Supplementary Dispatches*, H. Wellesley to Wellington, July 31, 1811, VII: 192.

29. P.R.O., F.O. 72/125, Cortes to Deputies of Santa Fé, Aug. 25, 1811.

30. Ibid., American Deputies to Cortes, Aug. 26, 1811.

31. Ibid., Cortes to American Deputies, Aug. 26, 27, 1811; American Deputies to Cortes, Aug. 27, 1811.

32. P.R.O., F.O. 72/125, Puñomostro to Cortes, Aug. 29, 1811, Cortes to Puñomostro, Aug. 29, 1811; P.R.O., F.O. 72/113, Projet for a Constitution, Aug. 31, 1811, H. Wellesley to R. Wellesley, Aug. 31, 1811; Wellesley Papers, Add. MSS. 49,983, H. Wellesley to R. Wellesley, Aug. 31, 1811.

33. P.R.O., F.O. 72/113, H. Wellesley to R. Wellesley, Aug. 31, 1811; Wellesley Papers, Add. MSS. 49,983, H. Wellesley to R. Wellesley, July 17, Aug. 31, 1811; Vaughan Papers, E:2:7, Vaughan memorandum, July 15, 1811; Holland, *Foreign Reminiscences*, pp. 100—101; Wellington, *Dispatches*, Wellington to H. Wellesley, Aug. 14, 1811, V: 215; Wellington, *Supplementary Dispatches*, H. Wellesley to Wellington, Aug. 8, 1811, VII: 197.

34. Wellesley Papers, Add. MSS. 49,983, H. Wellesley to R. Wellesley, Aug. 31, 1811; P.R.O., F.O. 72/113, H. Wellesley to R. Wellesley, Aug. 31, 1811.

35. P.R.O., F.O. 72/113, H. Wellesley to Bardaxi, Aug. 29, 1811, to R. Wellesley, Aug. 31, 1811.

36. P.R.O., F.O. 72/113, Bardaxi to H. Wellesley, Aug. 30, 1811, H. Wellesley to R. Wellesley, Aug. 31, 1811; Wellesley Papers, Add. MSS. 49,983, H.

Wellesley to R. Wellesley, Aug. 31, Oct. 28, 1811 (Henry reported good progress by Oct. 20, 1811); P.R.O., F.O. 72/114, Doyle to H. Wellesley, Oct. 20, 1811.

37. P.R.O., F.O. 72/113, H. Wellesley to R. Wellesley, Aug. 31, 1811.

38. Wellesley Papers, Add. MSS. 37,295, R. Wellesley to Perceval, July 15, 1811, Perceval to R. Wellesley, n.d.

39. Butler, *The Eldest Brother*, p. 457; 1st Duke of Buckingham and Chandos, *Memoirs of the Court of England during the Regency, 1811–1820*, I: 121; Torrens, *The Marquess Wellesley*, pp. 459, 471; *Morning Chronicle*, Oct. 11, 1811, also believed the cabinet deficient in energy: "The Marquis Wellesley only, in whose department the business upon which they met is, being left to make up the dispatches agreeable to the determination of the Cabinet, and he has been indefatigably employed in doing this ever since. It is believed that the Noble Marquis has at length succeeded in persuading his colleagues to pursue a more decisive system than has heretofore been attempted.—And surely it is time!"

40. Torrens, *The Marquess Wellesley*, pp. 449–71; Buckingham, *Memoirs of the Regency*, I: 126–27; Huskisson Papers, Add. MSS. 38,738, Canning to Huskisson, Sept. 18, 1811, Huskisson to Canning, Aug. 6, 1811.

41. Wellesley Papers, Add. MSS. 37,293, R. Wellesley to Alexander I, Aug. 16, 1811; Mr. Thorton's notes on a conference with R. Wellesley, Sept. 14, 1811, R. Wellesley to Thorton, Oct. 9, 1811; ibid., Add. MSS. 37,295, R. Wellesley to Alexander I, Aug. 9, 1811; A.H.N., Sección de Estado, Legajo 5463, Apodaca to Bardaxi, July 29, Sept. 4, 1811, Legajo 5464, Infantado to Bardaxi, Sept. 18, 1811; Wellesley Papers, Add. MSS. 37,314, R. Wellesley to Bathurst, Aug. 10, 1811.

42. Wellesley purchased Apsley House in 1807 for £16,000 and sold it to his brother, the Duke of Wellington, in 1816 for £42,000. Apsley House now serves as the Wellington Museum.

43. P.R.O., F.O. 72/117, Apodaca to R. Wellesley, Aug. 29, 31, 1811; A.H.N., Sección de Estado, Legajo 5463, Apodaca to Bardaxi, July 10, 1811.

44. P.R.O., F.O. 72/108, R. Wellesley to H. Wellesley, July 27, 1811.

45. P.R.O., F.O. 72/117, Apodaca to R. Wellesley, July 8, 1811.

46. P.R.O., F.O. 72/113, Vega to H. Wellesley, Sept. 4, 1811.

47. Ibid., H. Wellesley to Vega, Sept. 4, 1811.

48. Wellesley Papers, Add. MSS. 49,983, H. Wellesley to R. Wellesley, Sept. 13, 1811; P.R.O., F.O. 72/113, H. Wellesley to R. Wellesley, Sept. 13, 17, 1811.

49. P.R.O., F.O. 72/113, H. Wellesley to R. Wellesley, Sept. 13, 1811; Wellesley Papers, Add. MSS. 49,983, H. Wellesley to R. Wellesley, Sept. 13, 1811; Vaughan Papers, C:107:6, Stuart to Vaughan, October 11, 1811. Stuart writes that Wellesley referred to the princess as the "Bloody Bitch of the Indies."

50. Wellesley Papers, Add. MSS. 49,983, H. Wellesley to R. Wellesley, Aug. 31, 1811; P.R.O., F.O. 72/113, H. Wellesley to R. Wellesley, Aug. 31, 1811; A.H.N., Sección de Estado, Legajo 5464, Infantado to Bardaxi, Oct. 6, 30, 1811.

51. P.R.O., F.O. 72/113, H. Wellesley to R. Wellesley, Sept. 13, 1811; Wellesley Papers, Add. MSS. 49,983, H. Wellesley to R. Wellesley, Sept. 13, Oct. 28, 1811; P.R.O., F.O. 72/114, H. Wellesley to R. Wellesley, Sept. 13, 1811.

52. Vaughan Papers, E:2:9–10, Vaughan's notes, Sept. 10, 1811; P.R.O., F.O. 72/114, H. Wellesley to R. Wellesley, Oct. 28, 1811.

264 *Notes to pp. 194–97*

53. Wellesley Papers, Add. MSS. 49,983, H. Wellesley to R. Wellesley, Sept. 21, 1811; P.R.O., F.O. 72/113, H. Wellesley to Bardaxi, Sept. 19, 1811.

54. P.R.O., F.O. 72/113, Bardaxi to H. Wellesley, Sept. 22, 1811.

55. Ibid., H. Wellesley to Bardaxi, Sept. 25, 1811.

56. Wellesley Papers, Add. MSS. 49,983, H. Wellesley to R. Wellesley , Sept. 30, 1811.

57. Ibid., Add. MSS. 37,293, R. Wellesley to H. Wellesley, Sept. 30, 1811, to Infantado, Sept. 30, 1811; P.R.O., F.O. 72/156, Croker to Hamilton, Oct. 1, 1811; A.H.N., Sección de Estado, Legajo 5464, Regency to Infantado, Dec. 4, 1811, Infantado to Bardaxi, Oct. 5, 1811.

58. *Morning Chronicle*, Oct. 2, 1811; *Examiner*, Oct. 6, 1811; Wellesley Papers, Add. MSS. 37,310, Yorke to R. Wellesley, Oct. 3, 1811; P.R.O., F.O. 72/156, Croker to Hamilton, Oct. 1, 1811.

59. Wellesley Papers, Add. MSS. 37,293, Souza to R. Wellesley, Oct. 3, 1811; P.R.O., F.O. 72/108, R. Wellesley to H. Wellesley, Oct. 1, 1811; Wellesley Papers, Add. MSS. 37,415, H. Wellesley to R. Wellesley, Nov. 17, 1811; Vaughan Papers, C:107:5, Stuart to Vaughan, Sept. 20, 1811. "The affairs of Spain look blacker . . . and as the gentleman of the Cortes now constitute the executive gov't. of the country I see no probability of improvement there. This is precisely what might be expected from attorneys, clerks & coffee house politicians: Hatred of the nobility & a determination to render a people democratical who by habit & inclination always were and will remain monarchists and aristocrats."

60. Vaughan Papers, E:3:1, Vaughan's notes, Nov. 2, 1811; Wellesley Papers, Add. MSS. 49,983, H. Wellesley to R. Wellesley, Sept. 17, 1811; Wellington, *Supplementary Dispatches*, H. Wellesley to R. Wellesley to Wellesley, Oct. 1, 1811, VII: 220.

61. Vaughan Papers, E:3:1, Vaughan's notes, Nov. 2, 1811, ibid., C:118:4, H. Wellesley to Vega, Oct. 30, 1811; Wellesley Papers, Add. MSS. 49,983, H. Wellesley to R. Wellesley, Oct. 28, 1811; P.R.O., F.O. 72/114, H. Wellesley to R. Wellesley, Oct. 28, 1811.

62. P.R.O., F.O. 72/114, Junta of Cádiz to Regency, Oct. 30, 1811, to H. Wellesley, Oct. 30, 1811; Wellesley Papers, Add. MSS. 49,984, H. Wellesley to R. Wellesley, Nov. 17, 1811; ibid., Add. MSS. 37,415, H. Wellesley to R. Wellesley, Nov. 23, 1811.

63. P.R.O., F.O. 72/114, H. Wellesley to R. Wellesley, Nov. 18, 1811; to Bardaxi, Nov. 12, 15, 1811, Bardaxi to H. Wellesley, Nov. 13, 1811; Wellesley Papers, Add. MSS. 49,984, H. Wellesley to R. Wellesley, Nov. 18, 1811.

64. Wellesley Papers, Add. MSS. 49,984, H. Wellesley to R. Wellesley, Nov. 18, Dec. 7, 1811; P.R.O., F.O. 72/114, H. Wellesley to R. Wellesley, Nov. 18, 1811.

65. P.R.O., F.O. 72/114, H. Wellesley to R. Wellesley, Nov. 18, 1811; Wellesley Papers, Add. MSS. 49,984, H. Wellesley to R. Wellesley, Nov. 18, Dec. 7, 1811; Vaughan Papers, C:118:15, H. Wellesley memorandum, n.d.

66. Vaughan Papers, E:10:4, H. Wellesley to Vaughan, Dec. 16, 1811; ibid., E:5A, H. Wellesley's memorandum, Dec. 12, 1811; P.R.O., F.O. 72/109, H. Wellesley to R. Wellesley, Jan. 13, 1811. About Vaughan's services, Wellesley states: "indeed they are invaluable just now from his extensive knowledge of the language, & his habits of communicating with Spaniards."

67. P.R.O., F.O. 72/115, Bardaxi to H. Wellesley, Dec. 19, 1811 (confidential);

Wellesley Papers, Add. MSS. 49,984, H. Wellesley to R. Wellesley, Dec. 20, 1811.

68. Vaughan Papers, E:10:4, H. Wellesley to Vaughan, Dec. 16, 1811; Wellesley Papers, Add. MSS. 49,984, H. Wellesley to R. Wellesley, Dec. 20, 1811.

69. Vaughan Papers, E:10:1, Clive to Vaughan, Dec. 20, 1811.

70. Wellesley, Papers, Add. MSS. 49,984, H. Wellesley to R. Wellesley, Dec. 20, 1811; P.R.O., F.O. 72/115, H. Wellesley to R. Wellesley, Dec. 20, 1811; Vaughan Papers, E:10:4, H. Wellesley to Vaughan, Dec. 16, 1811; ibid., E:11:1, H. Wellesley to Vaughan, Dec. 20, 1811.

71. Wellesley Papers, Add. MSS. 37,296, Perceval to R. Wellesley, Nov. 2, 7, 12, Dec. 25, 1811, R. Wellesley to Perceval, Nov. 4, 7, Dec. 26, 1811.

72. Buckingham, *Memoirs of the Regency*, I:127; Wellesley Papers, Add. MSS. 37,296, R. Wellesley to Perceval, Nov. 27, 1811. The Regency Bill expired in February 1812.

73. Liverpool Papers, Add. MSS. 38,378, York to Liverpool, Dec. 7, 1811 (this letter was passed on to Wellesley).

74. Butler, *The Eldest Brother*, p. 457.

75. Wellesley Papers, Add. MSS. 37,296, R. Wellesley to Perceval, Dec. 18, 1811. Intercabinet communications on the new regency provisions are contained ibid. and Liverpool Papers, Add. MSS. 38,362.

76. Vaughan Papers, E:11:6, Vaughan to H. Wellesley, Jan. 10, 1812; ibid., E:11:9, Vaughan to H. Wellesley, Jan. 20, 1812. "I have been delighted with Ld. Wellesley's frank and kind treatment of me & the very zealous & active manner in which he has taken up the business you sent me about."

77. Ibid., E:11:7, Vaughan to H. Wellesley, Jan. 12, 1812.

78. P.R.O., F.O. 72/127, R. Wellesley to H. Wellesley, Jan. 2, 17, 1812; Wellesley Papers, Add. MSS. 49,980, R. Wellesley to H. Wellesley, Jan. 2, 17, 1812.

79. Wellesley Papers, Add. MSS. 49,980, R. Wellesley to H. Wellesley, Jan. 17, 1812, P.R.O., F.O. 72/127, R. Wellesley to H. Wellesley, Jan. 17, 1812.

80. P.R.O., F.O. 72/115, Bardaxi to H. Wellesley, Dec. 29, 1811; P.R.O., F.O. 72/134, Infantado to R. Wellesley, Jan. 7, 1812.

81. P.R.O., F.O. 72/115, H. Wellesley to Bardaxi, Dec. 30, 1811, to R. Wellesley, Dec. 31, 1811; Wellesley Papers, Add. MSS. 49,984, H. Wellesley to R. Wellesley, Dec. 31, 1811.

82. Wellesley Papers, Add. MSS. 49,984, H. Wellesley to R. Wellesley, Jan. 13, 1812; P.R.O., F.O. 72/129, H. Wellesley to R. Wellesley, Jan. 13, 1812; Vaughan Papers, E:10:3, Clive to Vaughan, Jan. 13, 1812; A.H.N., Sección de Estado, Legajo 5464, Infantado to R. Wellesley, Feb. 5, 1812.

83. Wellesley Papers, Add. MSS. 37,296, Canning to R. Wellesley, Jan. 9, 1812.

84. *Parliamentary Debates*, XXI: 7–10; A.H.N., Sección de Estado, Legajo 5464, Infantado to Bardaxi, Jan. 10, 1812.

85. *Parliamentary Debates*, XXI: 408–78.

86. Wellington, *Supplementary Dispatches,* Liverpool to Wellington, Jan. 20, 1812, VII: 256–57; Buckingham, *Memoirs of the Regency,* II: 195–96; Wellesley Papers, Add. MSS. 37,296, Perceval to R. Wellesley, Jan. 17, 1812.

87. Bathurst Papers, loan no. 57, vol. 5, no. 433, Bathurst Memorandum, Jan. 17, 1812.

88. Ibid., no. 435, R. Wellesley to Perceval, Jan. 18, 1812.

89. Ibid., no. 439, Bathurst Memorandum, Feb. 17, 1812.
90. Buckingham, *Memoirs of the Regency*, I: 224–25; Michael Roberts, *The Whig Party: 1807–1812*, p. 380.
91. Wellesley Papers, Add. MSS. 37,296, Prince Regent to Lord Eldon, Feb. 18, 1812, Perceval to Wellington, Feb. 10, 1812; P.R.O., F.O. 72/134, Infantado to R. Wellesley, Feb. 21, 1812; Buckingham, *Memoirs of the Regency*, I: 261; A.H.N., Sección de Estado, Legajo 5464, Infantado to Bardaxi, Feb. 27, 1812.
92. *Examiner*, Feb. 23, 1812.

Chapter 10

1. Wellesley Papers, Add. MSS. 49,984, H. Wellesley to R. Wellesley, Jan. 22, Feb. 3, 1812; P.R.O., F.O. 72/129, H. Wellesley to R. Wellesley, Jan. 22, Feb. 3, 1812.
2. P.R.O., F.O. 72/129, H. Wellesley to R. Wellesley, Feb. 3, 1812; Wellesley Papers, Add. MSS. 49,984, H. Wellesley to R. Wellesley, Feb. 3, 1812.
3. P.R.O., F.O. 72/134, Cortes to R. Wellesley, Feb. 5, 1812; Vaughan Papers, E:3:2, Vega to H. Wellesley, Feb. 24, 1812; P.R.O., F.O. 72/129, Bardaxi to H. Wellesley, Jan. 29, 1812, H. Wellesley to R. Wellesley, Jan. 22, 1812; Wellesley Papers, Add. MSS. 49,984, H. Wellesley to R. Wellesley, Jan. 22, 1812. Count Fernan-Nuñez was appointed to take Infantado's place as ambassador to th Court of St. James.
4. *Parliamentary Debates*, XXI: 707–12, 842–81; the *Examiner* (Feb. 23, 1812), not overly fond of Wellington, approved of Parliament's action: " . . . though his Lordship is rather a patient and brave officer, than a great one, yet he actually does something for his money;—he undergoes a toil for it, and to a certain degree has upheld the British reputation in arms."
5. Wellington, *Supplementary Dispatches*, Wellington to R. Wellesley, March 12, 1812, VII: 303.
6. Wellesley Papers, Add. MSS. 37,296, T. Sydenham to R. Wellesley, March 31, 1812 (Sydenham forwarded Stuart's letter, dated March 17, 1812, to Wellesley); ibid., Add. MSS. 37,293, Wm. Bentinck to R. Wellesley, May 7, 1812, Villiers to Wellesley, March 3, 1812.
7. Bathurst Papers, loan no. 57, vol. 5, no. 442, R. Wellesley to Bathurst, Feb. 26, 1812.
8. Wellesley Papers, Add. MSS. 37,314, contains numerous letters from Bathurst updating Wellesley on events in the peninsula.
9. *Parliamentary Debates*, XXI: 1262–63, 1294–1309; P.R.O., F.O. 72/127, Castlereagh to H. Wellesley, March 30, 1812.
10. Wellesley Papers, Add. MSS. 37,296, Memorandum on reasons for quitting office; Add. MSS. 37,296 contains the political correspondence between Canning and Wellesley for the months of March through May 1812.
11. *Parliamentary Debates*, XXII: 45.
12. Butler, *The Eldest Brother*, pp. 466–67.
13. *Parliamentary Debates*, XXII: 1069–73, 1042–48.
14. The *Times*, the *Morning Post*, and the *Morning Chronicle*, all of May 12, 1812.
15. Wellesley Papers, Add. MSS. 37,296, Canning to R. Wellesley, May 17, 18, 1812, Minutes of Wellesley's meeting with Liverpool, May 18, 1812, R. Wellesley to Liverpool, May 18, 1812.

16. Huskisson Papers, Add. MSS. 38,738, copy of a Wellesley note on his refusal to join Liverpool, May 18, 1812.

17. *Parliamentary Debates*, XXII: 1014. See also George D. Knight, "Lord Liverpool and the Peninsular War, November 1809 through March 1811" (thesis).

18. The *Times*, May 21, 1812; the *Morning Chronicle* and the *Morning Post* followed with similar articles.

19. *Morning Chronicle*, May 21, 1812.

20. Wellesley Papers, Add. MSS. 37,296, Memorandum on Wellesley's reasons for quitting office. The memorandum also stated: "In fact, he was convinced by experience, that the Cabinet neither possessed ability, nor knowledge to *devise* a good plan, nor temper and discernment to adopt what he now thought necessary, unless Mr. Perceval should concur with Lord Wellesley. To Mr. Perceval's judgement or attainments, Lord Wellesley (under the same experience) could not pay any deference, without injury to the public service."

21. Thomas Sydenham had much to do with the writing of the memorandum. One of the copies is in his handwriting. Benjamin, his brother, was still a confidant of Wellesley's and ever present at Apsley House.

22. *Morning Post*, May 21, 1812.

23. Huskisson Papers, Add. MSS. 38,738, Arbuthnot to Huskisson, May 23, 1812; Bathurst Papers, Loan no. 57, vol. 5, no. 458, Richmond to Bathurst, May 27, 1812. Some Tories were absolutely outraged with Wellesley. The Duke of Richmond commented: "Nothing can go on well when Lord Wellesley has anything to do. How that man has lowered himself." He also sugggested that Wellesley be sent to India just to get him out of Britain.

24. Huskisson Papers, Add. MSS. 38,738, Canning to R. Wellesley, May 23, 1812; Wellesley Papers, Add. MSS. 37,296, Minutes of Wellesley's meetings with Grenville and Grey, May 23, 1812, Grey to R. Wellesley, May 23, 1812, Moira to R. Wellesley, May 23, 1812, Holland to R. Wellesley, May 23, 1812, Lansdowne to R. Wellesley, May 23, 1812, R. Wellesley to Prince Regent, May 24, 1812.

25. *Creevey Papers*, Creevey to wife, May 27, 1812, I:158–59.

26. The *Morning Chronicle*, the *Times*, and the *Morning Post*, all of June 3, 1812; Wellesley Papers, Add. MSS. 37,296, R. Wellesley to Grenville, June 1, 1812, to Grey, June 1, 1812, Grenville to R. Wellesley, June 2 1812; Huskisson Papers, Add. MSS. 38,738, Huskisson to Arbuthnot, June 2, 1812, Arbuthnot to Huskisson, June 2, 1812.

27. *Creevey Papers*, Creevey to wife, June 3, 1812, I:165; the *Times*, the *Morning Chronicle*, and the *Morning Post*, all of June 4, 1812.

28. *Morning Chronicle*, June 5, 1812.

29. *Creevey Papers*, Creevey to wife, June 8, 1812, I:163; the *Morning Post*, the *Morning Chronicle*, and the *Times*, all of June 8, 1812.

30. *Examiner*, May 24, 1812.

31. P.R.O., F.O. 72/130, H. Wellesley to Castlereagh, June 20, 1812; P.R.O., F.O. 72/156, H. Wellesley to British Commissioners, July 17, 1812.

32. P.R.O., F.O. 72/134, Infantado to Castlereagh, March 2, April 24, 1812, Castlereagh to Infantado, March 25, May 1, 1812; P.R.O., F.O. 72/129, H. Wellesley to R. Wellesley, March 10, 1812, to Castlereagh, April 12, 1812; Londonderry, *Correspondence of Castlereagh*, H. Wellesley to Castlereagh, April 10, 1812, VIII:246–47; P.R.O., F.O. 72/130, H. Wellesley to Castlereagh, May 15, 1812; P.R.O., F.O. 72/127, Castlereagh to H. Wellesley, June 2, 1812.

33. Charles Arbuthnot, *Correspondence of Charles Arbuthnot,* H. Wellesley to Arbuthnot, Sept. 20, 1812, p. 65.

34. Cowley Papers, P.R.O., F.O. 519/67, H. Wellesley's Diary.

35. Butler, *The Eldest Brother,* p. 479.

36. Malleson, *Life of Marquess Wellesley,* pp. 201, 218; Torrens, *The Marquess Wellesley,* p. 123; Pearce, *Memoirs and Correspondence of Marquess Wellesley,* III:241; Butler, *The Eldest Brother,* pp. 501–13.

37. Butler, *The Eldest Brother,* pp. 514–24; Malleson, *Life of Marquess Wellesley,* p. 212.

38. Malleson, *Life of Marquess Wellesley,* p. 228; Butler, *The Eldest Brother,* pp. 569–79.

Bibliography

Primary Sources

Public Documents

London. Public Record Office.
Foreign Office. General Correspondence. Before 1906. Spain (F.O. 72).
(F.O. 72/75. To Lord Wellesley. June–November, 1809.
F.O. 72/76–78. From Lord Wellesley. August–November 1809.
F.O. 72/79. From Bartholomew Frere. November–December, 1809.
F.O. 72/80. Consular reports. 1809.
F.O. 72/81–82. Foreign. Various, 1809.
F.O. 72/83–90. Domestic. Various. 1809.
F.O. 72/91. South America. June 1809.
F.O. 72/92. From Bartholomew Frere. January–March, 1810.
F.O. 72/93. To Henry Wellesley. December 1809–December 1810.
F.O. 72/94–98. From Henry Wellesley. March–December, 1810.
F.O. 72/99. Consuls George White, James Duff, Bernard Athy, and Peter C. Tapper, Generals Whittingham, Doyle, and Walker, Colonels Carrol, Roche, and Downies, C. R. Vaughan, L. Briarly, and Foreign. Various. 1810.
F.O. 72/100–101. Admiral Apodaca. January–December 1810.
F.O. 72/102–5. Domestic. Various. January December, 1810.
F.O. 72/106. Bolívar and Méndez. South America. June–September 1810.
F.O. 72/107. Alexander MacKinnon, Don M. Trigoyen, and various. South America. 1810.
F.O. 72/108. To Henry Wellesley. 1811.
F.O. 72/109–15. From Henry Wellesley. 1811.
F.O. 72/116. Commissioner George White, and Consuls James Duff,

Bernard Athy, Louis Hargrove, Generals Whittingham, Doyle, Colonel Carrol, Captain Landmann, and various. 1811.

F.O. 72/117–18. Admiral Apodaca. 1811. Domestic.

F.O. 72/119. Duke del Infantado. August–December 1811.

F.O. 72/120–24. Domestic. Various. 1811.

F.O. 72/125. Spanish America—North. General Miranda, etc. Domestic. Joseph Hibberson, and Don L. Mendes. 1811.

F.O. 72/126. Spanish America—South. Alexander MacKinnon, Consul Robert P. Staples, John C. Rawlinson, etc., Messrs. Trigoyen, Moreno, and Guido. 1811.

F.O. 72/127–28. To Henry Wellesley. 1812.

F.O. 72/129–32. From Henry Wellesley. 1812.

F.O. 72/133. Consuls James Duff, Bernard Athy, John and Richard Allen, Marquis of Wellington, Generals Doyle, Carrol, Roche, and Whittingham, Colonel Green, C. R. Vaughan, and various. 1812.

F.O. 72/134. Duke del Infantado. January–May 1812.

F.O. 72/137–39. Domestic. Various. January–June 1812.

F.O. 72/156. Commissioners George Cockburn, Thomas Sydenham, and John Philip Morier, America. October 1811–February 1813.

F.O. 72/157. Robert P. Staples, Don Manuel Moreno, Don Luis Lopez Méndez, and various, America. 1812–13.

Foreign Office. Great Britain and General (F.O. 83).

F.O. 83/18–19. Collection of anonymous letters from Spain. 1808–11.

F.O. 83/20, 23. Various. 1811–12.

Foreign Office. Protocols of Treaties (F.O. 93).

F.O. 93/77–6, 7. Treaty of alliance and friendship. February 19, 1810. Portugal. Treaty of commerce and navigation. Portugal. February 19, 1810.

F.O. 93/99–6. Treaty of peace, friendship, and alliance. Spain. January 14, 1809. Additional articles. March 21, 1809.

Foreign Office. Ratification of Treaties (F.O. 94).

F.O. 94/286–7. Treaty of peace, friendship and alliance. January 14, February 16, 1809. Additional article to the foregoing. March 21, April 16, 1809.

Foreign Office. Embassy and Consular Archives (F.O. 185).

F.O. 185/16–18. From Foreign Office. 1809–10.

F.O. 185/19. To Foreign Office. 1810.

F.O. 185/20. From Spanish Government. 1810.

F.O. 185/21. To Spanish Government. 1810.

F.O. 185/24. From Foreign Office, 1811.

F.O. 185/25. To Foreign Office. 1811.

F.O. 185/26. Spanish Government. 1811.

F.O. 185/29–30. Consuls and various. 1811.

F.O. 185/31. From Foreign Office. 1812.

F.O. 185/32. To Foreign Office. 1812.

F.O. 185/33. Spanish Government. 1812.

F.O. 185/36. Consuls and various. 1812.

F.O. 187/1. Registers to Foreign Office. March 1810–May 1812.

Foreign Office. Private Collections. Cowley Papers (F.O. 519).

F.O. 519/30. Letters to Charles Stuart, March 1810–June 1811.

F.O. 519/34–35. Letters to Wellington. March 1810–August 1810.

F.O. 519/36. Letters to Marquess Wellesley. March 1810–October 1811.

F.O. 519/66–9. Memoirs and Diary.

Madrid. Archivo Histórico Nacional (A.H.N.)

Sección de Estado.

Legajo 3002. Cortes de Cadíz. Decretos.

Legajo 2962. Defensa de Junta Suprema.

Legajo 2987, 3003, 3119, 3099, 3112, 3113, 3110, 3111, 3104, 3121, 3130. Correspondencia interceptada.

Legajo 5459–64. Correspondencia diplomatica con Inglaterra.

Legajo 5488. Inglaterra. Cuentas.

Legajo 5608–14, 5619, 5620, 5623, 5627. Inglaterra. Expedientes.

Legajo 1–84. Junta Central Suprema Gubernativa del Reino y del Consejo de Regencia. Años 1808–10.

Legajo 3072, 3110, 3066. Junta Central Suprema Gubernativa del Reino y del Consejo de Regencia. Varios. 1809–14.

Legajo 3566. Regencia. Asuntos varios. 1808–14.

Legajo 3010, 2994. Guerra de la Independencia. Confidentes. 1808–12.

Washington, D.C. National Archives.

Department of State. General Correspondence. Spain.

No. 59. Vol. 11. To Secretary of State. 1809–10.

Manuscripts

London. British Museum. Manuscript Collection.

Bathurst Papers. Loan No. 57, vol. 3–5, 60, 95. Private and official correspondence, 1809–13.

Canning Papers. Additional Manuscripts 46841, 49597. Private correspondence, 1810–12.

Herries Papers. Additional Manuscripts 57367–77, 57393, 57415, 57428–9. Memoranda and accounts from the office of the Commissary-in-Chief, 1810–12.

Hobart Papers. Additional Manuscript 34455.

Huskisson Papers. Additional Manuscripts 38737–39, 38759–60, 39948. General and private correspondence, and official financial reports.

Lenox Papers. Loan No. 57. Vol. 106.

Liverpool Papers. Additional Manuscripts. 38243–47, 38323–26, 38360–62, 38378, 38473, 38566, 38571. General and official correspondence.

Melville Papers. Loan No. 57. Vol. 108.

Original Letters and Autographs of Foreign Statesmen, Officers, and Others, from 1494 to 1830. Additional Manuscript 15945.

Paget Papers. Additional Manuscripts 48387–88.

Peel Papers. Additional Manuscript 40605.

Pelham Papers. Additional Manuscript 33124.

Perceval Papers. Additional Manuscripts 49177, 49185, 49188, 49190. Official and general correspondence.

Vansittart Papers. Additional Manuscripts 31230–31. General correspondence.

Wellesley Papers. Series I.
  Additional Manuscripts 13804–06. Miscellaneous letters and papers,
    1802–22, and *Playfair's* account of the Wellesley family.
  Additional Manuscript 13914. Pedigree of the families of Wellesley, Cusack,
    and Colley.
  Additional Manuscripts 13473–99. Private and official correspondence,
    1798–1805.
Wellesley Papers. Series II.
  Additional Manuscripts 37286–88. Correspondence relating to Spain and
    Portugal, chiefly as ambassador extraordinary in 1809.
  Additional Manuscript 37289. Copies of dispatches to George Canning
    while ambassador to Spain.
  Additional Manuscripts 37291–94. Correspondence and papers relating to
    foreign affairs while foreign secretary.
  Additional Manuscripts 37295–97. Select political correspondence 1799–
    1835.
  Additional Manuscripts 37309–10. General correspondence.
  Additional Manuscript 37314. Letters to Lord Bathurst and Henry Welles-
    ley, 1809.
  Additional Manuscript 37315–16. Family correspondence.
  Additional Manuscript 37317. Legal papers.
  Additional Manuscript 37415. Correspondence with Wellington (1806–42)
    and Henry Wellesley (1803–41).
  Additional Manuscript 37416. Personal and private correspondence, family
    records and the beginnings of an autobiography.
  Additional Manuscripts 49979–92. Précis books of dispatches to and from
    Spain, Portugal, and Brazil, 1809–12.
Oxford. All Souls College Library.
  Vaughan Papers. Manuscripts of Charles Richard Vaughan.
    C:48:1–10; C:49:1–10. Correspondence with William Hamilton, 1810–
      11.
    C:56:2–10; C:57:1. Correspondence with Lord Holland.
    C:60:1–7; C:61:1–4. Correspondence with Lady Holland.
    C:103:1–10; C:104:1–11; C:105:1–6; C:106:1–9; C:107:5–9. Corres-
      pondence with Charles Stuart.
    C:118:1–5. Vega correspondence.
    E:1:5; E:2:5–10; E:3:1–11; E:5A; E:10:1–4; E:11:1–9. Spanish papers.

Newspapers and Periodicals

  Edinburgh Review
  Examiner
  Hampshire Chronicle
  Hull Packet
  Le Moniteur
  Morning Chronicle
  Morning Post
  Quarterly Review
  Shrewsbury Chronicle
  Times (London)

Memoirs, Letters, Diaries, and Other Published Primary Sources

Andrews, John. *Characteristical Views of the Past and of the Past and of the Present State of the People of Spain and Italy.* London: C. Chapple, 1808.

Anglesey, George Charles Henry Victor Paget, 7th Marquis of. *One-Leg: The Life and Letters of Henry William Paget, First Marquess of Anglesey, K.G.* New York: William Morrow and Co., 1961.

Arbuthnot, Charles. *Correspondence of Charles Arbuthnot.* Camden Series. Vol. 65. London: Royal Historical Society, 1941.

Artola, Miquel. *Los orígenes de la España contemporánea.* 2 vols. Madrid: Instituto de Estudios Políticos, 1959.

Bagot, Joceline. *George Canning and His Friends.* 2 vols. London: John Murray, 1909.

Blayney, Andrew Thomas Blayney, baron. *Narrative of a Forced Journey Through Spain and France, as a Prisoner of War, in Years 1810–1814.* 2 vols. London: E. Kerby, 1814.

Bourrienne, Louis Antoine Fauvelet de. *Memoirs of Napoleon Bonaparte.* Edited by R. W. Phipps. 5 vols. New York: Charles Scribner's Sons, 1892.

Bragge, William. *Peninsular Portrait, 1811–1814: The Letters of Captain William Bragge, Third Dragoons.* Edited by S. A. C. Cassals. London and New York: Oxford University Press, 1963.

Brougham, Henry Lord. *Historical Sketches of Statesmen Who Flourished in the Time of George III.* 2 vols. Philadelphia: Lea and Blanchard, 1839.

———. *The Life and Times of Henry Lord Brougham.* 3 vols. New York: Harper and Bros., 1871–72.

Buckingham and Chandos, 1st Duke of. *Memoirs of the Court of England during the Regency, 1811–1820.* 2 vols. London: Hurst and Blackett, 1856.

Cobbett, William. *History of the Regency and the Reign of George IV.* 2 vols. London: William Cobbett, 1830.

Creevey, Thomas. *The Creevey Papers: A Selection From the Correspondence and Diaries of the Late Thomas Creevey, M.P.* Edited by Sir Herbert Maxwell. 2 vols. New York: E. P. Dutton, 1903.

Croker, John Wilson. *The Croker Papers: The Correspondence and Diaries of the Late Right Honourable John Wilson Croker.* Edited by Louis J. Jennings. 3 vols. London: John Murray, 1884.

Dundas, Henry, and Wellesley, Richard Colley. *Two Views of British India: The Private Correspondence of Mr. Dundas and Lord Wellesley, 1798–1801.* Edited by Edward Ingram. London: Adams and Dort, 1970.

D'Urban, Sir Benjamin. *The Peninsular Journal of Major General Sir Benjamin D'Urban.* Edited, with an introduction, by I. J. Rousseau. London: Longmans, Green, 1930.

Foy, Maximilien Sébastien, comte. *History of the War in the Peninsula, under Napoleon. To Which is Prefixed a view of the Political and Military State of the Four Belligerent Powers.* 2 vols. London: Treuttel and Wurtz, 1827.

Frere, Bartholomew. *The Works of the Right Honourable John Hookam Frere.* London: Basil Montago Pickering, 1874.

George III, King of England. *The Later Correspondence of George III,* Vol. V. *January, 1808 to December, 1810.* Edited by A. Aspinall. Cambridge: At the University Press, 1970.

Gordon, Alexander. *A Cavalry Officer in the Corunna Campaign, 1808–1809: The Journal of Captain Gordon of the 15th Hussars.* Edited by H. C. Wylly. London: John Murray, 1913.

Grasilier, Léonce. *Adventuriers politiques sous le Consulat et l'Empire. Le baron de Kolli. Le comte Pagowski.* Paris: Ollendorff, 1902.

Great Britain. *Cobbett's Parliamentary History of England from the Earliest Period to the Year 1803.* London: T.C. Hansard, 1816.

———. *Hansard's Catalogue and Breviate of Parliamentary Papers, 1696–1834.* Reprinted in facsimile, with an introduction by P. Ford and G. Ford. Oxford: Blackwell, 1953.

———. *The Parliamentary Debates from the Year 1803 to the Present Time.* 1st ser. London: T.C. Hansard, 1820.

———. Historical Manuscripts Commission. *Report on the Manuscripts of J. B. Fortescue, Esq., Preserved at Dropmore.* Edited by Walter Fitzpatric. Hereford: Hereford Times Limited for H.M. Stationery Office, 1915 and 1927.

———. Parliament. House of Commons. Board of General Officers Appointed to Inquire into the . . . Convention, etc. in Portugal. A Copy of the Proceedings upon the Inquiry Relative to the Armistice and Convention etc., Made and Concluded in Portugal, in August 1808, between the Commanders of the British and French Armies;—Held at the Royal Hospital at Chelsea, on Monday the 14th of November; and continued by Adjournments until Tuesday the 27th of December, 1808. London, 1809.

Hamilton, Thomas. *Annals of the Peninsular Campaigns.* A new ed. rev. and augmented by Frederick Hardman. Edinburgh: Blackwood, 1849.

Harris, James, First Earl of Malmesbury. *Diaries and Correspondence of James Harris, First Earl of Malmesbury.* Edited by his grandson, the third Earl. 4 vols. London: Richard Bentley, 1844.

Harris, John. *Recollections of Rifleman Harris.* Edited by Henry Curling with an introduction by the Hon. Sir John Fortescue. Portway and Bath: Cedric Chivers, 1966.

Hay, Sir Andrew Leith. *A Narrative of the Peninsular War.* 4th ed. London: J. Hearne, 1850.

Hazlitt, William. *Memoirs of William Hazlitt.* 2 vols. London: n.p., 1867.

Herries, John Charles. "A Review of the Controversy Respecting the High Price of Bullion and the State of our Currency." In [a collection of seven] *Bullion and Currency Tracts.* N.p., 1811–12.

Herries, John Charles. *Memoir of the Public Life of the Rt. Hon. J.C. Herries.* 2 vols. London: John Murray, 1880.

Hertslet, Edward Cecil. *Hertslet's Commercial Treaties. A Collection of Treaties and Conventions Between Great Britain and Foreign Powers and of the Laws, Decrees, Orders in Council, etc. Concerning the Same* . . . . 31 vols. London: Statistical Office, 1822–1925.

Holland, Lady Elizabeth. *The Journal of Elizabeth, Lady Holland.* Edited by the Earl of Ilchester. 2 vols. London: Longman's Green, 1909.

Holland, Henry Richard Lord. *Foreign Reminiscences.* Edited by his son, Henry Edward Lord Holland. New York: Harper, 1851.

———. *Memoirs of the Whig Party during My Time.* Edited by his son, Henry Edward Lord Holland. 2 vols. London: Longman, Brown, Green, and Longman's, 1852–54.

Horner, Francis. *Memoirs and Correspondence of Francis Horner, M.P.* Edited by L. Horner. 2 vols. London: John Murray, 1843.

Huskisson, William. *The Question Concerning the Depreciation of our Currency Stated and Examined.* London: John Murray, 1810.

Jackson, George. *The Diaries and Letters of Sir George Jackson, K.C.H., from the Peace of Amiens to the Battle of Talavera.* Edited by Lady Jackson. 2 vols. London: Bentley, 1872.

Jacob, William. *Travels in the South of Spain.* London: T. Johnson and Company, 1811.

Jones, Sir John Thomas, bart. *Accounts of the War in Spain, Portugal, and the South of France from 1808 to 1814 Inclusive.* London: T. Egerton, 1818.

————. *Memoranda Relative to the Lines Thrown up to Cover Lisbon in 1810.* London: C. Rowrath, 1829.

Kincaid, Sir John. *Adventures in the Rifle Brigade, in the Peninsula, France, and the Neatherlands from 1809 to 1815.* 3d ed. London: T. and W. Boone, 1847.

Knighton, Sir William. *Memoirs.* Edited by Lady Knighton, London: n.p., 1838.

Kolli, Charles Leopold Baron de. *Mémoires du baron de Kolli et de la reine d'Éturie.* Paris: Michaud, 1923.

Landmann, George Thomas. *Recollections of My Military Life.* London: Hurst and Blackett, 1854.

Leach, Jonathan. *Rough Sketches of the Life of an Old Soldier: During a Service in the West Indies: At the Siege of Copenhagen in 1807: In the Peninsula and the South of France in the Campaigns from 1808 to 1814, with the Light Division: In the Netherlands in 1815: Including the Battles of Quatre Bras and Waterloo: With a Slight Sketch of the Three Years Passed by the Army of Occupation in France.* London: Longmans, Rees, Orme, Brown and Green, 1831.

Leveson-Gower, Granville. *Private Correspondence of Granville Leveson-Gower.* Edited by Countess Granville. 2 vols. London: John Murray, 1916.

Lewin, Harry Ross. *With the Thirty-Second in the Peninsula and Other Campaigns.* Edited by John Wardell. Dublin: Hodges, Figgis, 1904.

Londonderry, Charles William Vane, 3d Marquis of. *Narrative of the Peninsular War from 1808 to 1813.* By Lieut. General Charles William Vane, Marquess of Londonderry. 3d ed. with an appendix of correspondence. London: H. Colburn, 1829.

Londonderry, Robert Stewart, 2d Marquis of. *Correspondence, Despatches and Other Papers of Viscount Castlereagh.* Edited by Charles W. Vane. 12 vols. London: William Shobrel, 1851.

Mampel, Johan Christian. *The Adventures of a Young Rifleman in the French and English Armies during the War in Spain and Portugal from 1806 to 1816.* London: H. Colburn, 1826.

Maxwell, William Hamilton. *Peninsular Sketches: By Actors on the Scene.* 2 vols. London: H. Colburn, 1845.

Milburne, Henry. *A Narrative of Circumstances Attending the Retreat of the British Army Under the Command of Lieut. Gen. Sir John Moore, K.B. With a Concise Account of the Memorable Battle of Corunna . . . And a Few Remarks Connected with These Subjects in a Letter Addressed to the Right Honourable Lord Viscount Castlereagh.* London: T. Edgerton, 1809.

Moore, James Carrick. *The Life of Lieutenant General Sir John Moore, K.B. by His Brother.* 2 vols. London: John Murray, 1834.

————. *A Narrative of the Campaign of the British Army in Spain, Commanded by His Excellency Lieut. General Sir John Moore, K.B. Authenticated by Official Papers and Original Letters.* London: J. Johnson, 1809.

Moore, Sir John. *The Diary of Sir John Moore.* Edited by Major-General Sir J. F. Maurice. 2 vols. London: E. Arnold, 1904.

Munster, George Augustus Frederick Fitzclarence, 1st Earl of. *An Account of the British Campaign in 1809, under Sir Arthur Wellesley, in Portugal and Spain.* London: H. Colburn and R. Bentley, 1831.

Napier, Sir William Francis Patrick. *History of the War in the Peninsula and in the South of France, from the Year 1807 to the Year 1814.* 6 vols. London: Barthés and Lowell, 1876.

Napoléon I. *The Confidential Correspondence of Napoleon Bonaparte with His Brother Joseph, Sometime King of Spain.* 2 vols. London: John Murray, 1835.

————. *Correspondance de Napoléon Ier, publiée par ordre de l'empereur Napoléon III.* 32 vols. Paris: Imprimerie Impériale, 1865.

Pearce, Robert Rouiere. *Memoirs and Correspondence of the Most Noble Richard Marquess Wellesley, K.P.* 3 vols. London: R. Bentley, 1846.

Pelet, Jean Jacques. *The French Campaign in Portugal, 1810–11: An Account by Jean Jacques Pelet.* Edited, annotated, and translated by Donald D. Horward. Minneapolis: University of Minnesota Press, 1973.

Pellew, George. *The Life and Correspondence of the Right Honourable Henry Addington, 1st Viscount Sidmouth.* London: John Murray, 1847.

Picton, Sir Thomas. *Memoirs of Lieutenant General Sir Thomas Picton, Including His Correspondence From Originals in Possession of His Family.* Edited by Heaton Bowstead Robinson. 2d ed. rev. with additions. 2 vols. London: Bentley, 1836.

Romilly, Samuel. *Memoirs of the Life of Sir Samuel Romilly.* 3 vols. London: J. Fairburn, 1841.

Rose, George. *The Diaries and Correspondence of the Right Honourable George Rose Containing Original Letters of the Most Distinguished Statesmen of His Day.* Edited by Leveson Vernon Harcourt. London: R. Bentley, 1860.

Sarrazin, Jean. *History of the War in Spain and Portugal from 1807 to 1814.* London: Collins, 1815.

Sheridan, R. B. *Memoirs of the Life of the Rt. Hon. R. B. Sheridan.* London: Longman, 1825.

Southey, Robert. *History of the Peninsular War.* 3 vols. London: John Murray, 1823–32.

Spain. Laws, statutes, etc. *Colección de los decretos y órenes que han expedido las cortes generales y extraordinarias desde su instalación de 24 setiembre de 1810 hasta . . . mandada publicar de orden de las mismas.* Madrid: Imprenta nacional, 1820–21.

————. *Constitución, 1812. Constitution politique de la monarchie Espanole, promulguée à Cadix le 19 Mars 1812, et jurée à Madrid par le Roi Ferdinand VII, le 7 Mars 1820. Précédée du rapport de la commission des Cortès chargée de presenter le projet de constitution.* Traduit de l'espagnol en français par E. Nuñez de Taboado. Bruxelles: Maubach, 1820.

————. *Junta de iconografía nacional. Guerra de la Independencia: Retratos.* Madrid: Revista de Archivos, Bibliotecas y Museos, 1908.

Stothert, William. *A Narrative of the Principal Events of the Campaigns of 1809, 1810, and 1811, in Spain and Portugal: Interspersed with Remarks on Local Scenery and Manners.* London: W. Smith, 1812.

Toreno, José María Queipo de Llano Ruiz de Saravía, conde de. *Historia del levantamiento, guerra y revolución de España.* Madrid: Biblioteca de Autores Españoles, 1953.

———. *Historia del Levantamento Guerra y Revolución de España: Precedida de la Biografía del Autor.* Escrita por el exemo. Sr. D. Leopoldo Augusto de Cueto. Madrid: Hernando, 1926.

Walton, William. *The Revolutions of Spain from 1808 to the End of 1836. With Biographical Sketches of the Most Distinguished Personages, and a Narrative of the War in the Peninsula Down to the Present Time, from the Most Authentic Sources.* 2 vols. London: Bentley, 1877.

Wellesley, Henry, First Lord Cowley. *The Diary and Correspondence of Henry Wellesley, First Lord Cowley, 1790–1846.* Edited by F.A. Wellesley. London: Hutchinson and Co., Ltd., 1930.

Wellesley, Richard Marquess. *The Despatches, Minutes, and Correspondence of the Marquess Wellesley, K.G., during the Administration in India.* Edited by Montgomery Martin. 5 vols. London: W. H. Allen, 1840.

———. *The Dispatches and Correspondence of the Marquess Wellesley, K.G. during His Lordship's Mission to Spain as Ambassador Extraordinary to the Supreme Junta in 1809.* Edited by Montgomery Martin. London: John Murray, 1838.

———. *The Wellesley Papers.* Edited by the editor of the "Windham Papers." 2 vols. London: Herbert Jenkins, Ltd., 1904.

Wellington, Arthur Wellesley, 1st Duke of. *The Dispatches of Field Marshal the Duke of Wellington during His Various Campaigns in India, Denmark, Portugal, Spain, the Low Countries, and France, from 1799 to 1818.* Compiled from official and other authentic documents, by the late Colonel Gurwood. New and enlarged ed. 8 vols. London: John Murray, 1852.

———. *General Orders.* 5 vols. London: T. Egerton, 1811–14.

———. *Some Letters of the Duke of Wellington to His Brother, William Wellesley-Pole.* Edited by Sir Charles Webster. London: Royal Historical Society, 1948.

———. *Supplementary Dispatches, Correspondence, and Memoranda of Field Marshal Arthur, Duke of Wellington.* Edited by the 2d Duke of Wellington. 14 vols. London: John Murray, 1863.

———. *Wellington at War, 1794–1815: A Selection of Wartime Letters.* Edited and introduced by Antony Brett-James. London: Macmillan, 1961.

Wheeler, William. *The Letters of Private Wheeler.* Edited and with a foreword by B. H. Liddell Hart. London: Michael Joseph, 1952.

Wyld, James, pub. *Memoir Annexed to an Atlas Containing Plans of the Principal Battles, Sieges, and Affairs, in Which the British Troops Were Engaged During the War in the Spanish Peninsula and the South of France, from 1808 to 1814.* London: J. Wyld, 1841.

Theses and Dissertations

Fryman, Mildred L. "Charles Stuart and the Common Cause: The Anglo-Portuguese Alliance, 1810–1814." Ph.D. dissertation, Florida State University, 1974.

Goldstein, Morton. "Great Britain in Spain, 1807–1809." Ph.D. dissertation, University of Chicago, 1969.

Goodwin, Winslow Copley. "The Political and Military Career of Don Pedro Caro Y Sureda, Marques de la Romana." Ph.D. dissertation, Florida State University, 1973.

Horward, Donald D. "The French Invasion of Portugal: 1810–1811." Ph.D. dissertation, University of Minnesota, 1962.

Knight, George D. "Lord Liverpool and the Peninsular War, November, 1809 through March, 1811." Master's thesis, Florida State University, 1970.

Vichness, Samuel Edison. "The Early Military Career of William Carr Beresford: 1768–1810." Master's thesis, Florida State University, 1971.

Secondary Sources

Bibliographical Aids and Reference Works

Bindoff, S. T.; Smith, E. F. M.; and Webster, C. K. *British Diplomatic Representatives: 1789–1852.* London: Royal Historical Society, 1934.

The Complete Peerage of England, Scotland, Ireland, Great Britain, and the United Kingdom, Extant, Extinct, or Dormant. New ed. rev. and much enlarged. Edited by Hon. Vicary Gibbs. London: St. Catherine's Press, 1912.

Diccionario bibliografico de la guerra de la indendencia española (1808–1814). Referencias y notas comentadas de obras impresas, documentos y manuscritos de autores nacionales y extranjeros, que tratan de asuntos militares, historicos, politicos, religiosos, economicos, etcetera, etc., relacionados con dicha guerra y su epoca. 3 vols. Madrid: Talleres del Servicio Geografico del Ejercito, 1944–52.

Dictionary of National Biography. Edited by Sir Leslie Stephen and Sir Sidney Lee. 1885–1900. Reprint. London: Oxford University Press, 1921–22.

Horward, Donald D. *The French Revolution and Napoleon Collection at Florida State University.* Tallahassee, Florida: Friends of the Florida State University Library, 1973.

Articles and Books

Aldington, Richard. *The Duke: Being an Account of the Life and Achievements of Arthur Wellesley, First Duke of Wellington.* New York: Viking, 1943.

Alexander , James Edward. *Life of Field Marshal, His Grace, The Duke of Wellington. Embracing His Civil, Military, and Political Career to the Present Time.* 2 vols. London: H. Colburn, 1840.

Anderson, John Henry. *The Peninsular War, March 1, 1811 to the Close of the War in 1814.* London: Rees, 1906.

Archivo Militar. *La Guerra de la Independencia.* Madrid: Servicio Militar, 1966.

Arteche y Moro, Don José Gómez de. *Guerra de la Independencia.* 14 vols. Madrid: Credito Commercial, 1868.

Ashton, John. *Social England under the Regency.* London: Chatto and Windus, 1899.

Aspinal, A. *Lord Brougham and the Whig Party.* Manchester: Manchester University Press, 1927.

Aspinall, A. "The Canningite Party." *Transactions of the Royal Historical Society,* 4th ser. XVII (1934): 177–226.

Azcarate, Pablo de. *Wellington y España.* Madrid: Desposa Calpe, 1960.

Balagny, Dominique. *Campagne de l'empereur Napoléon en España, 1808–1809.* 5 vols. Paris: Nancy, Berger-Levrault et Cie, 1906.

Bartlett, C. J. *Castlereagh.* New York: Charles Scribner's Sons, 1966.

Brodrick, George C., and Fotheringham, J. K. *The History of England: From Addington's Administration to the Close of William IV's Reign: 1808–1837.* London: Longmans, Green and Co., 1919.

Brooke, John. *King George III: A Biography of America's Last Monarch.* New York: McGraw-Hill Book Company, 1972.

Bryant, Arthur. *The Age of Elegance, 1812–1822.* New York: Harper, 1950.

———. *The Great Duke: Or, the Invincible General.* London: Collins, 1971.

———. *The Years of Endurance, 1793 to 1802.* London: Collins, 1951.

———. *The Years of Victory, 1802 to 1812.* London: Collins: 1944.

Butler, Iris. *The Eldest Brother: The Marquess Wellesley, the Duke of Wellington's Eldest Brother.* London: Hodder and Stoughton, 1973.

Butler, Lewis William George. *Wellington's Operations in the Peninsula, 1808–1814.* 2 vols. London: T. F. Unwin, 1904.

Carr, Raymond. *Spain: 1808–1939.* Oxford: The Clarendon Press, 1966.

———. "Spain and Portugal, 1793 to 1840." In *The New Cambridge Modern History.* vol. IX, *War and Peace in an Age of Upheaval, 1793–1830,* edited by C. W. Crawley. Cambridge: At the University Press, 1965.

Chapman, Charles E. *A History of Spain.* New York: The Macmillan Company, 1948.

Chandler, David. *The Campaigns of Napoleon.* New York: The Macmillan Company, 1966.

Christiansen, Eric. *The Origins of Military Power in Spain, 1800–1854.* London: Oxford University Press, 1967.

Clinton, Herbert R. *The War in the Peninsula and Wellington's Campaigns in France and Belgium.* (With original maps and plans.) London: F. Warne, 1878.

Cooper, Leonard. *The Age of Wellington: The Life and Times of the Duke of Wellington, 1769–1852.* London: Macmillan and Co., Ltd., 1964.

Curtis, Edith Roelker. *Lady Sarah Lennox, an Irrepressible Stuart, 1745–1826.* New York: Putnam, 1946.

Curzon of Kedleston, The Marquess. *British Government in India.* 2 vols. London: Cassell, 1925.

Davies, Godfrey. *Wellington and His Army.* Oxford: Blackwell, 1954.

———. "The Whigs and the Peninsular War." *Transactions of the Royal Historical Society,* 4th ser. II (1919): 113–31.

Fayle, C. Ernest, et al. *The Trade Winds: A Study of British Overseas Trade during the French Wars, 1793–1815.* Edited by C. Northcote Parkinson. London: George Allen and Unwin, Ltd., 1948.

Festing, Gabrielle. *John Hookham Frere and His Friends.* London: James Nisbet and Co., Ltd., 1899.

Fitchett, William Henry. *How England Saved Europe: The Story of the Great War.* London: Smith, Elder, 1899–1900.

———. *The Great Duke.* London: Smith, Elder, 1911.

Fortescue, Sir John William. *British Statesmen of the Great War, 1793–1814.* Oxford: The Clarendon Press, 1911.

———. *A History of the British Army.* 20 vols. London: Macmillan, 1910–17.

———. *Wellington.* London: E. Benn, 1960.

Fuente, Don Modesto de la. *Historia General de España.* 17 vols. Barcelona: Montanes y Simon, 1930.

Glover, Michael. *Britannia Sickens: Sir Arthur Wellesley and the Convention of Cintra.* London: Leo Cooper Ltd., 1970.

———. *Wellington as Military Commander.* London: Batsford, Princeton, Van Nostrand, 1968.

Gray, Denis. *Spencer Perceval: The Evangelical Prime Minister, 1762–1812.* Manchester: Manchester University Press, 1963.

Griffiths, Sir Perceval. *The British Impact on India.* London: MacDonald and Co., 1952.

Guedalla, Philip. *Wellington.* New York: Literary Guild, 1931.

Hawes, Frances. *Henry Brougham.* New York: St. Martin's Press, n.d.

Heckscher, Eli Filip. *The Continential System: An Economic Interpretation.* Edited by Harold Westergaard. Oxford: Clarendon Press, 1922.

Hinde, Wendy. *George Canning.* New York: St. Martin's Press, 1973.

Howard, Donald D. *The Battle of Bussaco: Masséna vs. Wellington.* Tallahassee: Florida State University Press, 1965.

Hume, Martin A.S. *Modern Spain: 1788–1898.* London: G. B. Putnam's Sons, 1900.

Hunt, William. *The History of England from the Accession of George III to the Close of Pitt's First Administration.* London: Longmans, Green, 1905.

Hutton, W. H. *The Marquess Wellesley, K.G.* Rulers of India Series. Oxford: Clarendon Press, 1893.

Iribarren, José Maria. *Espoz y Mina: El Liberal.* Madrid: Aguilar, 1967.

Kaufmann, William W. *British Policy and the Independence of Latin America, 1804–1828.* New Haven: Yale University Press, 1951.

Lenanton, Carola Mary Anima Oman. *Sir John Moore.* London: Hodder and Stoughton, 1953.

Longford, Elizabeth. *Wellington: The Years of the Sword.* New York: Harper and Row, 1969.

Lovett, Gabriel H. *Napoleon and the Birth of Modern Spain.* New York: New York University Press, 1965.

Lyall, Sir Alfred. *The Rise and Expansion of the British Dominion in India.* New York: Howard Fertig, 1968.

Mahan, Alfred Thayer. *The Influence of Seapower Upon the French Revolution and Empire, 1793–1812.* 2 vols. Boston: Little Brown, 1898.

Malleson, G. B. *The Life of Marquess Wellesley, K.G.* London: W. H. Allen and Co., 1889.

Marshall, Dorothy. *The Rise of George Canning.* London: Longmans, Green, 1938.

Maxwell, William Hamilton, *Life of Field Marshal His Grace the Duke of Wellington.* London: A.H. Baily, 1839–41.

Oliver, Robert Tarbell. *Four Who Spoke Out: Burke, Fox, Sheridan, Pitt.* Syracuse, N.Y.: Syracuse University Press, 1946.

Oman, Sir Charles William Chadwick. *A History of the Peninsular War.* 7 vols. Oxford: Clarendon Press, 1902–30.

———. *Wellington's Army, 1809–1814.* London: E. Arnold, 1912.

Petrie, Sir Charles Alexander. *George Canning.* London: Eyre and Spottiswoode, 1946.

Pidal, Ramon Menendez. *The Spaniards in Their History.* New York: W. W. Norton, 1950.

Roberts, Michael. *The Whig Party: 1807–1812.* London: Macmillan and Co., Ltd., 1965.

Roberts, P. E. *India under Wellesley.* London: G. Bell and Son, Ltd., 1929.

Rose, John Holland. "Canning and the Spanish Patriots in 1808." *American Historical Review* XII (1906): 39–52.

———. "The Contest with Napoleon, 1802–1812." In *The Cambridge History of British Foreign Policy, 1783–1919,* edited by A. W. Ward and G. P. Gooch. Vol. I, *1783–1815.* New York: The Macmillan Co., 1922.

Rosebery, Archibald Philip Primrose, 5th Earl of. *Pitt.* London: Macmillan, 1892.

Ross, Steven T. *European Diplomatic History, 1789–1815: France against Europe.* Garden City, N.Y.: Doubleday, 1969.

Shand, Alexander Innes. *The War in the Peninsula, 1808–1814.* New York: Scribner, 1898.

Sherwig, John M. *Guineas and Gunpowder: British Foreign Aid in the Wars with France, 1793–1815.* Cambridge: Harvard University Press, 1969.

Smith, Vincent A. *The Oxford History of India.* Oxford: The Clarendon Press, 1958.

Solís, Ramon. *El Cádiz de las Cortes: La Vida en la cuidad en los años de 1810 a 1813.* Madrid: Ministituto de Estudios Politicos, 1958.

Spear, Percival. *The Nabobs: A Study of the Social Life of the English in 18th Century India.* London: Oxford University Press, 1963.

Tilley, John, and Gasilee, Stephen. *The Foreign Office.* The Whitehall Series. London: G. P. Putnam's, 1933.

Torrens, W. M. *The Marquess Wellesley, Architect of Empire.* London: Chatto and Windus, 1880.

Walpole, Spencer. *The Life of Spencer Perceval.* 2 vols. London: Hurst and Blackett, 1874.

Ward, Stephen George Peregrine. *Wellington's Headquarters: A Study of the Administration Problems in the Peninsula, 1809–1814.* London: Oxford University Press, 1957.

Webster, C. K. *The Foreign Policy of Castlereagh, 1812–1815: Britain and the Reconstruction of Europe.* London: G. Bell and Sons, Ltd., 1931.

Weller, Jac. *Wellington in the Peninsula, 1808–1814.* London: N. Vane, 1962.

Wilson, Philip Whitewell. *William Pitt, the Younger.* Garden City, N.Y.: Doubleday, 1930.

Yonge, Charles. *The Life and Administration of Robert Banks, Second Earl of Liverpool, K.G., Late First Lord of the Treasury.* 3 vols. Compiled from original documents. London: Macmillan, 1868.

Ziegler, Phillip. *Addington, A Life of Henry Addington, First Viscount Sidmouth.* New York: The John Day Company, 1965.

Index